SCOTLAND'S GARDENS 2017 GUIDEBOOK

Printed by Bell & Bain Ltd. Cover image Tyninghame House © Judy Riley.
Maps produced by Alan Palfreyman Graphics @APalfreyman Contains OS data © Crown copyright MiniScale 2015

Scotland's Gardens, 2nd Floor, 23 Castle Street, Edinburgh EH2 3DN
T: 0131 226 3714   E: info@scotlandsgardens.org   W: www.scotlandsgardens.org

CHAIRMAN'S MESSAGE

Printing deadlines dictate that I must write my chairman's statement for 2017 before the autumn has really got underway. It is early September and I am sitting in my office at home surrounded by the heady scent of sweet peas and a glorious bowl of dahlias. The long dark winter nights and their associated opportunities for planning for next summer's work in the garden, are still ahead of us.

It is too early to know how the numbers for 2016 will turn out but we do know that the reorganisation we put in place last year has seen our costs fall substantially, and the evidence to date is that our revenue streams have been steady. The spring was not kind to us with a number of cold and wet weekends but latterly things have been much better and visitor numbers have been solid. I am anticipating that we will see an improvement in our cost:income ratio. None of this would have been possible without the dedicated support of our wonderful Garden Owners, our District and Area Organisers and a host of volunteers who have lent a helping hand at events and openings. So I would like to thank them all very much for their unstinting and loyal support. I would also like to pay tribute to the staff in Castle Street who have borne a very significant burden over the last eighteen months whilst the office reorganisation took place. Without their enthusiasm and good humour in difficult circumstances we could not have completed our reorganisation with such little visible disruption.

We have been very occupied over the last several months reviewing carefully all aspects of our activities so that we can look forward to the years ahead with confidence and vigour. We have engaged widely with our stakeholders and our plans have been heavily influenced by their input. This period of introspection and consultation has been a fascinating exercise and one which will stand us in good stead for the foreseeable future.

My five year stint as chairman of Scotland's Gardens will come to an end in March when I will hand over the baton to David Mitchell. I know that David will continue with the evolutionary changes that are now underway. One of his first tasks will be to oversee the upgrading of our database.

The database is creaking at the seams and needs to be replaced and thereafter there will be a significant improvement to our rather clunky website. These are major projects and we want to make sure that we get them right first time round so the current preparatory work now being undertaken by our National Organiser, Terrill Dobson, is essential before we embark on the upgrades themselves.

I have very much enjoyed my time with Scotland's Gardens and I would like to thank all those people who have been so supportive of both myself and the charity over that time. I know that I will be leaving a reformed and healthy organisation in good hands and I will follow its fortunes from my vantage point as a continuing garden owner. I wish you a very contented and fertile 2017 and a very happy season visiting some of Scotland's most beautiful gardens.

Mark Hedderwick
Chairman

As the proud President of Scotland's Gardens, it was an honour and a huge pleasure to be invited to the 85th birthday party of this unique charity at Winton House last summer. I had a glimpse of the warm welcome which all the Scotland's Gardens owners give to their guests every summer!

How fitting that we celebrated this milestone at Winton House, which is the longest-opening garden in the scheme, welcoming visitors for the last 84 years. As I walked through the beautiful gardens, I was able to thank in person some of the garden owners, enthusiastic volunteers and staff members who all work together to make Scotland's Gardens so successful.

It was fascinating to see the display of some of the archives dating back to the very first Guidebook in 1931. There is a wealth of material illustrating the long history of Scotland's Gardens and I was pleased to hear that plans are afoot to make more of this valuable resource.

It was a wonderful party, celebrating 85 years of opening gardens to visitors and raising money for charities in Scotland. It also celebrated the hard work of owners, gardeners and volunteers who make it all possible.

Looking back brings happy memories, but I feel sure that the hard work and enthusiasm shown over the last 85 years will have an enduring legacy and that Scotland's Gardens is a charity that will thrive and blossom in the future.

Camilla

WHO'S WHO IN SCOTLAND'S GARDENS

WHO'S WHO IN SCOTLAND'S GARDENS

PRESIDENT
HRH The Duchess of Rothesay

HEAD OFFICE
23 Castle Street,
Edinburgh EH2 3DN
T: 0131 226 3714
E: info@scotlandsgardens.org
W: www.scotlandsgardens.org

Terrill Dobson
National Organiser

Christina Smith
Adminstrator

Hazel Reid
Office Manager

BANKERS
Handelsbanken, 18 Charlotte Square,
Edinburgh EH2 4DF

SOLICITORS
J & H Mitchell WS, 51 Atholl Road,
Pitlochry PH16 5BU

ACCOUNTANTS
Douglas Home & Co,
47-49 The Square, Kelso TD5 7HW

SCOTTISH CHARITY NO SC011337

ISSN   2054-3301
ISBN   978-0-901549-32-7

Offices at: Bath Belfast Birmingham Bournemouth Cheltenham Edinburgh Exeter Glasgow Guildford Leeds Liverpool London Manchester Reigate Sheffield

Cultivating relationships, growing investments

We are proud to sponsor Scotland's Gardens. With 15 offices across the UK, we are a national network with a local feel, and our offices in Glasgow and Edinburgh are well placed to tend to your investments, pensions or other financial matters.

Our specialist teams manage £27.5 billion* on behalf of our clients, seeking the best and most tax-efficient returns on their capital. To see how we could best be of service to you please visit our website.

Please bear in mind that the value of investments and the income derived from them can go down as well as up and that you may not get back the amount that you have put in.

For more information on how we have supported Scotland's Gardens please visit **investecwin.co.uk/sponsorships**

Edinburgh – please contact Murray Mackay on **0131 226 5000**
Glasgow – please contact Stuart Light on **0141 333 9323**

WHAT HAPPENS TO THE MONEY RAISED?

All garden owners who participate in the Scotland's Gardens programme are able to nominate a charity of their choice to receive 40% of the funds raised at their openings. 226 different charities will be supported in this manner in 2017 and these vary from small and local to large and well known organisations. These charities are listed below and are also detailed within each garden listing.

Accord Hospice • Acting for Others • ACTS • Adoption Scotland • ADSHG • Advocacy Service Aberdeen • All Saints Church, Glencarse • Alzheimer Scotland • Amnesty International • Ankizy Gasy - Children of Madagascar Foundation • Anthony Nolan • Appin Parish Church • Appin Village Hall • Archie Foundation (for the new children's ward at Ninewells Hospital) • Ardgowan Hospice • Ardwell Community Kirk • Argyll Animal Aid • Artlink Central • Association of Local Voluntary Organisations • Barnardos • Befriend a Child, Aberdeen • Bennachie Guides • Black Isle Bee Gardens • Black Watch Army Cadet Force • Blythswood Care • Borders and Kirkton Manor & Lyne Churches • British Heart Foundation • British Horse Society Scotland • British Limbless Ex-Servicemen's Association • Brooke | Action for Working Horses and Donkeys • Bumblebee Conservation Trust • Cambo Heritage Trust • Camphill Blair Drummond • Cancer Research UK • Canine Concern Scotland Trust • Canine Partners • Castle Loch, Lochmaben Community Trust • Children 1st • Children's Hospice Association Scotland (CHAS) • Christ Church Kincardine O'Neil • Christchurch Episcopal Church, Lochgilphead • Circle Scotland • CLIC Sargent • Compassion in World Farming • Corsock and Kirkpatrick Durham Church • Coulter Library Trust • Craigrothie Village Hall • Crail Cubs • Crail Preservation Society • Crisis • Croick Church • Crossroads Caring Scotland (West Stirling Branch) • Cruickshank Botanic Gardens Trust • Dalhousie Day Care • Diabetes UK • Dogs for Good • Dogs Trust • Dr Neil's Garden Trust • Dumfries Music Club • Dumfriesshire and Cumbria Greyhound Rescue • East Fife Members' Centre of the National Trust for Scotland • East Lothian Special Needs Play Schemes • Ellon & District Legion Scotland • Elvanfoot Trust • Erskine Hospital • Fauna and Flora International • Feedback Madagascar • Fenwick Church Hall Development Fund • Fettercairn Community Allotments • Fife Voluntary Action • Fingask Follies • Forfar Open Garden Scheme • Forgan Arts Centre • Forgandenny Parish Church • Forget Me Not Children's Hospice • Forth Driving Group RDA • Fortingall Church • Freedom From Fistula Foundation • Friends of Anchor • Friends of Camperdown House • Friends of Kirkcudbright Swimming Pool • Friends of Loch Arthur Community • Friends of St Modan's • Friends of the Neuro Ward at Aberdeen Royal Infirmary • Friends of Thor House, Thurso • Garden Organic • Gargunnock Community Centre • Gargunnock Community Trust • Girl Guiding Dundee Outdoor Centre • Girl Guiding Montrose • GKOPC Thrums Tots and Messy Church • Glasserton Parish Church • Guide Dogs For the Blind • Gunsgreen House Trust • Help for Heroes • Hessilhead Wildlife Rescue Trust • Highland Disability Sport Swim Team • Highland Hospice • Hillfoot Harmony Barbershop Singers • Hobkirk Church • Homestart • Hope Kitchen -Oban • Horatio's Gardens • Hospitalfield Trust • Insch Parish Church Restoration Fund • Julia Thomson Memorial Trust • Juvenile Diabetes Research Foundation • Kilbarchan Old Library • Kirkandrews Church • Kirkmahoe Parish Church • Kirkpatrick Durham Church • Laggan Church • Lamancha & District Community Association • Lanark Development Trust (Castlebank Regeneration Fund) • Leighton Library • Leuchie House • Loch Arthur Community (Camphill Trust) • Logie & St John's (Cross) Church, Dundee • Lothian Cat Rescue • LUPUS UK • MacMillan Cancer Care, Black Isle • Macmillan Cancer Support • Macmillan Centre at Borders General Hospital • Macmillan Nurses • Mamie Martin Fund • Margaret Kerr Unit Borders General Hospital • Marie Curie • Mary's Meals • Médecins Sans Frontières • Mercy Ships UK • Milnathort Guide Group • MIND • Morningside Heritage Association • MS Society • MS Therapy Centres • National Trust for Scotland (Threave Ospreys) • Netherthird Community Development Group • Nicholls Spinal Injury Foundation • Orkidstudio • Oxfam • Parkinson's UK • Perth & Kinross District Nurses • Peter Pan Moat Brae Trust • PF Counselling Service • Pinmill Village Association • Pittenweem Community Library • Plant Heritage • Plant Life Scotland for Coronation Meadows • Poppy Scotland • Port Logan Hall • Practical Action • Prostate Cancer UK • RAF Benevolent Fund • Rafford Church • Royal Botanic Garden Edinburgh • RBLS (Borders Area) • Red Cross • Riding for the Disabled Association • RIO Community Centre • RNLI • ROKPA Tibetan Charity • Royal Voluntary Service • RUDA • Saline Environmental Group • Sandpiper Trust • SANDS • Save the Children • Scooniehill Riding for the Disabled • Scotland's Charity Air Ambulance • Scots Mining Company Trust • Scottish Civic Trust • Scottish Motor Neurone Disease • Scottish Refugee Council • Scottish Wildlife Trust • Scout Group (Newburgh) • SG Development Fund • Soldiers Off The Street • Southdean Hall (SC044518) • Southton Smallholding • SSPCA • St Athernase Church, Leuchars • St Columba's Church • St Columba's Hospice • St Margaret's Parish Church, Dalry • St Mary's Episcopal Church • St Saviour's Church • St Vigeans Church Fund • St Vincent's Hospice • STAR Children's Charity • Strathcarron Hospice • Student Foodbank, Dundee & Angus College • Survival International • Sustrans • Tarland Development Group • Teapot Trust • The Ben Walton Trust • The Buccleuch and Queensberry Pipebank • The Conservation Foundation • The Coronation Hall, Muckhart • The Craigentinny Telferton Allotments • The Crichton Trust • The Divine Innocence Trust • The Dunscore Gala • The Euan Macdonald Centre for Motor Neurone Disease Research • The Gurkha Welfare Trust • The Jo Walters Trust • The Kirkcudbright Hospital League of Friends • The Library Renewed • The Little Haven • The Red Cross, Dunoon Branch • The Samaritans • The Scottish Dark Sky Observatory • The Thornhill Scottish Dancers • The Woodland Trust • Triple Negative Breast Cancer Research (Anne Konishi Memorial Fund) • Type 1 Juvenile Diabetes Research Fund • UCAN • Unicorn Preservation Society • University of Strathclyde Ross Priory Gardens • Westerkirk Parish Trust • Whithorn Trust • World Cancer Research • World Horse Welfare • Yorkhill Childrens Charity

The remaining 60%, net of expenses, of the funds raised at each opening is given to Scotland's Gardens beneficiary charities which are currently: The Queen's Nursing Institute Scotland, Maggie's Cancer Caring Centres, The Gardens Fund of the National Trust for Scotland and Perennial. Information about how ths money has helped our beneficiaries can be found on the following pages. Money is also donated via the Cattanach bequest to the National Trust for Scotland to train an apprentice gardener.

INTRODUCTION TO THE GUIDEBOOK

We have a fantastic selection of just shy of 500 gardens opening under our banner to raise money for charity, some 70 of which are new and have never opened before. These include a selection of village openings, special trail events in East Lothian, Fife and Orkney, and even a Christmas-time Festive Floral Evening in Stirlingshire.

opened for 78 years for Scotland's Gardens. In our feature article (p18-20) you will see that their history extends for many more fascinating years. Do be sure to visit this year. And there are also more gardens with a long history of opening for Scotland's Gardens and these with special anniversaries are highlighted on our Long Service Award pages (p25-26).

You may notice a slight "history slant" to this year's guidebook. 2017 has been designated by VisitScotland as the year of History, Heritage and Archaeology. Founded in 1931, and facilitating garden openings across our country, Scotland's Gardens has a special opportunity to support this exciting initiative. We entered into the spirit of this initiative last June when we celebrated our 85th birthday (p22-24) with our garden openers, volunteers, and President, The Duchess of Rothesay. At this event we displayed a selection of material from our historical archive collection and have started a project to catalogue our fascinating history (donations gratefully received through our Head Office).

SCOTLAND'S GARDENS SCHEME

IN AID OF THE QUEEN'S INSTITUTE (SCOTTISH BRANCH) AND DISTRICT NURSING

By the courtesy of the Owners, the following Gardens will be open to the public on the dates named, for the benefit of the Queen's Institute, Scottish Branch, and District Nursing. Copies of the general list and all information as to the Gardens may be obtained from the Secretary of the Gardens Scheme, 26 Castle Terrace, Edinburgh. Telephone 27801.

Unless otherwise stated, the Gardens are open from 11 a.m. to 7 p.m. on week-days and from 2 p.m. to 7 p.m. on Sundays. The usual charge for admission is 1/-.

GENERAL LIST
FOR 1931

PUBLISHED BY
The Queen's Institute of District Nursing
Scottish Branch
Head Office—26 Castle Terrace, Edinburgh

June 1931.

This year we have also joined forces with Historic Environment Scotland, through one of our volunteers, to highlight which garden openings include historic "designed landscapes" (p25), many of which are private and not otherwise available to the public. West Linton Village, in Peeblesshire, seems to have also caught the bug, as their conservation village will be offering a special Garden and Historical Trail.

So whether you're a garden lover, history buff, or just enjoy a great day out with a good cuppa, please support Scotland's Gardens and all of our many charities generously with your visits.

Terrill Dobson
National Organiser

This year's featured garden, with its photograph on our cover, is Tyninghame Garden which has

Find your way through cancer

Come to Maggie's

Maggie's provides free practical, emotional and social support for people with cancer and their family and friends.

Built in the grounds of NHS hospitals, our network of Centres across the UK are warm and welcoming places, with professional staff on hand to offer the support you need to find your way through cancer.

Maggie's Centres are open Monday to Friday, 9am – 5pm, and no referral is required.

Maggie's Centres across Scotland receive vital funds from every garden opening. Our heartfelt thanks go to everyone who supports Scotland's Gardens by opening their garden, volunteering or visiting a garden.

www.maggiescentres.org

SCOTLAND'S GARDENS
GARDENS OPEN FOR CHARITY

maggie's

Maggie Keswick Jencks Cancer Caring Centres Trust (Maggie's) is a registered charity, No. SC024414

BENEFICIARY MESSAGES

maggie's

When designing the blueprint for Maggie's Centres, our co-founder, Maggie Keswick Jencks, talked about the need for 'thoughtful lighting, a view out to trees, birds and sky'.

Her legacy is a growing network of Centres which give people with cancer, their families and friends somewhere to turn to at an extremely difficult moment in their lives. Always close to a major cancer hospital, they are

Sheltered inside, it helps to be reminded by a seasonal and changing scene outside, that you are still part of a living world. Our landscape gardeners incorporate scent as well as sight, consider how their planting will behave in the rain as well as in the sun, plant trees and shrubs that bud and blossom and berry, and plants that even 'die well' before returning the following year.

Our Centres provide many opportunities to look outside from wherever you are in the building, even if it is to an internal planted courtyard. Sometimes, when in acute distress, all that a person can bear is to look out of the window from a sheltered place, at the branch of a tree moving in the wind. Pictured, our beautiful Reflection Garden at Maggie's Glasgow features a unique mirror installation, as part of the wooded glade surrounding the Centre. Designed by Lily Jencks, daughter of our co-founders Maggie and Charles, the garden allows visitors a moment to contemplate, not on cancer, but on how the sun reflects on the glass, or how the humidity condenses on a surface.

calm, friendly places which help people find the hope, determination and resources they need to cope with one of the toughest challenges any of us is likely to have to face.

Early in 2017 we will celebrate the opening of our 20th Centre in our 20th year, in the grounds of Forth Valley Royal Hospital in Larbert. Nestling beside a lochan and surrounded by woodland, Maggie's Forth Valley is thoughtfully designed to celebrate the beauty of the landscape and the hope that nature offers.

Our buildings - and their surrounding landscapes - set the scene and the tone for everything that happens at Maggie's.

I would like to take this opportunity to thank you all for your support of Maggie's in Scotland again this year. Our Centres benefit from every Scotland's Gardens opening throughout the year.

With warmest wishes,

Laura Lee
Chief Executive

Please call 0300 123 1801 or visit www.maggiescentres.org for more information

BENEFICIARY MESSAGES

THE QUEEN'S NURSING INSTITUTE SCOTLAND

Throughout the 85 year history of Scotland's Gardens we have worked together to make a difference to our communities by supporting care at home. Established in 1889, our original work saw us training Scotland's Queen's Nurses. From 1931, Scotland's Gardens helped pay for their training, salaries, and pensions.

Queen's Nurses provided excellent care and support to individuals and families within the home, with their distinctive uniform marking them out as a welcome guest. An important part of their role was health improvement, encouraging families to adopt healthier ways of living.

Queen's Nurse Annie Meredith with recently extended family group, c1950

As training of nurses moved to colleges, and salaries and pensions moved to the NHS, our charitable objectives changed, while our principles remain the same. Our purpose is to promote excellence in community nursing across Scotland, to improve the health and wellbeing of the people of Scotland, and to ensure that nurses who work in Scotland's communities are the very best they can be.

As part of this aim, 2017 will see the reintroduction of the Queen's Nurse title to Scotland. It will be awarded for the first time since January 1969. The reintroduced title will be awarded as a mark of excellence, with successful candidates taking part in a nine month programme enhancing their skills and working on a development project.

The programme is designed to allow candidates the time to flourish. It consists of a five day residential workshop with masterclasses, action learning sets and inspirational conversations with invited guests. There will be opportunities for monthly coaching sessions, and two further workshop days. Each new Queen's Nurse will have a development project to work on during the programme, which clearly benefits their community, and this, along with their professional development, will be the focus of the coaching.

These new Queen's Nurses will follow in the footsteps of the previous generation, providing excellent care. We will select 20 candidates each year and because of the generous funding from Scotland's Gardens we can confidently plan the first three years of the programme.

Our historic and ongoing relationship is a core part of who we are and we appreciate your continued support of community nursing in Scotland.

Clare Cable
Chief Executive and Nurse Director
Queen's Nursing Institute Scotland

the National Trust
for Scotland

Spectacular

**SEASONAL
GARDENS**

OPEN
ALL YEAR

www.nts.org.uk/visitgardens

BENEFICIARY MESSAGES

the National Trust
for Scotland
a place for everyone

On behalf of the National Trust for Scotland, I would like to thank all of Scotland's Gardens owners for their ongoing support and commitment to the National Trust for Scotland and its own gardens. We are grateful not only for your financial support but for the help that you provide to us in so many other ways. At times of great change in the world, increasing numbers of people seek comfort and inspiration in gardens and those cared for by the members of Scotland's Gardens set high standards for us all to aspire to.

With its mild winter, late spring and late summer weather 2016 proved a reasonable year for gardening and garden visiting; our staff were able to get on top of their work and enjoy the late summer sunshine as well as attracting a significant number of visitors. Our open days in support of Scotland's Gardens were generally well supported with 28 of our gardens opening 51 times hosting guided walks, plant & produce sales, garden quizzes and craft stalls, daffodil teas, vegetable days and specialist craft-skills workshops in pruning and maintaining herbaceous borders all in support of Scotland's Gardens.

Through the School of Heritage Gardening, in part supported by Scotland's Gardens, the Trust continues to play an important part in growing future gardeners. There is a high quality framework to support gardener training in our gardens across the country with student placements at Threave Garden.

Broughton House, Kirkcudbrightshire

Thanks to your generous financial donation our gardens continue to flourish, visitors can enjoy the varied seasonal highlights across our gardens and appreciate the expertise and labours of our dedicated garden staff, who help develop and conserve these beautiful places.

Simon Skinner
Chief Executive

PERENNIAL
GARDENERS' ROYAL BENEVOLENT SOCIETY

Vincent's Story

Vincent* spent almost his entire working life as a gardener on private estates. When a stroke dramatically changed his retirement plans, Perennial has been there to help him look forward to a brighter future.

His 37-year career in horticulture came to an abrupt end in 2012. The stroke left him with limited mobility and affected his sight, hearing and memory. Perennial then helped Vincent claim the statutory benefits to which he was entitled. Sadly, his health continued to deteriorate. By 2015 he was confined to a wheelchair and could no longer access his own garden. For someone whose life had been devoted to horticulture, it was a shattering blow.

Vincent* spent almost his entire working life as a gardener

Perennial stood by him again. Our support has enabled Vincent to work on the garden while in his wheelchair. It's made a massive difference.

Being able to pursue his passion has greatly improved his quality of life, and his mental wellbeing. Vincent is looking forward to a happier retirement now. "I did not think I would ever be able to enjoy gardening again but Perennial has made it possible for me.

I can now relive memories from my past and my life has colour in it again."

*We've changed his name to protect his identity.

Gifts that Transform Lives

Perennial's virtual gifts were introduced three years ago and have raised over £14,500, supplying essential items such as winter coats, microwaves, Christmas food vouchers or paying for heating and fuel bills for those who could not otherwise afford them.

Your support could help a Perennial client keep their independence.

£50

Your gift could help someone pay for an essential heating service.

£75

See the full range on the website at:
www.perennial.org.uk/VirtualGifts

· ·

Help Line:	0800 093 8543
Debt Advice:	0800 093 8546
Donation Line:	0800 093 8792

Perennial
115-117 Kingston Road,
Leatherhead,
Surrey,
KT22 7SU.

www.perennial.org.uk

A company limited by guarantee. Registered in England & Wales company no: 8828584. Charity no: 1155156. | Registered in Scotland. Charity no: SC040180. VAT no. 991 2541 09. Perennial's Debt Advice Service is regulated by the Financial Conduct Authority.

BENEFICIARY MESSAGES

PERENNIAL
GARDENERS' ROYAL BENEVOLENT SOCIETY
Helping Horticulturists In Need Since 1839

Perennial – at the heart of horticulture

Perennial is the only UK charity dedicated to helping all those who work in horticulture.

Perennial offers free, confidential advice and support to everyone working in or retired from horticulture and their families, including gardeners, landscapers, nursery and garden centre staff, parks and grounds care staff and tree surgeons, for as long as it is needed. People turn to Perennial for financial and emotional help in times of need because of disability, sickness, poverty, financial hardship and old age – although increasingly younger people are seeking assistance.

Many individuals describe the services Perennial offers simply as a 'lifeline'. The work of Perennial depends entirely on voluntary donations from the horticulture industry and the garden-loving public.

A message from Carole

Thank you!

The money that Perennial receives from Scotland's Gardens quite simply, saves lives.

My sincerest thanks to each and every one of you, for supporting both charities and ensuring that Scotland's most glorious outdoor spaces help gardeners and horticulturists in times of crisis.

Carole Baxter
Perennial Trustee

A message from our Chairman

Since the charity's inception over 175 years ago, Perennial has been helping gardeners and horticulturists in need. We provide much needed help and advice for vulnerable gardeners and other horticulturists, as well as their families.

Dougal Philip, Chairman

However we can only continue to provide these services with support from the garden loving public. Your visits to gardens through the Scotland's Gardens scheme helps our charity throughout the year.

Daily we continue to see how difficult people find it to cope, and to maintain a decent life, particularly when things go wrong through illness, financial hardship and/or disability, for both individuals and their families.

It is particularly heartening to recognise and thank the individuals, businesses and organisations who support us, most especially Scotland's Gardens which has increased its funding to Perennial up to £25,000 in the last year.

Dougal Philip
Chairman of Perennial Trustees

Carole Baxter, Trustee

WILDERNESS AND WALLED GARDEN
THE GARDENS AND POLICIES
OF TYNINGHAME HOUSE

Elaborate beds in the south lawn at the end of the 19th century

The story of Tyninghame begins in the eighth century when St Baldred established a monastic cell here on the banks of the Tyne. It became a centre of monastic life and in the 12th century a fine chapel was built which became the Parish church until 1761. At this time a new village had been built and the church moved to Whitekirk. Of the monastic garden, nothing remains nor is there any sign of the original village of Tyninghame which occupied the North bank of the river.

The designed landscape we see today was laid out by the young Thomas, 6th Earl of Haddington and Helen, his wife, following the faltering steps of his father and grandfather, who had begun to enclose and drain fields, and plant some trees, with little success. It was Helen who encouraged her husband to furnish their estate with designed woodlands, at first near the house, then on the adjacent Tyninghame Muir (now Binning Wood) and finally on a sandy rabbit warren near the sea. Three formal tree lined avenues linked the various parts: The Sea Avenue, Lime Tree Walk and the Garleton Avenue.

It was Helen who began the planting each time. When Thomas saw how well Helen had executed her first plans he decided he wanted to create what he called 'The Wilderness'. He chose land near the bowling green and laid it out with a centre and fourteen walks radiating from it. Later they enlarged it, but of this formal design, little is discernible today although many of the original trees remain: lime, beech and chestnut. The hedges

The Wilderness in spring with Tulipa sylvestris

Tyninghame House from South Lawn

which originally lined the walks have long disappeared, including the double holly hedges for which Tyninghame was famous.

Helen's enthusiasm for planting trees knew no bounds and her husband worked out by trial and error how to raise and plant them so they would succeed. After thirty years he set down his experience in **A Treatise on the Manner of Raising Forest Trees**. Written in 1733 but not

The Apple Walk

published until 1756, this small book is of the greatest historical interest. It is the earliest account of estate forestry in Scotland. By the time of his death in 1735 he and his wife had established woodland on some 800 acres of unpromising land, planted extensive shelterbelts and enclosed and drained the surrounding land.

The planting and development that has taken place since has respected the framework that they established. A walled garden with greenhouses was built about 1750, before Helen died, age 91, in 1768. The original four quadrants, central feature and boundary path remain, although the layout within these sections has been modified over the years and the heated walls of the greenhouses, introduced in the 1800s, no longer function.

The 19th century saw many introductions of new tree species and rhododendrons into the Wilderness and the Garleton Walk. Robert Brotherston, Head Gardener for almost 50 years (1874-1923) re-planned parts of the Walled Garden planting parallel yew hedges on the north-south central axis, with double herbaceous borders and a gravel path. Robert was as interested in flowers and fruit as he was in vegetables. He was a prolific contributor to **The Gardener** magazine and the author of three books, including the first book on flower arranging, published in 1906. He also planted the 120 yard long Apple Walk to the south of the Walled Garden. During his time there were at least sixteen gardeners working at Tyninghame, excluding the foresters and gamekeepers who managed the woodlands.

The house itself underwent extensive remodelling by William Burn in 1828; its harled exterior was faced with pink sandstone, pepper pot turrets added, some windows enlarged and the garden to the south terraced. An obelisk dedicated to Thomas and Helen was erected in 1856 at the head of the Sea Avenue. The parterre, terrace and steps and the South lawn with its stone planters, were all to Burns' designs.

Little changed until 1965, when Lady Sarah, wife of the 12th Earl of Haddington, created 'The Secret Garden' to the West of the Parterre. Conceived as an intimate garden for old roses and based on an early 18th century French design, in mid-summer the borders overflow with pale colours and scented roses. The statue of Flora is from the 20th century but the fountain basin is much older. The Apple Walk here has been recently replanted.

The house remained in the possession of the Haddington family until 1987 when it was sold and divided into individual apartments. At the same time, garden buildings were converted into separate dwellings including a house that was built at the head of The Walled Garden.

The Obelisk at the head of the Sea Avenue, dedicated to Thomas 6th Earl of Haddington and his wife Helen

Today the residents own about 38 acres surrounding the house, the core of the original estate. The Head Gardener, Chas Lowe, is assisted by one other gardener.

The appearance of the house is much as Burns envisaged it. And the design of the landscape itself is much as it was in the 18th century. It was practical and it has endured.

We look forward to welcoming you on our open days which are:

Sunday 14 May and Sunday 18 June
1:00pm to 5:00pm
Please see p245 for further details.

Double yew hedges in the Walled Garden

The decorative urn was once a chimney for the heated wall. The original greenhouse has been demolished.

DIANA MACNAB AWARD
FOR OUTSTANDING SERVICE

The Diana Macnab Award, presented annually at our Conference, is granted to someone who has given outstanding service to Scotland's Gardens. In 2016 the recipient was Lady Edmonstone of Duntreath Castle.

Julie's involvement with Scotland's Gardens Scheme began in 1975 and continues to this day. Over the years she has been Vice Chairman, a long serving member of the Executive and Finance Committees and Stirling District Organiser for 25 years.

Last summer Char Hunt, Trish Kennedy, the office staff and Julie selected items of historical interest for display at the elegant garden party at Winton House, East Lothian, to celebrate Scotland's Gardens 85th birthday which was attended by our President, The Duchess of Rothesay.

Julie was also invited to contribute to our 75th celebrations and wrote "Sharing and Caring - A History of Scotland's Gardens" for our 2006 Guidebook which still acts as a reference for people interested in our history.

Julie also founded and created the high profile and hugely popular Stirling Autumn Lectures which still help greatly in raising awareness of the charity. She particularly enjoyed having the celebrities to stay the night before.

In 2010 Scotland's Gardens invited our President, The Duchess of Rothesay to visit one of our gardens and she chose Duntreath. Julie managed the event with poise and style, serving a private lunch in the house and then introducing the Duchess to almost every garden owner and volunteer who attended.

Julie says she has hugely enjoyed all her days supporting Scotland's Gardens and all the friendliness of the gardening community. In particular the fact that our charity supports such a wonderful variety of good and worthwhile causes.

We would like to thank Julie for her enormous contribution to Scotland's Gardens and congratulate her on this well deserved award.

Lady Edmonstone

Duntreath Castle

85TH BIRTHDAY CELEBRATIONS

A Royal Visit...

On 22nd June we held a special party to celebrate our 85th birthday at Winton House, the garden which has opened the longest (84 years) for Scotland's Gardens. Limited to only 220 guests, we invited our volunteer organisers and our garden owners who have opened for us for a number of years. Guests were asked to dress with a touch of the 1930s and many embraced the spirit of the day with much imagination.

Guests arrived for 11am, required to be in place before the arrival of Her Royal Highness, the Duchess of Rothesay, who was to come by helicopter, but she surprised us all by arriving earlier than expected by car! The Duchess was greeted by the Lord-Lieutenant for East Lothian, Michael Williams, the owners of Winton House, Sir Francis and Lady Ogilvy, David Mitchell (SG Deputy Chair) and Terrill Dobson (SG National Organiser) and piped in by Calum, the Ogilvy's son. With Toby Subiotto, the Winton Gardener, on hand the group set off for a tour of the garden.

The Duchess first toured the walled garden where she was introduced to several of Scotland's Gardens' long service garden owners, including:

The Countess Haig & Dowager Countess Haig
Bemersyde Opened 74 years

The Hon Mrs Mary Ramsay
Bughtrig
Opened 66 years

Colonel S J Furness
Netherbyres
Opened 66 years

Jeanette and Ruaraidh Ogilvie
Pitmuies House
Opened 50 years

Next in her garden tour the Duchess was introduced to some of the helpers who have supported the many years of Winton openings. These introductions took place at a special patio created by Sir Francis to commemorate the occasion. It included a carved stone:

The Duchess seemed genuinely touched by the gesture.

The Duchess then walked on to meet several of our District Organisers who have volunteered many years of their time and energy to support Scotland's Gardens. These included:

Leslie Stein
Past Stirling Area Organiser, District Organiser and Garden Owner since 1976

Jeni Auchinleck
Fife Area Organiser,
organiser of Crail village opening since 1988

Vicki Reid Thomas
District Organiser for Edinburgh & West Lothian for 18 years

Rose-Ann Cuninghame
District Organiser and Area Organiser for Ayrshire for 24 years

With our organisers, the Duchess helped to plant a commemorative Mulberry Tree. There is a bit of a story about mulberry trees which is linked to Winton House. King James VI/I ordered acres of Mulberry trees when he'd planned to compete with the French in the silk industry. Apparently King James VI/I was set to visit Winton and the laird of the day arranged to

have a beautiful ceiling constructed in his honour and this included mulberry trees. But sadly James VI/1 did not come so the ceiling had to be presented to Charles II. Possibly even more sad, James IV/I introduced the wrong type of Mulberry tree (nigra), not the one enjoyed by silkworms, and we maintained that tradition by planting a Morus nigra.

For the final stop in the tour, the Duchess was shown inside Winton House where she met the Ogilvy family and was able to see the elaborate plasterwork ceiling mentioned above.

Meanwhile during the Duchess' garden tour, the other guests in the party marquee were treated to a display of Scotland's Gardens' archives and a short talk by David Rae OBE. David, recently retired Director of Horticulture and current Director of the Stanley Smith Horticultural Trust, spoke about his experiences with the value of archives, encouraging us to "grasp the challenge" and explore our archives.

The Duchess then joined the party in the marquee and spoke to various guests and staff. She was shown the displays of our archive project and introduced to our beneficiaries and party sponsor. The Duchess then cut our birthday cake, a spectacular carrot cake topped with a huge marzipan carrot, which quite hilariously and spontaneously broke in half just as The Duchess was preparing to cut the cake. She then spoke to the guests, very kindly telling us how proud she was to be our President and thanking all of our garden openers and volunteer organisers.

Just before her departure there was an amusing moment, which the frustrated photographers could not capture, when the youngest Ogilvy son, Hamish, enticed The Duchess to pose with him for an iPhone selfie. A delicious garden party style lunch was served and guests were invited to visit the garden and the house.

Special thank you

A huge thank you to **Investec** who very generously sponsored the party.

SCOTLAND'S GARDENS AND DESIGNED LANDSCAPES

It is exciting to note the importance which gardens play in our historic environment and landscape, and all the more so in 2017, which has been designated the Year of History, Heritage and Archaeology by the Scottish Government.

A number of gardens which appear in our 2017 guidebook are recognised nationally and appear in Scotland's Inventory of Gardens and Designed Landscapes, compiled by Historic Environment Scotland.

More information on the Inventory, and a wealth of information on the historical, architectural and horticultural aspects of these gardens can be found at http://portal.historicenvironment.scot/

ABERDEENSHIRE
Castle Fraser Garden
Fyvie Castle
Haddo House
Hatton Castle
Kildrummy Castle Gardens
Leith Hall Garden
Pitmedden Garden
Tillypronie

ANGUS & DUNDEE
Brechin Castle
Dunninald Castle
Pitmuies Gardens

ARGYLL
Achnacloich
Ardchattan Priory
Ardkinglas Woodland Garden
Arduaine Garden
Benmore Botanic Garden
Crarae Garden
Inveraray Castle Gardens

AYRSHIRE
Blair House, Blair Estate
Carnell
Craigengillan Estate & Observatory
Culzean
Glenapp Castle

BERWICKSHIRE
Netherbyres

CAITHNESS & SUTHERLAND
Castle & Gardens of Mey

DUMFRIESSHIRE
Cowhill Tower
Dalswinton House

DUNBARTONSHIRE
Glenarn
Ross Priory

EAST LOTHIAN
Belhaven House /Belhaven Hill School
Tyninghame House
Winton House

EDINBURGH, MID & W LOTHIAN
Newhall
Newliston

ETTRICK & LAUDERDALE
Bemersyde

FIFE
Balcarres
Balcaskie
Cambo Gardens
Earlshall Castle
Falkland Palace and Garden
Hill of Tarvit
Kellie Castle

GLASGOW & DISTRICT
Greenbank Garden

ISLE OF ARRAN
Brodick Castle & Country Park

KINCARDINE & DEESIDE
Crathes Castle Garden
Drum Castle Garden
Fasque House
Glenbervie House
Inchmarlo House Garden

KIRKCUDBRIGHTSHIRE
Brooklands
Broughton House Garden
Cally Gardens
Threave Garden

LANARKSHIRE
Scots Mining Company House

LOCHABER
Ardtornish

MORAY & NAIRN
Brodie Castle
Gordonstoun

PEEBLESSHIRE
Dawyck Botanic Garden
Kailzie Gardens
Portmore
Stobo Japanese Water Garden

PERTH & KINROSS
Blair Castle Gardens
Bolfracks
Braco Castle
Branklyn Garden
Drummond Castle Gardens
Glendoick
Fingask Castle
Megginch Castle

RENFREWSHIRE
Duchal

ROSS, CROMARTY...
Dundonnell House
Dunvegan Castle and Gardens
Inverewe Garden and Estate

ROXBURGHSHIRE
Floors Castle
Monteviot

STIRLINGSHIRE
Duntreath Castle
Gargunnock House Garden

WIGTOWNSHIRE
Ardwell House Gardens
Castle Kennedy and Gardens
Galloway House Gardens
Logan Botanic Garden
Logan House Gardens

LONG SERVICE AWARDS

Congratulations to the following gardens, which will receive long service awards from Scotland's Gardens in 2017. We are thankful for their commitment and dedication to our worthy causes

75 YEARS

Bemersyde **(Ettrick & Lauderdale)**

Brechin Castle **(Angus & Dundee)**

Glenarn **(Dunbartonshire)**

Glenbervie **(Kincardineshire)**

Bemersyde

Brechin Castle

Glenarn

Glenbervie

50 YEARS

Dundonnell House **(Ross, Cromarty, Skye & Inverness)**

Earlshall Castle **(Fife)**

Kailzie Gardens **(Peeblesshire)**

Megginch **(Perth & Kinross)**

25 YEARS

Kilarden **(Dunbartonshire)**

Logan Botanic Garden **(Wigtownshire)**

Dundonnell House

Kilarden

Earlshall Castle © Ray Cox

Logan Botanic Garden

Kailzie Gardens

Megginch © Ray Cox

NEW GARDENS FOR 2017

Aberdeenshire

Drumrossie Mansion House

Angus & Dundee

12 Glamis Drive
Arbroath Collection of Gardens
Inchmill Cottage
Langley Park Gardens

Argyll

2 Broadcrosft Lane
Dalnashean

Ayrshire

Barnweil Garden
Netherthird Community Garden
The Gardens of Fenwick

Caithness, Sutherland, Orkney & Shetland

The Garden at the Auld Post Office B&B

Dumfriesshire

Holehouse
Shawhead
Whiteside

12 Glamis Drive

The Garden at the Auld Post Office B&B

Langley Park Gardens

Carey, Abernethy Open Gardens

Dunbartonshire

Dean Cottage with Ortona

East Lothian

Gullane Coastal Gardens

Edinburgh, Midlothian & West Lothian

39 Nantwich Drive
Colinton Gardens
Riccarton Mains Farmhouse

Glasgow & District

44 Gordon Road
Horatio's Gardens
Partickhill Gardens East
Partickhill Gardens West

Kincardine & Deeside

Clayfolds

Kirkcudbrightshire

Barmagachan House
Drumstinchall Cottage
Drumstinchall House

Lanarkshire

The Quothquan Gardens

Moray & Nairn

Balnabual Cottage
Burgie
Knock House

Peeblesshire

Peebles Gardens

Perth & Kinross

Abernethy Open Gardens
The Garden at Craigowan

Riccarton Mains Farmhouse

Drumstinchall House

Ravens Craig, Peebles Gardens

Renfrewshire

Bridge of Weir Road Gardens
Craig Hepburn Memorial Garden
St Vincent's Hospice Garden

Ross, Cromarty, Skye & Inverness

Bhlaraidh House

Roxburghshire

Pirnie
Westerhouses

Wigtownshire

Fernlea Garden

Galloway House Gardens
Lisieux Garden

Bhlaraidh House

Westerhouses

Fernlea Garden

39 Nantwich Drive

PLANT SALES

Fife

Cambo Gardens Spring Plant Sale, Kingsbarns	Sunday 16 April	11:00am - 4:00pm

Renfrewshire

Kilmacolm Plant Sale, Outside Kilmacolm Library, Lochwinnoch Road, Kilmacolm	Saturday 22 April	10:00am - 12:00pm

Stirlingshire

Gargunnock House Garden Plant Sale, Gargunnock	Sunday 23 April	2:00pm - 5:00pm

Fife

Kellie Castle Spring Plant Sale, Pittenweem	Sunday 7 May	10:30am - 3:00pm

Angus & Dundee

NEW Angus Plant Sale, Logie Walled Garden, Logie	Friday 12 May	5:00pm - 7:00pm

Peeblesshire

8 Halmyre Mains, West Linton	Sunday 4 June	10:00am - 12:00pm

Dunbartonshire

Hill House Plant Sale, Helensburgh	Sunday 3 September	11:30am - 4:00pm

Renfrewshire

Kilmacolm Plant Sale, Outside Kilmacolm Library, Lochwinnoch Road, Kilmacolm	Saturday 9 September	10:00am - 12:00pm

Fife

Hill of Tarvit Plant Sale & Autumn Fair, Cupar	Sunday 1 October	10:30am - 3:00pm

SNOWDROP OPENINGS

Celebrate the first signs of spring by exploring our beautiful Snowdrop Gardens.

Discover Scottish Gardens, VisitScotland and Scotland's Gardens will work together to support the popular Snowdrop Festival and promote this very special time of year for visiting gardens.

The following properties will be opening for charity under Scotland's Gardens for the 2017 Snowdrop Festival:

Aberdeenshire

Bruckhills Croft

Angus & Dundee

Langley Park Garden

Lawton House

Argyll

Maolachy's Garden

Ayrshire

Blair House, Blair Estate

Dumfriesshire

Barjarg Tower

Craig

East Lothian

Shepherd House

Fife

Lindores House

Kincardine & Deeside

Ecclesgreig Castle

Kirkcudbrightshire

Brooklands

Danevale Park

Lanarkshire

Cleghorn

Kilgraston, Perth & Kinross

Lawton House, Angus & Dundee

SCOTTISH SNOWDROP FESTIVAL
SATURDAY 28 JAN - SUNDAY 12 MARCH

Moray & Nairn
10 Pilmuir Road West

Peeblesshire
Kailzie Gardens

Perth & Kinross
Braco Castle
Fingask Castle
Kilgraston School

Ross, Cromarty, Skye & Inverness
Abriachan Garden Nursery

Stirlingshire
Duntreath Castle
Gargunnock House Garden
Kilbryde Castle

Wigtownshire
Craichlaw

If you have some lovely
snowdrops please get in touch.
Perhaps we can feature
your garden in 2018!

Galanthus Merlin   Galanthus elwesii Mrs McNamara   Galanthus plicatus Madelaine   Galanthus Reverend Hailstone

Just four of the 320+ named varieties of snowdrop at Bruckhills Croft, Aberdeenshire.

EAST LOTHIAN GARDEN TRAIL JUNE - JULY 2017

Scotland's Gardens is proud to announce another East Lothian Garden Trail after the first successful venture in 2014.

This trail provides an opportunity to see twelve magnificent spacious gardens and well tended allotments in close proximity over a day or days, making it worthwhile to come from afar. Six gardens have featured in the previous trail but five new gardens have been added and new ground is broken with the addition of the Musselburgh Allotments.

This is an opportunity to see splendid plants in a mix of settings, some many generations old, some relatively recent; both coastal and inland; both rugged and manicured – and with those who created the gardens on hand. Picking the brains of the owner, or custodian – for many of these gardens are but held in custody for the next generation – must surely be one of the highlights of wandering around the fruits of someone else's labour. See also page 242.

Charities

60% net of the proceeds is shared between Scotland's Gardens' beneficiary charities. The remainder is shared equally between Trellis and MND Scotland.

Opening times

Wednesday 28 June - Sunday 2 July
1:00pm - 6:00pm   All gardens except The Hopes and Musselburgh Allotments

Wednesday 28 June - Thursday 29 June
1:00pm - 6:00pm   The Hopes

Saturday 1 July - Sunday 2 July
1:00pm - 6:00pm   Musselburgh Allotments

Preston Hall

Green House at Eskhill

Fairnielaw House

Bowerhouse

The Hopes, Gifford

The Gardens

Blackdykes North Berwick EH39 5PQ

Bowerhouse Dunbar EH42 1RE

Bowerhouse Walled Garden Dunbar EH42 1RE

Congalton House North Berwick EH39 5JL

Fairnielaw House Athelstaneford EH39 5BE

Frostineb Pathhead EH37 5TB

Garvald Grange Garvald EH41 4LL

Green House at Eskhill Inveresk EH21 7TD

Musselburgh Allotments Inveresk EH21 7TF

Preston Hall Pathhead EH37 5UG

Redcliff Whittingehame, Haddington EH41 4QA

The Hopes Gifford EH41 4PL

Admission

£25.00 for entrance to all gardens on all dates. Accompanied children free.

£5.00 for a single garden on a single day at the gate.

Tickets available at **www.scotlandsgardens.org/elgt2017** or by cheque, payable to Scotland's Gardens and accompanied by a stamped addressed A5 envelope, from Ian Orr, 6 Grannus Mews, Inveresk EH21 7TT E: ianandisabel@mac.com.

Congalton

Garvald Grange

Bowerhouse Walled Garden

Frostineb

Blackdykes

FIFE GARDEN TRAIL
JUNE - JULY 2017

Running over late June and early July, the Fife Garden Trail provides an opportunity to see nine privately owned gardens five of which have never or rarely admitted visitors before.

It also offers a very flexible way to visit the gardens whether you wish to visit the area and see all gardens in three days (20-22 June, 27- 29 June or 4-6 July) or take the four weeks to see them all. The gardens can also be visited at different times, with some open all day, some in the afternoon, and others in the afternoon and evening. Some gardens have plants for sale, others the option of teas.

The Gardens

Balcaskie
Pittenweem KY10 2RE

Edenside
Strathmiglo KY14 7PX

Freelands
Ceres KY15 5LW

Gilston House
by Largoward, Leven KY8 5QP

Lucklaw House
Logie KY15 4SJ

St Mary's Farm
St Mary's Road, Cupar KY15 4NF

Teasses Gardens
Near Ceres KY8 5PG

Whinhill
Lahill Mains, Upper Largo KY8 5QS

Willowhill
Forgan, Newport-on-Tay DD6 8RA

From recently developed to rejuvenated historic all the gardens opening for the Trail are unique and reflect great gardening and creative talent. All are different, but have one thing in common - their owners would love to share their garden and passion for gardening with you and raise funds for charity in the process.

A ticket for the Fife Garden Trail makes a perfect gift and do treat yourself as well!

See page 123 for further details.

Charities

60% net of the proceeds goes to Scotland's Gardens' beneficiary charities. The remainder will be split equally between RNLI Anstruther and RHET Fife.

Opening times

Tuesdays					
Freelands	10am-4pm	20 June	27 June	4 July	-
Teasses	10am-4pm	20 June	27 June	4 July	11 July
Whinhill	1pm-5pm	20 June	27 June	4 July	11 July

Wednesdays					
Edenside	1pm-6pm	21 June	28 June	5 July	-
Lucklaw House	11am-5pm	21 June	28 June	5 July	12 July
St Mary's Farm	4pm-8pm	21 June	28 June	5 July	12 July
Willowhill	10am-7pm	21 June	28 June	5 July	12 July

Thursdays					
Balcaskie	10am-4pm	22 June	29 June	6 July	13 July
Gilston House	1pm-5pm	22 June	29 June	6 July	13 July

Balcaskie

Willowhill

Admission

£20.00 (plus £1 P&P) for entrance to all gardens. Accompanied children free.

Tickets are available online at:

http://www.scotlandsgardens.org/FGF2017

or by cheque payable to Scotland's Gardens from S Lorimore, Willowhill, Forgan, Newport on Tay, Fife DD6 8RA.

St Mary's Farm

Gilston House

Teasses

Freelands

Lucklaw House

Edenside

Whinhill

ORKNEY GARDEN FESTIVAL 17 - 25 JUNE 2017

A full week of delights for gardeners in Orkney, including four trails supporting Scotland's gardens.

SATURDAY 17 JUNE 2017
SECRET GARDENS OF KIRKWALL

11:30am - 4:00pm
£10 for all gardens or £2 per garden
All proceeds to SG Beneficiaries

1.   30 Queen Sonja Kloss KW15 1FJ
2.   4 Lynn Crescent KW15 1FF
3.   10 Slater Street KW15 1PQ
4.   Eight Bells 3 Soulisquoy Place KW15 1TJ
5.   14a Victoria Street KW15 1DN
6.   Kirkness and Gorie Deli KW15 1DH

This selection of eclectic gardens can mainly be viewed on foot and are accessible from the town centre, apart from Eight Bells and Lynn Crescent. Many of the gardens are tiny but demonstrate what can be done in a small space. Slater Street has a wonderful range of perennial geraniums whilst Eight Bells is a larger garden well worth hopping back into the car for. It is packed with some real little treasures and has been planned beautifully with great ideas for a more suburban setting. The tiniest garden is planted under the shade of an stunted oak in a small courtyard adjoining Kirkness and Gorie where there will be tasting sessions on the day! 14a Victoria Street in the shadow of the ancient palace is a haven for pots and containers, aviary and a fabulous tiny teapot collection.

Cream teas will be provided in conjunction with Marie Curie at the Town Hall 11:00am - 4:00pm. Plant Market in Kirkwall town centre. No disabled access at 10 Slater Street.

**Kirkwall Plant Market
in aid of Friends of the Neuro Ward ARI 11am - 2pm

**Cream Teas at Kirkwall Town Hall
in aid of Marie Curie 11:30am - 4pm

**A Wander through the Woods at Woodwick House, Evie
with music by Jo Philby, Prosecco and Petit Fours
in aid of Friends of the Neuro Ward ARI

**Independent events not organised by Scotland's Gardens

SUNDAY 18 JUNE 2017
ORKNEY GARDEN TRAIL ONE

11:30am - 4:00pm
£12 for all gardens or £2.50 per garden
All proceeds to SG Beneficiaries

7.   Annies Place Birsay KW17 2LX
8.   Aviedale Rendall KW17 2PB
9.   Quarry Field Orphir KW17 2RF
10. Dalkeith Polytunnel Finstown KW17 1TT
11. Gyre Cottage Orphir KW17 2RD
12. Kierfold House Sandwick KW16 3JE
13. Stenwood Finstown KW17 2JX
     (as seen on *The Beechgrove Garden*)
14. Quoy of Houton Orphir KW17 2RD
     (as seen on *The Beechgrove Garden*)
15. Community Garden Finstown KW17 2JX
16. Muckle Jocks Herston KW17 2RH
17. Fiddlers Green Herston KW17 2RH
18. Merengo Gardens Herston KW17 2TD

A chance to explore Orkney from its most northerly point to southerly Herston, a mixture of small and larger gardens in a variety of locations, many of them demonstrating excellent coastal planting. Wander through the woods at Stenwood and marvel at the fabulous plantings of water loving plants at the Community garden. See the 60 foot water rill at The Quoy stretching towards the sea and Kierfold House with its ancient walled garden bursting with perennial treasures. Go south to Herston to see three small wonderful gardens by the sea, featured in Scottish Field magazine. The gardens survive the harshest weather but are filled with roses and vegetables, they are not to be missed!

Cream teas at Merengo Gardens and refreshments at Dalkeith Polytunnel.

Monday 19 June 2017
**Gardeners Lunch at the Merkister Hotel
with guest speaker Rosa Steppanova
in aid of Friends of the Neuro Ward ARI

TUESDAY 20 JUNE 2017

Open Garden at the Quoy of Houton 11am - 2pm
Coffee and chat with Rosa Steppanova. Refreshments available. 40% to Friends of the Neuro Ward ARI, the net remaining goes to SG Beneficiaries.

SATURDAY 24 JUNE 2017
HOY GARDEN TRAIL

Times according to ferry timetable
£12 for all gardens or £2.50 per garden
Please note you should book the ferry prior to
purchasing tickets to the trail.
All proceeds to SG Beneficiaries

19. St Johns Manse KW16 3NY

20. Kingshouse KW17 2LQ

21. Halyel KW16 3NY

22. Greenhill KW17 2LU

23. The Garrison KW16 3NX

24. Daisy Bank

25. Old Hall KW17 2PR

This is going to be a real adventure; take the ferry
across to the island of Hoy and Longhope, follow the
yellow signs to see seven gardens open for the very
first time some of them right on the beach with their
very own seals! Others on the moors that battle with
wind, salt and mountain climate. It is marvellous to see
what these previously unseen gardens have in store for
lovers of gardens. There is even an ingenious vegetable
growing set up. Unmissable!

SUNDAY 25 JUNE 2017
ORKNEY GARDEN TRAIL TWO

11:30am - 4:00pm
£12 for all gardens or £2.50 per garden
All proceeds to SG Beneficiaries

26. Annies Place Birsay KW17 2LX

27. Aviedale Rendall KW17 2PB

28. Quarry Field Orphir KW17 2RF

29. Dalkeith Polytunnel Finstown KW17 1TT

30. Gyre Cottage Orphir KW17 2RD

31. Kierfold House Sandwick KW16 3JE

32. Stenwood Finstown KW17 2JX

33. Midhouse Corrigal, Harray KW17 2LQ

34. Finstown Community Garden KW17 2JX

A chance to see some of the gardens you missed,
with cream teas being served in the lovely gardens of
Aviedale overlooking Eynhallow Sound with spectacular
views towards Rousay. Homemade treats at Dalkeith
Polytunnel where some prize winning vegetables will
be on show along with champion chickens and a new
greenhouse. Take time to travel north to Birsay to see
Annies Place demonstrating some beautiful annual
planting right by the beach. Quarrybank is a garden
owned by two florists and the mixture of ponds, hillside
planting with a wonderful collection of hostas and wild
life gardening demonstrates their excellent eye for
colour and structure. Midhouse is only open on this day
and will demonstrate some spectacular ways to garden
on steep slopes; a newly planted garden with some truly
innovative ideas. No disabled access at Midhouse.

***Free Open Air Concert at the Quoy of Houton
in aid of Friends of the Neuro Ward ARI
with music by the Polkadots 5pm - 7pm
Entrance by ticket only. Bring your own Picnic. Raffle.*

For further details see page 66-67, visit
https://www.facebook.com/orkneygardentrail
or contact Caroline Kritchlow
E: c.kritchlow258@btinternet.com

Please see our Facebook page -
facebook.com/orkneygardentrail
All tickets available at Scapa Travel, Kirkwall
E: scapa@barrheadtravel.co.uk

Quoy of Houton, Orkney

brightwater
holidays

SCOTLAND'S
GARDENS
GARDENS OPEN FOR CHARITY

PRIVATE GARDENS OF ROYAL DEESIDE
TOUR FROM 20 - 23 JUNE 2017

We are delighted to organise another exclusive garden tour in association with Scotland's Gardens. This special tour will not only raise more funds for deserving causes that they support but also give us the chance to visit some wonderful private gardens in the north-east of Scotland, most of which are not regularly open to the public.

COST FROM £545

Included in the price:

- Three nights' accommodation on dinner bed and full breakfast basis at the 4-star Ardoe House Hotel and Spa, near Aberdeen. All rooms have private facilities.
- Comfortable coaching throughout.
- Visits to the gardens of Crathes Castle, Drum Castle, Leith Hall, Kildrummy, Findrack, Kincardine, Glenbervie and a guided tour of the Cruickshank Botanic Garden, Aberdeen.
- Services of a Brightwater Holidays Tour Manager

A PERCENTAGE OF THE PROFITS FROM THIS TOUR IS DONATED TO SCOTLAND'S GARDENS.

For full details on the tour contact
01334 657155

Brightwater Holidays Ltd
Eden Park House
Cupar, Fife KY15 4HS
info@brightwaterholidays.com
www.brightwaterholidays.com

Glenbervie

Drum Castle © NTS

Kildrummy Castle Gardens

Leith Hall © NTS

ARGYLE®
CONSULTING LIMITED

Independent Financial Advice
for Individuals & Businesses

CORNEY&BARROW

INDEPENDENT WINE MERCHANTS-1780

For tastings, personal cellar advice,
gift suggestions and event planning
please visit or telephone our
Edinburgh office and tasting room.

Corney & Barrow
Oxenfoord Castle
Pathhead
EH37 5UB

Call **01875 321921**
email
edinburgh@corneyandbarrow.com

www.corneyandbarrow.com

NEW HOPETOUN GARDENS

...so much more than just a garden centre

The perfect place for a relaxed visit at any time of year. Set in six acres of woodland with 20 small themed gardens to explore and probably the biggest range of garden plants for sale in Scotland. The Scottish Home of Miniature and Fairy Gardening.

The Orangery tearoom will revive you and the gift shop will tempt you with the most exciting range of presents for everyone.

art in the garden runs during July and August and features original works of art by artists working in Scotland installed in the gardens.

(Entry is always free to our gardens.)

OPEN EVERY DAY 10.00AM – 5.30PM
New Hopetoun Gardens, by Winchburgh
West Lothian EH52 6QZ   01506 834433
www.newhopetoungardens.co.uk

Visit four Botanic Gardens to see one of the richest plant collections on Earth.

Royal Botanic Garden Edinburgh

Arboretum Place and Inverleith Row, Edinburgh EH3 5LR
Tel 0131 248 2909 | www.rbge.org.uk
Open every day from 10 am (except 1 January and 25 December) | Garden is free | Entry charges apply to Glasshouses

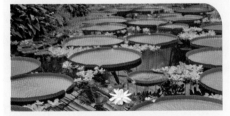

Royal Botanic Garden Edinburgh at **Logan**

Port Logan, Stranraer, Dumfries and Galloway DG9 9ND
Tel 01776 860231 | www.rbge.org.uk/logan
Open daily 15 March to 31 October
Admission charge applies

Royal Botanic Garden Edinburgh at **Benmore**

Dunoon, Argyll PA23 8QU
Tel 01369 706261 | www.rbge.org.uk/benmore
Open daily 1 March to 31 October
Admission charge applies

Royal Botanic Garden Edinburgh at **Dawyck**

Stobo, Scottish Borders EH45 9JU
Tel 01721 760254 | www.rbge.org.uk/dawyck
Open daily 1 February – 30 November
Admission charge applies

The Royal Botanic Garden Edinburgh is a Charity registered in Scotland (number SC007983) and is a Non Departmental Public Body (NDPB) sponsored and supported through Grant-in-Aid by the Scottish Government's Environment and Forestry Directorate (ENFOR).

Local relationship banking

At Handelsbanken relationship banking still lives up to its name. You only ever deal with people you know by name and decisions are made locally at the branch. Our simple aim is to provide the best possible service to our customers.

With over 200 branches across the UK, our branches in Scotland are based in Aberdeen, Dundee, Edinburgh, Dunfermline, Glasgow, Inverness, Perth and Stirling.

Contact us at your local branch where we would be delighted to talk to you about your specific needs and longer-term plans, and how we can support you.

handelsbanken.co.uk   **Handelsbanken**

GENERAL INFORMATION

MAPS
A map of each region and district is provided. These show the general areas and location of gardens. Directions can be found in the garden descriptions.

HOUSES
Houses are not open unless specifically stated; where the house or part of the house is open, an additional charge is usually made.

TOILETS
Private gardens do not normally have outside toilets. For security reasons owners have been advised not to admit visitors into their houses.

PHOTOGRAPHY
No photographs taken in a garden may be used for sale or reproduction without the prior permission of the garden owner.

CHILDREN
Children are generally welcome but must be accompanied by an adult. Some of our gardens have children's activities; details in the garden descriptions.

CANCELLATIONS
All cancellations will be posted on our website www.scotlandsgardens.org

KEY TO SYMBOLS

	New in 2017		Homemade teas		Accommodation
	Teas		Dogs on a lead allowed		Plant stall
	Cream teas		Wheelchair access		Scottish Snowdrop Festival

GARDEN LISTINGS

REGIONAL MAP OF SCOTLAND

Scotland's Gardens 2017 Guidebook is sponsored by INVESTEC WEALTH & INVESTMENT

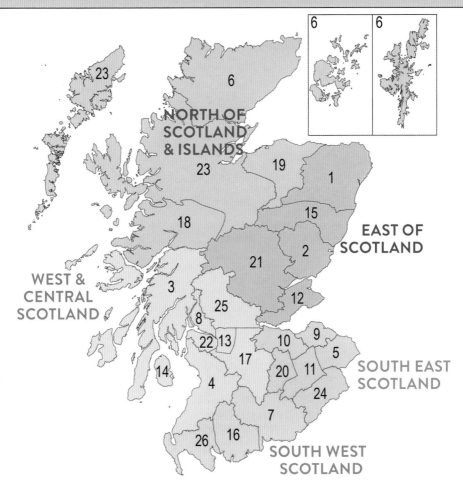

1. Aberdeenshire
2. Angus & Dundee
3. Argyll
4. Ayrshire
5. Berwickshire
6. Caithness, Sutherland, Orkney & Shetland
7. Dumfriesshire
8. Dunbartonshire
9. East Lothian
10. Edinburgh , Midlothian & West Lothian
11. Ettrick & Lauderdale
12. Fife
13. Glasgow & District
14. Isle of Arran
15. Kincardine & Deeside
16. Kirkcudbrightshire
17. Lanarkshire
18. Lochaber
19. Moray & Nairn
20. Peeblesshire
21. Perth & Kinross
22. Renfrewshire
23. Ross, Cromarty, Skye & Inverness
24. Roxburghshire
25. Stirlingshire
26. Wigtownshire

NORTH OF SCOTLAND & ISLANDS

Scotland's Gardens 2017 Guidebook is sponsored by **INVESTEC WEALTH & INVESTMENT**

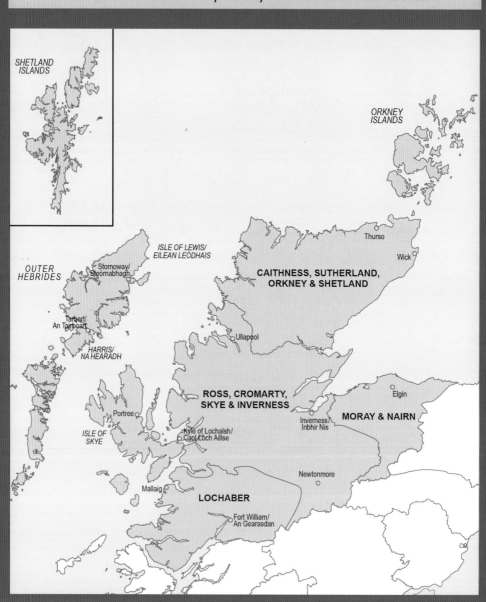

SHETLAND ISLANDS

ORKNEY ISLANDS

Thurso

Wick

ISLE OF LEWIS/ EILEAN LEÒDHAIS

OUTER HEBRIDES

Stornoway/ Steòrnabhagh

CAITHNESS, SUTHERLAND, ORKNEY & SHETLAND

Tarbert/ An Tairbeart

HARRIS/ NA HEARADH

Ullapool

Portree

Elgin

ROSS, CROMARTY, SKYE & INVERNESS

MORAY & NAIRN

ISLE OF SKYE

Inverness/ Inbhir Nis

Kyle of Lochalsh/ Caol Loch Aillse

Newtonmore

Mallaig

LOCHABER

Fort William/ An Gearasdan

CAITHNESS & SUTHERLAND

Scotland's Gardens 2017 Guidebook is sponsored by **INVESTEC WEALTH & INVESTMENT**

District Organisers

To be advised

E: caithness@scotlandsgardens.org

Area Organisers

Sara Shaw

Amat, Ardgay, Sutherland IV24 3BS

Treasurer

To be advised

Gardens open on a specific date

Amat, Ardgay	Saturday 10 June	2:00pm	- 5:00pm
Amat, Ardgay	Sunday 11 June	2:00pm	- 5:00pm
Duncan Street Gardens, Thurso	Sunday 11 June	1:00pm	- 5:00pm
Bighouse Lodge, by Melvich	Sunday 2 July	2:00pm	- 5:00pm
The Castle & Gardens of Mey, Mey	Wednesday 5 July	10:00am	- 5:00pm
The Castle & Gardens of Mey, Mey	Wednesday 12 July	10:00am	- 5:00pm
House of Tongue, Tongue	Saturday 29 July	2:00pm	- 6:00pm
Langwell, Berriedale	Sunday 6 August	1:00pm	- 5:00pm
Springpark House, Thurso	Saturday 12 August	1:00pm	- 5:00pm
Springpark House, Thurso	Sunday 13 August	1:00pm	- 5:00pm
The Castle & Gardens of Mey, Mey	Saturday 19 August	10:00am	- 5:00pm
The Garden at the Auld Post Office B&B, Spittal-by-Mybster	Sunday 27 August	2:00pm	- 5:00pm

Key to symbols

	New in 2017		Homemade teas		Accommodation
	Teas		Dogs on a lead allowed		Plant stall
	Cream teas	&#9855;	Wheelchair access		Scottish Snowdrop Festival

GARDEN LOCATIONS IN CAITHNESS & SUTHERLAND

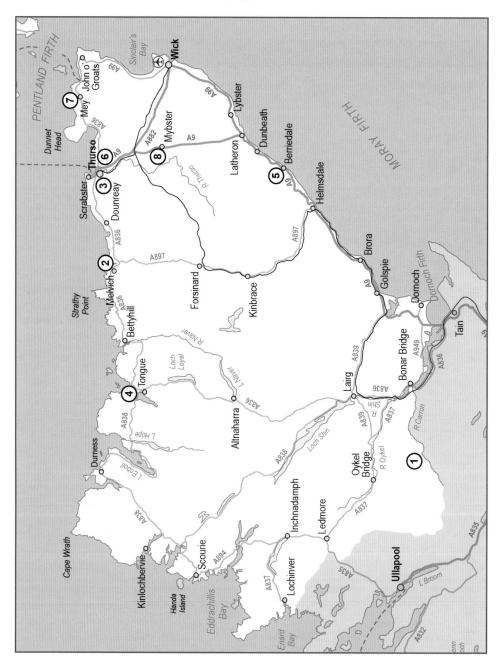

AMAT
Ardgay IV24 3BS
Jonny and Sara Shaw
E: sara.amat@aol.co.uk

Riverside garden surrounded by the old Caledonian Amat Forest. Herbaceous borders and rockery set in a large lawn looking onto a salmon pool. Old and new rhododendrons with woodland and river walk plus large specimen trees in policies.

Other Details: Homemade teas £3.50.

Directions: Take the road from Ardgay to Croick nine miles. Turn left at the red phone box and the garden is 500 yards on the left.

Disabled Access:
Partial

Opening Times:
Saturday 10 June &
Sunday 11 June
2:00pm - 5:00pm

Admission:
£4.50, accompanied children free

Charities:
Alzheimer Scotland (40 nips project) receives 20%, Croick Church receives 20%, the net remaining to SG Beneficiaries

BIGHOUSE LODGE
by Melvich KW14 7YJ
Bighouse Estate
E: info@bighouseestate.co.uk   www.bighouseestate.co.uk

Bighouse Lodge is situated on the north coast of Sutherland at the mouth of the River Halladale. The two acre walled garden, originally laid out in 1715, consists of a central axis leading to a charming bothy with lawn, herbaceous borders, a sunken garden and four separate conceptual gardens behind the hedgerows. Each garden contains a sculpture to reflect the aspects of the Bighouse Estate namely the River, the Forest, the Strath and the Hill. The garden has recently been restored and is now a most interesting place to visit.

Other Details: There are gravelled paths. Homemade teas available priced £3.50.

Directions: Off the A836 ½ mile East of Melvich.

Disabled Access:
Partial

Opening Times:
Sunday 2 July
2:00pm - 5:00pm

Admission:
£4.00, children under 12
£1.00

Charities:
RNLI receives 40%, the net remaining to SG Beneficiaries

DUNCAN STREET GARDENS
Thurso KW14 7HU
The Gardeners of Duncan Street

Three beautiful gardens open on Duncan Street to include:

"Lazy Glade" 50 Duncan Street: A secluded walled garden in the centre of the town overflowing with plants, shrubs and small trees featuring a small glade, water feature and stream.

36 Duncan Street: A compact, centrally located town garden which is densely planted, and features a collection of bonsai.

7 Duncan Street: A town garden with a mix of trees, shrubs, ferns and herbaceous plants including many interesting and unusual species.

Other Details: Wheelchair access is limited due to narrow paths and steps.

Directions: Visitors to the gardens should start at 7 Duncan Street, Thurso.

Disabled Access:
Partial

Opening Times:
Sunday 11 June
1:00pm - 5:00pm

Admission:
£5.00, accompanied children free

Charities:
Friends of Thor House, Thurso receives 14%, The Samaritans receive 13%, Anthony Nolan receives 13%, the net remaining to SG Beneficiaries

HOUSE OF TONGUE
Tongue, Lairg IV27 4XH
The Countess of Sutherland
E: richardrowe37@gmail.com

Seventeenth century house on the Kyle of Tongue. Walled garden with herbaceous borders, lawns, old fashioned roses, vegetables, soft fruit and small orchard.

Other Details: Teas available at the hostel at beginning of the causeway.

Directions: Half a mile from Tongue village. The house is just off the main road approaching the causeway. The garden is well signposted.

Disabled Access:
Partial

Opening Times:
Saturday 29 July
2:00pm - 6:00pm

Admission:
£4.00, accompanied children free

Charities:
Children 1st receives 40%, the net remaining to SG Beneficiaries

---

LANGWELL
Berriedale KW7 6HD
Welbeck Estates T: 01593 751278/751237
E: macanson@hotmail.com

A beautiful and spectacular old walled garden with outstanding borders situated in the secluded Langwell Strath. Charming wooded access drive with a chance to see deer.

Other Details: Teas will be served in the Berriedale Portland Hall which is just off the A9 on the north side of Berriedale Braes 100 metres downhill from and opposite the Berriedale Church. Also open by arrangement 1 April - 31 October.

Directions: Turn off the A9 at Berriedale Braes, up the private (tarred) drive signposted Private - Langwell House. It is around 1¼ miles from the A9.

Disabled Access:
Partial

Opening Times:
Sunday 6 August
1:00pm - 5:00pm

Admission:
£4.00, accompanied children free

Charities:
RNLI receives 40%, the net remaining to SG Beneficiaries

SPRINGPARK HOUSE
Laurie Terrace, Thurso KW14 8NR
Ronald and Kirsty Gunn T: 01847 894797

Several individually styled gardens within one walled garden. Collection of old farming implements and household memorabilia on show. Vegetable garden and poly-tunnel. The garden is on one level with good wheelchair access and plenty of parking places close to the garden. Disabled parking spaces in the driveway.

Other Details: Teas £2.00.

Directions: In Thurso turn off the A836 Castletown road at Mount Pleasant Road, continue up the hill until you see Laurie Terrace (last road on the right), the house is at the end of the street.

Disabled Access:
Full

Opening Times:
Saturday 12 August &
Sunday 13 August
1:00pm - 5:00pm

Admission:
£3.50, accompanied children
free

Charities:
Cancer Research UK receives
40%, the net remaining to
SG Beneficiaries

THE CASTLE & GARDENS OF MEY
Mey KW14 8XH
The Queen Elizabeth Castle of Mey Trust T: 01847 851473
E: enquiries@castleofmey.org.uk   www.castleofmey.org.uk

Originally a Z plan castle bought by the Queen Mother in 1952 and then restored and improved. The walled garden and the East Garden were also created by the Queen Mother. An animal centre has been established over the last three years and is proving very popular with all ages. New herbaceous border, east facing, nestled under the west wall contains agapanthus, phlox, pink aconitum, sidalcea, verbascum and knautia among others.

Other Details: Tearoom, shop and animal centre. Visitor Centre, Animal Centre and Gardens open 10:00am - 5:00pm. Castle opens 10:20am and last entries are at 4:00pm. Open from mid May 2017 to the end of September 2017.

Directions: On the A836 between Thurso and John O'Groats.

Disabled Access:
Partial

Opening Times:
Wednesday 5 July,
Wednesday 12 July
& Saturday 19 August
10:00am - 5:00pm

Admission:
Gardens only: £6.50, children
£3.00, family £19.00
Castle & Gardens: £11.50,
concessions £9.75, children
£6.50, family £30.00

Charities:
Donation to SG Beneficiaries

NEW THE GARDEN AT THE AULD POST OFFICE B&B
Spittal-by-Mybster KW1 5XR
Lynne and Weyland Read
www.auldpostoffice.com

Surrounded by eight acres of Alaskan Lodgepole pine trees, this secluded garden has a variety of beds and borders containing evergreen plants, shrubs, grasses and perennials. Ten years and younger, the one third acre garden provides a meandering walk under the pergola to beds set in the lawn. The fish share their new pond with grasses and lilies and the garden walk continues beneath 20 year old pine trees, under-planted with shade loving perennials. Heather, junipers and conifers provide an all year centrepiece. There are many seating areas to rest awhile, and for the hardy, a stout footwear walk can be taken through the surrounding woodland. Planting has been chosen to encourage bees, birds and butterflies and the hens potter in their woodland enclosure.

Other Details: Homemade teas available priced £3.00.

Directions: A9 at Spittal

Disabled Access:
Partial

Opening Times:
Sunday 27 August
2:00pm - 5:00pm

Admission:
£3.50, accompanied children
free

Charities:
Cancer Research receives
40%, the net remaining to
SG Beneficiaries

LOCHABER

Scotland's Gardens 2017 Guidebook is sponsored by **INVESTEC WEALTH & INVESTMENT**

District Organiser & Treasurer

To be advised   E: lochaber@scotlandsgardens.org

Gardens open on a specific date

Canna House Walled Garden, Isle of Canna	Saturday 6 May	10:00am - 4:30pm
Ardverikie with Aberarder, Kinlochlaggan	Sunday 28 May	2:00pm - 5:30pm
Canna House Walled Garden, Isle of Canna	Saturday 12 August	10:00am - 4:30pm

Gardens open regularly

Ardtornish, By Lochaline, Morvern	Daily	10:00am - 6:00pm

Ardverikie

Key to symbols

New in 2017	Homemade teas	Accommodation
Teas	Dogs on a lead allowed	Plant stall
Cream teas	Wheelchair access	Scottish Snowdrop Festival

GARDEN LOCATIONS IN LOCHABER

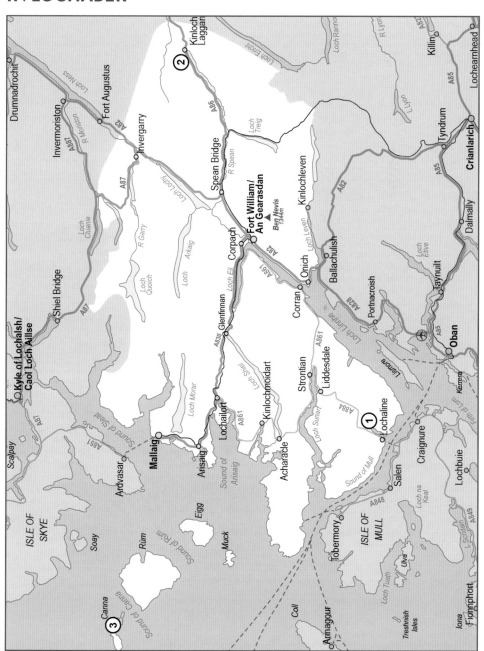

LOCHABER

ARDTORNISH
By Lochaline, Morvern PA80 5UZ
Mrs John Raven

Wonderful gardens of interesting mature conifers, rhododendrons, deciduous trees, shrubs and herbaceous, set amid magnificent scenery.

Directions: On the A884 Lochaline three miles.

Disabled Access:
None

Opening Times:
Daily 10:00am - 6:00pm

Admission:
£4.00

Charities:
Donation to SG Beneficiaries

ARDVERIKIE WITH ABERARDER
Kinlochlaggan PH20 1BX
Mrs E T Smyth-Osbourne, Mrs P Laing and The Feilden Family

Ardverikie T: 01528 544300
Lovely setting on Loch Laggan with magnificent trees. Walled garden with large collection of acers, shrubs and herbaceous. Architecturally interesting house (not open). Site of the filming of the TV series *Monarch of the Glen*.

Aberarder T: 01528 544300
The garden has been laid out over the last 20 years to create a mixture of spring and autumn plants and trees, including rhododendrons, azaleas and acers. The elevated view down Loch Laggan from the garden is exceptional.

Other Details: Teas at Aberarder for an additional charge.

Directions: On A86 between Newtonmore and Spean Bridge. Ardverikie's entrance is at the east end of Loch Laggan by the gate lodge over the bridge. For Aberarder go up the drive 200 yeards west of the Ardverikie entrance Lodge, adjoining a cottage

Disabled Access:
Partial

Opening Times:
Sunday 28 May
2:00pm - 5:30pm

Admission:
£5.00 includes entrance to both gardens

Charities:
Highland Hospice receives 20%, Laggan Church receives 20%, the net remaining to SG Beneficiaries

CANNA HOUSE WALLED GARDEN
Isle of Canna PH44 4RS
National Trust for Scotland T: 01687 462473
E: fmackenzie@nts.org.uk www.nts.org.uk/canna

Formerly derelict two acre walled garden brought back to life following a five year restoration project. There are soft fruits, top fruits, vegetables, ornamental lawns and flower beds. There is also a stunning 80 foot Escallonia arch. The garden has been replanted to attract bees, butterflies and moths. The woodland walks outside walls are not to be missed along with the spectacular views of neighbouring islands. Don't miss your chance to see this gem.

Other Details: No on site catering but cafe Canna may be open.

Directions: Access Isle of Canna via Calmac ferry from Mallaig pier.

Disabled Access:
Partial

Opening Times:
Saturday 6 May
& Saturday 12 August
10:00am - 4:30pm

Admission:
By donation

Charities:
Donation to SG Beneficiaries

MORAY & NAIRN

Scotland's Gardens 2017 Guidebook is sponsored by **INVESTEC WEALTH & INVESTMENT**

District Organiser

James Byatt	Lochview Cottage, Scarffbanks, Pitgaveny IV30 5PQ E: moraynairn@scotlandsgardens.org

Area Organisers

Lorraine Dingwall	10 Pilmuir Road West, Forres IV36 2HL
Gwynne & David Hetherington	Haugh Garden, Long Finals, College of Roseisle IV30 5YE
Rebecca Russell	12 Duff Avenue, Elgin, Moray IV30 1QS
Annie Stewart	33 Albert Street, Nairn IV12 4HF

Treasurer

Michael Barnett	Drumdelnies, Nairn IV12 5NT

Gardens open on a specific date

Brodie Castle, Brodie	Sat/Sun 22/23 April	10:30am	-	4:00pm
Balnabual Cottage, Dalcross	Sunday 28 May	2:00pm	-	5:00pm
Haugh Garden, College of Roseisle	Saturday 24 June	2:00pm	-	5:00pm
10 Pilmuir Road West , Forres	Sunday 2 July	2:00pm	-	5:00pm
Knock House, Rafford, Forres	Sat/Sun 15/16 July	1:30pm	-	5:30pm
Haugh Garden, College of Roseisle	Sats 22 July & 19 August	2:00pm	-	5:00pm
Gordonstoun, Duffus	Sunday 10 September	2:00pm	-	4:30pm

Gardens open regularly

Burgie, Between Forres and Elgin	1 April - 31 October	8:00am	-	5:00pm

Gardens open by arrangement

10 Pilmuir Road West , Forres	28 January - 12 March	01309 674634
Haugh Garden, College of Roseisle	1 May - 31 August	01343 835790

Key to symbols

	New in 2017		Homemade teas		Accommodation
	Teas		Dogs on a lead allowed		Plant stall
	Cream teas		Wheelchair access		Scottish Snowdrop Festival

GARDEN LOCATIONS IN
MORAY & NAIRN

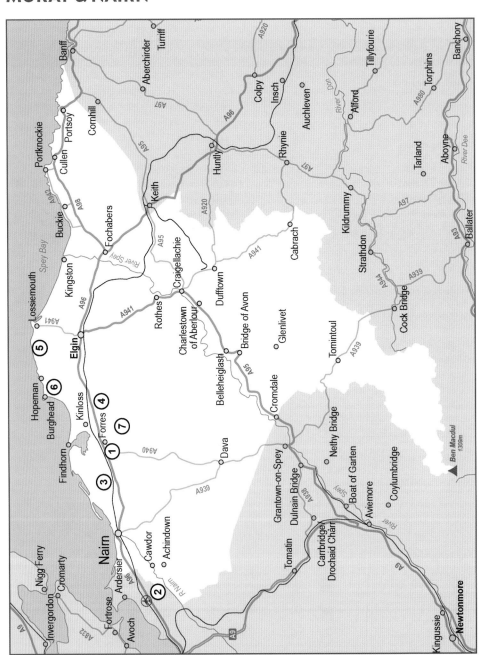

10 PILMUIR ROAD WEST
Forres IV36 2HL
Mrs Lorraine Dingwall T: 01309 674634
E: fixandig@aol.com

Plantsman's small town garden with over 300 cultivars of hostas, an extensive collection of hardy geraniums together with many other unusual plants. Managed entirely without the use of artificial fertilizers or chemicals, the owner encourages hedgehogs, toads and wild birds to control slugs. In early spring there are approximately 150 named snowdrops to be seen, some of which are very rare.

Other Details: During snowdrop season please phone to arrange a visit as parking is limited and weather variable.

Directions: From Tesco roundabout at Forres continue along Nairn Road. Take the first left onto Ramflat Road, then go right at the bottom and first left onto Pilmuir Road West.

Disabled Access:
None

Opening Times:
Sunday 2 July
2:00pm - 5:00pm
Also by arrangement
28 January - 12 March
for the Snowdrop Festival

Admission:
£3.00

Charities:
Macmillan Cancer Support
receives 40%, the net
remaining to SG Beneficiaries

NEW BALNABUAL COTTAGE
Dalcross IV2 7JJ
Mr and Mrs Hamish Mackintosh

One acre mixed garden with rhododendrons, azaleas, large rockeries and alpine beds, pond, stream and water features, greenhouse and alpine house and organic fruit and vegetables.

Directions: Eight miles from Inverness, ten miles from Nairn. From the A96 turn off at Tornagrain and go up the hill for one mile.

Disabled Access:
None

Opening Times:
Sunday 28 May
2:00pm - 5:00pm

Admission:
£4.00

Charities:
All proceeds to
SG Beneficiaries

MORAY & NAIRN

BRODIE CASTLE
Brodie, Forres IV36 2TE
The National Trust for Scotland T: 01309 641371
E: sferguson@nts.org.uk www.nts.org.uk/Property/Brodie-Castle/

The grounds of Brodie Castle are carpeted with daffodils in the spring and include a National Collection of over 110 different cultivars bred at the property by a former laird. Good displays of other spring bulbs and shrubs including dog's tooth violet and rhododendrons. On these special SG open days garden staff will be leading guided tours of the garden and talking about the history of the daffodil collection at Brodie. See the NTS website nearer the date for the tour times.

Other Details: National Plant Collection®: Narcissus (Brodie cvs.). Tea, coffee and cakes will be available to purchase in the tea room. The servery in the castle will be open. Pots of daffodils, including a very limited stock of Brodie cultivars will be available to purchase. Contact the property for further information.

Directions: Off A96 4½ miles west of Forres and 24 miles east of Inverness.

Disabled Access:
Full

Opening Times:
Saturday 22 April
10:30am - 4:00pm
Sunday 23 April
10:30am - 4:00pm

Admission:
Normal NTS admission applies.
Garden tour £3.00 (including NTS members)

Charities:
Donation to SG Beneficiaries

© NTS

NEW BURGIE
Between Forres and Elgin IV36 2QU
Hamish Lochore T: 01343 850231
E: hamish@burgie.org

A rare opportunity to see a sizeable woodland garden/arboretum in its infancy. It has a good collection of rhododendrons, sorbus, alder, birch and tilia but also includes many unusual trees from around the world. The arboretum is zoned into geographic areas and species type. It includes a Japanese garden, bog garden, bog wood, loch and quarry garden. First created in 2005 and is on going. Most plants are grown from hand collected seed and propagated in the Georgian greenhouse.

Other Details: Most woodland walks and paths are suitable for disabled chairs. Dogs welcome on leads. Tours by arrangement.

Directions: A96 between Forres and Elgin. Four miles East of Forres. Six miles west of Elgin. Road end sign Burgie Mains in wrought iron sign with horses and cattle on the top. South off the main road and 1 mile to the Woodland Garden car park.

Disabled Access:
Partial

Opening Times:
1 April - 31 October
8:00am - 5:00pm

Admission:
£3.00, accompanied children free (please use honesty box)

Charities:
Sandpiper Trust receives 20%, World Horse Welfare receives 20%, the net remaining to SG Beneficiaries

GORDONSTOUN

Duffus, near Elgin IV30 5RF
Gordonstoun School T: 01343 837837
E: richardss@gordonstoun.org.uk www.gordonstoun.org.uk

The gardens consist of good formal herbaceous borders around lawns, a terrace and an orchard. The school grounds include Gordonstoun House, a Georgian House of 1775/6 incorporating an earlier 17th century house built for the First Marquis of Huntly, and the school chapel, both of which will be open to visitors. There is also a unique circle of former farm buildings known as the Round Square and a scenic lake.

Directions: Entrance off B9012, four miles from Elgin at Duffus Village.

Disabled Access:
Full

Opening Times:
Sunday 10 September
2:00pm - 4:30pm

Admission:
£4.00, children £2.00

Charities:
All proceeds to
SG Beneficiaries

HAUGH GARDEN

College of Roseisle IV30 5YE
Gwynne and David Hetherington T: 01343 835790

We are now in the fifth year of developing our two acre garden with walks through mature woodland extensively planted with shade loving plants, rhododendrons and spring flowering bulbs and young woodland. Large lawns bordered by extensive herbaceous borders. Ongoing work to develop the garden around the ruins of an 18th century farmhouse continues. There is a wildlife pond with adjacent bog garden, fruit trees and a soft fruit and vegetable garden. The garden also has a greenhouse and large polytunnel.

Other Details: Car parking at Roseisle Village Hall but drop-off available at the house. There will be a well-stocked plant stall.

Directions: From Elgin take the A96 west, then the B9013 Burghead Road to the crossroads at the centre of College of Roseisle. The garden is on the right, enter from the Duffus Road. Village Hall car parking is to the left off Kinloss Road.

Disabled Access:
Partial

Opening Times:
Saturdays 24 June, 22 July
& 19 August
2:00pm - 5:00pm
Also by arrangement
1 May - 31 August

Admission:
£4.00, accomp. children free

Charities:
CHAS receives 20%,
Alzheimer's Scotland receives
20%, the net remaining to
SG Beneficiaries

NEW KNOCK HOUSE

Rafford, Forres IV36 2UH
Mr and Mrs J A Bruce Jones

Our garden surrounds a new eco house and was started five years ago. Being retired we planted mostly shrubs and easy maintenance plants. The two spectacular glacial kettles and a dew pond have become planted features. Round the house are herbaceous plants for extra colour. There is a fruit and vegetable garden with a polytunnel used to propagate plants for the garden and a wildflower meadow. The garden extends into the surrounding woodland, run on a continuous cover basis, with woodland walks and a viewpoint down to Findhorn Bay and the hills to the north.

Directions: Turn east at the war memorial at the north end of Rafford on the B9010. Go uphill 400m and take the drive into the wood on your right marked Knock House.

Disabled Access:
Partial

Opening Times:
Saturday 15 July
Sunday 16 July
1:30pm - 5:30pm

Admission:
£4.00

Charities:
Rafford Church receives
40%, the net remaining to
SG Beneficiaries

ORKNEY

Scotland's Gardens 2017 Guidebook is sponsored by **INVESTEC WEALTH & INVESTMENT**

District Organiser and Treasurer

As per Caithness & Sutherland

Area Organiser

Caroline Critchlow

The Quoy of Houton, Orphir KW17 2RD
E: caithness@scotlandsgardens.org

Gardens open on a specific date

Orkney Garden Festival: Secret Gardens of Kirkwall	Saturday 17 June	11:30am - 4:00pm
Orkney Garden Festival: Trail One	Sunday 18 June	11:30am - 4:00pm
The Quoy of Houton, Orphir	Tuesday 20 June	11:00am - 4:00pm
Orkney Garden Festival: Hoy Garden Trail, Hoy	Saturday 24 June	Check ferry timetable
Orkney Garden Festival: Trail Two	Sunday 25 June	11:30am - 4:00pm

Mucklejocks, part of Orkney Garden Festival: Trail One

Key to symbols

	New in 2017		Homemade teas		Accommodation
	Teas		Dogs on a lead allowed		Plant stall
	Cream teas		Wheelchair access		Scottish Snowdrop Festival

GARDEN LOCATIONS IN ORKNEY

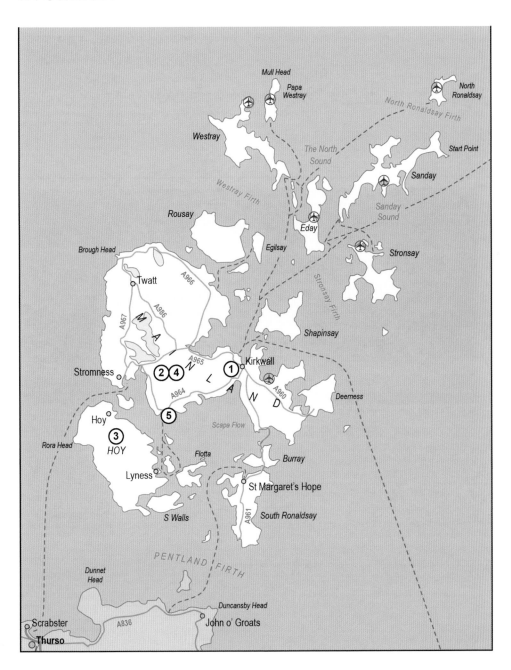

ORKNEY

NEW ORKNEY GARDEN FESTIVAL: SECRET GARDENS OF KIRKWALL
Orkney KW15
The Gardeners of Orkney

Six gardens in Kirkwall. Please see pages 38-39 for further details.

Cream teas will be provided in conjunction with Marie Curie at the Town Hall 11:00am - 4:00pm. Plant Market in Kirkwall town centre.

Other Details: These gardens are opening as part of the Orkney Garden Festival which runs from Saturday 17 June - Sunday 25 June.

For further details visit **https://www.facebook.com/orkneygardentrail** or contact Caroline Kritchlow E: c.kritchlow258@btinternet.com.

Disabled Access:
Partial

Opening Times:
Saturday 17 June
11:30am - 4:00pm

Admission:
£10.00 for all gardens or
£2.00 per garden.
Tickets for all events available
at Scapa Travel, Kirkwall.
E: scapa@barrheadtravel.co.uk

Charities:
All proceeds to
SG Beneficiaries

4 Lynn Crescent, Orkney, One of the Secret Gardens of Kirkwall

NEW ORKNEY GARDEN FESTIVAL: TRAIL ONE
Orkney KW17
The Gardeners of Orkney

Twelve Orkney gardens. Please see pages 38-39 for further details.

Cream teas at Merengo Gardens and refreshments at Dalkeith Polytunnel.

Other Details: These gardens are opening as part of the Orkney Garden Festival which runs from Saturday 17 June - Sunday 25 June.

For further details visit **https://www.facebook.com/orkneygardentrail** or contact Caroline Kritchlow E: c.kritchlow258@btinternet.com.

Disabled Access:
Full

Opening Times:
Sunday 18 June
11:30am - 4:00pm

Admission:
£12.00 for all gardens or
£2.50 per garden
Tickets for all events available
at Scapa Travel, Kirkwall.
E: scapa@barrheadtravel.co.uk

Charities:
All proceeds to
SG Beneficiaries

3 NEW ORKNEY GARDEN FESTIVAL: HOY GARDEN TRAIL
Hoy, Orkney KW17
The Gardeners of Orkney

Seven gardens on the island of Hoy. Please see pages 38-39 for further details.

Other Details: These gardens are opening as part of the Orkney Garden Festival which runs from Saturday 17 June - Sunday 25 June.

For further details visit **https://www.facebook.com/orkneygardentrail** or contact Caroline Kritchlow E: c.kritchlow258@btinternet.com.

Disabled Access:
Partial

Opening Times:
Saturday 24 June
times dependent on ferry

Admission:
£12.00 for all or £2.50 per garden - please book the ferry prior to purchasing tickets. Tickets for all events available at Scapa Travel, Kirkwall.
E: scapa@barrheadtravel.co.uk

Charities:
All proceeds to
SG Beneficiaries

4 NEW ORKNEY GARDEN FESTIVAL: TRAIL TWO
Orkney KW17
The Gardeners of Orkney

Nine Orkney gardens. Please see pages 38-39 for further details.

Other Details: These gardens are opening as part of the Orkney Garden Festival which runs from Saturday 17 June - Sunday 25 June.

For further details visit **https://www.facebook.com/orkneygardentrail** or contact Caroline Kritchlow E: c.kritchlow258@btinternet.com.

Disabled Access:
Partial

Opening Times:
Sunday 25 June
11:30am - 4:00pm

Admission:
£12.00 for six gardens or £2.50 per garden. Tickets for all events available at Scapa Travel, Kirkwall.
E: scapa@barrheadtravel.co.uk

Charities:
All proceeds to
SG Beneficiaries

5 THE QUOY OF HOUTON
Orphir KW17 2RD
Kevin and Caroline Critchlow T: 01856 811237
E: c.kritchlow258@btinternet.com

An historic walled garden a stone's throw away from the sea and completely restored in 2008. The garden is planted to withstand winds in excess of 100 mph and features drystone walling features, raised beds and a 60 foot water rill. The planting reflects its coastal location and is planted in the cottage garden style with towering allium, many varieties of geranium and plants collected from around Europe. There are wildflower areas which encourage bees and butterflies. There is a separate walled vegetable garden and fruit cage which supplies the house and B&B and cottage guests.

Other Details: Opening as part of the Orkney Garden Festival. Coffee and chat with Rosa Steppanova. Refreshments available.

Directions: A964 from Kirkwall to Houton. Take ferry turning, straight across at first junction following tarmac road to a two storey yellow house across the bay.

Disabled Access:
None

Opening Times:
Tuesday 20 June
11:00am - 4:00pm

Admission:
£2.50

Charities:
Friends of the Neuro Ward at Aberdeen Royal Infirmary receives 40%, the net remaining to SG Beneficiaries

ROSS, CROMARTY, SKYE & INVERNESS

Scotland's Gardens 2017 Guidebook is sponsored by INVESTEC WEALTH & INVESTMENT

District Organiser

Lucy Lister-Kaye

House of Aigas, Beauly IV4 7AD
E: rosscromary@scotlandsgardens.org

Area Organiser

Emma MacKenzie

Glenkyllachy, Tomatin IV13 7YA

Treasurer

Sheila Kerr

Lilac Cottage, Struy, By Beauly IV4 7JU

Gardens open on a specific date

Dundonnell House, Little Loch Broom	Thursday 13 April	2:00pm	5:00pm
Inverewe Garden and Estate, Poolewe	Wednesday 17 May	10:00am	5:30pm
Aultgowrie Mill, Aultgowrie	Sunday 21 May	1:00pm	5:00pm
Skye Forest Gardens, Skye Permaculture, Rhuba Phoil	Sunday 21 May	Dawn	Dusk
House of Gruinard, Laide, by Achnasheen	Wednesday 24 May	Dawn	Dusk
Oldtown of Leys Garden, Inverness	Saturday 27 May	2:00pm	5:00pm
Hugh Miller's Birthplace Cottage & Museum, Cromarty	Sunday 28 May	12:00pm	5:00pm
Dundonnell House, Little Loch Broom	Thursday 1 June	2:00pm	5:00pm
Gorthleck, Stratherrick	Thursday 1 June	10:00am	9:00pm
Inverewe Garden and Estate, Poolewe	Thursday 1 June	9:30am	6:00pm
Field House, Belladrum	Sunday 4 June	2:00pm	4:30pm
Malin, Glenaldie, Tain	Saturday 10 June	11:00am	5:00pm
Malin, Glenaldie, Tain	Sunday 11 June	11:00am	5:00pm
Brackla Wood, Culbokie, Dingwall	Thursday 22 June	2:00pm	4:30pm
House of Aigas and Field Centre, By Beauly	Sunday 25 June	2:00pm	5:00pm
Aultgowrie Mill, Aultgowrie	Sunday 16 July	1:00pm	5:00pm
Dundonnell House, Little Loch Broom	Thursday 20 July	2:00pm	5:00pm
2 Durnamuck, Little Loch Broom	Saturday 22 July	12:00pm	5:00pm
House of Aigas and Field Centre, By Beauly	Sunday 23 July	2:00pm	5:00pm
Dundonnell House, Little Loch Broom	Thursday 17 August	2:00pm	5:00pm
2 Durnamuck, Little Loch Broom	Sunday 20 August	12:00pm	5:00pm
Highland Liliums, Kiltarlity	Sunday 27 August	12:00pm	4:30pm
Old Allangrange, Munlochy	Saturday 2 September	10:30am	5:00pm
2 Durnamuck, Little Loch Broom	Saturday 9 September	12:00pm	5:00pm
Dundonnell House, Little Loch Broom	Thursday 21 September	2:00pm	5:00pm

ROSS, CROMARTY, SKYE & INVERNESS

Gardens open regularly

Abriachan Garden Nursery, Loch Ness Side	1 February - 30 November	9:00am - 7:00pm
Attadale, Strathcarron	1 April - 28 October (exc. Sundays)	10:00am - 5:30pm
Balmeanach House, Balmeanach	2 May - 6 October (Tue and Fri only)	10:30am - 3:00pm
Bhlaraidh House, Glenmoriston	13 April - 30 September (Thur - Sun only)	10:00am - 6:00pm
Dunvegan Castle and Gardens, Isle of Skye	1 April - 15 October	10:00am - 5:30pm
Highland Liliums	Daily	9:00am - 5:00pm
Leathad Ard, Upper Carloway	15 May - 2 September (exc. Sundays)	10:00am - 6:00pm
Oldtown of Leys Garden, Inverness	Daily	Dawn - Dusk
The Lookout, Kilmuir	1 May - 31 August (Sundays only)	12:00pm - 4:00pm

Gardens open by arrangement

Dundonnell House, Little Loch Broom	3 April - 31 October (Monday - Friday only)	07789 390028
Glenkyllachy Lodge, Tomatin	1 May - 30 October	emmaglenkyllachy@gmail.com
House of Aigas and Field Centre, By Beauly	1 April - 28 October	01463 782443
Leathad Ard, Upper Carloway	1 April - 30 September (exc. Sundays)	01851 643204
The Lookout, Kilmuir	1 May - 31 August	01463 731489

Key to symbols

 New in 2017

 Teas

 Cream teas

 Homemade teas

 Dogs on a lead allowed

 Wheelchair access

 Accommodation

 Plant stall

 Scottish Snowdrop Festival

GARDEN LOCATIONS IN
ROSS, CROMARTY, SKYE & INVERNESS

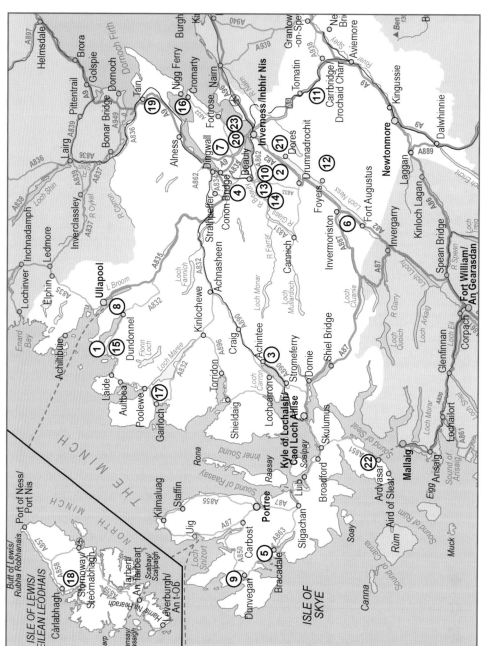

2 DURNAMUCK
Little Loch Broom, Wester Ross IV23 2QZ
Will Soos and Susan Pomeroy T: 01854 633761
E: sueandwill@icloud.com

Our garden is situated on the edge of Little Loch Broom and is south east facing. It is a coastal plantsman's garden with a rich mix of herbaceous borders, trees and shrubs, vegetables, drystone wall planting, South African plants, Mediterranean plants, wild meadow and stunning views. Many of the plants have been collected from all over the world and growing them in Durnamuck has provided the obvious challenges but with an overall pleasing outcome.

Other Details: The ground is a bit stony in places, including the drive. Teas are available Sunday 20 August and Saturday 9 September only.

Directions: On the west coast take the A832, then take the turning along the single track road signed Badcaul, continue to the yellow salt bin, turn right, go to bottom of the hill and it is the house with the red roof. There is parking down by the house if needed.

Disabled Access:
None

Opening Times:
Saturday 22 July,
Sunday 20 August
& Saturday 9 September
12:00pm - 5:00pm

Admission:
£3.00

Charities:
Ankizy Gasy - Children of Madagascar Foundatioon receives 40%, the net remaining to SG Beneficiaries

---

ABRIACHAN GARDEN NURSERY
Loch Ness Side IV3 8LA
Mr and Mrs Davidson T: 01463 861232
E: info@lochnessgarden.com www.lochnessgarden.com

This is an outstanding garden. Over four acres of exciting plantings with winding paths through native woodlands. Seasonal highlights - snowdrops, hellebores, primulas, meconopsis, hardy geraniums and colour-themed summer beds. Views over Loch Ness.

Other Details: Working retail nursery.

Directions: On A82 Inverness/Drumnadrochit road, approximately eight miles south of Inverness.

Disabled Access:
Partial

Opening Times:
1 February - 30 November
9:00am - 7:00pm

Admission:
£3.00

Charities:
Donation: Highland Hospice receives 40%, the net remaining to SG Beneficiaries

---

ATTADALE
Strathcarron IV54 8YX
Mr and Mrs Ewen Macpherson T: 01520 722603
E: info@attadalegardens.com www.attadalegardens.com

The Gulf Stream, surrounding hills and rocky cliffs, create a microclimate for 20 acres of outstanding water gardens, old rhododendrons, unusual trees and a fern collection in a geodesic dome. There is also a sunken fern garden developed on the site of an early 19th century drain, a waterfall into a pool with dwarf rhododendrons, sunken garden, peace garden and kitchen garden. Other features include a conservatory, Japanese garden, sculpture collection and giant sundial.

Other Details: Disabled car parking by main house.

Directions: On the A890 between Strathcarron and South Strome.

Disabled Access:
Partial

Opening Times:
1 April - 28 October
10:00am - 5:30pm
(exc. Sundays)

Admission:
£8.00, OAPs £6.00,
children £1.00, free entry for wheelchair users

Charities:
Donation to SG Beneficiaries

AULTGOWRIE MILL
Aultgowrie, Urray, Muir of Ord IV6 7XA
Mr and Mrs John Clegg T: 01997 433699
E: john@johnclegg.com

Aultgowrie Mill is an 18th century converted water mill set in gardens, river and woodlands of 13 acres. Features include a wooded island, a half acre wildflower meadow and a wildlife pond, all with outstanding views of the surrounding hills. The maturing gardens have terraces, lawns, two mixed orchards and raised vegetable beds with glasshouse and a third of a mile river walk. The BBC's *Beechgrove Garden* featured this garden in July 2014.

Other Details: Homemade cream teas are served on the balcony and millpond lawn. Maps and photographs of the gardens, island and river walks will be on display, ample field parking. Well behaved dogs on leads welcome. Large, extensive plant stall.

Directions: From the south, turn left at Muir of Ord Distillery, Aultgowrie Mill is 3.2 miles. From the north and west, after Marybank Primary School, Aultgowrie Mill is 1.7 miles up the hill.

Disabled Access:
Partial

Opening Times:
Sunday 21 May
Sunday 16 July
1:00pm - 5:00pm

Admission:
£4.50, children under 12 free

Charities:
RNLI receives 40%, the net remaining to SG Beneficiaries

 BALMEANACH HOUSE
Balmeanach House, Balmeanach, near Struan, Isle of Skye IV56 8FH
Mrs Arlene Macphie T: 01470 572320
E: info@skye-holiday.com   www.skye-holiday.com

During the late 1980s, a third of an acre of croft land was fenced in to create a garden. Now there is a glorious herbaceous border, bedding plants area and a small azalea/rhododendron walk. In addition, there is a woodland dell with fairies, three ponds and a small shrubbery. Lots of seating areas are provided and visitors are welcome to rest, or even picnic, remembering, please to take all litter away.

Other Details: Plant stall at Plants 'n' Stuff, Atholl Service Station. Teas at Waterside Cafe, Atholl Service Station.

Directions: A87 to Sligachan, turn left, Balmeanach is five miles north of Struan and five miles south of Dunvegan.

Disabled Access:
None

Opening Times:
2 May - 6 October
10:30am - 3:00pm
Tuesdays and Fridays only

Admission:
£3.00, children under 12 free

Charities:
SSPCA receives 40%, the net remaining to SG Beneficiaries

 NEW BHLARAIDH HOUSE
Glenmoriston, Inverness IV63 7YH
Harry and Jean Robinson

An acre of mature gardens around an old estate manager's cottage. The theme is a backdrop of Highland woodlands with heritage oak trees interspersed with drystone features and ponds. There are areas of conifers, evergreens and perennials for year round interest with drifts of spring bulbs and numerous seasonal plants.

Other Details: Self service tea/coffee and biscuits available in the garden studio. Website at http://historicalresearch.org/slide-show.html gives a good summary and will be updated regularly to show work done and what is in flower.

Directions: On the A887 road between Loch Ness and the Isle of Skye, four miles west of Invermoriston, turn off at Bhlaraidh Private Road sign and park by the Scotland's Gardens sign.

Disabled Access:
None

Opening Times:
13 April - 30 September
10:00am - 6:00pm
Thursdays - Sundays only)

Admission:
£3.00

Charities:
All proceeds to
SG Beneficiaries

7 BRACKLA WOOD
Culbokie, Dingwall IV7 8GY
Susan and Ian Dudgeon T: 01349 877765
E: smdbrackla@aol.com

Mature one acre plot consisting of woodland, wildlife features, ponds, mixed borders, a kitchen garden, rockery and mini-orchard. Spring bulbs and hellebores, rhododendrons, wisteria and roses followed by crocosmia, clematis and deciduous trees provide continuous colour and interest throughout the seasons. There is always the chance to see red squirrels.

Other Details: Strictly no dogs except guide dogs.

Directions:
From N - take A9 turn to Culbokie. At end of village, turn right to Munlochy. A mile up the road, turn right into No Through Road to Upper Braefindon.
From S - take A9 to Munlochy. At end of village, turn right and then sharp left up road signposted Culbokie and Killen. After about 4½ miles turn left onto road signposted Upper Braefindon. Brackla Wood is the first house on left.

Disabled Access:
Partial

Opening Times:
Thursday 22 June
2:00pm - 4:30pm

Admission:
£3.00, accompanied children free

Charities:
Black Isle MacMillan Cancer Care receives 40%, the net remaining to SG Beneficiaries

8 DUNDONNELL HOUSE
Little Loch Broom, Wester Ross IV23 2QW
Dundonnell Estates T: 07789 390028

CELEBRATING 50 YEARS OF OPENING FOR CHARITY WITH SCOTLAND'S GARDENS!

Camellias, magnolias and bulbs in spring, rhododendrons and laburnum walk in this ancient walled garden. Exciting planting in new borders gives all year colour centred around one of the oldest yew trees in Scotland. A new water sculpture, midsummer roses, restored Edwardian glasshouse, riverside walk, arboretum - all in the valley below the peaks of An Teallach.

Other Details: Champion Trees: Yew and Holly. On 1 June homemade teas are available at the house. On other dates teas are available at Maggie's Tearoom three miles towards Little Loch Broom.

Directions: Off A835 at Braemore on to A832. After 11 miles take Badralloch turn for half a mile.

Disabled Access:
Partial

Opening Times:
Thursdays 13 April, 1 June, 20 July, 17 August & 21 Sept
2:00pm - 5:00pm
Also by arrangement 3 April - 31 October (Mon - Fri only)

Admission:
£3.50, accomp. children free

Charities: Nicholls Spinal Injury Foundation and Bumblebee Conservation Trust both receive 20%, the net remaining to SG Beneficiaries

9 DUNVEGAN CASTLE AND GARDENS
Isle of Skye IV55 8WF
Hugh Macleod of Macleod T: 01470 521206
E: info@dunvegancastle.com www.dunvegancastle.com

Five acres of formal gardens dating from the 18th century. In contrast to the barren moorland of Skye, the gardens are an oasis featuring an eclectic mix of plants, woodland glades, shimmering pools fed by waterfalls and streams flowing down to the sea. After the Water Garden with its ornate bridges and islands replete with a rich and colourful plant variety, wander through the elegant surroundings of the formal Round Garden. The Walled Garden is worth a visit to see its colourful herbaceous borders and recently added Victorian style glasshouse. In what was formerly the castle's vegetable garden, there is a Garden Museum and a diverse range of plants and flowers which complement the features including a waterlily pond, a neoclassical urn and a larch pergola. Replanting and landscaping has taken place over the last 30 years to restore and develop the gardens.

Directions: One mile from Dunvegan Village, 23 miles west of Portree. Follow the signs for Dunvegan Castle.

Disabled Access:
Partial

Opening Times:
1 April - 15 October
10:00am - 5:30pm

Admission:
Gardens only admission:
Adults £11.00, children
£7.00, seniors/students/
groups £8.00

Charities:
Donation to SG Beneficiaries

10 FIELD HOUSE
Belladrum, Beauly IV4 7BA
Mr and Mrs D Paterson
www.dougthegarden.co.uk

An informal country garden in a one acre site with mixed borders, ponds and some unusual plants - a plantsman's garden. Featured on *Beechgrove Garden*.

Directions: Four miles from Beauly on A833 Beauly to Drumnadrochit road, then follow signs to Belladrum.

Disabled Access:
Partial

Opening Times:
Sunday 4 June
2:00pm - 4:30pm

Admission:
£4.00

Charities:
Highland Disability Sport
Swim Team receives 40%,
the net remaining to
SG Beneficiaries

11 GLENKYLLACHY LODGE
Tomatin IV13 7YA
Mr and Mrs Philip Mackenzie
E: emmaglenkyllachy@gmail.com

In a magnificent Highland glen, at 1150ft Glenkyllachy offers a glorious garden of shrubs, herbaceous plants, rhododendrons, trees and spectacular views down the Findhorn River. There are some rare specimens and an embryonic arboretum. Rhododendrons and bulbs flower in May/June, herbaceous plants bloom through July/August. Experience the wild flower meadow in summer and glorious autumn colours from September. Original sculptures and a 'Highgrove-inspired' wall provide year-round interest.

Other Details: Teas are available by prior arrangement.

Directions: Turn off A9 at Tomatin and take the Coignafearn/Garbole single track road down the north side of the River Findhorn, there is a cattle grid and gate on the right 500 metres *after* the humpback bridge and the sign to Farr.

Disabled Access:
Partial

Opening Times:
By arrangement
1 May - 30 October

Admission:
£5.00, under 10s free

Charities:
Marie Curie Cancer Care
receives 40%, the net
remaining to SG Beneficiaries

GORTHLECK

Stratherrick IV2 6UJ
Steve and Katie Smith T: 07710 325903

An unusual 20 acre woodland garden built in an unlikely place, on and around an exposed rocky ridge. The layout of the garden works with the natural features of the landscape rather than against them, with numerous paths, hedges and shelter belts creating clearly defined spaces that enable a large collection of plants and trees to thrive. It has extensive collections of both rhododendrons and bamboos. The challenges presented by the site become a bonus with the ridge offering long views of the surrounding countryside in the 'borrowed landscape' tradition of Japanese gardens. It didn't exist ten years ago and Gorthleck is very much a work-in-progress that is well-maintained by a team of enthusiastic gardeners.

Directions: From the A9, join the B862. Go through Errogie past a sharp left-hand bend. One mile after this there is a small church on the left. The Gorthleck drive is opposite the church and the house can be seen on the hill to the left as you follow the drive (to the left of the new house). Park on the grass verges.

Disabled Access:
None

Opening Times:
Thursday 1 June
10:00am - 9:00pm

Admission:
£5.00

Charities:
Maggie's Highlands receives 40%, the net remaining to SG Beneficiaries

HIGHLAND LILIUMS

10 Loaneckheim, Kiltarlity IV4 7JQ
Neil and Frances Macritchie T: 01463 741365
E: neil.macritchie@btconnect.com   www.highlandliliums.co.uk

A working retail nursery with spectacular views over the Beauly valley and Strathfarrar hills. A wide selection of home grown plants available including alpines, ferns, grasses, herbaceous, herbs, liliums, primulas and shrubs.

Other Details: Teas on 27 August only with discounted plant sale. Also open year round 9:00am - 5:00pm.

Directions: Signposted from Kiltarlity village, which is just off the Beauly to Drumnadrochit road (A833), approximately 12 miles from Inverness.

Disabled Access:
Full

Opening Times:
Sunday 27 August
12:00pm - 4:30pm
Daily 9:00am - 5pm

Admission:
Free but donations welcome

Charities:
Highland Hospice receives 40%, (August opening) the net remaining to SG Beneficiaries.
Donation to SG Beneficiaries given for other dates.

HOUSE OF AIGAS AND FIELD CENTRE

By Beauly IV4 7AD
Sir John and Lady Lister-Kaye T: 01463 782443
E: sheila@aigas.co.uk   www.aigas.co.uk

The House of Aigas has a small arboretum of named Victorian specimen trees and modern additions. The garden consists of extensive rockeries, herbaceous borders, ponds and shrubs. Aigas Field Centre rangers lead regular guided walks on nature trails through woodland, moorland and around a loch.

Other Details: Champion Trees: Douglas fir, Atlas cedar and Sequoiadendron. Homemade teas in the house on both 25 June and 23 July. Lunches/teas are available on request on other dates. Check out Aigas website for details of other events.

Directions: Four and a half miles from Beauly on A831 Cannich/Glen Affric road.

Disabled Access:
Partial

Opening Times:
Sunday 25 June
Sunday 23 July
2:00pm - 5:00pm
By arrangement
1 April - 28 October

Admission:
£4.00, accompanied children free

Charities:
Highland Hospice (Aird branch) receives 40%, the net remaining to SG Beneficiaries

HOUSE OF GRUINARD
Laide, by Achnasheen IV22 2NQ
The Hon Mrs A G Maclay T: 01445 731235
E: office@houseofgruinard.com

Superb hidden and unexpected garden developed in sympathy with stunning west coast estuary location. Wide variety of interesting herbaceous and shrub borders with water garden and extended wild planting.

Directions: On A832 twelve miles north of Inverewe and nine miles south of Dundonnell.

Disabled Access:
None

Opening Times:
Wednesday 24 May
Dawn - Dusk

Admission:
£3.50, children under 16 free

Charities:
Highland Hospice receives 40%, the net remaining to SG Beneficiaries

HUGH MILLER'S BIRTHPLACE COTTAGE & MUSEUM
Church Street, Cromarty IV11 8XA
The National Trust for Scotland T: 01381 600245 E: millermuseum@nts.org.uk
www.nts.org.uk/property/hugh-millers-birthplace-cottage-and-museum/

Domestic gardens, including the garden of wonders, created in 2008, with its theme of natural history, features fossils, exotic ferns, ornamental letter-cutting and a mystery stone. The sculptural centrepiece of this award-winning small but beautiful area is a scrap metal ammonite created by Helen Denerley. While at the birthplace, see the cobbled courtyard and the garden room - space for reflection and walk around the garden named after Hugh's wife, Lydia. The crescent-shaped, sandstone path of fragrant climbing roses, herbs and wild plant areas which reflect Miller's own love of nature and curiosity in the natural landscape.

Directions: By road via Kessock Bridge and A832 to Cromarty. Twenty-two miles north east of Inverness.

Disabled Access:
None

Opening Times:
Sunday 28 May
12:00pm - 5:00pm
(Last entry 4:30pm)

Admission:
Normal NTS admission applies. All donations welcome.

Charities:
Donation to SG Beneficiaries

INVEREWE GARDEN AND ESTATE
Poolewe, Achnasheen IV22 2LG
The National Trust for Scotland T: 01445 781200
E: inverewe@nts.org.uk www.nts.org.uk/Property/Inverewe-Garden-and-Estate

Magnificent 54 acre highland garden, surrounded by mountains, moorland and sea loch. Created by Osgood Mackenzie in the late 19th century, with a wealth of exotic plants from Australian tree ferns to Chinese rhododendrons to South African bulbs. Recent plantings include a grove of Wollemi pines and other 'fossil' trees. An electric buggy and two wheelchairs are available to use free of charge. Please book in advance to avoid disappointment.

Other Details: National Plant Collection®: Olearia, Rhododendron (subsect. Barbata, subsect. Glischra, subsect. Maculifera). Champion Trees: Over twenty. **17 May** - The Head Gardener's walk: Woodland Gardening. **1 June** - The First Gardener's walk: National Collection plantings. Meet at the Visitor Centre at 2:00pm for all walks. A shop and self-service restaurant are available.

Directions: Signposted on A832 by Poolewe, six miles northeast of Gairloch.

Disabled Access:
Partial

Opening Times:
Wednesday 17 May
10:00am - 5:30pm
Thursday 1 June
9:30am - 6:00pm

Admission:
Normal NTS admission applies

Charities:
Donation to SG Beneficiaries

18 LEATHAD ARD

Upper Carloway, Isle of Lewis HS2 9AQ
Rowena and Stuart Oakley T: 01851 643204
E: stuart.oakley1a@gmail.com   www.whereveriam.org/leathadard

A one acre sloping garden with stunning views over East Loch Roag. It has evolved along with the shelter hedges that divide the garden into a number of areas giving a new view at every corner. With shelter and raised beds, the different conditions created permit a wide variety of plants to be grown. Beds include herbaceous borders, cutting borders, bog gardens, grass garden, exposed beds, patio, a new pond and vegetable and fruit patches, some of which are grown to show.

Other Details: Rowena and Stuart are happy to show visitors around in the afternoons, although this could take a couple of hours.

Directions: A858 Shawbost - Carloway. First right after Carloway football pitch. First house on right. The Westside circular bus ex Stornoway to road end, ask for the Carloway football pitch.

Disabled Access:
None

Opening Times:
15 May - 2 September
10:00am - 6:00pm
(exc. Sundays)
By arrangement 1 April - 30
September (exc. Sundays)

Admission:
Recommended min. donation
£4.00 per head, children free

Charities:
Red Cross receives 40%,
the net remaining to
SG Beneficiaries

19 MALIN

Glenaldie, Tain IV19 1ND
Ivan Brockway
E: ikbrock@btinternet.com

The garden has a wide range of trees, shrubs and other plants including alpines, roses and perennials. In a damp area hostas and primulas grow with many ferns. A pergola has a vine and other climbers including wisteria and jasmine. Rhododendrons and azaleas have been planted in the woodland and main garden. There is a large pond with 60 ducks and geese, and a stream with rogersia, gunnera and meconopsis. The garden also has a polytunnel, greenhouses and an alpine house.

Other Details: The two acre garden has been lovingly developed by Mary and Ivan over the past 20 years mostly from a bare farm field. The garden is being opened in memory of Mary, who sadly died in April 2015.

Directions: From the south near Tain, on the A9, turn left signposted Glenaldie and Rosemount. Just over ½ mile along this road at the end of the woodland the garden entrance is on the left.

Disabled Access:
Partial

Opening Times:
Saturday 10 June
Sunday 11 June
11:00am - 5:00pm

Admission:
£3.00, homemade teas £3.00

Charities:
Highland Hospice receives
40%, the net remaining to
SG Beneficiaries

20 OLD ALLANGRANGE

Munlochy IV8 8NZ
J J Gladwin T: 01463 811304
E: jayjaygladwin@gmail.com

A 17th century lime washed house is the backdrop to a formal(ish) garden with many fine old trees including an ancient stand of yews. We use sculpted hedges to play with perspective. There is an ice house, vegetable garden, a mound, orchard and two large polytunnels where we grow vegetables bio-dynamically. We are establishing a nursery where plants attractive to invertebrates are grown. We plant particularly for wildlife so wildflowers and beneficial weeds are encouraged.

Other Details: Champion Trees: Yew. We garden and farm organically and increasingly bio-dynamically and are developing research programmes with Professor Dave Goulson, founder of the BBCT to know better what to plant for invertebrates.

Directions: From Inverness head four miles north on the A9, and follow the directions for Black Isle Brewery. Park in the brewery car park and you will be given directions in the shop.

Disabled Access:
Partial

Opening Times:
Saturday 2 September
10:30am - 5:00pm

Admission:
£7.50 including scones and
lots of cake, and a pot of tea.
Home baking using organic
ingredients.

Charities:
Black Isle Bee Gardens
receives 40%, the net
remaining to SG Beneficiaries

21 OLDTOWN OF LEYS GARDEN

Inverness IV2 6AE
David and Anne Sutherland T: 01463 238238
E: ams@oldtownofleys.com

Large garden established thirteen years ago on the outskirts of Inverness and overlooking the town. Herbaceous beds with lovely rhododendron and azalea displays in spring. There are specimen trees, three ponds surrounded by waterside planting and a small woodland area. A new rockery area was created in 2015 and is still developing.

Directions: Turn off Southern distributor road (B8082) at Leys roundabout towards Inverarnie (B861). At T-junction turn right. After fifty metres turn right into Oldtown of Leys.

Disabled Access:
Partial

Opening Times:
Saturday 27 May
2:00pm - 5:00pm
Open daily Dawn - Dusk

Admission:
27 May 2017: £4.00,
children £1.00, under 2s free
Other days: by donation

Charities:
Local Charities receive
40%, the net remaining to
SG Beneficiaries

---

22 SKYE FOREST GARDENS

Skye Permaculture, Rhuba Phoil, Armadale Pier Road, Ardvasar, Sleat IV45 8RS
Sandy Masson T: 01471 844700
E: rubhaphoil@yahoo.co.uk   www.skyeforestgarden.com

A wild natural forest garden managed on permaculture principles with a woodland walk to seal and bird islands. Look out for otters and other wildlife! There is an interesting Alchemy Centre with a composting display.

Other Details: Accommodation is available in tent/bothy retreat. Follow us on Facebook at *facebook.com/RubhaPhoil*

Directions: Turn right at the car park on Armadale Pier.

Disabled Access:
Partial

Opening Times:
Sunday 21 May
Dawn - Dusk

Admission:
Donations welcome

Charities:
Donation to SG Beneficiaries

---

23 THE LOOKOUT

Kilmuir, North Kessock IV1 3ZG
David and Penny Veitch T: 01463 731489
E: david@veitch.biz

A ¾ acre elevated coastal garden with incredible views over the Moray Firth which is only for the sure-footed. This award winning garden is created out of a rock base with shallow pockets of ground, planted to its advantage to encourage all aspects of wildlife. There is a small sheltered courtyard, raised bed vegetable area, pretty cottage garden, scree and rock garden, rose arbour, rhododendrons, flowering shrubs, bamboos, trees and lily pond with waterside plants.

Other Details: Coffee, tea and home baking outside if weather permits. Studio with exhibition of landscape pictures for sale.

Directions: From Inverness - take North Kessock left turn from A9, and third left at roundabout to underpass, then sharp left onto Kilmuir road. From Tore - take slip road for North Kessock and first right for Kilmuir. Follow signs for Kilmuir (3 miles) until you reach the shore. Garden is near far end of village with a large palm tree on the grass.

Disabled Access:
None

Opening Times:
1 May - 31 August
12:00pm - 4:00pm
(Sundays only)
Also by arrangement
1 May - 31 August

Admission:
£3.00, children under 16 free

Charities:
Alzheimers Scotland receives
40%, the net remaining to
SG Beneficiaries

SHETLAND

Scotland's Gardens 2017 Guidebook is sponsored by **INVESTEC WEALTH & INVESTMENT**

District Organiser and Treasurer

As per Caithness & Sutherland

Area Organisers

Mary Leask	VisitScotland, Market Cross, Lerwick ZE1 0LU
Steve Mathieson	VisitScotland, Market Cross, Lerwick ZE1 0LU

Gardens open regularly

Highlands, East Voe	1 May - 30 September	9:00am	-	9:00pm
Lee Gardens, Tresta	1 Mar - 31 Oct (exc. Thurs)	2:00pm	-	5:00pm
Nonavaar, Levenwick	14 Apr - 3 Sept (Fris & Suns)	11:00am	-	6:00pm
Norby, Burnside, Sandness	Daily	Dawn	-	Dusk

Gardens open by arrangement

Cruisdale, Sandness	On request	01595 870739
Keldaberg, Cunningsburgh	1 June - 31 October	01590 477331
Lindaal, Tingwall	1 June - 30 September	01595 840420
Nonavaar, Levenwick	14 April - 3 September	01950 422447

Key to symbols

	New in 2017		Homemade teas		Accommodation
	Teas		Dogs on a lead allowed		Plant stall
	Cream teas		Wheelchair access		Scottish Snowdrop Festival

GARDEN LOCATIONS
IN SHETLAND

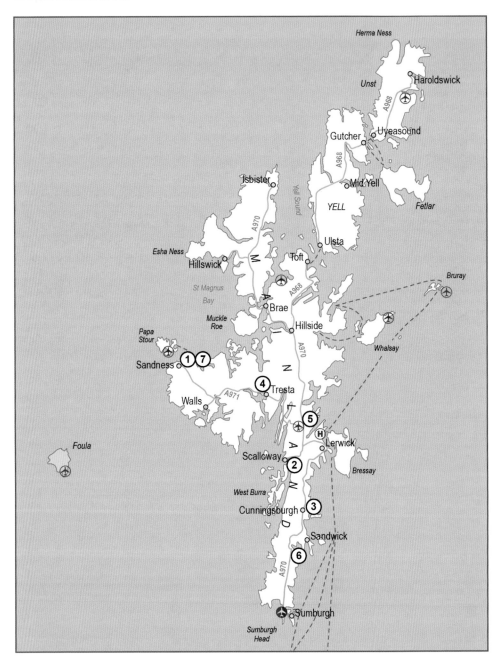

Herma Ness

Haroldswick

Unst

A968

Uyeasound

Gutcher

A968

Isbister

Mid Yell

Yell Sound

YELL

Fetlar

A970

Esha Ness

Ulsta

Toft

Bruray

Hillswick

St Magnus
Bay

M
A
A968

Brae

Muckle
Roe

Hillside

Whalsay

Papa
Stour

A970

Sandness ① ⑦

N

Foula

④ Tresta

A971

Walls

⑤

L
(H)
Lerwick

A
②
N
Scalloway

Bressay

West Burra

D
Cunningsburgh ③

Sandwick

⑥

A970

Sumburgh

Sumburgh
Head

CRUISDALE
Sandness ZE2 9PL
Alfred Kern T: 01595 870739

The garden is in a natural state with many willows, several ponds and a variety of colourful hardy plants that grow well in the Shetland climate. It is a work in progress, started about 15 years ago and growing bigger over the years with more work planned.

Directions: From Lerwick head north on the A970, then at Tingwall take the A971 to Sandness, on the west side of Shetland. Opposite the school, on the right hand side with a wind generator in the field.

Disabled Access:
None

Opening Times:
By arrangement on request

Admission:
£3.00, accompanied children free

Charities:
WRVS receives 40%, the net remaining to SG Beneficiaries

HIGHLANDS
East Voe, Scalloway ZE1 0UR
Sarah Kay T: 01595 880526
E: info@easterhoull.co.uk   www.easterhoull.co.uk

The garden is in two parts. The upper garden is mostly a rockery, with a large selection of plants, shallow pond, seating area and newly built 'polycrub' and green house. The lower garden is on a steep slope with a spectacular sea view over the village of Scalloway. There is a path to lead visitors around. The garden features a large collection of plants, vegetable patch, deep pond and pergola. It was awarded a 'Shetland Environmental Award' in 2014 for its strong theme of recycling.

Other Details: There is self catering accommodation available next to the garden. See website for details.

Directions: Follow the A970 main road towards the village of Scalloway. Near the top of the hill heading towards Scalloway take a sharp turn to the left, signposted Easterhoull Chalets. Follow the road to chalets (painted blue with red roofs) and you will see the yellow SG sign for the garden.

Disabled Access:
None

Opening Times:
1 May - 30 September
9:00am - 9:00pm

Admission:
£3.50, accompanied children free

Charities:
Yorkhill Childrens Charity receives 40%, the net remaining to SG Beneficiaries

SHETLAND

KELDABERG
Cunningsburgh ZE2 9HG
Mrs L Johnston T: 01590 477331
E: linda.keldaberg@btinternet.com

A 'secret garden' divided into four areas. A beach garden of grasses, flowers and driftwood. The main area is a sloping perennial border leading down to a greenhouse, vegetable plot, up to a decked area with containers and exotic plants including agaves, pineapple lilies, cannas and gunneras. The new part has trees, raised vegetable beds, a rockery, retaining walls and an arbour in which to rest. There is a pond complete with goldfish, golden orf and koi plus acquatic plants and a water lily.

Directions: On the A970 south of Lerwick is Cunningsburgh, take the Gord junction on the left after passing the village hall. Continue along the road to the first house past the Kenwood sign.

Disabled Access:
Partial

Opening Times:
By arrangement 1 June - 31 October. Phone first to avoid disappointment.

Admission:
£3.00

Charities:
Chest Heart & Stroke Scotland receives 40%, the net remaining to SG Beneficiaries

LEA GARDENS
Tresta ZE2 9LT
Rosa Steppanova T: 01595 810454

Lea Gardens, started in the early 1980s, now covers almost two acres. The plant collection, the largest north of Inverewe Gardens, consists of 1,500 different species and cultivars from all over the world, including phyto-geographic elements of collections of plants from New Zealand, South Africa and South America. Planted to provide all year round interest it has been divided into a variety of habitats: woodland and shade, borders, wetland, raised beds, and acid and lime lovers. A winner of the 2011 Shetland Environmental Award.

Directions: From Lerwick take the A970 north, turn left at Tingwall onto the A971 past Weisdale along Weisdale Voe and up Weisdale hill. Coming down, Lea Gardens is on your right surrounded by trees.

Disabled Access:
Partial

Opening Times:
1 March - 31 October
2:00pm - 5:00pm
(exc. Thursdays)

Admission:
£4.00, accompanied children free

Charities:
Donation to SG Beneficiaries

5 LINDAAL
Tingwall ZE2 9SG
Mr Adam Leslie T: 01595 840420
E: lindaal@btinternet.com

An established garden of almost one acre. Flat area around the house leading up a slope to a small woodland area with conifers and deciduous trees. In the garden there are four ponds and a well, tubs and hanging baskets with a mix of perennial plants and annuals. Good for wildlife with frogs and birds.

Directions: Go north from Lerwick to Tingwall taking the Laxfirth junction on your right past the local hall and school, round the end of the loch and straight up the hill to first wooden house on the right.

Disabled Access:
Partial

Opening Times:
By arrangement
1 June - 30 September

Admission:
£3.00, accompanied children free

Charities:
MS Society Shetland Branch receives 40%, the net remaining to SG Beneficiaries

---

6 NONAVAAR
Levenwick ZE2 9HX
James B Thomason T: 01950 422447

This is a delightful country garden, sloping within drystone walls and overlooking magnificent coastal views. It contains ponds, terraces, trees, bushes, varied perennials, annuals, vegetable garden and greenhouse.

Other Details: There is an Arts & Crafts studio.

Directions: Head south from Lerwick. Turn left at Levenwick sign soon after Bigton turnoff. Follow the road to third house on the left after Midway stores. Park where there is a 'Garden Open' sign.

Disabled Access:
None

Opening Times:
14 April - 3 September
11:00am - 6:00pm
(Fridays and Sundays only)
or other days by arrangement
(please phone first)

Admission:
£3.00, accompanied children free

Charities:
Cancer Research receives 40%, the net remaining to SG Beneficiaries

---

7 NORBY
Burnside, Sandness ZE2 9PL
Mrs Gundel Grolimund T: 01595 870246
E: gislinde@tiscali.co.uk

A small but perfectly formed garden and a prime example of what can be achieved in a very exposed situation. Blue painted wooden pallets provide internal wind breaks and form a background for shrubs, climbers and herbaceous plants, while willows provide a perfect wildlife habitat. There are treasured plants such as chionocloa rubra, pieris, Chinese tree peonies, and a selection of old-fashioned shrub roses, lilies, hellebores, grasses from New Zealand etc.

Directions: Head north on the A970 from Lerwick then west on the A971 at Tingwall. At Sandness, follow the road to Norby, turn right at the Methodist Church, *Burnside* is at the end of the road.

Disabled Access:
None

Opening Times:
Open daily
Dawn - Dusk
If no-one is in please feel free to wander around

Admission:
£3.00, accompanied children free

Charities:
Survival International receives 40%, the net remaining to SG Beneficiaries

CHARITIES SUPPORTED

Each visit you make to one of our gardens in 2017 will raise money for our beneficiary charities:

In addition, funds will be distributed to a charity of the owner's choice.
For South West Scotland, these include:

Alzheimer Scotland

Ankizy Gasy - Children of Madagascar Foundatioon

Anthony Nolan

Black Isle Bee Gardens

Black Isle MacMillan Cancer Care

Bumblebee Conservation Trust

Cancer Research UK

CHAS

Children 1st

Croick Church

Friends of the Neuro Ward at Aberdeen Royal Infirmary

Friends of Thor House, Thurso

Highland Disability Sport Swim Team

Highland Hospice

Laggan Church

Local Charities

Macmillan Cancer Support

Maggie's Cancer Caring Centre: Highlands

Marie Curie

MS Society Shetland Branch

Nicholls Spinal Injury Foundation

Rafford Church

Red Cross

RNLI

Royal Voluntary Service

Sandpiper Trust

SSPCA

Survival International

The Samaritans

World Horse Welfare

Yorkhill Childrens Charity

EAST OF SCOTLAND

Scotland's Gardens 2017 Guidebook is sponsored by **INVESTEC WEALTH & INVESTMENT**

ABERDEENSHIRE

District Organiser

Verity Walters	Tillychetly, Alford AB33 8HQ
	E: aberdeenshire@scotlandsgardens.org

Area Organisers

Gill Cook	Old Semeil, Strathdon AB36 8XJ
Jennie Gibson	6 The Chanonry, Old Aberdeen AB24 1RP
Anne Lawson	Asloun, Alford AB33 8NR
Penny Orpwood	Middle Cairncake, Cuminestown, Turriff AB53 5YS
Helen Rushton	Bruckhills Croft, Rothienorman, Inverurie AB51 8YB

Treasurer

Tony Coleman	Templeton House, Arbroath DD11 4QP

Gardens open on a specific date

Auchmacoy, Ellon	Sunday 16 April	12:00pm	- 4:00pm
Westhall Castle, Oyne, Inverurie	Sunday 30 April	1:00pm	- 4:00pm
Castle Fraser Garden, Sauchen, Inverurie	Saturday 6 May	11:00am	- 4:00pm
Castle Fraser Garden, Sauchen, Inverurie	Sunday 7 May	11:00am	- 4:00pm
Leith Hall Garden, Huntly	Thursday 25 May	7:00pm	
Kildrummy Castle Gardens, Alford	Sunday 4 June	10:00am	- 5:00pm
Tillypronie, Tarland	Sunday 4 June	2:00pm	- 5:00pm
Cruickshank Botanic Gardens, Aberdeen	Wednesday 7 June	6:00pm	- 8:30pm
Birken Cottage, Burnhervie, Inverurie	Sunday 11 June	2:00pm	- 5:00pm
Haddo House, Methlick, Ellon	Wednesday 28 June	11:00am	- 4:00pm
Leith Hall Garden, Huntly	Thursday 29 June	7:00pm	
Bruckhills Croft, Rothienorman, Inverurie	Sunday 9 July	12:00pm	- 5:00pm
Middle Cairncake, Cuminestown, Turriff	Saturday 22 July	1:00pm	- 5:00pm
Drumrossie Mansion House, Insch	Sunday 23 July	1:00pm	- 5:00pm
Middle Cairncake, Cuminestown, Turriff	Sunday 23 July	1:00pm	- 5:00pm
Leith Hall Garden, Huntly	Thursday 27 July	7:00pm	
Alford Village Gardens, Alford	Sunday 30 July	1:30pm	- 5:30pm
Haddo House, Methlick, Ellon	Wednesday 9 August	11:00am	- 4:00pm
Pitmedden Garden, Ellon	Sunday 13 August	10:00am	- 5:30pm
Leith Hall Garden, Huntly	Thursday 24 August	7:00pm	
Tarland Community Garden, Aboyne	Saturday 23 September	12:00pm	- 4:00pm

ABERDEENSHIRE

Kildrummy Castle Gardens, Alford	Sunday 1 October	10:00am - 5:00pm

Gardens open regularly

Fyvie Castle, Fyvie, Turriff	5 January - 22 December	9:00am - Dusk

Gardens open by arrangement

Airdlin Croft, Ythanbank, Ellon	21 May - 31 July	01358 761491
An Teallach, Largue, Huntly	1 June - 31 August	01464 871471
Birken Cottage, Burnhervie, Inverurie	1 May - 31 July	01467 623013
Blairwood House, South Deeside Road, Blairs	18 June - 27 August	01224 868301 07732 532276
Bruckhills Croft, Rothienorman, Inverurie	18 February - 19 March	01651 821596
Bruckhills Croft, Rothienorman, Inverurie	1 July - 31 July	01651 821596
Grandhome, Danestone, Aberdeen	1 April - 31 October	01224 722202
Hatton Castle, Turriff	On request	01888 562279
Laundry Cottage, Culdrain, Gartly, Huntly	On request	01466 720768
Middle Cairncake, Cuminestown, Turriff	On request	01888 544432

Key to symbols

 New in 2017
 Homemade teas
 Accommodation
 Teas
 Dogs on a lead allowed
 Plant stall
 Cream teas
 Wheelchair access
 Scottish Snowdrop Festival

GARDEN LOCATIONS
IN ABERDEENSHIRE

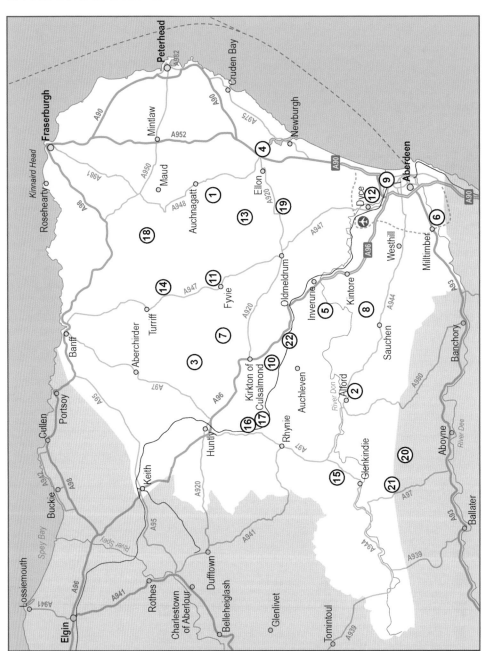

1 AIRDLIN CROFT
Ythanbank, Ellon AB41 7TS
Richard and Ellen Firmin T: 01358 761491
E: rsf@airdlin.com

A large woodland garden, eventually destined to fill our five-acre croft, features species rhododendrons, hydrangeas, viburnums, ferns, hostas and other shade tolerant plants. A sheltered, sunny terrace hosts some tender exotics. One of two polytunnels houses the 'library collection' of more than 450 hosta cultivars. We go out of our way to attract wildlife - 99 bird species recorded here since 1983.

Other Details: Disabled access to plant nursery only. Please, no dogs. Teas available at Haddo House or Formartine's, about five miles away.

Directions: From the A948, three miles north of Ellon, take the left turn towards Drumwhindle. After another couple of miles take the second left towards Cairnorrie. Proceed for nearly a mile, ignoring the first Airdlin Croft at Coalmoss, and turn left at the first bend down our 300 metre track, parking is in the field at the bottom.

Disabled Access:
Partial

Opening Times:
By arrangement
21 May - 31 July

Admission:
£4.00

Charities:
Fauna and Flora International receives 40%, the net remaining to SG Beneficiaries

2 ALFORD VILLAGE GARDENS
Alford AB33 8HH
Gardeners of Alford

In the heart of the beautiful Vale of Alford, the village lies near the River Don amid rolling farmland. The gardens, both mature and newly established, offer a fascinating range of planting and designs, some quirky, some traditional, but all inspirational, with colourful borders, roses, shrubs, and productive fruit and vegetable patches to enjoy. A warm welcome awaits you.

Other Details: Tickets and map available from the Public Hall in Kingsford Road with teas being served there from 2:30pm.

Directions: Look out for the yellow signs pointing the way to the gardens.

Disabled Access:
Partial

Opening Times:
Sunday 30 July
1:30pm - 5:30pm

Admission:
£8.00 includes entry to all gardens and teas, children under 12 free

Charities:
UCAN receives 20%, ACTS receives 20%, the net remaining to SG Beneficiaries

3 AN TEALLACH
Largue, Huntly AB54 6HS
Gary and Victoria Morrison T: 01464 871471
E: gary.k.morrison@gmail.com

This young cottage garden, of approximately one acre (and growing), was created in 2013 and has become established in a remarkably short time. Surrounded by uninterrupted views of rolling hills and farmland, the garden includes a charming variety of colourful herbaceous, mixed borders, a terraced woodland bank, rose garden, fruit and vegetable beds, and an (as-yet) untamed quarry area. The growing collection of plants and flowers provide interest from May to October.

Directions: Leaving Largue on the B9001, head towards Rothienorman. An Teallach is the first track on the left, after the national speed limit sign.

Disabled Access:
None

Opening Times:
By arrangement
1 June - 31 August

Admission:
£4.00

Charities:
Dogs Trust receives 40%, the net remaining to SG Beneficiaries

ABERDEENSHIRE

AUCHMACOY
Ellon AB41 8RB
Mr and Mrs Charles Buchan

Auchmacoy House's attractive policies feature spectacular displays of thousands of daffodils.

Other Details: Homemade teas and soup. Easter egg hunt. Buchan Pipe Band.

Directions: A90 from Aberdeen. Turn right to Auchmacoy/Collieston.

Disabled Access:
Partial

Opening Times:
Sunday 16 April
12:00pm - 4:00pm

Admission:
£3.00, concessions £2.50,
accompanied children free

Charities:
Ellon & District Legion
Scotland receives 40%,
the net remaining to
SG Beneficiaries

BIRKEN COTTAGE
Burnhervie, Inverurie AB51 5JR
Clare and Ian Alexander T: 01467 623013
E: i.alexander@abdn.ac.uk

This steeply sloping garden of just under one acre is packed with plants. It rises from a wet streamside gully and woodland, past sunny terraces and a small parterre, to dry flowery banks.

Directions: Burnhervie is about three miles west of Inverurie. Leave Inverurie by the B9170 (Blackhall Road) or B993 (St James' Place).

Disabled Access:
None

Opening Times:
Sunday 11 June
2:00pm - 5:00pm
Also by arrangement
1 May - 31 July

Admission:
£4.00

Charities:
Friends of Anchor receives
40%, the net remaining to
SG Beneficiaries

BLAIRWOOD HOUSE
South Deeside Road, Blairs AB12 5YQ
Ilse Elders T: 01224 868301 M:07732 532276
E: ilse.elders@yahoo.co.uk

Over the past couple of years the owners have changed their 18 year old, one acre garden in several ways. By re-routing part of the driveway they created space for a pond (using local stones) and a small stream. Many new flowering shrubs are used to extend seasonal interest and to provide a good backdrop for less substantial herbaceous perennials. They revamped the entire herb garden for ease of maintenance, and started a kitchen garden. The garden sits well in the surrounding countryside and provides pleasure through its plant combinations. The short walk from the garden to the river Dee is recommended.

Other Details: Refreshments are available at two nearby hotels. Teas available for parties of ten and over by request.

Directions: Blairs, on the B9077, five minutes by car from Bridge of Dee, Aberdeen. Very close to Blairs Museum.

Disabled Access:
Partial

Opening Times:
By arrangement
18 June - 27 August

Admission:
£4.00

Charities:
Elvanfoot Trust receives 40%, the net remaining to SG Beneficiaries

---

BRUCKHILLS CROFT
Rothienorman, Inverurie AB51 8YB
Paul and Helen Rushton T: 01651 821596
E: helenrushton1@aol.com

An informal country cottage garden extending to ¾ acre with a further acre as wildflower meadow and pond. There are several garden rooms which have different moods, from the bright sunny gravel garden to the shady and cool orchard. Borders are packed with a huge variety of plants, and include themes such as a white border, a butterfly alley and a blue and yellow border. There are various seating areas around the garden or you can head to the pavilion for a cuppa and homebake.

Other Details: Large selection of home grown plants and snowdrops for sale The snowdrop openings are by appointment only, due to limited parking in winter. Home bakes will include gluten free.

Directions: At Rothienorman take the B9001 north, just after Badenscoth Nursing Home turn left, in one mile you will be directed where to park depending if it is the winter or summer opening.

Disabled Access:
Partial

Opening Times:
Sunday 9 July
12:00pm - 5:00pm
Also by arrangement 18 Feb - 19 Mar for the Snowdrop Festival and 1 July - 31 July

Admission:
£4.00, accomp. children free

Charities:
Advocacy Service Aberdeen and Befriend a Child, Aberdeen both receive 20%, the net remaining to SG Beneficiaries

---

CASTLE FRASER GARDEN
Sauchen, Inverurie AB51 7LD
The National Trust for Scotland T: 01330 833463
E: castlefraser@nts.org.uk www.nts.org.uk/property/castle-fraser-garden-and-estate

Castle Fraser's designed landscape and parkland are the work of Thomas White dating from 1794. Castle Fraser, one of the most spectacular of the Castles of Mar, has a traditional walled garden of trees, shrubs and herbaceous plantings, a medicinal and culinary border and organically grown fruit and vegetables. You can stroll through the woodland garden with its azaleas and rhododendrons or take the young at heart to the Woodland Secrets adventure playground and trails.

Other Details: A sale of herbaceous plants lifted straight from the castle garden. Pick up a colourful addition to enhance your own garden from the Castle Fraser collection-reliably hardy for Aberdeenshire. There is also a cafe at Castle Fraser.

Directions: Near Kemnay, off the A944.

Disabled Access:
Partial

Opening Times:
Saturday 6 May &
Sunday 7 May
11:00am - 4:00pm

Admission:
Normal NTS admission applies. All donations welcome.

Charities:
Donation to SG Beneficiaries

9 **CRUICKSHANK BOTANIC GARDENS**
23 St Machar Drive, Aberdeen AB24 3UU
Cruickshank Botanic Garden Trust, Aberdeen University
www.abdn.ac.uk/botanic-garden/

An evening tour with the Curator, Mark Paterson and Head Gardener, Richard Walker. The garden comprises a sunken garden with alpine lawn, a rock garden built in the 1960s complete with cascading water and pond system, a long double sided herbaceous border, a formal rose garden with drystone walling, and an arboretum. It has a large collection of flowering bulbs and rhododendrons, and many unusual shrubs and trees including two mature Camperdown Elms. It is sometimes known as The Secret Garden of Old Aberdeen.

Directions: Come down St Machar Drive over the mini roundabout, just before the first set of traffic lights turn left into the Cruickshank Garden car park. The pedestrian garden entrance is off The Chanonry.

Disabled Access:
Partial

Opening Times:
Wednesday 7 June
6:00pm - 8:30pm

Admission:
£5.00 includes tea/coffee and biscuits.

Charities:
Cruickshank Botanic Gardens Trust receives 40%, the net remaining to SG Beneficiaries

---

10 **NEW DRUMROSSIE MANSION HOUSE**
Insch AB52 6LJ
Mr and Mrs Hugh Robertson

The property, which can be traced back to the Crusades, is surrounded by three acres of landscaped lawns, formal walled garden, veg and greenhouse area and a newly planted orchard. There are 27 acres of wooded walks, paddocks and a large wildlife pond. Vegetables are grown in raised beds. The walled garden is laid out in lawns of a very high standard, with herbaceous borders and fruit trees on the south facing wall. There is a large collection of hostas and alstroemerias, as well as herbaceous plants, heathers and azaleas, a productive vegetable garden, plant raising area and polytunnel for early veg and flowers, a large glasshouse for tomatoes and a sunken greenhouse which provides over wintering heat for tender plants. The main feature is the well which in days gone by provided the water supply to the house.

Directions: Enter drive from Drumrossie Street which leads off the crossroads in centre of village. The drive is through trees at back of Costcutter Supermarket. Do not follow sat nav.

Disabled Access:
Full

Opening Times:
Sunday 23 July
1:00pm - 5:00pm

Admission:
£4.00, accompanied children free

Charities:
Insch parish church restoration fund receives 40%, the net remaining to SG Beneficiaries

---

11 **FYVIE CASTLE**
Fyvie, Turriff AB53 8JS
The National Trust for Scotland T: 01651 891363 / 891266
E: gthomson@nts.org.uk   www.nts.org.uk/Property/Fyvie-Castle/

An 18th century walled garden developed as a garden of Scottish fruits and vegetables. There is also the American garden, Rhymer's Haugh woodland garden, a loch and parkland to visit. Expert staff are always on hand to answer any questions. Learn about the collection of Scottish fruits and their cultivation, and exciting projects for the future. Check the Fyvie Castle Facebook page for up-to-date information on fruit and vegetable availability.

Other Details: A wide selection of seasonal fresh organically grown produce for sale from our 'Fruit Store' shop in the walled garden from approx mid-July, proceeds donated to Scotland's Gardens. The walled garden is closed during the Christmas holidays. Opening times are for the garden, check website for castle opening times.

Directions: Off the A947 eight miles south east of Turriff and twenty-five miles north west of Aberdeen.

Disabled Access:
Full

Opening Times:
5 January - 22 December
9:00am - Dusk

Admission:
Free admission to the garden and grounds

Charities:
Donation to SG Beneficiaries

GRANDHOME
Danestone, Aberdeen AB22 8AR
Mr and Mrs D R Paton T: 01224 722202
E: davidpaton@btconnect.com

Eighteenth century walled garden incorporating a rose garden (replanted 2010) and policies with daffodils, tulips, rhododendrons, azaleas, mature trees and shrubs.

Directions: From the north end of North Anderson Drive, continue on the A90 over Persley Bridge, turning left at the Tesco roundabout. 1¾ miles on the left, through the pillars on a left hand bend.

Disabled Access:
Partial

Opening Times:
By arrangement
1 April - 31 October

Admission:
£4.00

Charities:
Children 1st receives
40%, the net remaining to
SG Beneficiaries

HADDO HOUSE
Methlick, Ellon AB41 7EQ
The National Trust for Scotland T: 01651 851 440
E: haddo@nts.org.uk www.nts.org.uk/Property/Haddo-House/

The gardens at Haddo have recently been restored to their original Victorian glory and showcase geometric beds planted in a modern interpretation of Victorian formal bedding schemes. Meet the gardeners and learn about this project, the history of the gardens and our plans for the future. Visitors will also enjoy the secluded glades and knolls. A magnificent avenue of lime trees leads to adjacent Haddo country park with its lakes, monuments, walks and wildlife.

Other Details: Garden quiz and crafts for kids – get creative with our gardeners and bring home your own little piece of Haddo. The guided tours will set off at 12:30pm and 3:30pm.

Directions: Off B999 near Tarves, at Raxton crossroads, 19 miles N of Aberdeen, 4 miles N of Pitmedden and 10 miles NW of Ellon. Cycle - one mile from NCN 1. Bus - Stagecoach Bluebird from Aberdeen bus station 01224 212666, c. 4 mile walk.

Disabled Access:
Partial

Opening Times:
Wednesday 28 June &
Wednesday 9 August
11:00am - 4:00pm

Admission:
Normal NTS admission
applies.
Guided tours £4.00, children
under 12 £2.00.
Kid's quiz £1.00 and kid's
crafts by donation

Charities:
Donation to SG Beneficiaries

HATTON CASTLE
Turriff AB53 8ED
Mr and Mrs D James Duff T: 01888 562279
E: jjdgardens@btinternet.com

Hatton Castle has a two acre walled garden featuring mixed borders and shrub roses with yew and box hedges and alleys of pleached hornbeam. Also, a kitchen garden, fan trained fruit trees, a lake and woodland walks.

Directions: On A947, two miles south of Turriff.

Disabled Access:
Full

Opening Times:
By arrangement on request

Admission:
£5.00, accompanied children
free

Charities:
Juvenile Diabetes Research
Foundation receives 40%,
the net remaining to
SG Beneficiaries

ABERDEENSHIRE

 15 KILDRUMMY CASTLE GARDENS
Alford AB33 8RA
Kildrummy Garden Trust
www.kildrummy-castle-gardens.co.uk

These gardens were created in the ancient quarry below the Castle. The bridge spanning the garden is a copy of famous Brig o'Balgownie and reflects beautifully on the largest of the four ponds which plays host to a wide range of water plants. Rhododendrons and azaleas feature from April (frost permitting). In June the lovely blue of the meconopsis can be enjoyed and September/October brings colchicums and brilliant colour with acers, fothergillas and viburnums.

Directions: On the A97, ten miles from Alford, seventeen miles from Huntly. Car park free inside the hotel main entrance. Coaches park up at the hotel delivery entrance.

Disabled Access:
Partial

Opening Times:
Sunday 4 June
Sunday 1 October
10:00am - 5:00pm

Admission:
£4.50, concessions £4.00, accompanied children free

Charities:
Aberdeen Branch Multiple Sclerosis Society receives 40%, the net remaining to SG Beneficiaries

---

 16 LAUNDRY COTTAGE
Culdrain, Gartly, Huntly AB54 4PY
Simon and Judith McPhun T: 01466 720768
E: simon.mcphun@btinternet.com

An informal, cottage-style garden of about 1½ acres. Upper garden around the house of mixed borders, vegetables and fruit. Steep grass banks to the south and east are planted with native and non-native flowers, specimen trees and shrubs. Narrow grass paths, not suitable for wheelchairs, lead down to the River Bogie.

Directions: Four miles south of Huntly on the A97.

Disabled Access:
Partial

Opening Times:
By arrangement 1 January - 31 December

Admission:
£4.00, accompanied children free

Charities:
Amnesty International receives 40%, the net remaining to SG Beneficiaries

---

 17 LEITH HALL GARDEN
Huntly AB54 4NQ
The National Trust for Scotland T: 01464 831148
E: leithhall@nts.org.uk www.nts.org.uk/property/leith-hall-garden-and-estate/

A series of evening guided tours with the Head Gardener. The west garden was made by Charles and Henrietta Leith-Hay around the beginning of the 20th century. In summer the magnificent zigzag herbaceous and serpentine catmint borders provide a dazzling display. A lot of project work has been ongoing in the garden, including a rose catenary along with large borders which have been redeveloped in a Gertrude Jekyll style and a laburnum archway with spring interest borders. The carefully reconstructed rock garden is an ongoing work in progress with new planting being added throughout the season.

Other Details: The guided tours with the Head Gardener start at 7:00pm and include refreshments. Booking is essential.

Directions: On the B9002 one mile west of Kennethmont.

Disabled Access:
Partial

Opening Times:
Thursday 25 May 7:00pm
Thursday 29 June 7:00pm
Thursday 27 July 7:00pm
Thursday 24 August 7:00pm

Admission:
£5.00 for the guided tour

Charities:
Donation to SG Beneficiaries

MIDDLE CAIRNCAKE
Cuminestown, Turriff AB53 5YS
Mr and Mrs N Orpwood T: 01888 544432

Our garden has evolved from grass circling the house and steading to a series of small garden areas with places to sit and enjoy the surroundings. Our aim has been to create a pleasing environment to delight the senses through different garden themes and planting. It includes cottage gardens, a pond, formal rose garden, heathers and a productive kitchen garden for self-sufficiency. We have many trees and the lower woodland walk completes the garden.

Directions: Middle Cairncake is on the A9170 between New Deer and Cuminestown. It is clearly signposted.

Disabled Access:
Partial

Opening Times:
Saturday 22 July
& Sunday 23 July
1:00pm - 5:00pm
Also by arrangement
1 June - 10 September

Admission:
£3.50, accompanied children free

Charities:
Parkinson's UK receives 40%, the net remaining to SG Beneficiaries

PITMEDDEN GARDEN
Ellon AB41 7PD
The National Trust for Scotland T: 01651 842352
E: sburgess@nts.org.uk www.nts.org.uk/Property/Pitmedden-Garden/

Pitmedden is a seventeenth century walled garden on two levels. Original garden pavilions with ogival roofs look down on an elaborate spectacle of four rectangular boxwood parterres flanked by fine herbaceous borders and espalier trained apple trees on south and west facing granite walls. An avenue of yew obelisks runs from east to west and up to 30,000 bedding plants add to the wow factor of this immaculately kept formal garden.

Other Details: Guided Walk with Head Gardener/Property Manager, 2:30pm - 4:30pm with an in depth look behind the scenes and an opportunity to discuss the history of Pitmedden and what it takes to maintain such a special place. Gift shop. Self-catering accommodation available. Tearoom open 10:30am – 4:30pm.

Directions: On the A920, one mile west of Pitmedden Village and fourteen miles north of Aberdeen.

Disabled Access:
Partial

Opening Times:
Sunday 13 August
10:00am - 5:30pm
(Last entry 5:00pm)

Admission:
Normal NTS admission charges apply, £10.00 for guided walk, includes refreshments.

Charities:
Donation to SG Beneficiaries

20 TARLAND COMMUNITY GARDEN
Aboyne AB34
The Gardeners of Tarland

Tarland Community Gardens opened in 2013 and is a Tarland Development Group project. It provides an inclusive and accessible community growing space for local residents. It has indoor (polytunnel) and outdoor raised beds for rent plus communal planting areas including a soft fruit cage, fruit trees, and a herb garden. The community bee group also manages a hive at the site. It is a place for members to grow produce, learn, share and have fun.

Other Details: The garden is open as part of the Tarland Food and Music Festival, a weekend of concerts, talks, workshops and food. To see the programme and find out what is going on, see *www.facebook.com/TarlandFoodMusicFest/*.

Directions: Take the B9094 from Aboyne or the A96 and B9119 from Aberdeen. Arriving at the village square the gardens will be clearly signposted.

Disabled Access:
Full

Opening Times:
Saturday 23 September
12:00pm - 4:00pm

Admission:
£3.00, accompanied children free, homemade teas £3.00

Charities:
Tarland Development Group receives 40%, the net remaining to SG Beneficiaries

---

21 TILLYPRONIE
Tarland AB34 4XX
The Hon Philip Astor

Late Victorian house, for which Queen Victoria laid the foundation stone, with superb views over the Dee Valley. There are herbaceous borders, heather beds, a water garden and rockery with alpines. The Golden Jubilee garden contains trees, shrubs and plants of a golden hue. There is a fine collection of trees, including recently planted acers and a well-established pinetum with rare specimens. There is also a fruit garden and greenhouses. In June there is a wonderful show of azaleas, rhododendrons and spring heathers.

Other Details: Please note there is no disabled toilet.

Directions: Off the A97 between Ballater and Strathdon.

Disabled Access:
Partial

Opening Times:
Sunday 4 June
2:00pm - 5:00pm

Admission:
£5.00, children £2.00

Charities:
All proceeds to
SG Beneficiaries

---

22 WESTHALL CASTLE
Oyne, Inverurie AB52 6RW
Mr Gavin Farquhar and Mrs Pam Burney T: 01224 214301
E: enquiries@ecclesgreig.com

Set in an ancient landscape in the foothills of the impressive foreboding hill of Bennachie. A circular walk through glorious daffodils with outstanding views. Interesting garden in early stages of restoration, with large groupings of rhododendrons and specimen trees. Westhall Castle is a 16th century tower house, incorporating a 13th century building of the bishops of Aberdeen. There were additions in the 17th, 18th and 19th centuries. The castle is semi-derelict, but stabilised from total dereliction. A fascinating house encompassing 600 years of alteration and additions.

Directions: Marked from the A96 at Old Rayne and from Oyne Village.

Disabled Access:
Partial

Opening Times:
Sunday 30 April
1:00pm - 4:00pm

Admission:
£4.00, accompanied children free

Charities:
Bennachie Guides receives 40%, the net remaining to SG Beneficiaries

ANGUS & DUNDEE

Scotland's Gardens 2017 Guidebook is sponsored by **INVESTEC WEALTH & INVESTMENT**

District Organiser

Terrill Dobson	Logie House, Kirriemuir DD8 5PN
	E: angus@scotlandsgardens.org

Area Organisers

Helen Brunton	Cuthlie Farm, Arbroath DD11 2NT
Pippa Clegg	Easter Derry, Kilry, Blairgowrie PH11 8JA
Moira Coleman	Templeton House, Arbroath DD11 4QP
Katie Dessain	Lawton House, Inverkeilor, by Arbroath DD11 4RU
Mary Gifford	Kinnordy House, Kinnordy, Kirriemuir DD8 5ER
Jan Oag	Lower Duncraig, 2 Castle Street, Brechin DD9 6JN
Jeanette Ogilvie	House of Pitmuies, Guthrie DD8 2SN
Mary Stansfeld	Dunninald Castle, By Montrose DD10 9TD
Gladys Stewart	Ugie-Bank, Ramsay Street, Edzell DD9 7TT
Claire Tinsley	Ethie Mains, Ethie DD11 5SN

Treasurer

Terrill Dobson	Logie House, Kirriemuir DD8 5PN

Gardens open on a specific date

Langley Park Gardens, Montrose	Saturday 11 March	10:00am	-	4:00pm
Lawton House, Inverkeilor	Sunday 12 March	2:00pm	-	5:00pm
Inchmill Cottage, Glenprosen	Thursday 4 May	2:00pm	-	5:00pm
Brechin Castle, Brechin	Sunday 7 May	2:00pm	-	5:00pm
Angus Plant Sale, Logie Walled Garden, Logie	Friday 12 May	5:00pm	-	7:00pm
Dalfruin, Kirriemuir	Sunday 14 May	2:00pm	-	5:00pm
Inchmill Cottage, Glenprosen	Thursday 18 May	2:00pm	-	5:00pm
Dundee & Angus College Gardens, Dundee	Sunday 21 May	11:00am	-	4:00pm
Dunninald Castle, Montrose	Sunday 21 May	1:00pm	-	5:00pm
The Shrubbery, Dundee	Friday 26 May	2:00pm	-	5:00pm
Gallery, Montrose	Saturday 27 May	2:00pm	-	5:00pm
The Shrubbery, Dundee	Saturday 27 May	2:00pm	-	5:00pm
The Shrubbery, Dundee	Sunday 28 May	2:00pm	-	5:00pm
Inchmill Cottage, nr Kirriemuir	Thursday 1 June	2:00pm	-	5:00pm
Arbroath Collection of Gardens, Arbroath	Saturday 3 June	1:00pm	-	5:00pm
Forfar Open Garden, Forfar	Saturday 10 June	2:00pm	-	5:00pm

ANGUS & DUNDEE

Inchmill Cottage, Glenprosen	Thursday 15 June	2:00pm	5:00pm
Kilry Village Gardens, Kilry	Saturday 17 June	12:00pm	5:00pm
Kilry Village Gardens, Kilry	Sunday 18 June	12:00pm	5:00pm
Newtonmill House, by Brechin	Sunday 25 June	2:00pm	5:00pm
Hospitalfield Gardens, Westway	Saturday 8 July	2:00pm	5:00pm
Gallery, Montrose	Saturday 15 July	2:00pm	5:00pm
The Herbalist's Garden at Logie, Kirriemuir	Saturday 29 July	2:00pm	5:00pm
The Herbalist's Garden at Logie, Kirriemuir	Sunday 30 July	2:00pm	5:00pm
Inchmill Cottage, Glenprosen	Thursday 3 August	2:00pm	5:00pm
Inchmill Cottage, Glenprosen	Thursday 17 August	2:00pm	5:00pm
12 Glamis Drive, Dundee	Saturday 19 August	2:00pm	5:00pm
12 Glamis Drive, Dundee	Sunday 20 August	2:00pm	5:00pm
Inchmill Cottage, Glenprosen	Thursday 7 September	2:00pm	5:00pm
Inchmill Cottage, Glenprosen	Thursday 21 September	2:00pm	5:00pm

Gardens open regularly

Gallery, Montrose	1 June - 31 Aug (Tues only)	1:00pm	5:00pm
Pitmuies Gardens, Guthrie	1 April - 30 October	10:00am	5:00pm

Gardens open by arrangement

3 Balfour Cottages, Menmuir	3 May - 17 May	01356 660280
Gallery, Montrose	1 June - 31 August	01674 840550
Kirkton House, Montrose	1 May - 30 September	01674 673604

Plant sales

Angus Plant Sale, Logie Walled Garden, Logie	Friday 12 May	5:00pm	7:00pm

Key to symbols

	New in 2017		Homemade teas		Accommodation
	Teas		Dogs on a lead allowed		Plant stall
	Cream teas		Wheelchair access		Scottish Snowdrop Festival

GARDEN LOCATIONS IN
ANGUS & DUNDEE

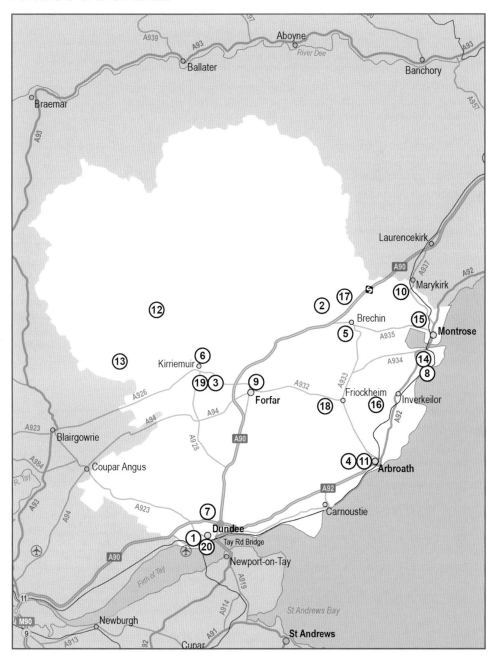

ANGUS & DUNDEE

1 NEW 12 GLAMIS DRIVE
Dundee DD2 1QL
John and Frances Dent

This established garden with mature trees occupies a half-acre south-facing site overlooking the River Tay and Fife hills. The tennis court lawn has herbaceous borders. The woodland area includes hidden features, garden ornaments and a miniature topiary garden and bower. A small rose garden and fountain and two oriental-themed water gardens complete the tour in time for tea in the marquee.

Other Details: The afternoon will include musical performance and a children's quiz.

Directions: Please note there is no roadside parking on Glamis Drive. Limited disabled parking available at the house.

Disabled Access:
Partial

Opening Times:
Saturday 19 August
Sunday 20 August
2:00pm - 5:00pm

Admission:
£4.00, accompanied children free

Charities:
Girl Guiding Dundee Outdoor Centre and Logie & St John's (cross) Church, Dundee each receive 20%, the net remaining to SG Beneficiaries

2 3 BALFOUR COTTAGES
Menmuir DD9 7RN
Dr Alison Goldie and Mark A Hutson T: 01356 660280
E: alisongoldie@btinternet.com www.angusplants.co.uk

Small cottage garden packed with rare and unusual plants. It comprises various 'rooms', containing myriad plants from potted herbs, spring bulbs and alpines in a raised bed, to a 'jungle' with a range of bamboos. Many other interesting plants include primula, hosta, meconopsis, fritillaria, trillium, allium, a large display of bonsai and auriculas.

Other Details: National Plant Collection®: *Primula auricula* (alpine).

Directions: Leave the A90 two miles south of Brechin and take the road to Menmuir (3½ miles). At the T-junction turn right and it is in the first group of cottages on your left (175 yards).

Disabled Access:
None

Opening Times:
By arrangement
3 May - 17 May

Admission:
£3.00, accompanied children free

Charities:
All proceeds to
SG Beneficiaries

3 NEW ANGUS PLANT SALE
Logie Walled Garden, Logie DD8 5PN
Scotland's Gardens Angus & Dundee Organisers
E: pippaclegg@hotmail.com

This will be the first plant sale for our Angus & Dundee District - Plants and Prosecco. We will offer a selection of unusual plants, all grown locally and sourced from private gardens. We also welcome donations of plants prior to the sale and on the day.

Other Details: Admission price includes a glass of Prosecco and nibbles. The garden will also be open to visit.

Directions: From the A90, take A926 towards Kirriemuir. Just after the *Welcome to Kirriemuir* sign take a sharp left on to single track road, or from Kirriemuir take A926 towards Forfar and fork right on to single track road at Beechwood Place. Then take the first left onto drive and follow signs.

Disabled Access:
Partial

Opening Times:
Plant sale
Friday 12 May
5:00pm - 7:00pm
garden also open

Admission:
£3.00, accompanied children free

Charities:
All proceeds to
SG Beneficiaries

NEW ARBROATH COLLECTION OF GARDENS
DD11 4ED and DD11 2NT
Gardens of Arbroath

An interesting collection of gardens that benefit from the shelter of mature trees. The smallest in St Vigeans is a lovely cottage garden with a range of ferns. Visitors may also visit the village museum and church. Balcathie and Cuthlie are larger farmhouse gardens. Both have wonderful old trees under planted with mature shrubs, azalea and rhododendrons. A gentle slope at Balcathie provides the backdrop for a cascading water feature surrounded by mixed shrubs, iris and primula. Hospitalfield's garden will also support the day (see separate entry) along with nearby Hope, an organic fruit and veg garden which provides training and work experience for adults with learning and/or physical disabilities.

Other Details: Teas in the St Vigeans Hall, ice-cream at Cuthlie Farm, Arbirlot.

Directions: Tickets & maps on 3 Jun at St Vigeans Hall DD11 4ED and Cuthlie Farm, Arbirlot DD11 2NT. Also from 1 Apr at Ashbrook Nursery, Forfar Rd, DD1 3RB.

Disabled Access:
Partial

Opening Times:
Saturday 3 June
1:00pm - 5:00pm

Admission:
£4.00, accompanied children free

Charities:
St Vigeans Church Fund receives 20%, Archie Foundation receives 20% for the new children's ward at Ninewells Hospital, the net remaining to SG Beneficiaries

BRECHIN CASTLE
Brechin DD9 6SG
The Earl and Countess of Dalhousie T: 01356 624566
E: mandyferries@dalhousieestates.co.uk   www.dalhousieestates.co.uk

CELEBRATING 75 YEARS OF OPENING FOR CHARITY WITH SCOTLAND'S GARDENS!

The uniquely curving walls of the garden at Brechin Castle are just the first of many delightful surprises in store. The luxurious blend of ancient and modern plantings is the second. Find charm and splendour in the wide gravelled walks, secluded small paths and corners. May sees the rhododendrons and azaleas hit the peak of their flowering to wonderful effect; and with complementary underplanting and a framework of great and beautiful trees set the collection in the landscape. This is a lovely garden at any time of year and a knockout in the spring.

Other Details: Dogs on leads please.

Directions: A90 southernmost exit to Brechin, one mile past Brechin Castle Centre, Castle gates are on the right.

Disabled Access:
Partial

Opening Times:
Sunday 7 May
2:00pm - 5:00pm

Admission:
£5.00, accompanied children free

Charities:
Dalhousie Day Care receives 20%, Unicorn Preservation Society receives 20%, the net remaining to SG Beneficiaries

DALFRUIN
Kirktonhill Road, Kirriemuir DD8 4HU
Mr and Mrs James A Welsh

A well-stocked connoisseur's garden of about a third acre situated at the end of a short cul-de-sac. There are many less common plants like varieties of trilliums, meconopsis (blue poppies), tree peonies (descendants of ones collected by George Sherriff and grown at Ascreavie), dactylorhiza and dodonopsis. There is a scree and collection of ferns. The vigorous climbing rose Paul's Himalayan Musk grows over a pergola. Interconnected ponds encourage wildlife.

Other Details: Good plant stall with many unusual plants including Trilliums, Meconopsis, tree peonies and two year old monkey puzzle saplings. Teas served at St Mary's Episcopal Church.

Directions: From the centre of Kirriemuir turn left up Roods. Kirktonhill Road is on the left near top of the hill. Park on Roods or at St Mary's Episcopal Church. Disabled parking only in Kirktonhill Road.

Disabled Access:
Partial

Opening Times:
Sunday 14 May
2:00pm - 5:00pm

Admission:
£4.00, accompanied children free

Charities:
St Mary's Episcopal Church receives 40%, the net remaining to SG Beneficiaries

DUNDEE & ANGUS COLLEGE GARDENS
Kingsway Campus, Old Glamis Road, Dundee DD3 8LE
Horticulture Department, D&A College
www.dundeeandangus.ac.uk

Dundee and Angus College gardens have been developed and re-developed over the past 40 years. Currently the gardens display many different garden rooms along with finished show areas. Other 'rooms' are constantly in a state of construction (and occasional destruction) by our students. This year we are particularly proud of our fruit and vegetable garden, Japanese garden, pond area, our new rose garden, herbaceous border and our new rock garden which is still very much under construction. The glass houses and frame yard are always busy with a fine range of bedding plants, alpines and herbaceous plants and a selection of shrubs and trees many of which will be for sale. We always have a few 'specials' on the go as well.

Other Details: Students and staff will be available to help with any questions and demonstrations will go on throughout the day. Tea, coffee and cakes will be available, prepared and served by the college hospitality students.

Directions: Along the Kingsway at the roundabout with Old Glamis Road. National Express buses (18, 19, 21) run along Old Glamis Road to/from Dundee town centre.

Disabled Access:
Partial

Opening Times:
Sunday 21 May
11:00am - 4:00pm

Admission:
£4.00, accompanied children free

Charities:
Student Foodbank, Dundee & Angus College receives 40%, the net remaining to SG Beneficiaries

DUNNINALD CASTLE
Montrose DD10 9TD
The Stansfeld Family T: 01674 672031
E: visitorinformation@dunninald.com www.dunninald.com

Dunninald Castle is a family home built in 1824, set in policies developed during the 17th and 18th centuries. It offers many attractive features to the visitor including a beech avenue planted around 1670. Snowdrops in spring and bluebells in May carpet the woods and wild garden. At its best in July, the highlight of Dunninald is the walled garden with traditional mixed borders, vegetables, soft fruits, fruit trees and greenhouse.

Other Details: Gardens open from 21 May - 31 August, 1:00pm - 5:00pm. Castle Tours from 1 - 30 July 1:00pm - 5:00pm (closed Mondays). See our website for additional information. Groups welcome with prior appointment.

Directions: Three miles south of Montrose, ten miles north of Arbroath, signposted from the A92.

Disabled Access:
Partial

Opening Times:
Sunday 21 May
1:00pm - 5:00pm
for Bluebell Sunday

Admission:
£4.00, accompanied children free

Charities:
Girl Guiding Montrose receives 40%, the net remaining to SG Beneficiaries

FORFAR OPEN GARDEN

36 Lochside Road, Forfar DD8 3JD
Forfar Open Garden Scheme T: 01307 469090
E: craichie@aol.com

This new therapeutic garden has been developed by local gardeners banded together into the charity, Forfar Open Garden Scheme. The quarter acre garden caters for people of all abilities and provides sessions of horticulture therapy in an informal setting. The planting strives for a balance of ornamental, sensory and seasonal productive plants. The garden houses a large greenhouse, polytunnel, and meeting room where the gardeners can mix socially.

Other Details: Conducted tours are available for groups by arrangement.

Directions: Lochside Road is opposite the entrance to Tesco in Forfar. The garden is 200 yards along Lochside Road on the right.

Disabled Access:
Full

Opening Times:
Saturday 10 June
2:00pm - 5:00pm

Admission:
£3.00, accompanied children free

Charities:
Forfar Open Garden Scheme receives 40%, the net remaining to SG Beneficiaries

GALLERY

Montrose DD10 9LA
Mr John Simson T: 01674 840550
E: galleryhf@googlemail.com

The redesign and replanting of this historic garden, featured in *Homes & Gardens*, have preserved and extended its traditional framework of holly, privet and box. A grassed central alley, embellished with circles, links themed gardens, including the recently replanted gold garden and hot border, with the fine collection of old roses and the fountain and pond of the formal white garden. A walk through the woodland garden, home to rare breed sheep, with its extensive border of mixed heathers, leads to the River North Esk. From there rough paths lead both ways along the bank.

Other Details: Teas available only on 27 May and 15 July open days. Groups welcome by appointment.

Directions: From the A90 south of Northwater Bridge take the exit to Hillside and next left to Gallery and Marykirk. From the A937 west of rail underpass follow signs to Gallery and Northwater Bridge.

Disabled Access:
Partial

Opening Times:
Saturday 27 May
Saturday 15 July
2:00pm - 5:00pm
1 June - 31 August
1:00pm - 5:00pm (Tues only)
By arrangement 1 Jun - 31 Aug

Admission:
£4.00, accomp children free

Charities:
Practical Action receives 40%, the net remaining to SG Beneficiaries

HOSPITALFIELD GARDENS

Hospitalfield House, Westway, Arbroath DD11 2NH
Hospitalfield Arts
E: info@hospitalfield.org.uk www.hospitalfield.org.uk

At Hospitalfield in Arbroath the artist Patrick Allan-Fraser (1813–1890) remodelled a 13th-century hospital to create his 19th-century Arts & Crafts home. The walled gardens have been cultivated from the early medieval period, from the medicinal and the orchard to the Victorian passion for collecting ferns. This lovely flower and vegetable garden, set against the red sandstone neo Gothic architecture is maintained by a part time Gardener and a team of volunteers through their Garden Club. They run an international cultural programme rooted in the contemporary visual arts, inspired by the long and extraordinary heritage of the site.

Other Details: Garden is also open Saturdays from 20 May to 23 Sept, 2:00pm - 5:00pm. Hospitalfield House is open for weekly guided tours, quarterly open weekends and a varied international cultural programme. See website.

Directions: See website for directions.

Disabled Access:
Partial

Opening Times:
Saturday 8 July
2:00pm - 5:00pm

Admission:
£4.00, accompanied children free

Charities:
Hospitalfield Trust receives 40%, the net remaining to SG Beneficiaries

NEW INCHMILL COTTAGE
Glenprosen, nr Kirriemuir DD8 4SA
Iain Nelson T: 01575 540452

This is a long, sloping and terraced garden at over 800 feet in the Braes of Angus, developed to be a garden for all seasons. Half is dominated by bulbs, rhododendrons, azaleas, primulas, meconopsis and clematis. The other half mainly later summer bulbs, herbaceous plants and roses. There is also a rockery/scree and fernery.

Other Details: Car parking beside the church (50 yards away) and by the village hall opposite, where a pop-up coffee facility will be set up hopefully! There will be a plant stall.

Directions: From Kirriemuir take the B955 (signposted *The Glens*) to Dykehead (about five miles). From there follow the *Prosen* sign for about five miles. Inchmill is the white fronted cottage beside the phone box.

Disabled Access:
None

Opening Times:
Thursdays: 4 & 18 May
1 & 15 June
3 & 17 August
7 & 21 September
2:00pm - 5:00pm

Admission:
£3.00, accomp. children free

Charities:
Archie Foundation receives 40% (Ninewells Hospital for new Children's Ward), the net remaining to SG Beneficiaries

---

KILRY VILLAGE GARDENS
Kilry, Glen Isla PH11 8HS
Kilry Garden Club

A varied selection of delightful and interesting gardens in a beautiful glen setting with two new additions this year. Plantings include meconopsis, primulas, rhododendrons and attractive wild flower areas around water. Also vegetable plots, unusual trees and shrubs.

Other Details: Soup, teas and plants with tickets, toilet and maps from the central point of Kilry Village Hall (PH11 8HS).

Directions: From Perth take the A94 to Coupar Angus and just before Meigle take the B964 and follow signs to Glen Isla and then to Kilry with sign on the left. From Dundee take the B954 to Coupar Angus and follow as from Perth.

Disabled Access:
Partial

Opening Times:
Saturday 17 June
Sunday 18 June
12:00pm - 5:00pm

Admission:
£5.00, accompanied children free

Charities:
Scotland's Charity Air Ambulance receives 40%, the net remaining to SG Beneficiaries

---

KIRKTON HOUSE
Kirkton of Craig, Montrose DD10 9TB
Campbell Watterson T: 01674 673604
E: campbellkirktonhouse@btinternet.com

A regency manse set in over two acres of garden. The walled garden includes herbaceous borders, a sunken garden, lime allee, statuary and formal rose garden. The wild garden includes a pond and water lilies. There is also a large flock of Jacobs sheep in the adjoining glebe.

Directions: One mile south of Montrose, off the A92 at the Balgove turn-off.

Disabled Access:
Partial

Opening Times:
By arrangement
1 May - 30 September

Admission:
£4.00, accompanied children free

Charities:
All proceeds to SG Beneficiaries

15 NEW LANGLEY PARK GARDENS
Montrose DD10 9LG
Marianne and Philip Santer T: 01674 810735
E: philip@psanter.wanadoo.co.uk www.langleyparkgardens.co.uk

Set overlooking Montrose basin, Langley Park Gardens include 27 acres of policies containing woodland walks with snowdrops nestling at the base of ancient and younger trees. Large drifts of snowdrops of many varieties can be admired around the wall of the three walled gardens and in the small arboretum. Walk down through the 20 acre wildflower meadow to see the snowdrops along the bank of the wildlife pond, enjoying the views of Montrose basin, Montrose, the hills and sea beyond. You will also be welcome to wander around the walled gardens to see them coming to life after their winter slumbers and see the promise of things to come.

Other Details: Gardens also open from the first weekend in May until the last Sunday in September, 10:00am-4:00pm, Friday, Saturday and Sunday only. Disabled toilet available.

Directions: Just off the A935 Montrose to Brechin Road, 1.5 miles from Montrose.

Disabled Access:
Partial

Opening Times:
Saturday 11 March
10:00am - 4:00pm
for the Snowdrop Festival

Admission:
£4.00, accompanied children free

Charities:
MS Therapy Centre (Tayside Ltd) receives 40%, the net remaining to SG Beneficiaries

16 LAWTON HOUSE
Inverkeilor, by Arbroath DD11 4RU
Katie & Simon Dessain

Woodland garden of beech trees carpeted with snowdrops and crocuses in spring set around a Georgian House. There is also a walled garden planted with fruit trees and vegetables. The property was owned for many years by Elizabeth and Patrick Allan Fraser who built Hospitalfield House in Arbroath.

Directions: Take B965 between Inverkeilor and Friockheim, turn right at sign for Angus Chain Saws. Drive approximately 200 metres, then take first right.

Disabled Access:
Partial

Opening Times:
Sunday 12 March
2:00pm - 5:00pm
for the Snowdrop Festival

Admission:
£3.00, accompanied children free

Charities:
Julia Thomson Memorial Trust receives 40%, the net remaining to SG Beneficiaries

17 NEWTONMILL HOUSE
by Brechin DD9 7PZ
Mr and Mrs S Rickman
E: rrickman@srickman.co.uk www.newtonmillhouse.co.uk

Newtonmill House looks over and into the semi-formal walled garden. The entrance to the garden is through a wrought iron gate that reflects the mill wheel from which Newtonmill derives its name. The central pathway is flagged by herbaceous borders, sheltered by a fine *Prunus Cerasifera 'Pissardii'* hedge. The garden is divided into four squares of kitchen garden, spring garden, croquet lawn with summer house, and the recently completed autumn garden. Through the rose arch at the south end of the garden are peony and shrub rose beds, a small pond area and doocot. Adjacent to the house is a rose-garlanded terrace and raised beds.

Directions: From the A90, exit B966 Brechin/Edzell towards Edzell.

Disabled Access:
Full

Opening Times:
Sunday 25 June
2:00pm - 5:00pm

Admission:
£4.00, accompanied children free

Charities:
RNLI (Montrose Ladies Branch) receives 40%, the net remaining to SG Beneficiaries

PITMUIES GARDENS
House of Pitmuies, Guthrie, By Forfar DD8 2SN
Jeanette & Ruaraidh Ogilvie
E: ogilvie@pitmuies.com www.pitmuies.com

Two semi-formal walled gardens adjoin the 18th century house and shelter long borders of herbaceous perennials, superb delphiniums, old fashioned roses and pavings with violas and dianthus. Spacious lawns, river and lochside walks beneath fine trees. There is a wide variety of shrubs with good autumn colour and an interesting picturesque turreted doocot and 'Gothick' wash house. Myriad spring bulbs include carpets of crocus following the massed snowdrops.

Other Details: Dogs on leads, please.

Directions: A932. Friockheim 1½ miles.

Disabled Access:
Partial

Opening Times:
1 April - 30 October
10:00am - 5:00pm

Admission:
£5.00, accompanied children free

Charities:
Donation to SG Beneficiaries

THE HERBALIST'S GARDEN AT LOGIE
Logie House, Kirriemuir DD8 5PN
Terrill and Gavin Dobson
E: terrill@angusherbalists.co.uk www.angusherbalists.co.uk

This garden, featured on the *Beechgrove Garden* in 2014, is set amid an 18th century walled garden and large Victorian styled greenhouse within Logie's organic farm. Featuring more than 150 herbs, the physic garden is divided into eight rectangles including medicinal herbs for different body systems. All the herbs are labelled with a brief description of actions to help novices learn more about this ancient art. The garden also features a herbaceous border and productive fruit and vegetable garden.

Other Details: Children's wildlife activities.

Directions: From the A926 leaving Kirriemuir, fork left at Beechwood Place onto the single track road or if approaching Kirriemuir take sharp left after *Welcome to Kirriemuir* sign. Take the first left and follow signs to The Walled Garden.

Disabled Access:
Partial

Opening Times:
Saturday 29 July
Sunday 30 July
2:00pm - 5:00pm

Admission:
£4.00, accompanied children free

Charities:
GKOPC Thrums Tots and Messy Church receives 40%, the net remaining to SG Beneficiaries

---

THE SHRUBBERY
67 Magdalen Yard Rd, Dundee DD2 1AL
Mrs Elaine Kuwahara

Home of famed Dundee artist McIntosh Patrick for many years, the garden and house were the subject of several of his paintings. The Georgian townhouse was designed and built by Dundee architect David Neave in 1817. The garden has been sympathetically restored to McIntosh Patrick's time and features mainly herbaceous perennials and shrubs. It also includes surviving fruit trees from its original layout as a working garden. There is a pond with goldfish and koi carp.

Other Details: Celebrating the 200th anniversary of The Shrubbery. Dogs on lead please. Disabled parking on the driveway, if required.

Directions: From Riverside Drive in Dundee, take the slip road at the old rail bridge and follow road to the left round Magdalen Green.

Disabled Access:
Full

Opening Times:
Friday 26 May
Saturday 27 May
Sunday 28 May
2:00pm - 5:00pm

Admission:
£3.00, accompanied children free

Charities:
Friends of Camperdown House receives 40%, the net remaining to SG Beneficiaries

FIFE

Scotland's Gardens 2017 Guidebook is sponsored by **INVESTEC WEALTH & INVESTMENT**

District Organisers

Louise Roger	Chesterhill, Boarhills, St Andrews KY16 8PP
Catherine Erskine	Cambo House, Kingsbarns KY16 8QD
	E: fife@scotlandsgardens.org

Area Organisers

Jeni Auchinleck	2 Castle Street, Crail KY10 3SQ
Oenone Baillie	West Mill Cottage, Dunino, St Andrews KY16 8LT
Pauline Borthwick	96 Hepburn Gardens, St Andrews KY16 9LP
Evelyn Crombie	Keeper's Wood, Over Rankeilour, Cupar KY15 4NQ
Caroline Macpherson	Edenside, Strathmiglo KY14 7PX
Lorna McHardy	Gardeners Cottage, Shore Road, Crombie Point Crombie KY12 8LQ
Lindsay Murray	Craigfoodie, Dairsie, Cupar KY15 4RU
April Simpson	The Cottage, Boarhills, St Andrews KY16 8PP
Fay Smith	37 Ninian Fields, Pittenweem, Anstruther KY10 2QU
Julia Young	South Flisk, Blebo Craigs, Cupar KY15 5UQ

Treasurer

David Buchanan Cook	Helensbank, 56 Toll Road, Kincardine FK10 4QZ

Gardens open on a specific date

Lindores House, By Newburgh	Sunday 5 March	11:00am	- 3:00pm
Backhouse at Rossie Estate, By Collessie	Saturday 15 April	2:00pm	- 5:00pm
Cambo Gardens Spring Plant Sale, Kingsbarns	Sunday 16 April	11:00am	- 4:00pm
The Tower, 1 Northview Terrace, Wormit	Saturday 29 April	12:00pm	- 5:00pm
Kellie Castle Spring Plant Sale, Pittenweem	Sunday 7 May	10:30am	- 3:00pm
Tayfield with St Fort Woodland Garden and Willowhill Newport-on-Tay	Sunday 14 May	1:00pm	- 5:00pm
Earlshall Castle, Leuchars	Sunday 21 May	2:00pm	- 5:00pm
Kirklands, Saline	Sunday 21 May	2:00pm	- 5:00pm
46 South Street, St Andrews	Sunday 28 May	2:00pm	- 5:00pm
Lindores House, By Newburgh	Sunday 4 June	2:00pm	- 5:00pm
Three Gardens in Blebo Craigs, Blebo Craigs	Sunday 4 June	2:00pm	- 5:00pm
Craigrothie Village Gardens	Sunday 11 June	2:00pm	- 5:00pm
Culross Palace Garden, Culross	Sunday 18 June	12:00pm	- 5:00pm

FIFE

Scotland's Gardens 2017 Guidebook is sponsored by **INVESTEC WEALTH & INVESTMENT**

Greenhead Farmhouse, Greenhead of Arnot	Sunday 18 June	2:00pm	-	5:00pm
Kinghorn Village Gardens	Sunday 18 June	12:00pm	-	4:30pm
The Fife Garden Trail	Tuesday 20 June	10:00am	-	5:00pm
The Fife Garden Trail	Wednesday 21 June	10:00am	-	8:00pm
The Fife Garden Trail	Thursday 22 June	10:00am	-	5:00pm
The Tower, Wormit	Saturday 24 June	12:00pm	-	5:00pm
Backhouse at Rossie Estate, By Collessie	Sunday 25 June	2:00pm	-	5:00pm
Pittenweem: Gardens in the Burgh	Sunday 25 June	11:00am	-	5:00pm
The Fife Garden Trail	Tuesday 27 June	10:00am	-	5:00pm
The Fife Garden Trail	Wednesday 28 June	10:00am	-	8:00pm
The Fife Garden Trail	Thursday 29 June	10:00am	-	5:00pm
Earlshall Castle, Leuchars	Sunday 2 July	2:00pm	-	5:00pm
Wormistoune House, Crail	Sunday 2 July	12:00pm	-	5:00pm
The Fife Garden Trail	Tuesday 4 July	10:00am	-	5:00pm
The Fife Garden Trail	Wednesday 5 July	10:00am	-	8:00pm
The Fife Garden Trail	Thursday 6 July	10:00am	-	5:00pm
Crail: Small Gardens in the Burgh	Saturday 8 July	1:00pm	-	5:00pm
Crail: Small Gardens in the Burgh	Sunday 9 July	1:00pm	-	5:00pm
The Fife Garden Trail	Tuesday 11 July	10:00am	-	5:00pm
The Fife Garden Trail	Wednesday 12 July	10:00am	-	8:00pm
The Fife Garden Trail	Thursday 13 July	10:00am	-	5:00pm
Balcarres, Colinsburgh	Sunday 16 July	2:00pm	-	5:00pm
Balcaskie with Kellie Castle, Pittenweem	Sunday 23 July	12:00pm	-	5:00pm
Boarhills Village Gardens, St Andrews	Sunday 23 July	1:00pm	-	5:00pm
Falkland Palace and Garden, Falkland	Sunday 23 July	12:00pm	-	4:30pm
The Tower, Wormit	Saturday 29 July	12:00pm	-	5:00pm
Hill of Tarvit Plant Sale and Autumn Fair, Cupar	Sunday 1 October	10:30am	-	3:00pm

Gardens open regularly

Glassmount House, By Kirkcaldy	1 May - 30 September (Mon - Sat only)	2:00pm	-	5:00pm
Willowhill, Forgan	5 August - 26 August (Saturdays only)	2:00pm	-	5:00pm

FIFE

Gardens open by arrangement

Helensbank, Kincardine	1 June - 31 July	07739 312912
Kirklands, Saline	1 April - 30 September	01383 852737
Logie House, Crossford	1 April - 31 October	07867 804020
Rosewells, Pitscottie	1 April - 30 September	birgittamac@hotmail.co.uk
St Fort Woodland Garden, Newport-on-Tay	1 May - 30 November	07974 083110
Teasses Gardens, near Ceres	1 April - 30 September	07966 529205
The Tower, Wormit	1 April - 30 September	01382 541635 M: 07768 406946
Willowhill, Forgan	1 April - 31 August	01382 542890
Wormistoune House, Crail	1 April - 30 September	07905 938449

Plant sales

Cambo Gardens Spring Plant Sale, Kingsbarns	Sunday 16 April	11:00am - 4:00pm
Kellie Castle Spring Plant Sale, Pittenweem	Sunday 7 May	10:30am - 3:00pm
Hill of Tarvit Plant Sale and Autumn Fair, Cupar	Sunday 1 October	10:30am - 3:00pm

Key to symbols

	New in 2017		Homemade teas		Accommodation
	Teas		Dogs on a lead allowed		Plant stall
	Cream teas		Wheelchair access		Scottish Snowdrop Festival

GARDEN LOCATIONS IN FIFE

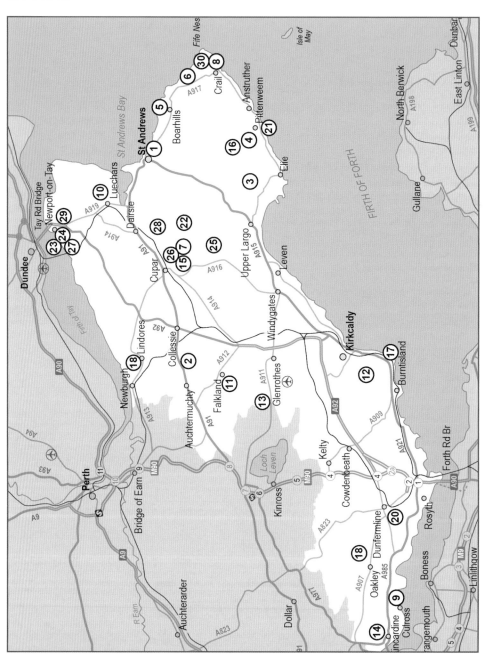

1 46 SOUTH STREET
St Andrews KY16 9JT
Mrs June Baxter T: 01334 474 995

Renowned town garden in medieval long rig, with orchard, clematis, spring bulbs and many spring flowering shrubs. An historic and unique feature in St Andrews, but also a wonderfully planted space where different styles of planting complement the range of plants used.

Other Details: Teas will be served under cover.

Directions: Entry for the garden is off South Street.

Disabled Access:
Partial

Opening Times:
Sunday 28 May
2:00pm - 5:00pm

Admission:
£5.00

Charities:
East Fife Members' Centre of the National Trust for Scotland receives 40%, the net remaining to SG Beneficiaries

2 BACKHOUSE AT ROSSIE ESTATE
By Collessie KY15 7UZ
Mr & Mrs Andrew and Caroline Thomson
E: caroline.thomson@rofsie-estate.com www.rofsie-estate.com

It is in the DNA - 10 years in the making, you are welcomed into the unfolding story of the many generations of one family, the remarkable Quaker Backhouse horticulturalists whose legacy is being brought back to life by the current 6th generation. See the Backhouse Centre, Walled Garden, cafe and plant sales, now an RHS Partner Garden. For April opening see the rare Backhouse daffodils recently awarded National Collection status, for children there is a fun Easter themed Woodland Trail.
The genesis for the garden's design concept was the coincidental realisation the owner's co-joined initials C-G A-T form the two base pairs of DNA, these letters are carved into the centromere sculpture which sits in the centre of the double helix pathway with scented roses scrambling over interrupted archways above. Herbaceous borders with wispy grasses, colourful perennials and rarities. Allium plantings, surround a grass labyrinth. A water feature, short rill and formal pond functions as a reservoir supporting the garden's watering requirements. Culinary and medicinal herbs, vegetables and cut flowers fill the pottager with old espaliered fruit trees trained on the stone walls. Interesting scree and rock garden and peat bed plantings. A woodland walk, with daffodils in season, leads to a ruined tomb.

Other Details: National Plant Collection®: daffodils. Information area and short video. The Backhouse Centre welcomes academic and horticultural enquiries, please contact Caroline Thomson. No dogs apart from Guide Dogs.

Directions: Between Auchtermuchty and Collessie on A91. One mile east of Auchtermuchty turn right for Charlottetown, turn first right into Rossie Estate onto an untarred drive.

Disabled Access:
Partial

Opening Times:
Saturday 15 April
& Sunday 25 June
2:00pm - 5:00pm

Admission:
£5.00

Charities:
Fife Voluntary Action receives 40%, the net remaining to SG Beneficiaries

FIFE

BALCARRES
Colinsburgh KY9 1HN
The Earl and Countess of Crawford and Balcarres

Superb 19th century formal and extensive woodland gardens with a wide variety of perennial plants and ornamental trees. The gardens are planted over a number of terraces surrounded by formal yew hedges. The terraces offer spectacular views over the Firth of Forth.

Directions: Half a mile north of Colinsburgh off A942.

Disabled Access:
None

Opening Times:
Sunday 16 July
2:00pm - 5:00pm

Admission:
£6.00, accompanied children free

Charities:
Riding for the Disabled Association receives 40%, the net remaining to SG Beneficiaries

BALCASKIE WITH KELLIE CASTLE
Pittenweem KY10 2RF
The Anstruther Family and The National Trust for Scotland

Balcaskie: In 1905 George Elgood wrote that Balcaskie was 'one of the best and most satisfying gardens in the British Isles'. Over the centuries, the gardens have seen input from Gilpin, Bryce & Nesfield. Today the gardens are at the start of a period of restoration with help from the National Trust for Scotland.

Kellie Castle: This superb garden, around 400 years old, was sympathetically restored by the Lorimer family in the late 19th century. The Arts and Crafts style garden has a selection of old-fashioned roses and herbaceous plants, cultivated organically and hosts an amazing 30 varieties of rhubarb and 75 different types of apple.

Directions: Access to Balcaskie and Kellie Castle via Kellie Castle only, a free minibus will transport visitors between the gardens. B9171, three miles NNW of Pittenweem. There is bus from local villages available by pre-booking.

Disabled Access:
Partial

Opening Times:
Sunday 23 July
12:00pm - 5:00pm

Admission:
£8.00 for entrance to both gardens

Charities:
Donation to SG Beneficiaries

BOARHILLS VILLAGE GARDENS
St Andrews KY16 8PP
The Gardeners of Boarhills T: 01334 880 238

Seven delightfully varied village gardens exhibiting a range of styles. Colourful, richly planted herbaceous borders at Kenly Green Farm; traditional mixed cottage garden style at The Dirdale and No 2 Old Edinburgh, with kitchen gardens and orchard; spectacular bedding and sweet peas at No 5 Old Edinburgh; clever use of different levels and existing built features at The Cottage, Sea View and No 1 Old Edinburgh, where the design beautifully complements stunning ranges of herbaceous and shrub planting.

Other Details: Teas in the Village Hall.

Directions: Enter the Village off the A917. Parking at Kenly Green Farm.

Disabled Access:
Partial

Opening Times:
Sunday 23 July
1:00pm - 5:00pm

Admission:
£5.00

Charities:
Scooniehill Riding for the Disabled receives 40%, the net remaining to SG Beneficiaries

CAMBO GARDENS SPRING PLANT SALE
Kingsbarns KY16 8QD
Trustees of Cambo Heritage Trust T: 01333 451040
E: mail@camboheritagetrust.org.uk www.camboheritagetrust.org.uk

Invited nurseries will join Cambo gardens to provide a wide range of rare and interesting plants. A great day out for the family. Childrens' activities, daffodil meadow, walled garden and woodland walk to the sandy beach. 'First Look' chance to see the newly converted stables (due to open as an education and training centre in June 2017). Tours throughout the day.

Other Details: National Plant Collection®: *Galanthus*. Champion Trees: Bundle Beech. 40% of funds raised on this day will go to the development of Cambo Heritage Centre and Gardens.

Directions: A917 between Crail and St Andrews.

Disabled Access:
Full

Opening Times:
Plant sale
Sunday 16 April
11:00am - 4:00pm
garden also open

Admission:
£2.50

Charities:
Cambo Heritage Trust receives 40%, the net remaining to SG Beneficiaries

---

CRAIGROTHIE VILLAGE GARDENS
KY15 5QA
The Gardeners of Craigrothie Village T: 01334 828 425

At least five gardens will be open in this delightful, picturesque village. Traditional in style, and many of them walled, they feature beautiful landscaping, making the most of the sloping valley setting through which the Craigrothie Burn runs. Ranging from a plant collector's garden to beautifully integrated examples of hard and soft landscaping, there is something for every visitor to enjoy.

Other Details: Parking is available at the Village Hall. Tickets and maps available at some gardens and the Village Hall.

Directions: On the A916 between Kennoway and Cupar, situated at the junction to Ceres on the B939

Disabled Access:
None

Opening Times:
Sunday 11 June
2:00pm - 5:00pm

Admission:
£5.00, accompanied children free

Charities:
Craigrothie Village Hall receives 40%, the net remaining to SG Beneficiaries

---

CRAIL: SMALL GARDENS IN THE BURGH
KY10 3SQ
The Gardeners of Crail

A number of small gardens in varied styles: cottage, historic, plantsman's and bedding. The stunning coastal location of the gardens presents some challenges for planting but also allows a great range of more tender species to flourish.

Other Details: Tickets and maps available from Mrs Auchinleck, 2 Castle Street, Crail and Ian and Margaret Moonie, 52 Marketgate South, Crail.

Directions: Approach Crail from either St Andrews or Anstruther by A917. Park in the Marketgate.

Disabled Access:
None

Opening Times:
Saturday 8 July
Sunday 9 July
1:00pm - 5:00pm

Admission:
£5.00

Charities:
Crail Cubs receives 10%, Crail Preservation Society receives 30%, the net remaining to SG Beneficiaries

FIFE

 CULROSS PALACE GARDEN
Culross KY12 8JH
The National Trust for Scotland T: 01383 880359
E: larnot@nts.org.uk www.nts.org.uk/property/royal-burgh-of-culross/

Relive the domestic life of the 16th and 17th centuries amid the old buildings and cobbled streets of this Royal Burgh on the River Forth. Explore the recreated 17th century garden behind the Culross Palace laid out to show the range of plants that were grown for culinary, medicinal and ornamental use. Don't miss the Scot's Dumpy chickens!

Other Details: Fruit and vegetable stalls from produce grown at Culross Palace. Meet the Head Gardener. Tours with Head Gardener at 12:30pm and 3:30pm. Partial access with difficulties for wheelchair users.

Directions: Off A985, three miles east of Kincardine Bridge, six miles west of Dunfermline. Buses Stagecoach, Stirling to Dunfermline or First, Edinburgh to Dunfermline. Falkirk station twelve miles, Dunfermline station six miles.

Disabled Access:
Partial

Opening Times:
Sunday 18 June
12:00pm - 5:00pm

Admission:
Normal NTS admission price applies, £6.00 for tour with Head Gardener

Charities:
Donation to SG Beneficiaries

EARLSHALL CASTLE
Leuchars KY16 0DP
Paul & Josine Veenhuijzen T: 01334 839205

CELEBRATING 50 YEARS OF OPENING FOR CHARITY WITH SCOTLAND'S GARDENS!

Extensive and interesting garden designed by Sir Robert Lorimer. Fascinating topiary lawn, for which Earlshall is renowned, rose terrace, croquet lawn with herbaceous borders, shrub border, box garden, orchard, kitchen and herb garden.

Directions: On Earlshall Road, three quarters of a mile east of Leuchars Village (off A919).

Disabled Access:
Partial

Opening Times:
Sunday 21 May
Sunday 2 July
2:00pm - 5:00pm

Admission:
£5.00, accomp. children free

Charities:
RAF Benevolent Fund receives 40% (May opening), St Athernase Church, Leuchars receives 40% (July opening), the net remaining to SG Beneficiaries

FALKLAND PALACE AND GARDEN
Falkland, Cupar KY15 7BU
The National Trust for Scotland T: 01337 857397
E: wpurvis@nts.org.uk www.nts.org.uk/property/falkland-palace-and-gardens/

Set in a medieval village, the Royal Palace of Falkland is a superb example of Renaissance architecture. Garden enthusiasts will appreciate the work of Percy Cane, who designed the gardens between 1947 and 1952. Come and enjoy this fantastic Herb Day - see details below.

Other Details: Champion Trees: *Acer platanoides* 'Crimson King'. This unique open day, will provide a fantastic opportunity for visitors to learn more about herbs including how these versatile plants have been used through the ages – from creating perfumes and flavouring foods, to treating ailments and providing a staple ingredient for traditional crafts.

Take a guided tour of the Palace's 'Physic Garden' to see herbs traditionally grown in the time of Mary, Queen of Scots and find out how they were used by the Royal Physician to heal the Kings' and Queen ailments.

- Pick up growing tips from horticultural experts.
- Take part in arts and crafts activities for all the family.
- Browse a wide selection of food, drink and herb-related market stalls.
- Enjoy cookery demonstrations and tastings with local chefs.
- Purchase locally grown herbs and plants.
- Enjoy the peaceful and tranquil arts and craft gardens by Percy Cane, the ancient orchard and the wildlife meadow.
- Visit Falkland Palace, the country residence of the Stuart monarchs for 200 years.

Directions: A912, 10 miles from M90, junction 8, 11 miles north of Kirkcaldy. Bus - Stagecoach Fife stops in the High Street (about 100 metres from the garden). OS Ref: NO252075.

Disabled Access:
Partial

Opening Times:
Sunday 23 July
12:00pm - 4:30pm

Admission:
Normal NTS admission applies

Charities:
Donation to SG Beneficiaries

GLASSMOUNT HOUSE
By Kirkcaldy KY2 5UT
Peter, James and Irene Thomson T: 01592 890214
E: mcmoonter@yahoo.co.uk

Densely planted walled garden with surrounding woodland. An A-listed sun dial, Mackenzie & Moncur greenhouse and historical doocot are complemented by a number of newer built structures. Daffodils are followed by a mass of candelabra and cowslip primula, meconopsis and *Cardiocrinum giganteum*. Hedges and topiary form backdrops for an abundance of bulbs, clematis, rambling roses and perennials, creating interest through the summer into September.

Other Details: Artists studio, gallery, wood store. Featured in *Country Living*, The *English Garden 2012*, *The Scottish Field 2013*. Winner of *The Times/Fetzer Back Gardens of the Year 2008* green garden category.

Directions: From Kirkcaldy - Head west on the B9157. Turn left immediately after the railway bridge on the edge of town. Follow the single track road for 1½ miles and cross the crossroads. Glassmount House is the first turning on your right.

Disabled Access:
None

Opening Times:
1 May - 30 September
2:00pm - 5:00pm
(Mon - Sat only)

Admission:
£4.00

Charities:
Parkinsons UK receives 40%, the net remaining to SG Beneficiaries

FIFE

GREENHEAD FARMHOUSE
Greenhead of Arnot KY6 3JQ
Mr and Mrs Malcolm Strang Steel T: 01592 840459
www.fife-bed-breakfast-glenrothes.co.uk

The south facing garden combines a sense of formality in its symmetrical layout, with an informal look of mixed herbaceous and shrub borders and a large display of alliums throughout. The garden is constantly evolving with new themes and combinations of plants, all unified by a fantastic use of colour. There is also a well stocked polytunnel which is used to augment the highly productive fruit and vegetable garden.

Other Details: Dogs on leads.

Directions: A911 between Auchmuir Bridge and Scotlandwell.

Disabled Access:
None

Opening Times:
Sunday 18 June
2:00pm - 5:00pm

Admission:
£5.00, accompanied children free

Charities:
Milnathort Guide Group receives 40%, the net remaining to SG Beneficiaries

---

HELENSBANK
Kincardine FK10 4QZ
David Buchanan-Cook and Adrian Miles T: 07739 312912
E: Helensbank@aol.com

An 18th century walled garden, with main feature a Cedar of Lebanon, reputedly planted in 1750 by the sea captain who built the house. It provides challenges for planting in terms of shade and needle fall. Distinctive garden 'rooms' in part of the garden comprise a perennial blue and white cottage garden, a formal rose garden and an 'Italian' garden with citrus trees in pots. A 'hot' courtyard contains exotics such as bananas, acacias, lochromas, melianthus and brugmansia. A shaded walk along the bottom of the garden leads to a Japanese pagoda. A large conservatory/greenhouse houses various climbing plants including varieties of passiflora.

Other Details: Homemade teas available for groups on request.

Directions: On request.

Disabled Access:
None

Opening Times:
By arrangement
1 June - 31 July

Admission:
£4.00

Charities:
Marie Curie receives 40%, the net remaining to SG Beneficiaries

---

HILL OF TARVIT PLANT SALE AND AUTUMN FAIR
Hill of Tarvit, Cupar KY15 5PB
The National Trust for Scotland/Scotland's Gardens Fife
E: s.a.lorimore@dundee.ac.uk   www.scotlandsgardens.org or www.nts.org.uk

This long established plant sale is a fantastic opportunity to purchase bare root and potted plants from an enormous selection on offer. We also welcome donations of plants prior to the sale and on the day! Bring and buy! Hill of Tarvit is one of Scotland's finest Edwardian mansion houses. Surrounding the mansion house are spectacular gardens designed by Robert Lorimer, woods, open heath and parkland to explore.

Other Details: House (reduced entry fee) and Garden Tea Room open 11:00am to 4:00pm.

Directions: Two miles south of Cupar off A916.

Disabled Access:
Partial

Opening Times:
Plant sale Sunday
1 October
10:30am - 3:00pm
garden also open.

Admission:
£2.50, children under 16 free

Charities:
All proceeds to
SG Beneficiaries

KELLIE CASTLE SPRING PLANT SALE
Pittenweem KY10 2RF
The National Trust for Scotland/Scotland's Gardens Fife
E: s.a.lorimore@dundee.ac.uk www.scotlandsgardens.org or www.nts.org.uk

Stock up your borders with a wide selection of interesting and unusual plants, grown locally and sourced from private gardens, at Scotland's Gardens Spring Plant Sale held in this this beautiful Arts and Crafts style garden. Enjoy the garden in spring with *Clematis montana* and apple blossom in flower, red *Euphorbia griffithii*, forget-me-nots, young vegetables and a great collection of rhubarb.

Directions: Road - B9171, three miles NNW of Pittenweem. Bus - Flexible from local villages by pre-booking.

Disabled Access:
Full

Opening Times:
Plant sale
Sunday 7 May
10:30am - 3:00pm
garden also open

Admission:
£2.50, children under 16 free

Charities:
All proceeds to
SG Beneficiaries

KINGHORN VILLAGE GARDENS
KY3 9RN
The Gardeners of Kinghorn Village
E: kinghorninbloom@gmail.com

Kinghorn is a large coastal village boasting an interesting variety of gardens, some directly on the sea front and some hidden treasures. Kinghorn in Bloom is a community gardening group which strives to make Kinghorn a greener,cleaner, more attractive place. Awarded Gold by Beautiful Fife for the last three years and in 2016 Awarded Best Coastal Village in Fife.

Other Details: Tickets and maps from Carousel Coffee Shop, Pettycur Road KY3 9RN.

Directions: Kinghorn village is between Kirkcaldy and Burntisland.

Disabled Access:
None

Opening Times:
Sunday 18 June
12:00pm - 4:30pm

Admission:
£5.00

Charities:
The Library Renewed receives
40%, the net remaining to
SG Beneficiaries

FIFE

18 KIRKLANDS
Saline KY12 9TS
Peter & Gill Hart   T: 01383 852737
E: gill@i-comment360.com   www.kirklandshouseandgarden.co.uk

Kirklands, built in 1832 on the site of an older house, has been the Hart family home for nearly 40 years. Peter and Gill began creating a garden and it is still a work in progress. There are herbaceous borders, a bog garden by the burn, a woodland garden with rhododendrons and a carpet of bluebells, a terraced wall garden with raised beds and espalier fruit trees. Saline Burn divides the garden from ancient woodland and the woodland walk.

Other Details: A tree house for the grandchildren was built recently, as seen on the *Beechgrove Garden* programme.

Directions: Junction 4, M90, then B914. Parking in the centre of the village, then a short walk to the garden. Limited disabled parking at Kirklands.

Disabled Access:
Partial

Opening Times:
Sunday 21 May
2:00pm - 5:00pm
Also by arrangement
1 April - 30 September

Admission:
£5.00, accompanied children free

Charities:
Saline Environmental Group receives 40%, the net remaining to SG Beneficiaries

---

19 LINDORES HOUSE
By Newburgh   KY14 6JD
Mr and Mrs R Turcan

Stunning lochside position with snowdrops, leucojums, aconites, trillium, primulae and rhododendrons. Woodland walk and amazing 17th century yew believed to be the largest in Fife.

Other Details: Champion Trees: Yew.
March Opening: Plant stall selling snowdrops and leucojum. Homemade soup and bread available from 11:30am, in the conservatory.
June Opening: Plant stall stocked with a variety of plants from the garden including trillium and candelabra primulae.

Directions: Off A913 two miles east of Newburgh.

Disabled Access:
Partial

Opening Times:
Sunday 5 March
11:00am - 3:00pm
for the Snowdrop Festival
Sunday 4 June
2:00pm - 5:00pm

Admission:
£4.00 March opening
£5.00 June opening
Accompanied children free

Charities:
ADSHG receives 40% March opening, Newburgh Scout Group receives 40% June opening, the net remaining to SG Beneficiaries

20 LOGIE HOUSE
Crossford, Dunfermline KY12 8QN
Mr and Mrs Jonathan Hunt T: 07867 804020

Central to the design of this walled garden is a path through a double mixed border. Long rows of vegetables and fruit also contribute to colour and design when seen from the house and terrace. A long border of repeat flowering roses and rose and annual beds contribute to an extended season of colour and interest. There is a magnificent and very productive Mackenzie & Moncur greenhouse in excellent condition with fully working vents and original benches and central heating system. The garden is surrounded by a belt of mixed woodland with walks.

Other Details: Dogs welcome outwith the walled garden.

Directions: M90 exit 1 for Rosyth and Kincardine Bridge (A985). After about two miles turn right to Crossford. At traffic lights, turn right and the drive is on the right at the end of the village main street.

Disabled Access:
Full

Opening Times:
By arrangement
1 April - 31 October

Admission:
£5.00

Charities:
Type 1 Juvenile Diabetes Research Fund receives 40%, the net remaining to SG Beneficiaries

---

21 PITTENWEEM: GARDENS IN THE BURGH

KY10 2PQ
The Gardeners of Pittenweem T: 01333 311988

A great variety in garden design: from well-established traditional, to open aspect landscaped and from organic permaculture to conventional allotment gardens, plus the recently refurbished Crazy Golf circuit for children is nearby, next to the West Braes car park.

Other Details: Tickets and maps obtainable at 3 Seaview Row, Pittenweem (near West Braes Car Park), 24 Milton Road (East side of Pittenweem) and from several gardens. Plant and book stalls. Refreshments are available in pubs, coffee shops and some gardens. Disabled access for some gardens.

Directions: On the A917 coast road enter Pittenweem following the signs to the West Braes car park next to the Crazy Golf. For traffic from the East, stop and park at Milton Road.

Disabled Access:
Partial

Opening Times:
Sunday 25 June
11:00am - 5:00pm

Admission:
£5.00

Charities:
STAR Children's Charity receives 20%, Pittenweem Community Library receives 20%, the net remaining to SG Beneficiaries

---

22 ROSEWELLS

Pitscottie KY15 5LE
**Birgitta and Gordon MacDonald
E: birgittamac@hotmail.co.uk**

Rosewells, designed by the garden owners, has developed over the last 20 years. It has an underlying theme that each part of the garden should work in relation to the rest to create one overall effect. Child friendly. The design centres on texture and foliage to provide a lively effect with structure and shape all year. The winter 'bones' are provided with trees and shrubs with features such as contorted stems and peeling or coloured bark. In spring and summer, texture and coloured foliage of shrubs and perennials add to the overall design. Birgitta sees flowers as an added bonus with scent and colour being important and combinations of yellow, blue and white colour schemes are preferred. The garden has many varieties of cornus, magnolias, trilliums, meconopsis, agapanthus, rhododendrons, auricular primulae, fritillaries, erythroniums, peonies and acers which are Birgitta and Gordon's favourites.

Directions: B940 between Pitscottie and Peat Inn, one mile from Pitscottie. Rosewells is the ochre coloured house.

Disabled Access:
Partial

Opening Times:
By arrangement
1 April - 30 September

Admission:
£4.00, accompanied children free

Charities:
Save the Children receives 40%, the net remaining to SG Beneficiaries

FIFE

23 ST FORT WOODLAND GARDEN
St Fort Farm, Newport-on-Tay DD6 8RE
Mr & Mrs Andrew Mylius T: 07974 083110
www.stfort.co.uk

Inspired by a visit to Ruskin's house and woodland garden at Brantwood. Azaleas and specimen rhododendrons are the principal plants as the acid soil within the wood makes them ideal, along with ability to withstand roe deer browsing. The rhododendrons include a wide selection of both specimen and hybrids. Azaleas are mainly *Azalea pontica* chosen for scent and autumn colour. Around 30 acres, Northwood is home to red squirrels, and offers spectacular views northwards over the River Tay. Also of interest are eucryphia, cercidiphyllum, tulip tree, various red acers, rowans, liquidambar, metasequoia and magnolias. Spectacular late autumn foliage!

Other Details: Approached by a 400m woodland walk from the car park/entrance. Teas can be provided for parties up to approx 25 by prior arrangement.

Directions: 1¾ miles south of the Tay Road Bridge off the A92, between the Forgan and Five Roads roundabouts.

Disabled Access:
None

Opening Times:
By arrangement
1 May - 30 November

Admission:
£4.00

Charities:
Brooke- Action for Working Horses & Donkeys receives 40%, the net remaining to SG Beneficiaries

24 TAYFIELD WITH ST FORT WOODLAND GARDEN AND WILLOWHILL
Newport-on-Tay DD6 8RA
Mr & Mrs William Berry, Mr & Mrs Andrew Mylius , Eric Wright & Sally Lorimore

Tayfield DD6 8RA: A wide variety of shrubs and fine trees, many to mark celebrations of the family who have lived here for over 200 years. Some trees are of great age and Tayfield has the tallest beech tree recorded in Scotland at 39 metres. A picturesque approach to Tayfield House is enhanced by wonderful large tree rhododendrons in May and views across the Tay all year round. The grounds are wildlife rich and contain two large ponds. Look out for red squirrels which are often seen.

St Fort DD6 8RE: see Fife entry for St Fort Woodland Garden.

Willowhill DD6 8RA: see Fife entry for Willowhill.

Other Details: Champion Trees: Beech (at Tayfield). Large Plant Sale at Willowhill.

Directions: 1½ miles south of Tay Road Bridge, take the B995 to Newport off the Forgan roundabout.

Disabled Access:
Partial

Opening Times:
Sunday 14 May
1:00pm - 5:00pm

Admission:
£5.00

Charities:
Forgan Arts Centre receives 40%, the net remaining to SG Beneficiaries

25 TEASSES GARDENS
near Ceres KY8 5PG
Sir Fraser and Lady Morrison T: 0796 6529205
E: craig@teasses.com

Teasses Gardens have been developed by the present owners for 16 years and now extend to approximately 60 acres. In addition to the restored Victorian walled garden with fruit, vegetables, cut flowers and a large greenhouse, there are formal and informal areas of the garden linked by numerous woodland walks, with several woodland gardens.

Other Details: For further information, contact Mr Craig Cameron, Head Gardener at the telephone number or email listed.

Directions: Between Ceres and Largo. Enter by Teasses Estate farm road, half a mile West of Woodside Village.

Disabled Access:
Partial

Opening Times:
By arrangement
1 April - 30 September

Admission:
£5.00

Charities:
Barnardos receives 40%, the net remaining to SG Beneficiaries

---

26 NEW THE FIFE GARDEN TRAIL

The Fife Gardeners
www.scotlandsgardens.org/FGT2017

Running over late June and early July, the Fife Garden Trail provides an opportunity to see nine privately owned gardens, all different, five of which have never or rarely admitted visitors before. It also offers a very flexible way to visit the gardens whether you wish to visit the area and see all gardens in three days (20-22 June, 27- 29 June or 4-6 July) or take the four weeks to see them all.

A ticket for the Fife Garden Trail makes a perfect gift - and do treat yourself as well!

Balcaskie	Pittenweem KY10 2RE
Edenside	Strathmiglo KY14 7PX
Freelands	Ceres KY15 5LW
Gilston House	by Largoward, Leven KY8 5QP
Lucklaw House	Logie KY15 4SJ
St Mary's Farm	St Mary's Road, Cupar KY15 4NF
Teasses Gardens	Near Ceres KY8 5PG
Whinhill	Lahill Mains, Upper Largo KY8 5QS
Willowhill	Forgan, Newport-on-Tay DD6 8RA

Other Details: A limited number of tickets are available and may be purchased by credit card at www.scotlandsgardens.org/FGF2017 or by cheque payable to Scotland's Gardens from S Lorimore, Willowhill, Forgan, Newport on Tay, Fife DD6 8RA. See pages 36 - 37 for further details.

Directions: Details will be shown in booklet provided on purchase of ticket(s).

Disabled Access:
Partial

Opening Times:
Tues 20 June 10am - 5pm
Wed 21 June 10am - 8pm
Thur 22 June 10am - 5pm
Tues 27 June 10am - 5pm
Wed 28 June 10am - 8pm
Thu 29 June 10am - 5pm
Tues 4 July 10am - 5pm
Wed 5 July 10am - 8pm
Thu 6 July 10am - 5pm
Tues 11 July 10am - 5pm
Wed 12 July 10am - 8pm
Thu 13 July 10am - 5pm
See pp36-37 for details.

Admission:
£20.00 (plus £1.00 P&P) for entrance to all gardens.
See other details.

Charities:
60% net of the proceeds goes to Scotland's Gardens' beneficiary charities. The remainder will be split equally between RNLI Anstruther and RHET Fife.

FIFE

27 THE TOWER

1 Northview Terrace, Wormit DD6 8PP
Peter and Angela Davey T: 01382 541635 M: 07768 406946
E: adavey541@btinternet.com

Situated four miles south of Dundee, this one acre Edwardian landscaped garden has panoramic views over the River Tay. Features include a rhododendron walk, rockeries, informal woodland planting schemes with native and exotic plants, offering year round interest. Original raised paths lead to a granite grotto with waterfall pool. Also of interest are raised vegetable beds made from granite sets.

Other Details: Garden is on a hillside with steep paths, therefore unsuited to those with poor mobility. Please contact Mr and Mrs Davey prior to visiting.

Directions: From B946 park on Naughton Road outside Spar shop and walk up path left following signs.

Disabled Access:
None

Opening Times:
Saturday 29 April,
Saturday 24 June,
& Saturday 29 July
12:00pm - 5:00pm
Also by arrangement
1 April - 30 September

Admission:
£4.00

Charities:
Barnados receives 40%,
the net remaining to
SG Beneficiaries

28 THREE GARDENS IN BLEBO CRAIGS

Blebo Craigs KY15 5UQ
Julia Young T: 01334 850859
E: julia@standrewspottery.co.uk   www.standrewspottery.co.uk

Three very different gardens in the pretty village of Blebo Craigs, each with stunning views.

South Flisk is a large garden created round a former quarry incorporating a pond with fish, a woodland area with meconopsis and trilliums and lots of rhododendrons. Recently featured on BBC TV's *Beechgrove Garden*.

Sunnybank recently renovated and includes stunning naturalistic planting and a Japanese water garden. Designer, Peter Christopher, will be on hand with advice on how to create this look.

Craighill Cottage garden has been resurrected from jungle status over the past two years. Highlights include an extensive stone dyking project which is now the backdrop for formal planting of herbaceous plants, shrubs, fruit trees and a rockery.

Other Details: Champion Trees: Nothofagus, planted in 1910 at South Flisk. George Young, the potter, will be giving demonstrations all day at South Flisk.

Directions: Blebo Craigs is off the B939 between Pitscottie and Strathkinness. There is a detailed map on the pottery website.

Disabled Access:
None

Opening Times:
Sunday 4 June
2:00pm - 5:00pm

Admission:
£5.00, accompanied children free

Charities:
RUDA receives 40%, the net remaining to SG Beneficiaries

South Flisk

South Flisk

29 WILLOWHILL

Forgan, Newport-on-Tay DD6 8RA
Eric Wright and Sally Lorimore T: 01382 542890
E: e.g.wright@dundee.ac.uk www.willowhillgarden.weebly.com

An evolving three acre garden featured in *Scotland for Gardeners* and *Scotland on Sunday*. The house is surrounded by a series of mixed borders designed with different vibrant colour combinations for effect all season and there is also a vegetable plot. Newly developed area containing borders of bulbs, roses and perennials. A stepped terrace of alpines leads to a wildlife pond in grassland planted with trees, bulbs and herbaceous perennials through which wide sweeping paths are mown.

Other Details: On Sunday 14 May Willowhill is opening with St Fort Woodland Garden and Tayfield.

Directions: 1½ miles south of Tay Road Bridge. Take the B995 to Newport off the Forgan roundabout. Willowhill is the first house on the left hand side next to the Forgan Arts Centre.

Disabled Access:
Partial

Opening Times:
5 - 26 August
2:00pm - 5:00pm
(Saturdays only)
Also by arrangement
1 April - 31 August

Admission:
£5.00

Charities:
RIO Community Centre
receives 40%, the net
remaining to SG Beneficiaries

30 WORMISTOUNE HOUSE

Crail KY10 3XH
Baron and Lady Wormiston T: Katherine Taylor, Head Gardener 07905 938449
E: ktaylor.home@googlemail.com

The 17th century tower house and gardens have been painstakingly restored over the last 20 years. The walled garden is a series of 'rooms', including a wildlife meadow, productive potager, magical Griselinia garden, wildlife ponds and rill, and recently planted mid and late season perennial borders. The garden's backbone is the splendid midsummer herbaceous border peaking in early July. Outside the walled garden, enjoy woodland walks around the newly re-landscaped lochan, surrounded by new planting.

Other Details: Teas available from 2:00pm on 2 July opening only.

Directions: One mile north of Crail on the A917 Crail to St Andrews road.

Disabled Access:
None

Opening Times:
Sunday 2 July
12:00pm - 5:00pm
Also by arrangement
1 April - 30 September

Admission:
£5.00, accompanied children
free

Charities:
Maggie's Cancer Care Centre
Fife receives 40%, the net
remaining to SG Beneficiaries

KINCARDINE & DEESIDE

Scotland's Gardens 2017 Guidebook is sponsored by **INVESTEC WEALTH & INVESTMENT**

District Organisers

Tina Hammond	Sunnybank, 7 Watson Street, Banchory AB31 5UB
Julie Nicol	Bogiesheil, Ballogie, Aboyne AB34 5DU
	E: kincardine@scotlandsgardens.org

Area Organisers

Andrea Bond	Rosebank, Crathes, Banchory AB31 5JE
Wendy Buchan	Inneshewen, Dess, Aboyne AB31 5BH
Gavin Farquhar	Ecclesgreig Castle, St Cyrus DD10 0DP
Helen Jackson	
Catherine Nichols	Westerton Steading, Dess, Aboyne AB34 5AY
Patsy Younie	Bealltainn, Ballogie, Aboyne AB34 5DL

Treasurer

Tony Coleman	Templeton House, Arbroath DD11 4QP

Gardens open on a specific date

Ecclesgreig Castle, St Cyrus	Sunday 5 March	1:00pm	-	4:00pm
Crathes Castle Garden, Banchory	Wednesday 17 May	5:30pm		
Inchmarlo House Garden, Inchmarlo	Sunday 21 May	1:30pm	-	4:30pm
Drum Castle Garden, Drumoak	Saturday 27 May	11:00am	-	4:00pm
Drum Castle Garden, Drumoak	Sunday 28 May	11:00am	-	4:00pm
Kincardine, Kincardine O'Neil	Sunday 11 June	1:30pm	-	5:00pm
Ecclesgreig Castle, St Cyrus	Sunday 18 June	1:00pm	-	5:00pm
Finzean House, Finzean	Sunday 18 June	2:00pm	-	5:00pm
Clayfolds, Bridge of Muchalls	Sunday 25 June	12:30pm	-	3:30pm
Drum Castle Garden, Drumoak	Wednesday 5 July	2:00pm		
Drum Castle Garden, Drumoak	Wednesday 12 July	2:00pm		
Douneside House, Tarland	Sunday 16 July	2:00pm	-	5:00pm
Drum Castle Garden, Drumoak	Wednesday 19 July	2:00pm		
Drum Castle Garden, Drumoak	Wednesday 26 July	2:00pm		
Glenbervie House, Drumlithie	Sunday 6 August	2:00pm	-	5:00pm
Fasque House, Fettercairn	Sunday 13 August	2:00pm	-	5:00pm
Crathes Castle Garden, Banchory	Saturday 30 September	2:00pm	-	4:00pm

KINCARDINE & DEESIDE

Glenbervie House

Key to symbols

 New in 2017

 Teas

 Cream teas

 Homemade teas

 Dogs on a lead allowed

 Wheelchair access

 Accommodation

 Plant stall

 Scottish Snowdrop Festival

GARDEN LOCATIONS IN KINCARDINE & DEESIDE

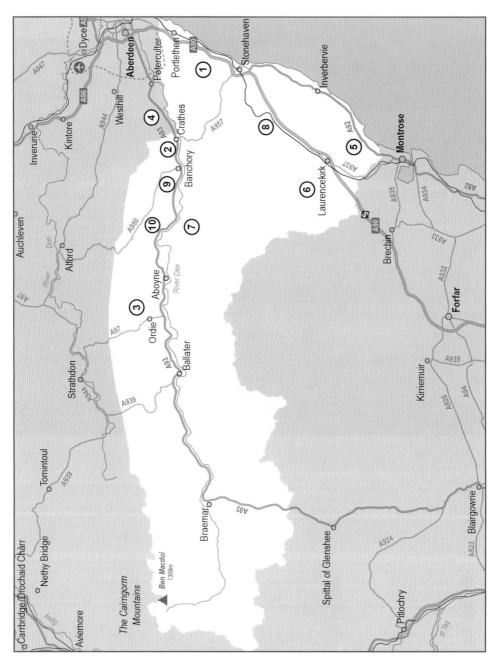

NEW CLAYFOLDS
Bridge of Muchalls, Stonehaven AB39 3RU
Andrea Sinclair

An informal country garden extending to a half acre, with a further six acres of wildflowers, native trees and a pond. Wildlife friendly mixed borders are filled with shrubs and perennials and include a 'hot' border with various flaxes and a variety of hot coloured plants. Follow the tracks through the recently developed 6 acre wildlife garden and see what native fauna and flora you can spot. Native northern marsh orchids are out in profusion from late May to July.

Other Details: Dogs on leads welcome.

Directions: SatNav – AB39 3RU but travel inland a further 1.5 miles to Clayfolds General Directions: Travelling in either direction on the A90, 3 miles north of Stonehaven, take the road signposted Netherley 3, continue travelling inland for approx. 1.5 miles and you will then be directed where to park.

Disabled Access:
Partial

Opening Times:
Sunday 25 June
12:30pm - 3:30pm

Admission:
£3.00

Charities:
SSPCA receives 40% (Scottish Society for Prevention of Cruelty to Animals), the net remaining to SG Beneficiaries

CRATHES CASTLE GARDEN
Banchory AB31 5QJ
The National Trust for Scotland T: 01330 844525
E: crathes@nts.org.uk www.nts.org.uk/property/crathes-castle-garden-and-estate

17 May - Join our expert Head Gardener for high tea followed by a garden walk within the beautiful setting of the gardens at Crathes Castle. Chance to ask questions of the Head Gardener during high tea.

30 October - Members of the garden team will lead you the autumn highlights of Crathes' gardens– a walk in the garden looking at autumn colour and planting.

Other Details: National Plant Collection®: *Dianthus* (Malmaison).
Champion Trees: Four champions including *Zelkova x verschaffeltii*.
May event - includes high tea and garden walk.
October event - meet at the front of the castle.
Booking essential via NTS website www.nts.org.uk for both events.

Directions: On A93, 15 miles west of Aberdeen and three miles east of Banchory.

Disabled Access:
Full

Opening Times:
Wednesday 17 May
5:30pm
Saturday 30 September
2:00pm - 4:00pm

Admission:
May event: £18.50
October event: £6.50
Admission also applicable to NTS members

Charities:
Donation to SG Beneficiaries

KINCARDINE & DEESIDE

3 **DOUNESIDE HOUSE**
Tarland AB34 4UD
The MacRobert Trust
www.dounesidehouse.co.uk

Douneside is the former home of Lady MacRobert who developed these magnificent gardens in the early to mid-1900s. Ornamental borders and water gardens surround a spectacular infinity lawn overlooking the Deeside hills. A large walled garden supplies vegetables and cut flowers and also houses a large ornamental greenhouse. A new arboretum displays over 130 trees amongst mown grass paths and walking trails behind Douneside offer breathtaking views across the Howe of Cromar and beyond.

Other Details: There will be a local pipe band and raffle.

Directions: B9119 towards Aberdeen. Tarland one mile.

Disabled Access:
Partial

Opening Times:
Sunday 16 July
2:00pm - 5:00pm

Admission:
£5.00, concession £3.00,
accompanied children free

Charities:
SG Development Fund
receives 40%, the net
remaining to SG Beneficiaries

4 **DRUM CASTLE GARDEN**
Drumoak, by Banchory AB31 5EY
The National Trust for Scotland T: 01330 700334
E: drum@nts.org.uk   www.nts.org.uk/property/drum-castle-garden-and-estate/

Join the Head Gardener for a walk through the historic rose garden each Wednesday at 2:00pm throughout July. The Trust has established a collection of old-fashioned roses which is at its peak for blossom and colour during July. Other garden areas include a pond and bog garden, wildlife meadow, wildlife garden, a cutting garden and new viewing platform and stumpery. The garden is open to visitors April - October with evening guided tours available on request.

Other Details: The May Chelsea Fringe weekend is the furthest north venue for harnessing and spreading excitement and energy that fizzes around gardens and gardening. There will be willow workshops and muddy puddle club sessions. There are garden workshops throughout the year. Booking essential via website.

Directions: On A93 three miles west of Peterculter. Ten miles west of Aberdeen and eight miles east of Banchory.

Disabled Access:
Partial

Opening Times:
Saturday 27 & Sunday 28 May
11:00am - 4:00pm
(for Chelsea Fringe event)
Weds 5, 12, 19 & 25 July
2:00pm (for guided walks)

Admission:
Chelsea Fringe £4.00,
conc. £2.00 (NTS members
free). Guided walks £5.00
(incl. NTS members)

Charities:
Donation to SG Beneficiaries

ECCLESGREIG CASTLE
St Cyrus DD10 0DP
Mr Gavin Farquhar T: 01224 214301
E: enquiries@ecclesgreig.com   www.ecclesgreig.com

Ecclesgreig Castle, Victorian Gothic on a 16th century core, is internationally famous as an inspiration for Bram Stoker's Dracula. The snowdrop walk (150+ varieties of snowdrop) starts at the castle, meanders around the estate, along woodland paths and the pond, ending at the garden. In the Italian balustraded gardens there is a 140 foot long herbaceous border, classical statues and stunning shaped topiary with views across St Cyrus to the sea. Started from a derelict site, development continues.

Other Details: Also to be found in the grounds is the well of St Cyrus a medieval hermit and the site of a Pictish monastery 8th centry AD.

Directions: Ecclesgreig will be signposted from the A92 Coast Road and from the A937 Montrose / Laurencekirk Road.

Disabled Access:
Partial

Opening Times:
Sunday 5 March
1:00pm - 4:00pm
for the Snowdrop Festival
Sunday 18 June
1:00pm - 5:00pm

Admission:
£4.00, accomp. children free

Charities:
Scottish Civic Trust receives 20%, Montrose Guides receives 20%, the net remaining to SG Beneficiaries

FASQUE HOUSE
Fettercairn, Laurencekirk AB30 1DN
Mr and Mrs Douglas Dick-Reid
www.fasquehouse.co.uk

The former family home of William Gladstone four-time Prime Minister under Queen Victoria is set deep within its own forested parkland at the end of a drive through a private deer park. The current owners have restored the house to its former glory and the gardens are becoming more stunning each year. Landscaping of the West Garden took place in 2013 with a sunken terrace garden containing a formal pond and a mixture of formal and herbaceous plants. There are some magnificent trees and beautiful long walks in the surrounding woodlands.

Other Details: Self catering accommodation is available. Partial disabled access but please note that there are many gravel paths where pushing a wheelchair is difficult.

Directions: Off B974 Cairn O'Mount road 1¼ miles north of Fettercairn.

Disabled Access:
Partial

Opening Times:
Sunday 13 August
2:00pm - 5:00pm

Admission:
£5.00, accompanied children free

Charities:
Fettercairn Community Allotments receives 20%, Home Start Stonehaven receives 20%, the net remaining to SG Beneficiaries

FINZEAN HOUSE
Finzean, Banchory AB31 6NZ
Mr and Mrs Donald Farquharson

Finzean House was the family home of Joseph Farquharson, the Victorian landscape painter, and the garden was the backdrop for several of his paintings. The garden has lovely views over the historic holly hedge to the front of Clachnaben. There is a spring woodland garden, extensive lawns with herbaceous and shrub borders and a working cut flower garden for late summer alongside a recently restored pond area.

Directions: On B976, South Deeside Road, between Banchory and Aboyne.

Disabled Access:
Full

Opening Times:
Sunday 18 June
2:00pm - 5:00pm

Admission:
£4.00, OAPs £3.00, accompanied children free

Charities:
Forget Me Not receives 40%, the net remaining to SG Beneficiaries

KINCARDINE & DEESIDE

8 GLENBERVIE HOUSE
Drumlithie, Stonehaven AB39 3YA
Mr and Mrs A Macphie

CELEBRATING 75 YEARS OF OPENING FOR CHARITY WITH SCOTLAND'S GARDENS.

The nucleus of the beautiful present day house dates from 15th century with additions in 18th and 19th centuries. A traditional Scottish walled garden on a slope with roses, herbaceous and annual borders along with fruit and vegetables. One wall is taken up with a Victorian style greenhouse with many species of pot plants and climbers including peach and figs. A woodland garden by a burn is punctuated with many varieties of plants, primula to name but one.

Other Details: Partial disabled access but please note some steep pathways and tree roots can make walking difficult in places. Gravel paths are not accessible for electric wheelchairs. **No dogs please.**

Directions: Drumlithie one mile. Garden one and a half miles off A90.

Disabled Access:
Partial

Opening Times:
Sunday 6 August
2:00pm - 5:00pm

Admission:
£5.00, accompanied children free

Charities:
Royal National Lifeboat Institute receives 40%, the net remaining to SG Beneficiaries

---

9 INCHMARLO HOUSE GARDEN
Inchmarlo, Banchory AB31 4AL
Skene Enterprises (Aberdeen) Ltd **T: 01330 826242**
E: info@inchmarlo-retirement.co.uk www.inchmarlo-retirement.co.uk

Beautiful five acre Woodland Garden filled with azaleas and rhododendrons beneath ancient Scots pines, Douglas firs and silver firs, some over 42 metres tall, beeches and rare and unusual trees, including pindrow firs, Pere David's maple, Erman's birch and a mountain snowdrop tree and the Oriental Garden features a Kare Sansui, a dry slate stream designed by Peter Roger, a RHS Chelsea gold medal winner. The Rainbow Garden, within the keyhole-shaped purple *Prunus cerasifera* hedge, has been designed by Billy Carruthers, an eight times gold medal winner at the RHS Scottish Garden Show.

Directions: From Aberdeen via North Deeside Road on A93, one mile west of Banchory turn right at the main gate to the Inchmarlo Estate.

Disabled Access:
Full

Opening Times:
Sunday 21 May
1:30pm - 4:30pm

Admission:
£4.50, accompanied children free

Charities:
Alzheimer Scotland receives 20%, Forget Me Not receives 20%, the net remaining to SG Beneficiaries

---

10 KINCARDINE
Kincardine O'Neil AB34 5AE
Mr and Mrs Andrew Bradford

A superb series of gardens around a Victorian Castle with great views across Deeside. Walled garden with a world-class laburnum walk, a mixture of herbaceous and shrub borders, vegetables and fruit trees. Extensive lawns and wildflower meadows and a thought-provoking Planetary Garden. A woodland garden with 120 varieties of rhododendrons and azaleas, many of recent planting, set amongst mature trees. Sculpture by Lyman Whittaker of Utah. A great day out.

Other Details: Children's treasure trail and excellent plant stall.

Directions: Kincardine O'Neil on A93. Gates and lodge are opposite the village school.

Disabled Access:
Partial

Opening Times:
Sunday 11 June
1:30pm - 5:00pm

Admission:
£5.00, children £2.00 (including entry to the treasure trail)

Charities:
Children 1st receives 20%, Christ Church Kincardine O'Neil receives 20%, the net remaining to SG Beneficiaries

PERTH & KINROSS

Scotland's Gardens 2017 Guidebook is sponsored by **INVESTEC WEALTH & INVESTMENT**

District Organisers

Margaret Gimblett	Fehmarn, Clayton Road, Bridge of Earn PH2 9AH
Miranda Landale	Clathic House, By Crieff PH7 4JY E:perthkinross@scotlandsgardens.org

Area Organisers

Mrs Sally Crystal	Little Tombuie, Killiechassie, Aberfeldy PH15 2JS
Henrietta Harland	Easter Carmichael Cottage, Forgandenny Road, Bridge of Earn PH2 9EZ
Elizabeth Mitchell	Woodlee, 28 St Mary's Drive, Perth PH2 7BY
Lizzie Montgomery	Burleigh House, Milnathort, Kinross KY13 9SR
Judy Nichol	Rossie House, Forgandenny PH2 9EH
Judy Norwell	Dura Den, 20 Pitcullen Terrace, Perth PH2 7EQ
Bumble Ogilvy Wedderburn	Garden Cottage, Lude, Blair Atholl PH18 5TR
Heather Wood	Mill of Forneth, Forneth, Blairgowrie PH10 6SP

Treasurer

Michael Tinson	Parkhead Hse, Parkhead Gdns, Burghmuir Rd PH1 1JF

Gardens open on a specific date

Kilgraston School, Bridge of Earn	Sunday 19 February	1:30pm	-	4:00pm
Megginch Castle, Errol	Sunday 16 April	2:00pm	-	5:00pm
Fingask Castle, Rait	Sunday 7 May	12:00pm	-	5:30pm
Branklyn Garden, Perth	Sunday 14 May	10:00am	-	4:00pm
Rossie House, Forgandenny	Friday 19 May	2:00pm	-	5:00pm
Rossie House, Forgandenny	Friday 26 May	2:00pm	-	5:00pm
Bradystone House, Murthly	Thursday 1 June	11:00am	-	4:00pm
Explorers Garden, Pitlochry	Sunday 4 June	10:00am	-	4:30pm
Bradystone House, Murthly	Thursday 8 June	11:00am	-	4:00pm
Bonhard House, Perth	Sunday 11 June	10:00am	-	4:00pm
Mill of Forneth, Forneth	Sunday 11 June	2:00pm	-	5:00pm
Bradystone House, Murthly	Thursday 15 June	11:00am	-	4:00pm
The Bield at Blackruthven, Tibbermore	Saturday 17 June	2:00pm	-	5:00pm
Bradystone House, Murthly	Thursday 22 June	11:00am	-	4:00pm
Abernethy Open Gardens, Abernethy	Saturday 24 June	10:00am	-	6:00pm
Blair Castle Gardens, Blair Atholl	Saturday 24 June	9:30am	-	5:30pm

PERTH & KINROSS

Wester House of Ross, Comrie	Saturday 24 June	2:00pm	-	5:00pm
Kincarrathie House, Perth	Sunday 25 June	12:00pm	-	4:00pm
Wester House of Ross, Comrie	Sunday 25 June	2:00pm	-	5:00pm
Bradystone House, Murthly	Thursday 29 June	11:00am	-	4:00pm
Bradystone House, Murthly	Thursday 6 July	11:00am	-	4:00pm
Bradystone House, Murthly	Thursday 13 July	11:00am	-	4:00pm
Bradystone House, Murthly	Thursday 20 July	11:00am	-	4:00pm
Bradystone House, Murthly	Thursday 27 July	11:00am	-	4:00pm
Drummond Castle Gardens, Crieff	Sunday 6 August	1:00pm	-	5:00pm

Gardens open regularly

Ardvorlich, Lochearnhead	1 May - 1 June	9:00am	-	Dusk
Bolfracks, Aberfeldy	1 April - 31 October	10:00am	-	6:00pm
Braco Castle, Braco	28 January - 31 October	10:00am	-	5:00pm
Fingask Castle	30 January - 9 March Mondays - Thursdays only	12:00pm	-	5:00pm
Glendoick, by Perth	1 April - 31 May	10:00am	-	4:00pm
Glenericht House Arboretum, Blairgowrie	Daily	9:00am	-	7:00pm

Gardens open by arrangement

Carig Dhubh, Bonskeid	1 May - 30 September	01796 473469
Glenlyon House, Fortingall	On request	01887 830233
Hollytree Lodge, Muckhart	1 April - 31 October	07973 374687
Kirkton Craig, Abernyte	15 May - 31 August	01828 686336
Latch House, Abernyte	1 May - 31 August	01828 686816
Mill of Forneth, Forneth	1 May - 30 September	gaw@gwpc.demon.co.uk
Pitcurran House, Abernethy	1 April - 30 September	01738 850933
The Garden at Craigowan, Ballinluig	15 April - 30 June	i.q.jones@btinternet.com
The Steading at Clunie, Newmill of Kinloch	29 April - 7 May & 14 June - 28 June	01250 884263

Key to symbols

	New in 2017		Homemade teas		Accommodation
	Teas		Dogs on a lead allowed		Plant stall
	Cream teas		Wheelchair access		Scottish Snowdrop Festival

GARDEN LOCATIONS IN
PERTH & KINROSS

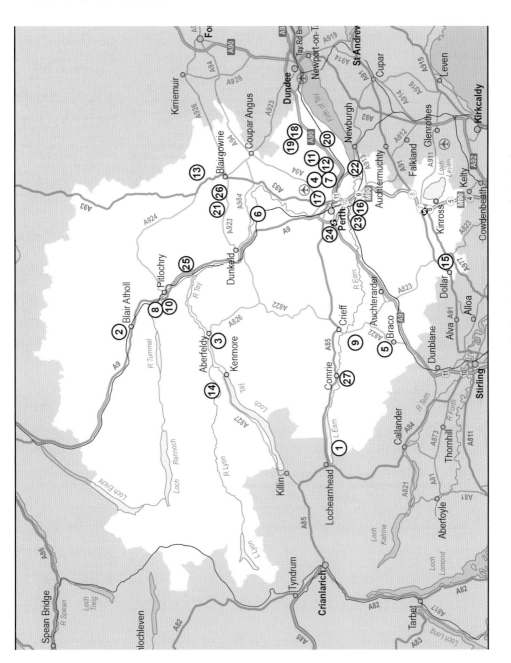

NEW ABERNETHY OPEN GARDENS
Abernethy PH2
The Gardeners of Abernethy

The beautiful and historic village of Abernethy will be opening at least five gardens, but more may be added. All gardens are non smoking and only guide dogs are allowed.
Carey House PH2 9N (Caroline and Alan Boyle): Six-year old two acre garden in the process of creation from fields rich in thistles and brambles. Includes small orchard, herbaceous beds, rose garden, pond area, cottage garden, cutting garden, vegetable and herb beds, lawns - all with panoramic views of the Ochils.
Bloomfield PH2 9LW (Claire Jones & Kyle Strachan): Half acre cottage garden, reclaimed from wilderness six years ago and beginning to mature. Mixed planting of trees, shrubs, perennials and bulbs. Two small nature ponds. Back garden has raised beds and children's play area.
Mornington Cottage (Keir Allen and Rachel Battilana): Located on the site of the Culdees monastery and just down the road from Abernethy's famous round tower, this kitchen garden has been producing food for the surrounding buildings for at least the last 210 years, possibly the last 1000. Fuelled by local horse manure, the rotating beds yield a wide variety of organic fruit and vegetables. Also features child and baby play equipment and a gigantic hen run. Disabled access may not be possible.
Eastbank Cottage PH2 9LR (Mike and Elsa Thomson): Traditional Scottish cottage, one third acre garden, walled and bounded by a small burn to the East. Azaleas, rhododendrons, erythroniums, varieties of wood anemones, trillium and a fine display of clematis. Altogether a little haven in the country.
5 Sutherland Crescent PH2 9GA (Gill Boardman): This garden has been designed and planted in late 2011 to 2012. Originally a very boring modern estate house garden with grass and decking! Mainly perennials and grasses were planted at side and front. More traditional back garden with shrubs for structure and some perennials. Silver birch trees, rowan trees, laurel hedges, beech hedge and golden privet on the boundaries

Other Details: Tickets, maps, teas, plant and produce stalls in the church hall at School Wynd. Tea and cake included in ticket price, light lunch available to purchase. Parking available at Crees Inn, Main Street for a donation to PADS and Second Chance.

Directions: Seven miles south of Perth. Leave the M90 at Junction 9 and follow signs for Newburgh and Cupar on the A912 for approximately five miles. Go left (straight on) at the mini roundabout, School Wynd is the first right after the zebra crossing, the Crees Inn carpark is the second right, it is a short walk between. The church hall and carpark will be signposted on the day.

Disabled Access:
Partial

Opening Times:
Saturday 24 June
10:00am - 6:00pm
(last entry 4pm)

Admission:
£8.00, includes tea and cake

Charities:
Abernethy in Bloom receives 19%, the Abernethy Museum, the Williamson Hall and the Abernethy Pavillion will each receive 7%, the net remaining to SG Beneficiaries

ARDVORLICH
Lochearnhead FK19 8QE
Mr and Mrs Sandy Stewart

Beautiful hill garden featuring over 300 different species and hybrid rhododendrons, grown in a glorious setting of oaks and birches on either side of the Ardvorlich Burn. The ground is quite steep in places and boots are advisable.

Directions: On South Loch Earn Road three miles from Lochearnhead, five miles from St Fillans.

Disabled Access:
None

Opening Times:
1 May - 1 June
9:00am - Dusk

Admission:
£4.00, children under 16 free

Charities:
The Gurkha Welfare Trust receives 40%, the net remaining to SG Beneficiaries

BLAIR CASTLE GARDENS
Blair Atholl PH18 5TL
Blair Charitable Trust T: 01796 481207
E: office@blair-castle.co.uk www.blair-castle.co.uk

Blair Castle stands as the focal point in a designed landscape of some 2,500 acres within a large and traditional estate. Hercules Garden is a walled enclosure of about nine acres recently restored to its original 18th century form with landscaped ponds, a Chinese bridge, plantings, vegetables and an orchard of more than 100 fruit trees. The glory of this garden in summer is the herbaceous border which runs along the 275 metre south facing wall. A delightful sculpture trail incorporates contemporary and century sculpture as well as eight new works, letter-carving on stone from the Memorial Arts Charity's Art and Memory Collection. Diana's Grove is a magnificent stand of tall trees including Grand Fir, Douglas Fir, Larch and Wellingtonia in just two acres.

Other Details: Also open 1 April - 27 October 9:30am - 5:30pm

Directions: Off the A9, follow signs to Blair Castle, Blair Atholl.

Disabled Access:
Partial

Opening Times:
Saturday 24 June
9:30am - 5:30pm

Admission:
£6.50, children £3.00, family ticket £16.00

Charities:
Donation to SG Beneficiaries

BOLFRACKS
Aberfeldy PH15 2EX
The Douglas Hutchison Trust T: 01887 820344
E: athel@bolfracks.com www.bolfracks.com

Special three acre garden with wonderful views overlooking the Tay Valley. Burn garden with rhododendrons, azaleas, primulas and meconopsis in a woodland garden setting. Walled garden with shrubs, herbaceous borders and rose rooms with old fashioned roses. There is also a beautiful rose and clematis walk. Peony beds are underplanted with tulips and Japanese anemone. The garden has a great selection of bulbs in spring and good autumn colour.

Other Details: Refreshments available for groups by prior arrangement.
Slippery paths in wet weather.

Directions: Two miles west of Aberfeldy on A827. White gates and Lodge are on the left. Look out for the brown tourist signs.

Disabled Access:
None

Opening Times:
1 April - 31 October
10:00am - 6:00pm

Admission:
£4.50, children under 16 free

Charities:
Donation to SG Beneficiaries

BONHARD HOUSE
Perth PH2 7PQ
Stephen and Charlotte Hay T: 01738552471

A traditional 19th century garden of five acres with mature trees including hollies, sequoias, Douglas Fir and a mid-19th century monkey puzzle. Extensive lawns, rhododendron and azalea beds, herbaceous borders, ponds, and an oak drive lined with primulas and daffodils. There is also a productive kitchen garden, wooded area and a walk up behind the house to a Pinetum containing more than 25 species.

Other Details: Sensible shoes should be worn.

Directions: From Perth take the A94 north to Scone. Before you reach Scone turn right at the sign to Murrayshall Hotel. Continue for about one mile. The house drive is on the right where the road turns sharp left.

From Balbeggie take the A94. Turn left, signposted for Bonhard one mile north of Scone and in half a mile turn right. House drive is on the left where the road turns sharp right shortly after Bonhard Nursery.

Disabled Access:
Partial

Opening Times:
Sunday 11 June
10:00am - 4:00pm

Admission:
£4.00 includes tea/homebakes

Charities:
Freedom From Fistula Foundation receives 40%, the net remaining to SG Beneficiaries

BRACO CASTLE
Braco FK15 9LA
Mr and Mrs M van Ballegooijen   T: 01786 880437

A 19th century landscaped garden with a plethora of wonderful and interesting trees, shrubs, bulbs and plants. An old garden for all seasons that has been extensively expanded over the last 26 years. The partly walled garden is approached on a rhododendron and tree lined path featuring an ornamental pond. Spectacular spring bulbs, exuberant shrub and herbaceous borders, and many ornamental trees are all enhanced by the spectacular views across the park to the Ochils. From snowdrops through to vibrant autumn colour this garden is a gem. Look out for the embothrium in June, hoheria in August, eucryphia in September and an interesting collection of rhododendrons and azaleas with long flowering season.

Other Details: Catering facilities are not available.

Directions: One to one and a half mile drive from the gates at the north end of Braco Village, just west of the bridge on the A822. Parking at the castle is welcome.

Disabled Access:
Partial

Opening Times:
28 January - 31 October
10:00am - 5:00pm
(open for the Snowdrop
Festival 28 January - 12
March)

Admission:
£4.00

Charities:
The Woodland Trust receives 40%, the net remaining to SG Beneficiaries

BRADYSTONE HOUSE
Murthly PH1 4EW
Mrs James Lumsden   T: 01738 710308
E: cwren@nts.org.uk   http://www.nts.org.uk/Property/Branklyn-Garden/

A true cottage garden converted 20 years ago from derelict farm steadings. It has been beautifully planted to produce an ever changing picture which in summer will take your breath away. Unusual plants complement others in wonderful combinations, and quite often there will be some plants for sale. The small woodland surrounding the garden and interplanted with many interesting shrubs and trees, has now matured, and there is a pretty winding grass walk through the trees. There is also a pond with free roaming ducks and hens. A gem of a garden.

Other Details: Refreshments available by prior arrangement. There is full disabled access, except perhaps the woodland walk which is grassy. Groups welcome.

Directions: From south/north follow A9 to Bankfoot, then sign to Murthly. At crossroads in Murthly take private road to Bradystone.

Disabled Access:
Partial

Opening Times:
Thursdays
1, 8, 15, 22, 29 June
& 6, 13, 20, 27 July
11:00am - 4:00pm

Admission:
£5.00

Charities:
Air Ambulance Scotland receives 40%, the net remaining to SG Beneficiaries

BRANKLYN GARDEN
116 Dundee Road, Perth PH2 7BB
The National Trust for Scotland   T: 01738 625535
E: cwren@nts.org.uk   http://www.nts.org.uk/Property/Branklyn-Garden/

This attractive garden in Perth was once described as "the finest two acres of private garden in the country". It contains an outstanding collection of plants particularly rhododendrons, alpine, herbaceous and peat-loving plants, which attract gardeners and botanists from all over the world.

Other Details: National Plant Collection®: Cassiope, Meconopsis (Himalayan poppy) and rhododendron subsect. Taliense. Champion Trees: *Pinus sylvestris* 'Globosa.' Head Gardener's walk at 2:00pm.

Directions: On A85 Perth/Dundee road.

Disabled Access:
Partial

Opening Times:
Sunday 14 May
10:00am - 4:00pm

Admission:
Normal NTS admission applies

Charities:
Donation to SG Beneficiaries

CARIG DHUBH
Bonskeid PH16 5NP
Jane and Niall Graham-Campbell T: 01796 473469
E: niallgc@btinternet.com

The garden is comprised of mixed shrubs and herbaceous plants with many species of meconopsis and primulas. It extends to about one acre on the side of a hill with some steep paths and uneven ground. The soil is sand overlying rock - some of which projects through the surface. There are beautiful surrounding country and hill views.

Directions: Take the old A9 between Pitlochry and Killiecrankie, turn west on the Tummel Bridge Road B8019, three quarters of a mile on north side of the road.

Disabled Access:
None

Opening Times:
By arrangement
1 May - 30 September

Admission:
£5.00, accompanied children free

Charities:
Poppies Scotland receives 40%, the net remaining to SG Beneficiaries

DRUMMOND CASTLE GARDENS
Crieff PH7 4HZ
Grimsthorpe & Drummond Castle Trust Ltd
www.drummondcastlegardens.co.uk

The Gardens of Drummond Castle were originally laid out in 1630 by John Drummond, second Earl of Perth. In 1830 the parterre was changed to an Italian style. One of the most interesting features is the multi-faceted sundial designed by John Mylne, Master Mason to Charles I. The formal garden is said to be one of the finest in Europe and is the largest of its type in Scotland.

Other Details: Also open 1 May - 31 October 1:00pm - 6:00pm. Admission £5.00, OAPs £4.00, children £2.00, family £12.00.

Directions: Entrance two miles south of Crieff on Muthill road (A822).

Disabled Access:
Partial

Opening Times:
Sunday 6 August
1:00pm - 5:00pm

Admission:
£4.00, OAPs £3.00, children £2.00, family £10.00

Charities:
British Limbless Ex-Servicemen's Association receives 40%, the net remaining to SG Beneficiaries

EXPLORERS GARDEN
Pitlochry PH16 5DR
Pitlochry Festival Theatre
www.explorersgarden.com

This 2.4ha (6 acre) woodland garden celebrates the Scottish Plant Hunters who risked their lives in search of new plants. The Explorers Garden is divided into geographic areas, each containing examples of the plants collected from that corner of the globe. Set in beautiful Highland Perthshire countryside, the garden is known for its meconopsis collection, stunning vistas and interesting sculptures and structures. Each year a photographic exhibition is held in the David Douglas Pavilion.

Other Details: National Plant Collection®: Meconopsis, large blue poppies.

Directions: Take the A9 to Pitlochry town, then follow signs to Pitlochry Festival Theatre.

Disabled Access:
Partial

Opening Times:
Sunday 4 June
10:00am - 4:30pm

Admission:
£4.00 or £5.00 with guided tour

Charities:
Acting for Others receives 40%, the net remaining to SG Beneficiaries

FINGASK CASTLE
Rait PH2 7SA
Mr and Mrs Andrew Murray Threipland T: 01821 670777
E: andrew@fingaskcastle.com www.fingaskcastle.com

Explore the large landscaped policies of the castle including (but not confined to) Belvederes, medieval wishing well, statues, topiary, Chinese bridge and much more. There are banks of snowdrops on the main drive, have a walk around the garden to find snowdrops in other areas.

Other Details: Champion Trees: Bhutan Pine. Cream teas will only be served at the May opening.

Directions: Half way between Perth and Dundee. From the A90 follow signs to Rait until small crossroad, turn right and follow signs to Fingask.

Disabled Access:
Partial

Opening Times:
Sun 7 May 12:00pm - 5:30pm
30 Jan - 9 Mar 12:00pm - 5:00pm (Mon - Thurs only) for the Snowdrop Festival

Admission:
Snowdrops: £3.00, May: £4.00, accomp. children free

Charities:
All Saints Church, Glencarse and Fingask Follies receive 40%, the net remaining to SG Beneficiaries

GLENDOICK
by Perth PH2 7NS
Peter, Patricia, Kenneth and Jane Cox T: 01738 860205
E: orders@glendoick.com www.glendoick.com

Glendoick is the ideal spring day out with a visit to both the gardens and garden centre in April and May. Glendoick was included in the *Independent on Sunday* survey of Europe's top 50 Gardens with a unique collection of plants from Cox plant-hunting expeditions in China & the Himalaya. Glendoick's 5 acres includes spectacular rhododendrons, magnolias, meconopsis, grown in the woodland garden, with its burn and waterfalls, the walled garden and the gardens surrounding the house. Many Glendoick plants have been bred by the Cox family, and new unnamed hybrids can be seen in the walled garden. The award-winning Glendoick Garden Centre and Cafe has one of Scotland's best selections of plants including their world-famous rhododendrons and azaleas as well as a gift shop and foodhall.

Other Details: National Plant Collection®: Rhododendron. Mail Order in winter months only. Refreshments for groups should be pre-booked contact Jane Cox by email: jane@glendoick.com. The woodland garden is challenging for wheelchairs. Disabled toilets at the garden centre only. Kenneth Cox's book *Scotland for Gardeners* describes 500 of Scotland's finest gardens.

Directions: Follow brown signs to Glendoick Garden Centre off A90 Perth - Dundee road. Gardens are ½ mile behind Garden Centre. After buying tickets at the garden centre, please drive up and park at gardens (free parking).

Disabled Access:
None

Opening Times:
1 April - 31 May
10:00am - 4:00pm

Admission:
£5.00, school age children free, no dogs. Tickets must be purchased from the garden centre.

Charities:
Donation to SG Beneficiaries

GLENERICHT HOUSE ARBORETUM
Blairgowrie PH10 7JD
Mrs William McCosh T: 01250 872092

Spectacular collection of Victorian planted trees and shrubs which are centred around a Grade 'A' listed suspension bridge (1846). Ninety-two tree varieties, mostly conifers including a top Douglas fir which is 171 feet and still growing, also a collection of younger trees. In May you will be able to view the wonderful daffodils and the rhododendrons in flower.

Directions: Off A93, the Lodge House is five miles north of Blairgowrie on the right hand side A93 from Blairgowrie. Follow the avenue to the bridge.

Disabled Access:
Partial

Opening Times:
Daily
9:00am - 7:00pm or Dusk

Admission:
£4.00

Charities:
SANDS receives 40%, the net remaining to SG Beneficiaries

GLENLYON HOUSE
Fortingall PH15 2LN
Mr and Mrs Iain Wotherspoon T: 01887 830233

Interesting garden framed by hedges, with colourful herbaceous borders and fruit trees underplanted with perennials and annuals. There is a kitchen and cutting garden as well as a wildlife pond.

Directions: Take the A827 Aberfeldy, B846 Coshieville then turn off for Fortingall and Glen Lyon.

Disabled Access:
Partial

Opening Times:
By arrangement on request

Admission:
£5.00

Charities:
Fortingall Church receives 40%, the net remaining to SG Beneficiaries

HOLLYTREE LODGE
Muckhart, Dollar FK14 7JW
Liz and Peter Wyatt T: 0797 337 4687
E: elizwyatt @aol.com

A tranquil garden, divided by internal hedges into smaller areas. These include a small Japanese garden, spring bulbs naturalised in grass, a mini orchard and wildflowers, a rill, a wildlife pond, mixed herbaceous borders, all within an acre plot. An interesting variety of unusual trees and shrubs, a good collection of rhododendrons and deciduous azaleas, a snow gum, a metasequoia glyptostroboides, a Persian ironwood, which colours beautifully in autumn, as do the acers. Tree trail. Our aim is to garden with nature, and organically, complementing our beekeeping interests; the best planting scheme often seems to happen by accident!

Other Details: Family friendly, pond dipping and nature hunt available for children, sensory garden plants. Groups up to 25 welcome. Tea/coffee available on request.

Directions: Approx 100m off the A91(between Dollar and Milnathort) down the small lane directly opposite the entrance to the Inn at Muckhart.

Disabled Access:
Full

Opening Times:
By arrangement
1 April - 31 October

Admission:
£4.00, accompanied children free
Tea/coffee £1.00

Charities:
The Coronation Hall, Muckhart receives 40%, the net remaining to SG Beneficiaries

KILGRASTON SCHOOL
Bridge of Earn PH2 9BQ
Kilgraston School T: 01738 815517
E: marketing@kilgraston.com www.kilgraston.com

Set within the grounds of Kilgraston School, this is a wonderful opportunity to see the snowdrops whilst exploring the woodlands and surroundings of this very unique garden. Statues and sculptures (including work by Hew Lorimer) intermingle with ancient trees, snowdrops and even the resident red squirrels. Spend a Sunday afternoon wandering along wild woodland pathways and through the extensive grounds, and explore the chapel, main hall and artworks within the school.

Other Details: Teas from the school's award-winning catering team are available (indoors, if the weather is against us), alongside a wide range of activities for children.

Directions: Three miles south of Perth on the A912. Kilgraston School is well signposted from the main road. Maps available at *www.kilgraston.com/contact*

Disabled Access:
Partial

Opening Times:
Sunday 19 February
1:30pm - 4:00pm
for the Snowdrop Festival

Admission:
£4.00

Charities:
Charity TBA and will receive 40%, the net remaining to SG Beneficiaries

---

KINCARRATHIE HOUSE
Pitcullen Crescent, Perth PH2 7HX
The Kincarrathie Trust T: 07402 215555
E: susan.eisner@sky.com

Kincarrathie House was originally the home of the whisky baron and philanthropist A.K. Bell (1868-1942). It is now a beautiful private residential care home for 44 residents. The house sits in extensive grounds, which incorporates 6.5 acres of parkland, a woodland walk and a walled garden of about an acre comprising of herbaceous borders, a small orchard and four large vegetable plots providing seasonal produce for use within the home.

Directions: Located on the north east edge of Perth on the A94.

From Perth: follow the A94 towards Coupar Angus/Scone and the entrance to the House is at the end of the row of guest houses.

From North-East: follow the A94 towards Perth. The entrance to the House is on the road from Scone to Perth just before the built up area begins on that side. Turn right at Kincarrathie House sign.

Disabled Access:
Full

Opening Times:
Sunday 25 June
12:00pm - 4:00pm

Admission:
£5.00 includes teas

Charities:
Donation to SG Beneficiaries

KIRKTON CRAIG
Abernyte PH14 9ST
Heather Berger T: 01828 686336
E: heather@thebergers.org.uk

This ¾ acre garden overlooks the Tay in the Braes of the Carse of Gowrie. The 150-year old high brick walls, which once enclosed the kitchen garden for nearby Abernyte House, today provide shelter for many colourful climbers and plants which are borderline hardy in Eastern Scotland, among them carpentaria californica, callistemon and crinodenron hookerianum. Mature trees and shrubs and colourful mixed borders. Spring bulbs.

Other Details: This garden is a short distance from Latch House, also opening by arrangement. As both are very different from each other, a visit to each is possible and suggested. Small groups and individual visitors are welcome. No dogs.

Directions: Coming from the A90 Inchture junction, take the B953 to Abernyte village. Opposite the school take a road signposted Church. Kirkton Craig is the second driveway on the left.

Disabled Access:
Full

Opening Times:
By arrangement
15 May - 31 August

Admission:
£5.00, to include tea/coffee/shortbread

Charities:
Crisis receives 40%, the net remaining to SG Beneficiaries

20 LATCH HOUSE
Abernyte PH14 9SU
Mrs Juliet McSwan T: 01828 686816

On top of a hill at 600 feet, giving wonderful views. The one plus acre garden flows round the house with lawns and mixed beds of trees, shrubs and perennials. To the rear, paths run through a wooded area with spring bulbs, rhododendrons and azaleas. There are interesting trees, including seven species of rowan. Little rockeries close to the house surround a paved sunken garden and a small, shelved pond where birds love to bathe. Varieties of poppies and trilliums are favourites with the owners.

Other Details: Very close to Kirkton Craig which also opens by arrangement. The two gardens are quite different and you might like to visit both on the same day.

Directions: Take the B953 from the A90 Inchture junction. Pass through the village of Abernyte. When the B953 bears to the left - approximately a half mile from Abernyte, keep to the right and continue up the hill for another half mile. Latch House is the first house on the left at the top of the hill.

Disabled Access:
Partial

Opening Times:
By arrangement
1 May - 31 August

Admission:
£5.00, includes tea/coffee

Charities:
Children's Hospice
Association Scotland (CHAS)
receives 40%, the net
remaining to SG Beneficiaries

---

21 MEGGINCH CASTLE
Errol PH2 7SW
Mr Giles Herdman and The Hon. Mrs Drummond-Herdman of Megginch

CELEBRATING 50 YEARS OF OPENING FOR CHARITY WITH SCOTLAND'S GARDENS!

Come and help us celebrate our 50th year of opening for charity with Scotland's Gardens on Easter Sunday afternoon. Join the great Megginch Easter Egg Hunt and see if the Lollipop Tree Fairy has decorated her Lollipop tree for this special occasion! Let your children run through the Heritage Orchard on a scavenger hunt and enjoy delicious home baked teas under the ancient Yew trees where monks once walked over a thousand years ago. Walk round the formal French parterre, past this romantic fifteenth century turreted castle (not open) through the unique Gothic stable yard and on to the double walled kitchen garden with its newly planted Cider Apple walk.

Directions: Approach directly off the A90, Perth-bound carriageway, half a mile on the left after Errol/Inchmichael flyover, between two stone lodge gatehouses. It is seven miles from Perth and eight from Dundee.

Disabled Access:
Full

Opening Times:
Sunday 16 April
2:00pm - 5:00pm
for Easter Sunday

Admission:
£5.00, concessions £4.00,
accompanied children free

Charities:
All proceeds to
SG Beneficiaries

---

22 MILL OF FORNETH
Forneth, Blairgowrie PH10 6SP
Mr and Mrs Graham Wood
E: gaw@gwpc.demon.co.uk

Built on the site of a watermill on the Lunan Burn, originally laid out in the 1970s by James Aitken, the Scottish landscape designer and naturalist. The sheltered four acre garden has a range of mature trees, including a Himalayan blue cedar, large rhododendrons, azaleas and a wide range of shrubs. The former mill lade feeds rocky waterfalls and a lily pond. Planting includes established perennials with seasonal colours, many bulbs, primulas and heathers, plus a vegetable garden on the site of an old tennis court.

Other Details: Grassy parking and picnic area available. Take care if weather has been wet and ground is soft!

Directions: Take the A923 Dunkeld to Blairgowrie road. Six miles east of Dunkeld turn south onto a minor road signposted Snaigow and Clunie. Mill of Forneth is the first gate on the left hand side.

Disabled Access:
Partial

Opening Times:
Sunday 11 June
2:00pm - 5:00pm
Also by arrangement
1 May - 30 September

Admission:
£4.00

Charities:
Perth & Kinross District
Nurses Blairgowrie & Black
Watch Army Cadet Force
both receive 20%, the net
remaining to SG Beneficiaries

23

PITCURRAN HOUSE
Abernethy PH2 9LH
The Hon Ranald and Mrs Noel-Paton T: 01738 850933
E: patricianp@pitcurran.com

End of village garden with an interesting combination of trees, shrubs and plants. Behind the house euphorbia mellifera and melianthus major grow happily amongst hebes and cistus. The garden also includes rhododendrons and azaleas, meconopsis, trilliums, tree peonies, *Smilacena racemosa* and a good *Caragana arborescens* 'Lorbergii'. There is a rose pergola covered in Blush Noisetta, Feicite Perpetue and 'Paul's Himalayan' Musk. A large west facing hydrangea border brightens up the late summer.

Other Details: There will be a few plants for sale.

Directions: South East of Perth. From M90 (exit 9) take A912 towards Glenfarg, go left at roundabout onto A913 to Abernethy. Pitcurran House is at the far eastern end of the village.

Disabled Access:
Partial

Opening Times:
By arrangement
1 April - 30 September

Admission:
£4.00, accompanied children free

Charities:
Juvenile Diabetes Research Foundation (JDRF) receives 40% the net remaining to SG Beneficiaries

24

ROSSIE HOUSE
Forgandenny PH2 9EH
Mr and Mrs David B Nichol T01738 812265
E: judynichol@rossiehouse.co.uk

This romantic garden has been establishing itself since 1657. It is a magical mystery tour of endless paths meandering under magnificent trees, unusual shrubs with a plethora of woodland bulbs and plants at your feet. Lift the branches of a *Hamamelis mollis* to find yourself by the pond in an oasis of scultured beauty. Look up 100 feet to the top of the *Abies alba* and climb the grass path to the sunken garden and the witches' hut. From snowdrops to hellebores then trillium and bluebells, flowering shrubs, roses and an abundance of water loving plants, this garden's interest goes on through to the magnificent autumn colours. In summer there are more formal gardens close to the house. Sculptures by David Annand and Nigel Ross. Look out for the 10 foot tea pot and the yew table ready for the Mad Hatters' tea party!

Other Details: Homemade teas on 26 May only.

Directions: Forgandenny is on the B935 between Bridge of Earn and Dunning.

Disabled Access:
Partial

Opening Times:
Friday 19 May
Friday 26 May
2:00pm - 5:00pm

Admission:
£4.00

Charities:
Forgandenny Parish Church receives 40% the net remaining to SG Beneficiaries

25 THE BIELD AT BLACKRUTHVEN
Blackruthven House, Tibbermore PH1 1PY
The Bield Christian Co Ltd T: 01738 583238
E: info@bieldatblackruthven.org.uk

The Bield is set in extensive grounds comprising well maintained lawns and clipped hedges, a flower meadow and a large collection of specimen trees. Visitors are encouraged to stroll around the grounds and explore the labyrinth cut into the grass of the old orchard. The main garden is a traditional walled garden containing extensive herbaceous borders, manicured lawns and an organic vegetable plot. The walled garden also contains a wide variety of trained fruit trees, a fruit cage, a glasshouse and a healing garden.

Directions: From Dundee or Edinburgh, follow signs for Glasgow, Stirling Crianlarich which lead onto the Perth bypass. Head west on the A85 signed to Crieff/Crianlarich to West Huntingtower. Turn left at the crossroads to Madderty/ Tibbermore. The entrance is on your left after ½ mile and is marked by stone pillars and iron gates. Take a left up the tarmac road passing the gate lodge. Turn right to park at the Steading.

Disabled Access:
Partial

Opening Times:
Saturday 17 June
2:00pm - 5:00pm

Admission:
£5.00 includes tea/coffee
and home baking

Charities:
Southton Smallholding
receives 40% the net
remaining to SG Beneficiaries

26 NEW THE GARDEN AT CRAIGOWAN
Ballinluig PH9 0NE
Ian and Christine Jones T: 01796 482244
E: i.q.jones@btinternet.com

'I am just bowled over! I have never ever seen so many and such a variety of species rhododendrons growing in a private garden in this country'. This was the reaction of an eminent gardener from Ireland when she saw the garden for the first time. Craigowan is truly a wonderful garden, a hidden gem situated on a quiet public road overlooking the Tay and Tummel valleys at an elevation of 600 ft. But this garden is not just for lovers of rhododendrons and azaleas. The garden now extends to five acres with woodland, lawns and formal herbaceous and planted areas. While the plant collection is mainly rhododendrons, magnolias, lilies and other traditional companion plants there is a wonderful show of meconopsis, followed by the giant Himalayan lilies in June, and the immaculate herbaceous borders are of interest and colour until mid-October. The rhododendron and azalea flowering period extends for almost 12 months but the most significant show is from mid-April until June. There is always a risk of frost which can wreck rhododendron flowering in the spring but there is a good collection of hardy species which have grown well and recent losses have been rare.

Other Details: Groups are welcome to visit the garden. Tea and coffee by prior arrangement only.

Directions: From north or south A9 to Ballinluig junction. Follow sign for Tulliemet and Dalcapon. Pass the filling station and Red Brolly Cafe. Turn right following the Tulliemet/Dalcapon sign. This is a steep narrow road so take care. About ½ mile up the road take a left turning with fields on either side and Craigowan is the first house on the left about ½ mile along. Park on paviours adjoining house.

Disabled Access:
Partial

Opening Times:
By arrangement
15 April - 31 July

Admission:
£6.00, includes tea

Charities:
LUPUS UK receives 40%,
the net remaining to
SG Beneficiaries

27 THE STEADING AT CLUNIE
Newmill of Kinloch, Clunie, Blairgowrie PH10 6SG
Jean and Dave Trudgill T: 01250 884263

The Steading at Newmill is situated on The Lunan Burn midway between Lochs Clunie and Marlee. There is a wild flower meadow that in spring is carpeted with Cowslips and in mid to late June several species of native orchids are in flower. In addition, there is a small cottage garden with a fish pond and a woodland walk along the banks of the Lunan Burn. The area is a haven for wildlife with beavers burrowing into the banks of the mill race.

Directions: Look for a track on a sharp right-hand bend just after a breeze-block wall on the south side of the A923 three miles west of Blairgowrie and 800 metres west of the Kinloch Hotel.

Disabled Access:
None

Opening Times:
By arrangement
29 April - 7 May
for spring flowers
and 14 June - 28 June
for wild orchids

Admission:
£5.00, includes tea/coffee

Charities:
Save the Children receives
40%, the net remaining to
SG Beneficiaries

28 WESTER HOUSE OF ROSS
Comrie PH6 2JS
Mrs Sue Young

Wester House of Ross is a four acre garden which has been developed over the last 15 years. Please visit us this year to enjoy the peonies, irises, roses, clematis and more.

Other Details: There will be a large interesting plant stall with plants from the garden and a great tea tent.

Directions: On the A85 drive westwards through Comrie, past the White Church and at the end of the village take a left turn over a small bridge, signposted Ross. Then take the first right, signposted Dalchonzie. After ¼ mile turn left at the three large dustbins and follow the signs to parking and the garden.

Disabled Access:
None

Opening Times:
Saturday 24 June
& Sunday 25 June
2:00pm - 5:00pm

Admission:
£4.00, accompanied children
free

Charities:
Blythswood Care receives
40%, the net remaining to
SG Beneficiaries

Each visit you make to one of our gardens in 2017 will raise money for our beneficiary charities:

In addition, funds will be distributed to a charity of the owner's choice. For the East of Scotland, these include:

Acting for Others

ACTS

ADSHG

Advocacy Service Aberdeen

All Saints Church, Glencarse and Fingask Follies

Alzheimer Scotland

Amnesty International

Archie Foundation

Barnados

Barnardos

Befriend a Child, Aberdeen

Bennachie Guides

Blairgowrie Black Watch Army Cadet Force

Blythswood Care

British Limbless Ex-Servicemen's Association

Brooke | Action for Working Horses & Donkeys

Cambo Heritage Trust

Children 1st

Children's Hospice Association Scotland (CHAS)

Christ Church Kincardine O'Neil

Craigrothie Village Hall

Crail Cubs

Crail Preservation Society

Crisis

Cruickshank Botanic Gardens Trust

Dalhousie Day Care

Dogs Trust

East Fife Members' Centre of the National Trust for Scotland

Ellon & District Legion Scotland

Elvanfoot Trust

Fauna and Flora International

Fettercairn Community Allotments

Fife Voluntary Action

Forfar Open Garden Scheme

Forgan Arts Centre

Forgandenny Parish Church

Forget Me Not

Fortingall Church

Freedom From Fistula Foundation

Friends of Anchor

Friends of Camperdown House

Girl Guiding Dundee Outdoor Centre

Girl Guiding Montrose

GKOPC Thrums Tots and Messy Church

Home Start Stonehaven

Hospitalfield Trust

Insch Parish Church Restoration Fund

Julia Thomson Memorial Trust

Juvenile Diabetes Research Foundation (JDRF)

Logie & St John's (Cross) Church, Dundee

LUPUS UK

Maggie's Cancer Caring Centre: Fife

Marie Curie

Milnathort Guide Group

MS Society (Aberdeen Branch)

MS Therapy Centre (Tayside Ltd)

Parkinson's UK

Perth & Kinross District Nurses

Pittenweem Community Library

Poppy Scotland

Practical Action

RAF Benevolent Fund

Riding for the Disabled Association

RIO Community Centre

RNLI

RUDA

Saline Environmental Group

SANDS

Save the Children

Scooniehill Riding for the Disabled

Scotland's Charity Air Ambulance

Scottish Civic Trust

Scout Group (Newburgh)

SG Development Fund

Southton Smallholding

SSPCA

St Athernase Church, Leuchars

St Mary's Episcopal Church

St Vigeans Church Fund

STAR Children's Charity

Student Foodbank, Dundee & Angus College

Tarland Development Group

The Coronation Hall, Muckhart

The Gurkha Welfare Trust

The Library Renewed

The Woodland Trust

Type 1 Juvenile Diabetes Research

UCAN

Unicorn Preservation Society

WEST & CENTRAL SCOTLAND

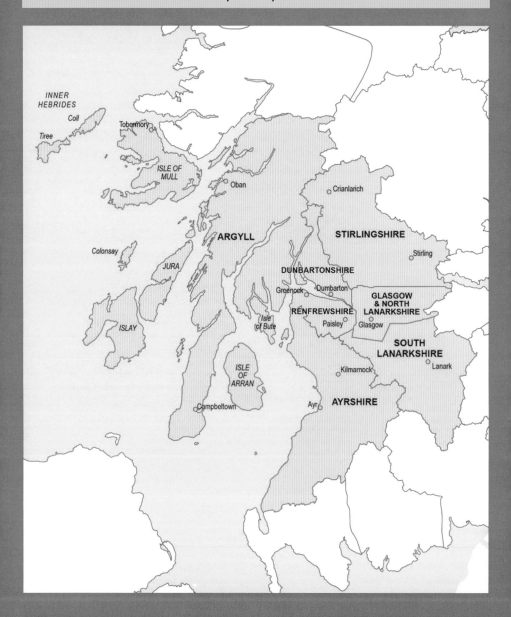

ARGYLL

Scotland's Gardens 2017 Guidebook is sponsored by **INVESTEC WEALTH & INVESTMENT**

District Organiser

Minette Struthers	Ardmaddy Castle, Balvicar, By Oban PA34 4QY E: argyll@scotlandsgardens.org

Area Organisers

Yvonne Anderson	Melfort House, Kilmelford, By Oban PA34 4XD
Grace Bergius	Craignish Hse, Ardfern, By Lochgilphead PA31 8QN
Mary Lindsay	Dal an Eas, Kilmore, Oban PA34 4XU
Patricia McArthur	Bute Cottage, Newton, Strachlachan PA27 8DB

Treasurer

Minette Struthers	Ardmaddy Castle, Balvicar, By Oban PA34 4QY

Gardens open on a specific date

Crarae Garden, Inveraray	Wednesday 19 April	10:00am	-	5:00pm
Benmore Botanic Garden, Benmore	Sunday 23 April	10:00am	-	6:00pm
Crarae Garden, Inveraray	Sunday 23 April	10:00am	-	5:00pm
Arduaine Garden, Oban	Sunday 30 April	9:30am	-	4:30pm
Kames Bay, Kilmelford	Saturday 6 May	1:30pm	-	5:00pm
Kames Bay, Kilmelford	Sunday 7 May	1:30pm	-	5:00pm
Dalnashean, Port Appin	Saturday 13 May	1:00pm	-	6:00pm
Knock Cottage, Lochgair	Saturday 13 May	1:30pm	-	5:00pm
Dalnashean, Port Appin	Sunday 14 May	1:00pm	-	6:00pm
Knock Cottage, Lochgair	Sunday 14 May	1:30pm	-	5:00pm
Braevallich Farm, by Dalmally	Saturday 20 May	1:00pm	-	5:30pm
Strachur House Flower & Woodland Gardens, Strachur	Saturday 20 May	1:00pm	-	5:00pm
Braevallich Farm, by Dalmally	Sunday 21 May	1:00pm	-	5:30pm
Strachur House Flower & Woodland Gardens, Strachur	Sunday 21 May	1:00pm	-	5:00pm
Maolachy's Garden, Lochavich	Saturday 27 May	1:00pm	-	6:00pm
Maolachy's Garden, Lochavich	Sunday 28 May	1:00pm	-	6:00pm
Knock Cottage, Lochgair	Saturday 3 June	1:30pm	-	5:00pm
Fasnacloich, Appin	Sunday 4 June	11:00am	-	5:00pm
Knock Cottage, Lochgair	Sunday 4 June	1:30pm	-	5:00pm
Dal an Eas, Kilmore, Oban	Saturday 24 June	1:00pm	-	6:00pm
Dal an Eas, Kilmore, Oban	Sunday 25 June	1:00pm	-	6:00pm
Caol Ruadh, Colintraive	Saturday 15 July	2:00pm	-	5:00pm

ARGYLL

Caol Ruadh, Colintraive	Sunday 16 July	2:00pm - 5:00pm
2 Broadcroft Lane, Rothesay	Saturday 29 July	1:00pm - 5:00pm
2 Broadcroft Lane, Rothesay	Sunday 30 July	1:00pm - 5:00pm

Gardens open regularly

Achnacloich, Connel	1 April - 31 Oct (Sats only)	10:00am - 4:00pm
Ardchattan Priory, North Connel	1 April - 31 October	9:30am - 5:30pm
Ardkinglas Woodland Garden, Cairndow	Daily	Dawn - Dusk
Ardmaddy Castle, by Oban	Daily	9:00am - Dusk
Ascog Hall, Ascog	1 April - 30 September	10:00am - 5:00pm
Barguillean's "Angus Garden", Taynuilt	Daily	9:00am - Dusk
Crinan Hotel Garden, Crinan	1 May - 31 August	Dawn - Dusk
Druimneil House, Port Appin	1 April - 31 October	Dawn - Dusk
Inveraray Castle Gardens, Inveraray	1 April - 31 October	10:00am - 5:45pm
Kinlochlaich Gardens, Appin	3 March - 15 October	10:00am - 4:00pm
Oakbank, Ardrishaig	1 May - 31 August	10:30am - 6:00pm

Gardens open by arrangement

Barochreal, Kilninver	1 May - 30 September	01852 316151
Dal an Eas, Kilmore	15 April - 10 September	01631 770246
Eas Mhor, Cnoc-a-Challtuinn	1 May - 30 September	01852 300469
Kinlochlaich Gardens, Appin	16 October - 2 March	07881 525754
Knock Cottage, Lochgair	15 April - 15 June	01546 886628
Maolachy's Garden, Lochavich	28 January - 12 March	01866 844212
Seafield, Hunter's Quay	1 June - 31 August	01369 703107

Key to symbols

	New in 2017		Homemade teas		Accommodation
	Teas		Dogs on a lead allowed		Plant stall
	Cream teas		Wheelchair access		Scottish Snowdrop Festival

GARDEN LOCATIONS IN ARGYLL

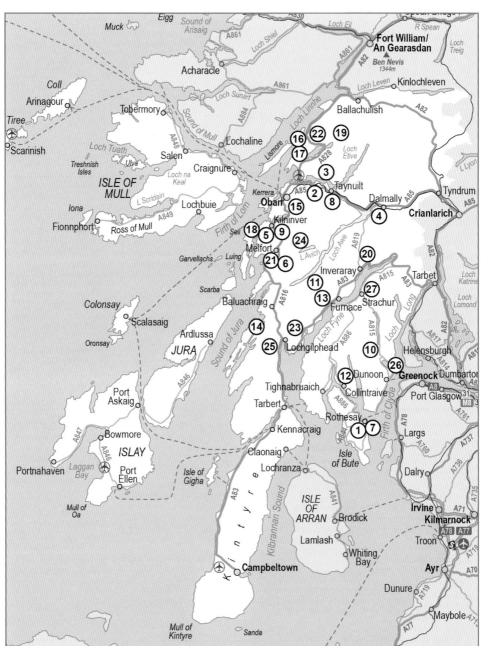

ARGYLL

NEW 2 BROADCROFT LANE
Rothesay, Isle of Bute PA20 9BA
Mrs Marlene Hill

A small but delightful hidden cottage garden with an emphasis on wildlife, there is a pond, unusual plantings, fruit and vegetables that are all growing in harmony.

Directions: In Rothesay proceed up High Street (B881) past the castle on the right till you come to Bussey's Carpet Shop in Broadcroft Lane - park in the lane and follow the arrows to our hidden garden.

Disabled Access:
Full

Opening Times:
Saturday 29 July
& Sunday 30 July
1:00pm - 5:00pm

Admission:
£3.00

Charities:
All proceeds to
SG Beneficiaries

ACHNACLOICH
Connel, Oban PA37 1PR
Mr T E Nelson T: 01631 710796
E: charlie_milne@msn.com

Scottish baronial house by John Starforth of Glasgow. Succession of wonderful bulbs, flowering shrubs, rhododendrons, azaleas, magnolias and primulas. Woodland garden with ponds above Loch Etive. Good autumn colours.

Directions: On the A85 three miles east of Connel. Parking is on the right at the bottom of the drive.

Disabled Access:
Partial

Opening Times:
1 April - 31 October
10:00am - 4:00pm
(Saturdays only)

Admission:
£4.00

Charities:
All proceeds to
SG Beneficiaries

ARDCHATTAN PRIORY
North Connel PA37 1RQ
Mrs Sarah Troughton T: 01796 481355
E: sh.troughton@gmail.com www.ardchattan.co.uk

Beautifully situated on the north side of Loch Etive. In front of the house there is a rockery, extensive herbaceous and rose borders, with excellent views over the loch. West of the house there are shrub borders and a wild garden, numerous roses and many different varieties of sorbus providing excellent autumn colour. The Priory, founded in 1230, is now a private house. The ruins of the chapel and graveyard are in the care of Historic Scotland and open with the garden.

Other Details: Sunday 30 July Garden Fete - soup lunches, homemade teas, plant and other stalls and other attractions.

Directions: Oban ten miles. From north: turn left off A828 at Barcaldine onto B845 for six miles. From East/Oban: on A85, cross Connel Bridge and turn first right, proceed east on Bonawe Road.

Disabled Access:
Partial

Opening Times:
1 April - 31 October
9:30am - 5:30pm

Admission:
£4.00, children under 16 free

Charities:
Donation to SG Beneficiaries

ARDKINGLAS WOODLAND GARDEN
Cairndow PA26 8BG
Ardkinglas Estate T: 01499 600261
www.ardkinglas.com

In a peaceful setting overlooking Loch Fyne the garden contains one of the finest collections of rhododendrons and conifers in Britain. This includes the mightiest conifer in Europe, a silver fir, as well as many other champion trees. There is a gazebo with unique "Scriptorium" based around a collection of literary quotes. The garden now has the only Gruffalo trail in Scotland, come and find him! It is a VisitScotland 3 star garden.

Other Details: Champion Trees: 'Grand Fir' tallest tree in Britain and other champion trees. Nearby is the Tree Shop, an independent garden centre and café which offers fabulous plants and food.

Directions: Entrance through Cairndow village off the A83 Loch Lomond/Inveraray road.

Disabled Access:
Partial

Opening Times:
Daily
Dawn - Dusk

Admission:
£5.00, family ticket £15.00

Charities:
Donation to SG Beneficiaries

ARDMADDY CASTLE
by Oban PA34 4QY
Mr and Mrs Charles Struthers T: 01852 300353
E: minette@ardmaddy.com www.gardens-of-argyll.co.uk

The gardens, in a most spectacular setting, are shielded by mature woodlands, carpeted with bluebells and daffodils and protected from the winds by the elevated castle. The walled garden is full of magnificent rhododendrons, a collection of rare and unusual shrubs and plants, the Clock Garden with its cutting flowers, the new crevice garden, fruit and veg grown with labour saving formality, all within dwarf box hedging. Beyond, a woodland walk, with its 60ft hydrangea, leads to the water gardens - in early summer a riot of candelabra primulas, irises, rodgersias and other damp loving plants and grasses. Lovely autumn colour. A plantsman's garden for all seasons.

Other Details: Seasonal vegetable and summer fruit stall. Toilet suitable for the disabled. Six self catering cottages, see our website for details.

Directions: Take A816 south of Oban for eight miles. Turn right B844 to Seil Island/ Easdale. Four miles on, turn left on to Ardmaddy road (signed) for a further two miles.

Disabled Access:
Full

Opening Times:
Daily
9:00am - Dusk

Admission:
£4.50, accompanied children free

Charities:
Donation to SG Beneficiaries

ARDUAINE GARDEN
Oban PA34 4XQ
The National Trust for Scotland T: 01852 200366
E: arduaine@nts.org.uk http://www.nts.org.uk/property/arduaine-garden

Outstanding 20 acre coastal garden created over 100 years ago on the south facing slope of a promontory separating Asknish Bay from Loch Melfort. This remarkable hidden paradise, protected by tall shelterbelts and influenced favourably by the North Atlantic Drift, grows a wide variety of plants from all over the globe Internationally known for its rhododendron species collection, the garden also features magnolias, camellias, azaleas and other wonderful trees and shrubs, many being tender and rarely seen. A broad selection of perennials, bulbs, ferns and water plants ensure year-long interest.

Other Details: Champion Trees: nine including *Gevuina avellana*. Garden also open 1 April - 30 Sept. Teas available in the local hotel. Dogs welcome on short leads.

Directions: Off the A816 Oban-Lochgilphead, sharing an entrance with the Loch Melfort Hotel.

Disabled Access:
Partial

Opening Times:
Sunday 30 April
9:30am - 4:30pm

Admission:
Normal NTS admission applies

Charities:
Donation to SG Beneficiaries

7 ASCOG HALL

Ascog, Isle of Bute PA20 9EU
Karin Burke T: 01700 503461
E: karin@ascogfernery.com www.ascogfernery.com

The outstanding feature of this three acre garden is the Victorian Fernery, a sunken structure fed by natural spring waters and housing many fern species, including a 1,000 year old King Fern and thought to be Britain's oldest exotic fern. Rare and unusual species await the visitor wandering the original garden "rooms" while the stables and coach house ruins feed the imagination of long lost times. The garden is generally well labelled and contains a plant hunter's trail. New for 2017 the "Golden Crown" Fernery.

Other Details: Restricted mobility parking at the top of the drive (close to the house). Personal assistance available for disabled access to the Fernery. Guide dogs are permitted. All proceeds are donated to the garden maintenance fund or to charity.

Directions: Three miles south of Rothesay on A844. Close to the picturesque Ascog Bay.

Disabled Access:
Partial

Opening Times:
1 April - 30 September
10:00am - 5:00pm

Admission:
£5.00

Charities:
Donation to SG Beneficiaries

---

8 BARGUILLEAN'S "ANGUS GARDEN"

Taynuilt PA35 1HY
The Josephine Marshall Trust T: 01866 822333
E: info@barguillean.co.uk www.barguillean.co.uk

Nine acre woodland garden around an eleven acre loch set in the Glen Lonan Hills. Spring flowering shrubs and bulbs, extensive collection of rhododendron hybrids, deciduous azaleas, conifers and unusual trees. The garden contains a large collection of North American rhododendron hybrids from famous contemporary plant breeders. Some paths can be steep. Three marked walks from 30 minutes to 1½ hours.

Other Details: Self catering accommodation available in separate comfortable wing of the main house. Coach tours by appointment.

Directions: Three miles south off A85 Glasgow/Oban road at Taynuilt; road marked Glen Lonan; three miles up single track road; turn right at the sign.

Disabled Access:
None

Opening Times:
Daily
9:00am - Dusk

Admission:
£3.50, children under 14 free

Charities:
Donation to SG Beneficiaries

---

9 BAROCHREAL

Kilninver, Oban, Argyll PA34 4UT
Nigel and Antoinette Mitchell T: 01852 316151
E: toni@themitchells.co.uk www.barochreal.co.uk

A young garden evolving since 2006. After much fencing, stone clearing and rewalling, digging and ditching, each year another area has been completed to provide a bank of rhododendrons and azaleas, a rose garden, water feature with rockery, a pond with island, raised vegetable beds and a wild garden with beehives, waterfalls and burns. Maintained walking tracks in the fields and to viewpoints. The two hard winters of 2010/11 and 2011/12 destroyed many plants in their infancy which are being replaced and constantly added to.

Directions: On the A816 Oban to Lochgilphead road just to the south of the village of Kilninver on the left hand side of the road.

Disabled Access:
Partial

Opening Times:
By arrangement
1 May - 30 September

Admission:
£3.00 children under 16 free

Charities:
Argyll Animal Aid receives 40%, the net remaining to SG Beneficiaries

BENMORE BOTANIC GARDEN
Benmore, Dunoon PA23 8QU
A Regional Garden of the Royal Botanic Garden Edinburgh T: 01369 706261
E: benmore@rbge.org.uk   www.rbge.org.uk

Benmore's magnificent mountainside setting is a joy to behold. Its 120 acres boast a world-famous collection of plants from the Orient and Himalayas to North and South America. An impressive avenue of giant redwoods, one of the finest entrances to any botanic garden in the world. Established in 1863, these majestic giants stand over 50m high. Seven miles of trails throughout lead to restored Victorian Fernery and dramatic viewpoint at 140m looking out to surrounding mountains and Holy Loch. Traditional Bhutanese and Chilean pavilions and the magnificent Golden Gates.

Other Details: National Plant Collection®: Abies, South American Temperate Conifers, Picea. Other opening times: 1 March - 31 October 10:00am-6:00pm (closing 5:00pm in March and October).

Directions: Seven miles north of Dunoon or 22 miles south from Glen Kinglass below *Rest and Be Thankful* pass. On A815.

Disabled Access:
Partial

Opening Times:
Sunday 23 April
10:00am - 6:00pm

Admission:
£6.50, concessions £5.50, children under 16 free (includes donation to garden, for prices without donation check rbge.org.uk)

Charities:
Donation to SG Beneficiaries

BRAEVALLICH FARM
by Dalmally PA33 1BU
Mr Philip Bowden-Smith T: 01866 844246
E: philip@brae.co.uk

Two gardens, one at the farm and another 300 metres above. The former is approx. 1.5 acres and developed over the last 40 years; its principal features include dwarf rhododendron, azaleas (evergreen and deciduous), large drifts of various primula and meconopsis, and mixed herbaceous/shrubs; there is also quite a serious kitchen garden. The garden above the farm, at approx. 7 acres, was developed over the last 25 years out of a birch and sessile oak wood and is a traditional glen garden intersected by two pretty burns with waterfalls. The peaceful setting and varied topography create attractive vistas. Plantings are predominantly rhododendron (120 plus varieties), deciduous azalea (30 varieties), camellia, magnolia, eucryphia, and many different shrubs and trees with large drifts of bluebell and other bulbs.

Other Details: Please note waterproof footwear is recommended.

Directions: SE of Loch Awe on B840, 15 miles from Cladich, 7 miles from Ford.

Disabled Access:
None

Opening Times:
Saturday 20 May
& Sunday 21 May
1:00pm - 5:30pm

Admission:
£5.00

Charities:
Mary's Meals receives 40%, the net remaining to SG Beneficiaries

CAOL RUADH
Colintraive PA22 3AR
Mr and Mrs C Scotland

Delightful seaside garden on the old B866 shore road looking out over Loch Riddon and the Kyles of Bute in this very beautiful corner of Argyll. There are water features with interesting new plantings and the added attraction of a unique outdoor sculpture park featuring works from a variety of Scottish artists.

Directions: Turn right off the A886 Strachur - Colintraive onto the B866 about 2½ miles before Colintraive. From Dunoon take the A815 north about 3½ miles, left on to B836 and then left on to the A886.

Disabled Access:
None

Opening Times:
Saturday 15 July
& Sunday 16 July
2:00pm - 5:00pm

Admission:
£5.00

Charities:
All proceeds to
SG Beneficiaries

CRARAE GARDEN
Inveraray PA32 8YA
The National Trust for Scotland T: 01546 886614
E: crarae@nts.org.uk   www.nts.org.uk/Property/Crarae-Garden/

Crarae is a rugged woodland garden which has a spectacular display of rhododendrons in May and June, a narrow gorge with waterfalls, pools, and varied wildlife from red squirrels and pine martens to otters. Above the garden is the forest garden, a very wild area which was planted in the 1930s as an experiment. This area now has stands of fine tall trees in a unique wild setting and is not open to the public.

Other Details: National Plant Collection®: *Nothofagus* (Southern Beech). This collection is the most northerly of its type in the UK. Champion Trees: abies, acer and chamaecyparis. Garden also open 1 April - 31 October. Disabled access only to part of the lower garden. Dogs on leads welcome. Plant sales, light refreshments and cakes available.

Directions: On A83 ten miles south of Inveraray.

Disabled Access:
Partial

Opening Times:
Wednesday 19 April
& Sunday 23 April
10:00am - 5:00pm

Admission:
Normal NTS admission applies

Charities:
Donation to SG Beneficiaries

CRINAN HOTEL GARDEN
Crinan PA31 8SR
Mr and Mrs N Ryan T: 01546 830261
E: nryan@crinanhotel.com   www.crinanhotel.com

Small rock garden with azaleas and rhododendrons created in a steep hillside over a century ago with steps leading to a sheltered, secluded garden with sloping lawns, herbaceous beds and spectacular views of the canal and Crinan Loch.

Other Details: Raffle of painting by Frances Macdonald (Ryan). Tickets at coffee shop, art gallery and hotel. Homemade teas available in the coffee shop.

Directions: Lochgilphead A83, then A816 to Oban, then A841 Cairnbaan to Crinan.

Disabled Access:
None

Opening Times:
1 May - 31 August
Dawn - Dusk

Admission:
By donation

Charities:
Feedback Madagascar receives 40%, the net remaining to SG Beneficiaries

---

DAL AN EAS
Kilmore, Oban PA34 4XU
Mary Lindsay T: 01631 770246
E: dalaneas@live.com

Recently created informal country garden with the aim of increasing the biodiversity of native plants and insects while adding interest and colour with introduced trees, shrubs and naturalised perennials. It has a structured garden with pond, a burn with pool, wildflower meadow with five different species of native orchid and a vegetable plot. Grass paths lead to waterfalls, views and ancient archaeological sites.

Other Details: Sturdy footwear is recommended.

Directions: Take A816 to Kilmore 3½ miles south of Oban. Turn left on road to Barran and Musdale. Keep left at junction for Connel. Dal an Eas is approximately one mile on the left before the big hedges.

Disabled Access:
Partial

Opening Times:
Saturday 24 June
& Sunday 25 June
1:00pm - 6:00pm
Also by arrangement
15 April - 10 September

Admission:
£4.00

Charities:
Mary's Meals receives 40%, the net remaining to SG Beneficiaries

16 **NEW DALNASHEAN**
Port Appin, Appin PA38 4DE
Kathleen Ferguson

Established garden sheltered by a beechwood hill giving views over Loch Linnhe and Lismore. Camellias, rhododendrons and magnolias as well as many unusual shrubs and trees. More recent planting in adjoining field with ponds surrounded by rhododendrons and azaleas and tree and shrub borders.

Other Details: Crafts and garden plants on sale. Teas available in Druimneil House garden which is one mile from Dalnashean, also open for SG.

Directions: Take the A828 to Appin then the road signposted to Port Appin and Lismore Ferry. After two miles, turn into the drive opposite the large mirror on roadside.

Disabled Access:
Partial

Opening Times:
Saturday 13 May
Sunday 14 May
1:00pm - 6:00pm

Admission:
£4.00

Charities:
Appin Parish Church receives 40%, the net remaining to SG Beneficiaries

17 **DRUIMNEIL HOUSE**
Port Appin PA38 4DQ
Mrs J Glaisher (Gardener: Mr Andrew Ritchie) T: 01631 730228
E: druimneilhouse@btinternet.com

Large garden overlooking Loch Linnhe with many fine varieties of mature trees and rhododendrons and other woodland shrubs. Nearer the house, an impressive bank of deciduous azaleas is underplanted with a block of camassia and a range of other bulbs. There is a small Victorian walled garden.

Other Details: Teas normally available. Lunch by prior arrangement.

Directions: Turn in for Appin off the A828 (Connel/Fort William Road). Two miles, sharp left at Airds Hotel, second house on the right.

Disabled Access:
None

Opening Times:
1 April - 31 October
Dawn - Dusk

Admission:
By donation

Charities:
All proceeds to
SG Beneficiaries

18 **EAS MHOR**
Cnoc-a-Challtuinn, Clachan Seil, Oban PA34 4TR
Mrs Kimbra Lesley Barrett T: 01852 300 469
E: kimbra1745@gmail.com

All the usual joys of a west coast garden plus some delightful surprises! A small contemporary garden on a sloping site - the emphasis being on scent and exotic plant material. Unusual and rare blue Borinda bamboos (only recently discovered in China) and bananas. The garden is at its best in mid to late summer when shrub roses and sweet peas fill the air with scent. The delightful sunny deck overlooks stylish white walled ponds with cascading water blades.

Other Details: Cream tea in small artist studio off the deck - enjoy the sound of gentle music. Small groups are welcome.

Directions: Turn off A816 from Oban onto B844 signed *Easdale*. Over the Bridge onto Seil Island, pass Tigh an Truish pub and turn right after ¼ mile up Cnoc-a-Challtuin road. Public car park on the left at the bottom, please park there and walk up the road. Eas Mhor on right after 2nd speed bump. Please do not block driveway.

Disabled Access:
None

Opening Times:
By arrangement
1 May - 30 September
(2017 open day
to be confirmed,
check SG website)

Admission:
Minimum donation £4.00,
refreshments are extra

Charities:
MS Therapy Centre (Oban)
receives 40%, the net
remaining to SG Beneficiaries

ARGYLL

19 FASNACLOICH
Appin PA38 4BJ
Mr David Stewart

South-facing 15 acre woodland garden sloping down to Loch Baile Mhic Cailein in Glen Creran. Partly laid out in the mid-19th century with extensive structural water features added in the early 20th century. The garden mainly consists of hybrid and species rhododendrons, azaleas and magnolias with, over the last 25 years, a more recent addition of trees from Eastern Europe, Central Asia and the Northern United States (including a small pinetum).

Directions: On the A828 at the roundabout on the north side of Creagan Bridge take the road for Invercreran. At the head of the loch go straight ahead for about 1½ miles. The house is on the right side.

Disabled Access:
Partial

Opening Times:
Sunday 4 June
11:00am - 5:00pm

Admission:
£5.00

Charities:
Mary's Meals receives 40%, the net remaining to SG Beneficiaries

20 INVERARAY CASTLE GARDENS
Inveraray PA32 8XF
The Duke and Duchess of Argyll T: 01499 302203
E: enquiries@inveraray-castle.com www.inveraray-castle.com

Rhododendrons and azaleas abound and flower from April to June. Very fine specimens of Cedrus deodars, Sequoiadendron wellingtonia, Cryptomeria japonica, Taxus baccata and others thrive in the damp climate. The 'Flag-Borders' on each side of the main drive with paths in the shape of Scotland's national flag, the St. Andrew's Cross, are outstanding in spring with Prunus 'Ukon' and P.subhirtella and are underplanted with rhododendrons, eucryphias, shrubs and herbaceous plants giving interest all year. Bluebell Festival during flowering period in May.

Other Details: Guide dogs allowed. Wheelchair users please note there are gravel paths.

Directions: Inveraray is 60 miles north of Glasgow on the banks of Loch Fyne on the A83 with a regular bus service from Glasgow and 15 miles from Dalmally on the A819.

Disabled Access:
Partial

Opening Times:
1 April - 31 October
10:00am - 5:45pm

Admission:
£5.00 (gardens only)

Charities:
Donation to SG Beneficiaries

21 KAMES BAY
Kilmelford PA34 4XA
Stuart Cannon T: 01852 200205
E: stuartcannon@kames.co.uk

The garden and house were first established from a wild hillside in 1982. The garden and woodland were extended in 2001. It is principally a spring garden with ornamental trees, azaleas and rhododendrons, the latter are mostly from Arduaine, Ardanasaig and various friends' gardens. A pond was created while landscaping the hill to provide a flatter area for a shed and greenhouse. Behind the garage is a new vegetable growing area. There are some pleasant walks in the woodland with wild primroses, violets, and other wild flowers, with various seats to rest and enjoy the special views over Loch Melfort and the Islands to the west.

Other Details: Some grass paths - suitable walking shoes are recommended as access is up a steep drive.

Directions: On A816 Oban to Lochgilphead road opposite Kames Bay and the fish farm. Two and a half miles south of Kilmelford and 2½ miles north of Arduaine.

Disabled Access:
None

Opening Times:
Saturday 6 May
Sunday 7 May
1:30pm - 5:00pm

Admission:
£4.00, children under 16 free

Charities:
St Columba's Church receives 40%, the net remaining to SG Beneficiaries

KINLOCHLAICH GARDENS
Appin PA38 4BD
Miss F M M Hutchison T: 07881 525754
E: fiona@kinlochlaich.plus.com www.kinlochlaichgardencentre.co.uk

Walled garden incorporating a large Nursery Garden Centre. Amazing variety of plants growing and for sale. Extensive grounds with woodland walk, spring garden. Many rhododendrons, azaleas, trees, shrubs and herbaceous, including many unusual - embothrium, davidia, stewartia, magnolia, eucryphia and tropaeolum. A quarter of the interior of the Walled Garden is borders packed with many unusual and interesting plants, espaliered fruit trees, and an ancient yew in the centre.

Other Details: Self catering accommodation.

Directions: On the A828 in Appin between Oban, 18 miles to the south, and Fort William, 27 miles to the north. The entrance is next to the Police Station.

Disabled Access:
Partial

Opening Times:
3 March - 15 October
10:00am - 4:00pm
Also by arrangement
16 October - 2 March

Admission:
£3.00

Charities:
Appin Village Hall receives 40%, the net remaining to SG Beneficiaries

KNOCK COTTAGE
Lochgair PA31 8RZ
Mr and Mrs Hew Service T: 01546 886628
E: corranmorhouse@aol.com

The six acre woodland garden is centred on a small waterfall, an 80 m lochan and lily pond. From the 1960s there was constant planting with major plantings in 1989 and the 90s. The storms of 2011/12 caused great damage to trees and bushes, thus a replanting phase of azaleas, rhododendron, camellias and other shrubs. There are over 80 species of rhododendron and hybrids. Among the mature and young trees are cut leaf oak and alder, specimen conifers, eucalyptus, acers, prunus and beech.

Other Details: Please note there is very limited parking. Waterproof footwear is recommended. Teas will be available on open weekends.

Directions: On the A83, from Lochgilphead, ½ mile before the Lochgair Hotel and on the left, and from Inveraray, ½ mile after the Lochgair Hotel and on the right between two sharp bends.

Disabled Access:
Partial

Opening Times:
Saturday & Sunday 13/14 May
Saturday & Sunday 3/4 June
1:30pm - 5:00pm
Also by arrangement
15 April - 15 June

Admission:
£4.00

Charities: Christchurch Episcopal Church, Lochgilphead & Marie Curie both receive 20%, the net remaining to SG Beneficiaries

MAOLACHY'S GARDEN
Lochavich, by Taynuilt PA35 1HJ
Georgina Dalton T: 01866 844212

Three acres of Woodland Garden with a tumbling burn - created in a small glen over 40 years. At an altitude of 450 feet and two weeks behind the coast we have a shorter growing season. By not struggling to grow tender or late species we can enjoy those that are happy to grow well here and give us all much pleasure. Snowdrops, followed by early rhodies, masses of daffodils in many varieties, bluebells, wild flowers and azaleas, primulas and irises. A productive veg patch and tunnel feed the gardener and family!

Other Details: Main path is gravelled, but some others are narrow, steep and not for the faint hearted! Sensible shoes recommended. The garden steps are being upgraded.

Directions: A816 to Kilmelford. Turn uphill between shop and church, signposted Lochavich 6, steep and twisty road with hairpin bend shortly after leaving village, check for passing places. Maolachy Drive is 4 miles from village. Cross 3 county cattle grids; after the third **ignore the forestry tracks** to left and right. Continue downhill towards Loch Avich, and Maolachy is up on the left, first house after Kilmelford. **Ignore Satnav.**

Disabled Access:
None

Opening Times:
Saturday 27 May
& Sunday 28 May
1:00pm - 6:00pm
also by arrangement 28 January - 12 March for the Snowdrop Festival

Admission:
£4.00, children under 16 free

Charities:
Hope Kitchen - Oban receives 40%, the net remaining to SG Beneficiaries

25 OAKBANK
Ardrishaig PA30 8EP
Helga Macfarlane T: 01546 603405
E: helga@macfarlane.one www.gardenatoakbank.blogspot.com

This unusual and delightful garden will appeal to adults and children alike with lots for each to explore, including a secret garden. It extends to some three acres of hillside with a series of paths winding amongst a varied collection of trees, shrubs, bulbs and wild flowers. There are several small ponds, many wonderful wood carvings, an active population of red squirrels and a viewpoint overlooking Loch Fyne to the Isle of Arran.

Other Details: Children can enjoy a play cafe, dragon's den, fairy glen, miniature village, secret garden, music corner, look-out house and wishing well.

Directions: On the Tarbert (South) side of Ardrishaig - entry to the garden is at the junction of Tarbert Road (A83) and Oakfield Road opposite the more southerly Scottish Water lay-by.

Disabled Access:
None

Opening Times:
1 May - 31 August
10:30am - 6:00pm

Admission:
£3.50, accompanied children free

Charities:
Diabetes UK receives 40%, the net remaining to SG Beneficiaries

---

26 SEAFIELD
173 Marine Parade, Hunter's Quay, Dunoon PA23 8HJ
Scoular Anderson T: 01369 703107
E: scoulara9@gmail.com

Behind the house lies a hidden gem of a stunning seaside garden on a hillside with clever plantings, divided into separate smaller gardens including gravel garden, damp pond garden, heather garden, shady garden, herbaceous beds, shrubs, ferns and grasses.

Directions: Situated on the Cowal Peninsula at Hunter's Quay on the A815 a few hundred yards south (Dunoon side) of the Western Ferries terminal. Parking is on the promenade.

Disabled Access:
Partial

Opening Times:
By arrangement
1 June - 31 August

Admission:
£4.00, accompanied children free

Charities:
Children's Hospice Association Scotland receives 40%, the net remaining to SG Beneficiaries

---

27 STRACHUR HOUSE FLOWER & WOODLAND GARDENS
Strachur PA27 8BX
Sir Charles and Lady Maclean

Directly behind Strachur House the flower garden is sheltered by magnificent beeches, limes, ancient yews and Japanese maples. There are herbaceous borders, a burnside rhododendron and azalea walk and a rockery. Old fashioned and species roses, lilies, tulips, spring bulbs and Himalayan poppies make a varied display in this informal haven of beauty and tranquillity. The garden gives onto Strachur Park, laid out by General Campbell in 1782, which offers spectacular walks through natural woodland with two hundred-year-old trees, rare shrubs and a lochan rich in native wildlife.

Directions: Turn off A815 at Strachur House Farm entrance. Park in farm square.

Disabled Access:
Full

Opening Times:
Saturday 20 May
Sunday 21 May
1:00pm - 5:00pm

Admission:
£4.00

Charities:
The Red Cross, Dunoon Branch receives 40%, the net remaining to SG Beneficiaries

AYRSHIRE

Scotland's Gardens 2017 Guidebook is sponsored by **INVESTEC WEALTH & INVESTMENT**

District Organiser

Rose-Ann Cuninghame	45 Towerhill Avenue, Kilmaurs, Kilmarnock KA3 2TS E: ayrshire@scotlandsgardens.org

Area Organisers

Margie Collins	Grougarbank House, Kilmarnock KA3 6HP
Anne MacKay	Pierhill, Annbank KA6 5AW
Wendy Sandiford	Harrowhill Cottage, Kilmarnock KA3 6HX
Jane Tait	The Wildings, Bankwood, Galston KA4 8LH

Treasurer

Kim Donald	19 Waterslap, Fenwick, Kilmarnock KA3 6AJ

Gardens open on a specific date

Blair House, Blair Estate, Dalry, Ayrshire	Sunday 19 February	11:00am - 4:00pm
Culzean, Maybole	Monday 1 May	12:00pm - 4:00pm
Craigengillan Estate and Scottish Dark Sky Observatory, Dalmellington	Sunday 7 May	2:00pm - 5:00pm & 10:00pm- 11:30pm
Holmes Farm, Drybridge, by Irvine	Sat & Sun 10/11 June	1:00pm - 5:00pm
Netherthird Community Garden, Cumnock	Saturday 24 June	1:00pm - 5:00pm
Barnweil Garden, Craigie, Nr Kilmarnock	Sunday 25 June	2:00pm - 5:00pm
The Gardens of Fenwick, Fenwick	Saturday 1 July	12:30pm - 5:00pm
Golf Course Road Gardens, Girvan	Sunday 9 July	1:00pm - 5:00pm
Carnell, By Hurlford	Sunday 16 July	2:00pm - 5:00pm

Gardens open by arrangement

Burnside, Littlemill Road, Drongan	1 April - 31 August	01292 592445
Glenapp Castle, Ballantrae, Girvan	17 March - 22 December	01465 831212
High Fulwood, Stewarton	1 May - 31 August	01560 484705

Key to symbols

	New in 2017		Homemade teas		Accommodation
	Teas		Dogs on a lead allowed		Plant stall
	Cream teas		Wheelchair access		Scottish Snowdrop Festival

GARDEN LOCATIONS IN AYRSHIRE

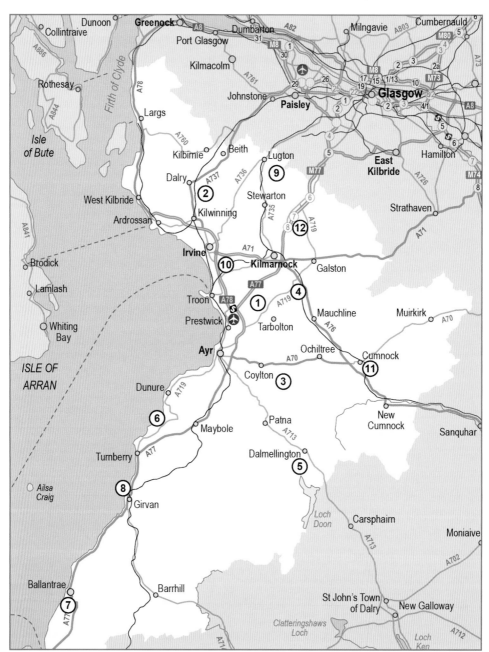

NEW BARNWEIL GARDEN

Craigie, Nr Kilmarnock KA1 5NE
Mr and Mrs Ronald W Alexander

Begun in 1972 this garden has evolved and developed ever since. With pure clay soil and being on the north side of the hill are two of the challenges and wind has also been a problem, but solved by planting beech hedging and shelter belts. The lawn on the south side of the early 19th century house is enclosed by herbaceous borders, giving way to shrub roses and then the woodland garden where the golden borders (a particular favourite as it always seems sunny even on a grey day) and a planting of meconopsis and *primula japonica* 'Postford White' are two of the sights amongst azaleas and species and hybrid rhododendrons. The north side has formal borders framing the view from the house to Craigie Castle and (on a clear day) Ben Lomond, with modern shrub rose borders on each side being a recent addition.

Other Details: Teas served in the house.

Directions: Craigie two miles. Right off the B730, two miles south of A77 to Tarbolton.

Disabled Access:
Partial

Opening Times:
Sunday 25 June
2:00pm - 5:00pm

Admission:
£5.00, children under 12 free

Charities:
Tarbolton Parish Church receives 40%, the net remaining to SG Beneficiaries

BLAIR HOUSE, BLAIR ESTATE

Dalry, Ayrshire KA24 4ER
Charles and Sallie Hendry T: 01294 833100
E: enquiries@blairestate.com   www.blairestate.com

Blair is a 'Sleeping Beauty' of a garden which is being lovingly restored. There is an atmosphere of a grand 19th century park with masses of changes in mood: sweeping vistas, magnificent trees, shady promenades, and secret groves - everything that is typical of the period. A start on the walled garden has been made with the removal of 600 Christmas trees and we are compiling ideas for future renovation. In February enjoy beautiful displays of snowdrops. Walks on the estate will include access to the private gardens. Please wear stout footwear.

Other Details: Selection of freshly baked produce to include homemade soup, coffee, teas, biscuits and afternoon tea with cakes. Gift stall. Full disabled access for catering and partial disabled access to the garden and grounds. Open for groups by arrangement.

Directions: From A737 in Dalry, take road signposted to the station and continue for ½ mile. Access via North Lodge Gates on the right. A one way system will be in place.

Disabled Access:
Partial

Opening Times:
Sunday 19 February
11:00am - 4:00pm
for the Snowdrop Festival

Admission:
£4.00, accompanied children free

Charities:
Girl Guiding Ayrshire North receives 40%, the net remaining to SG Beneficiaries

BURNSIDE

Littlemill Road, Drongan KA6 7EN
Sue Simpson and George Watt T: 01292 592445

This young six and a half acre garden was started in 2006. There is a wide range of plants from trees to alpines. Features include a 200 yard woodland border along the burn, herbaceous beds, screes, an ericaceous garden, three alpine houses, a collection of alpine troughs and a pond. The informal arboretum is underplanted with groups of daffodils, camassia and fritillaries.

Other Details: Dogs on a lead please. Teas and light refreshments by prior arrangement.

Directions: From A77 Ayr bypass take A70 Cumnock for 5¼ miles, at Coalhall, turn onto B730 Drongan (south) for 2½ miles. Burnside entrance immediately adjacent before black/white parapeted bridge. Ordnance Survey grid reference: NS455162

Disabled Access:
Partial

Opening Times:
By arrangement
1 April - 31 August

Admission:
£4.00, accompanied children free

Charities:
Alzheimers Scotland receives 40%, the net remaining to SG Beneficiaries

AYRSHIRE

CARNELL
By Hurlford KA1 5JS
Mr Michael Findlay T: 01563 884236
E: carnellestates@aol.com www.carnellestates.com

This lovely ten acre garden is featured in *Beechgrove Garden, Country Life, The Good Gardens Guide* and in Suki Urquhart's book *The Scottish Gardener*. This well known traditional walled garden is backed by a 100 yard long herbaceous border, facing a rock and water garden with gazebo and Burmese statues. Lawns, mature hedges, specimen trees and the Lime Avenue planted to commemorate the Battle of Dettingen in 1743, enhance the setting overlooked by the Peel Tower. Roses and phlox in particular are in full bloom during July.

Other Details: Ample parking available and delicious teas will be on offer.

Directions: From A77 (Glasgow/Kilmarnock) take A76 (Mauchline/Dumfries) then right on to the A719 to Ayr for 1½ miles.

Disabled Access:
Partial

Opening Times:
Sunday 16 July
2:00pm - 5:00pm

Admission:
£5.00, children under 12 free

Charities:
TBA receives 40%, the net remaining to SG Beneficiaries

© Ray Cox

CRAIGENGILLAN ESTATE AND SCOTTISH DARK SKY OBSERVATORY
Dalmellington KA6 7PZ
Mr Mark Gibson T: 01292 551118
E: info@scottishdarkskyobservatory.co.uk   www.scottishdarkskyobservatory.co.uk

Peacefully set in a rugged 'Highland' landscape recognised by Historic Scotland's *Inventory of Gardens and Designed Landscapes*. Beautiful gardens, recently uncovered 'rock and water garden' by James Pulham & Sons. Extensive displays of native bluebells - great swathes of vibrant blue under the fresh greens of newly forming leaf canopies, which form the focus of the opening. There are some of the darkest skies that most people will ever see with shooting stars, planets and comets visible.

Other Details: Visit as it gets dark (~10pm). Presentation by resident astronomer and, if the sky is clear you can stargaze using the Observatory's telescopes. Disabled access but call in advance to check for any limitations. Teas served in house.

Directions: A713 from Ayr, at the 30mph sign on entering Dalmellington turn right (signed *Craigengillan Stables*) - drive for approx 2¼ m. From Carsphairn side, stay on the main road and take first turning on left after the Jet petrol station.

Disabled Access:
Partial

Opening Times:
Sunday 20 May
2:00pm - 5:00pm (bluebells)
10:00pm - 11:30 pm (Scottish Dark Sky Observatory)

Admission:
£3.00, accompanied children free (for garden only)

Charities:
The Scottish Dark Sky Observatory receives 40%, the net remaining to SG Beneficiaries

CULZEAN
Maybole KA19 8LE
The National Trust for Scotland T: 0165 588 4400
E: culzean@nts.org.uk www.nts.org.uk/property/culzean-castle-and-country-park

The 18th century castle is perched on a cliff high above the Firth of Clyde. The Fountain Garden lies in front of the castle with terraces and herbaceous borders. The large walled garden contains a wide collection of fruit, vegetables and cut flowers plus an extensive vinery and peach house. The 560 acre Country Park offers beaches and rock pools, parklands, woodland walks and the new Adventure Cove.

Other Details: Guided walks at 1:00pm and 3:00pm, meet at the Walled Garden car park. Hanging basket demonstration at 12:00noon and 2:00pm. See NTS website for Castle and Estate details. Dogs welcome in the park however only assistance dogs have access to the walled garden and buildings.

Directions: On the A719 twelve miles south of Ayr, four miles west of Maybole. Bus 60 Stagecoach, Ayr/Girvan via Maidens to the entrance. One mile walk downhill from the stop to the Castle/Visitor Centre.

Disabled Access:
Full

Opening Times:
Monday 1 May
12:00pm - 4:00pm

Admission:
Normal NTS admission applies, guided walk £3.00 (including NTS members)

Charities:
Donation to SG Beneficiaries

GLENAPP CASTLE
Ballantrae, Girvan KA26 0NZ
Mr Paul Szkiler T: 01465 831212
E: gm@glenappcastle.com www.glenappcastle.com

The 36 acre grounds at Glenapp Castle are totally secluded and private. There are many rare and unusual plants and shrubs to be found, including magnificent specimen rhododendrons. Paths wander round the azalea pond, and through established woodland, leading to the wonderful walled garden with its 150 foot Victorian glasshouse. Fresh herbs and fruit from the garden are used every day in the castle kitchen. Much of the gardens were designed by Gertrude Jekyll (1843-1932) who was a world famous garden architect applying the principles of the arts and crafts movement and who worked in collaboration with Edwin Lutyens.

Directions: When approaching from the North take the A77 South. Pass through the village of Ballantrae, crossing the River Stinchar as you leave. Take the first turning on the right, 100 yards beyond the river (not sign posted). When approaching from the South take the A77 North and turn left 100 yards before the bridge over the River Stinchar at Ballantrae. The gates of the castle are located one mile along this road.

Disabled Access:
Partial

Opening Times:
By arrangement
17 March - 22 December

Admission:
£5.00 per person or complimentary if lunch or afternoon tea is purchased in the castle.

Charities:
Donation to SG Beneficiaries

AYRSHIRE

GOLF COURSE ROAD GARDENS
Girvan KA26 9HZ
The Gardeners of Golf Course Road

The Gardens of Golf Course Road face the Firth of Clyde and Ailsa Craig at one end, and fields and the Isle of Arran at the other. All the gardens suffer from wind and salt spray, however they have a great variety of herbaceous plants and shrubs. In general, the gardens to the front face the sea and therefore take the full brunt of the weather, with the rear gardens in some cases being walled and affording more protection. The soil conditions are light well drained and sandy.

Other Details: Entrance tickets, maps and stickers will be available at each garden. Girvan Golf Clubhouse is hosting the teas. The Clubhouse is in close proximity to the gardens.

Directions: From the north - on A77 turn right and follow signs for the Golf Course. From the south - on A77 come through Girvan, turn left at the lights, then first left and follow signs for the Golf Course.

Disabled Access:
Partial

Opening Times:
Sunday 9 July
1:00pm - 5:00pm

Admission:
£4.00, children under 12 free
for entrance to all gardens

Charities:
Macmillan Nurses receives
20%, Erskine Hospital
receives 20%, the net
remaining to SG Beneficiaries

HIGH FULWOOD
Stewarton KA3 5JZ
Mr and Mrs Crawford T: 01560 484705

One acre of mature garden, particularly fine in late spring with rhododendrons, azaleas, trillium, hellebore and other spring flowering plants and bulbs. There is also one acre of developing garden with herbaceous borders, vegetable garden and orchard at its best during July and August and two acres of native broadleaf woodland being created. No neat edges but lots to see at any time.

Directions: From Stewarton Cross take the B760 Old Glasgow Road for one mile - turn onto the road marked to Dunlop (from Glasgow this turning is half a mile past Kingsford. Continue for two miles and turn right at T junction. High Fulwood is a short distance on the right hand side.

Disabled Access:
None

Opening Times:
By arrangement
1 May - 31 August

Admission:
£4.00, accompanied children
free

Charities:
Hessilhead Wildlife Rescue
Trust receives 40%, the net
remaining to SG Beneficiaries

10 HOLMES FARM
Drybridge, by Irvine KA11 5BS
Mr Brian A Young T: 01294 311210
E: hfplants@live.co.uk   www.holmesfarmplants.com

Plantaholic's paradise! A plantsman's garden created by a confirmed plantaholic. An ever evolving selection of perennials, bulbs, alpines and shrubs. Meandering paths guide the eye through plantings predominantly herbaceous, with small trees and shrubs. The garden opening will hopefully be timed for peak bloom of some of the 400 iris in the garden. Some areas of the garden are currently undergoing a partial replant and redesign. There is a plant nursery with a wide selection of plant treasures from the garden and a gift shop and gallery too!

Directions: Holmes is the only farm between Drybridge and Dreghorn on B730.

Disabled Access:
None

Opening Times:
Saturday 10 June
& Sunday 11 June
1:00pm - 5:00pm

Admission:
£5.00, children under 12 free

Charities:
Plant Heritage receives 40%, the net remaining to SG Beneficiaries

11 NEW NETHERTHIRD COMMUNITY GARDEN
Craigens Road, Netherthird, Cumnock KA18 3AR
Netherthird Community Development Group
E: jamielor@aol.com

Netherthird Community Garden is an oasis of calm in the centre of the Ayrshire countryside. We have a lovely cottage garden, flower beds, vegetable beds, and wooden gazebos funded by Prince Charles' Foundation. There is also a beach, play area, vintage cafe, a new nature trail, fairy door hunt and lots more. Volunteers run the garden which is used by a wide range of community groups and all the children and nursery children from the adjacent Netherthird Primary during the week.

Other Details: Find us on Facebook by searching for Netherthird Community Development Group.

Directions: Driving south on the A76 Cumnock by-pass look for the roundabout signed B7083, take this exit which heads to Cumnock, after few hundred yards take right turn into Craigens Road, Netherthird Primary School is on the right. Parking available here, Community Garden nearby. Disabled parking at garden.

Disabled Access:
Partial

Opening Times:
Saturday 24 June
1:00pm - 5:00pm

Admission:
£3.00, accompanied children free

Charities:
Netherthird Community Development Group receives 40%, the net remaining to SG Beneficiaries

12 NEW THE GARDENS OF FENWICK
Fenwick KA3 6AJ
The Gardeners of Fenwick
E: kd581@aol.com

The attractive conservation village of Fenwick was home to the Fenwick Weavers' Society formed in 1761, possibly the world's first co-operative society. There will be gardens open in High, Low and new Fenwick - providing a wide variety, some new some old but all different. The gardens are full of a wide range of herbaceous and bedding plants, vegetables, trees and shrubs. Weather is a challenge in this area as we are quite high and exposed to south westerly winds and some frost!

Other Details: Tickets, maps & stickers at Fenwick Church Hall off Kirkton Road or 19 Waterslap off the S end of Main Road. Teas & plant stall at the Church Hall (also loos!).

Directions: From N: Take J7 off M77 Fenwick, turn left into village, right at roundabout and Kirkton Road is on left. From S: Take slip road off A77 Kilmarnock/Fenwick turn right for Fenwick (B7038) after two roundabouts enter village on to Main Road, turn right for Waterslap past Fenwick Deli.

Disabled Access:
Partial

Opening Times:
Saturday 1 July
12:30pm - 5:00pm

Admission:
£5.00 gives access to all gardens, children under 12 free

Charities:
Fenwick Church Hall Development Fund receives 40%, the net remaining to SG Beneficiaries

DUNBARTONSHIRE

Scotland's Gardens 2017 Guidebook is sponsored by **INVESTEC WEALTH & INVESTMENT**

District Organiser

Tricia Stewart	High Glenan, 24a Queen St, Helensburgh G84 9LG E:dunbartonshire@scotlandsgardens.org

Area Organisers

Joyce Goel	33 West Argyle Street, Helensburgh G84 8XR
Graham Greenwell	Avalon, Shore Rd, Mambeg Garelochhead G84 0EN
Rosemary Lang	Ardchapel, Shandon, Helensburgh G84 8NP

Treasurer

Kathleen Murray	7 The Birches, Shandon, Helensburgh G84 8HN

Gardens open on a specific date

Kilarden, Rosneath	Sunday 23 April	2:00pm	- 5:00pm
Ross Priory, Gartocharn	Sunday 21 May	2:00pm	- 5:00pm
Geilston Garden, Main Road, Cardross	Sunday 11 June	1:00pm	- 5:00pm
Dean Cottage with Ortona, Helensburgh	Sunday 20 August	2:00pm	- 5:00pm
Hill House Plant Sale, Helensburgh	Sunday 3 September	11:30am	- 4:00pm

Gardens open regularly

Glenarn, Glenarn Road, Rhu, Helensburgh	21 March - 21 September	Dawn	- Dusk

Plant sales

Hill House Plant Sale, Helensburgh	Sunday 3 September	11:30am	- 4:00pm

Key to symbols

	New in 2017		Homemade teas		Accommodation
	Teas		Dogs on a lead allowed		Plant stall
	Cream teas		Wheelchair access		Scottish Snowdrop Festival

GARDEN LOCATIONS
IN DUNBARTONSHIRE

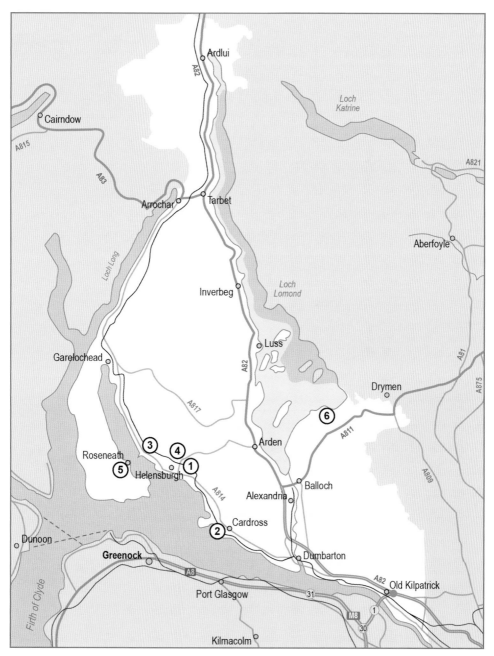

DUNBARTONSHIRE

1 NEW **DEAN COTTAGE WITH ORTONA**
Helensburgh G84 7ST
Mr & Mrs P Cairns and The Braid Family

Dean Cottage, 5 East Rossdhu Drive G84 7ST
The garden is only four years old - planted by the current owners. Twenty tons of gravel were laid over weed mat, designed to be low maintenance. There are lots of pots but also raised and herbaceous beds and a little pond. There is a small orchard, a fig tree, magnolias and soft fruit. Our speciality is hydrangeas - almost all grown from cuttings, likewise hebes and hostas. This is a wildlife friendly garden with birds, bees butterflies and a nocturnal hedgehog. The garden is disabled friendly, very level, but not suitable for wheelchairs as there is a lot of gravel.

Ortona, 41 Charlotte Street G84 7SE
About a third of an acre around a 1906 Leiper designed house. The east hedge was planted during wartime following removal of railings. The north and west side have leylandii hedges planted in 1971 to replace a mixed hawthorn hedge and is kept at its present height and width by one cut a year in late July. The terracing rockeries were constructed and enlarged since 1967 by the present owners, and all the trees and plants, some unusual, some delightlfully ordinary and floriferous, have been planted over the years.

Other Details: Homemade teas at Dean Cottage, plant stall at Ortona.

Directions: Head up Sinclair Street. Turn right into Abercromby Street and take first right into Charlotte Street. Ortona is 20 yards from the junction on the right. East Rossdhu Drive is on the right hand side of Sinclair Street as you head up the hill. Just before Helensburgh Upper Station.

Disabled Access:
Partial

Opening Times:
Sunday 20 August
2:00pm - 5:00pm

Admission:
£4.00, children under 12 free

Charities:
Macmillan Cancer Support receives 20%, Perennial receives 20%, the net remaining to SG Beneficiaries

---

2 **GEILSTON GARDEN**
Main Road, Cardross G82 5HD
The National Trust for Scotland T: 01389 849187
E: afarrell@nts.org.uk   www.nts.org.uk/Property/Geilston-Garden/

Geilston Garden has many attractive features including the walled garden with the herbaceous border providing summer colour, the tranquil woodland walks and a large working kitchen garden. This is the ideal season for viewing the Siberian iris in flower along the Geilston Burn and the Japanese azaleas. During the summer months, July to September, there is a range of fresh fruit and vegetables for sale from the large kitchen garden.

Other Details: There will be a plant stall selling Geilston-grown perennials together with some early produce.

Directions: On the A814, one mile from Cardross towards Helensburgh.

Disabled Access:
Partial

Opening Times:
Sunday 11 June
1:00pm - 5:00pm

Admission:
Normal NTS admission applies, children under 12 free

Charities:
Donation to SG Beneficiaries

GLENARN
Glenarn Road, Rhu, Helensburgh G84 8LL
Michael and Sue Thornley T: 01436 820493
E: masthome@btinternet.com www.gardens-of-argyll.co.uk

CELEBRATING 75 YEARS OF OPENING FOR CHARITY WITH SCOTLAND'S GARDENS!

Glenarn survives as a complete example of a ten acre garden which spans from 1850 to the present day. There are winding paths through glens under a canopy of oaks and limes, sunlit open spaces, a vegetable garden with beehives, and a rock garden with views over the Gareloch. It is famous for its collection of rare and tender rhododendrons but horticulturally there is much more besides.

Directions: On A814, two miles north of Helensburgh, up pier road. Cars to be left at the gate unless passengers are infirm.

Disabled Access:
Partial

Opening Times:
21 March - 21 September
Dawn - Dusk

Admission:
£5.00

Charities:
Donation to SG Beneficiaries

© Ray Cox

HILL HOUSE PLANT SALE
Helensburgh G84 9AJ
The National Trust for Scotland/SG T: 01436 673900
E: gsmith@nts.org.uk www.nts.org.uk/property/the-hill-house/

The plant sale is held in the garden of Hill House which has fine views over the Clyde estuary and is considered Charles Rennie Mackintosh's domestic masterpiece. The gardens continue to be restored to the patron's planting scheme with many features that reflect Mackintosh's design. The sale includes a wide selection of nursery grown perennials and locally grown trees, shrubs, herbaceous, alpine and house plants.

Other Details: Tearoom available inside Hill House.

Directions: Follow signs to The Hill House.

Disabled Access:
Full

Opening Times:
Plant sale
Sunday 3 September
11:30am - 4:00pm
garden also open.

Admission:
Free, but donations welcome
in aid of SG charities

Charities:
All proceeds to
SG Beneficiaries

DUNBARTONSHIRE

KILARDEN
Rosneath G84 0PU
Carol Rowe

CELEBRATING 25 YEARS OF OPENING FOR CHARITY WITH SCOTLAND'S GARDENS!

Sheltered hilly ten acre woodland with notable collection of species and hybrid rhododendrons gathered over a period of fifty years by the late Neil and Joyce Rutherford as seen on the *Beechgrove Garden*.

Other Details: Homemade teas served in the church hall. The church will be open and there will be organ music to enjoy.

Directions: A quarter of a mile from Rosneath off B833.

Disabled Access:
Partial

Opening Times:
Sunday 23 April
2:00pm - 5:00pm

Admission:
£3.00, accompanied children free

Charities:
Friends of St Modan's receives 40%, the net remaining to SG Beneficiaries

ROSS PRIORY
Gartocharn G83 8NL
University of Strathclyde

Mansion house with glorious views over Loch Lomond with adjoining garden. Wonderful selection of rhododendrons and azaleas which are the principal plants in the garden, with a varied selection of trees and shrubs throughout. Spectacular spring bulbs, border plantings of herbaceous perennials, shrubs and trees. Extensive walled garden with glasshouses, pergola and ornamental plantings. Play area and putting green beside house.

Other Details: Cream teas are served in the house. Please note that the house is not open to view. Dogs on leads welcome except in the walled garden. Plant stall in the walled garden.

Directions: Gartocharn one and a half miles off A811. The Balloch to Gartocharn bus leaves Balloch at 13:52.

Disabled Access:
Partial

Opening Times:
Sunday 21 May
2:00pm - 5:00pm

Admission:
£5.00, children under 12 free

Charities:
CHAS receives 20%
University of Strathclyde Ross Priory gardens receives 20%, the net remaining to SG Beneficiaries

GLASGOW & DISTRICT

Scotland's Gardens 2017 Guidebook is sponsored by **INVESTEC WEALTH & INVESTMENT**

District Organiser

Heidi Stone

0/1, 109 Hyndland Road G12 9JD
E: glasgow@scotlandsgardens.org

Area Organisers

Mandy Hamilton	Springfield, Colintravie, Argyll & Bute PA22 3AH
Audrey Mason	Hillend House, Drakemyre, Dalry KA24 5JR
Anne Murray	44 Gordon Road, Netherlee G44 3TW

Treasurer

Jim Murray

44 Gordon Road, Netherlee G44 3TW

Gardens open on a specific date

44 Gordon Road, Netherlee	Sunday 28 May	2:00pm	-	5:00pm
Partickhill Gardens East, Glasgow	Sunday 4 June	2:00pm	-	5:00pm
Greenbank Garden, Flenders Road, Clarkston	Saturday 10 June	11:00am	-	4:30pm
Greenbank Garden, Flenders Road, Clarkston	Sunday 11 June	11:00am	-	4:30pm
Kilsyth Gardens, Allanfauld Road, Kilsyth	Sunday 11 June	2:00pm	-	5:00pm
Partickhill Gardens West, Glasgow	Sunday 18 June	2:00pm	-	5:00pm
Strathbungo Gardens, March Street	Sunday 16 July	2:00pm	-	5:00pm
Horatio's Gardens, Queen Elizabeth Hospital	Sunday 30 July	2:00pm	-	5:00pm

Gardens open by arrangement

Kilsyth Gardens, Allanfauld Road, Kilsyth	1 April - 30 September	07743 110908

Key to symbols

	New in 2017		Homemade teas		Accommodation
	Teas		Dogs on a lead allowed		Plant stall
	Cream teas		Wheelchair access		Scottish Snowdrop Festival

GARDEN LOCATIONS IN GLASGOW & DISTRICT

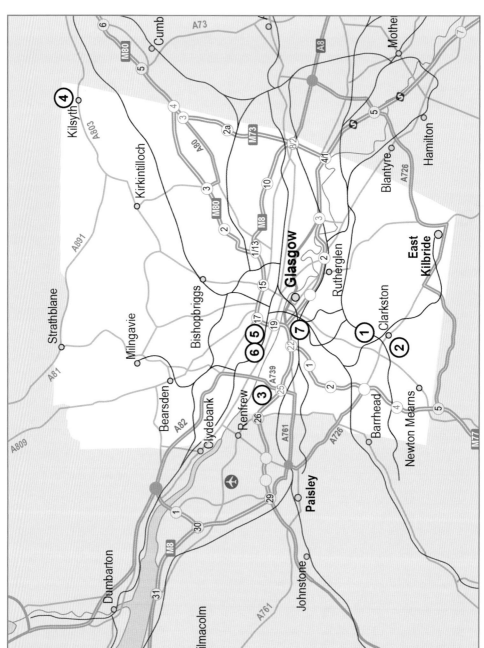

NEW 44 GORDON ROAD
Netherlee G44 3TW
Anne and Jim Murray

Mature town garden of approximately one acre containing large trees,
rhododendrons and magnolias, herbaceous borders with many unusual plants.
A Japanese garden and water feature, garden sculptures and large barbecue lodge.

Other Details: Plant stall.

Directions: B767 Clarkston Road past Linn Park gates, turn at Williamwood Drive
then second turning on the left.

Disabled Access:
Partial

Opening Times:
Sunday 28 May
2:00pm - 5:00pm

Admission:
£6.00 incl teas, children free

Charities:
Erskine Hospital receives
40%, the net remaining to
SG Beneficiaries

GREENBANK GARDEN
Flenders Road, Clarkston G76 8RB
The National Trust for Scotland T: 0141 616 5126
E: greenbankgarden@nts.org.uk www.nts.org.uk/property/greenbank-garden/

A unique walled garden with plants and designs of particular interest to suburban
gardeners. There is also a fountain and a woodland walk. Annual Schools'
Wheelbarrow Competition and Treasure Hunt. Come along and vote for your
favourite wheelbarrow, decorated by local school children. There will also be a
children's treasure hunt round the garden with prizes.

Other Details: National Plant Collection®: Bergenia cvs. & spp. All dogs on leads
are welcome in the woodland. Only assistance dogs are allowed in the garden. There
is no disabled access to Greenbank House but full access to the garden.

Directions: Flenders Road, off Mearns Road, Clarkston. Off M77 and A727, follow
signs for East Kilbride to Clarkston Toll. Busses - 4 and 4a, Glasgow to Newton
Mearns. Rail - Clarkston station 1¼ miles.

Disabled Access:
Full

Opening Times:
Saturday 10 June
& Sunday 11 June
11:00am - 4:30pm

Admission:
Normal NTS admission
applies, £2.00 per treasure
hunt ticket

Charities:
Donation to SG Beneficiaries

© NTS

GLASGOW & DISTRICT

NEW HORATIO'S GARDENS

Queen Elizabeth Hospital G51 4TF
Horatio's Gardens
E: sallie@horatiosgarden.org.uk   www.horatiosgarden.org.uk

Disabled Access:
Full

Opening Times:
Sunday 30 July
2:00pm - 5:00pm

Admission:
£6.00, including teas

Charities:
Horatio's Gardens receives
40%, the net remaining to
SG Beneficiaries

Opened in 2016, the garden was designed by award winning garden designer and RHS judge, James Alexander-Sinclair. It is for patients at The Scottish National Spinal Unit. The garden offers a haven for patients and their families during their long stay in hospital. The garden is divided into six distinct spaces, each with a different purpose and designed to stimulate different senses – sight, smell, touch and all providing a sense of wellbeing. The courtyard is at the heart of the unit with contemporary garden pods to enjoy the garden in all weathers. There is a woodland garden overlooked by the wards to encourage wildlife into the garden, a play garden for children who are visiting relatives and a physiotherapy garden which is functional as well as beautiful. Courtesy of Hartley Botanic, there is a greenhouse, which featured at Chelsea Flower Show and a Greenhouse Garden surrounded by raised beds and areas for horticultural therapy sessions. The scented garden is planted with carefully chosen shrubs growing around a stunning 'Coccolith' sculptures, donated by Brewin Dolphin.

Other Details: Charity chair Dr Olivia Chapple will give a talk about gardens and wellbeing at 3:00pm and guests will be guided on tours by Horatio's Garden volunteer team. Plants and the charity's merchandise will be on sale.

Directions: From the east or west of the city: On the M8 motorway to Junction 25, follow signs for the Clyde Tunnel (A739) for ¾ mile, then follow signs for the Queen Elizabeth Hospital. Turn left into Govan Road and the hospital is on the left. From north of the River Clyde: Go through the Clyde tunnel (A739) and follow signs for the hospital.

Dr Olivia Chapple and James Alexander Sinclair by the Medlar Tree donated by Scotland's Gardens' Trustees

4 KILSYTH GARDENS
Allanfauld Road, Kilsyth G65 9DE
Mr and Mrs A Patrick T: 07743 110908
E: alan.patrick3@googlemail.com

Aeolia: A third of an acre woodland garden developed since 1960 and designed to have something in flower every month of the year. The garden contains a large variety of mature specimen trees and shrubs, maples, primulas, hardy geraniums and herbaceous plants. Spring bulbs provide early colour and lilies and dahlias provide late season interest. There are a couple of small ponds for wildlife, two greenhouses and a fruit production area.The owners are members of the Scottish Rhododendron Society and have a collection of over 100 specimens, some grown from seed. Areas of the garden are often under development to provide something new to see and provide material for the extensive plant sale, which is all home-grown.

Blackmill: Across the road from Aeolia, Blackmill is a garden of two parts in that the Garrel Burn runs through the property. On one side is an acre of mature specimen trees, rhododendrons and shrubs on the site of an old water-powered sickle mill. There is an ornamental pond and a rock pool built into the remains of the mill building. On the other side a further two acres of woodland glen with paths along the Garrel Burn with views to many cascading waterfalls one with a seven metre drop. New is a large area of wildflowers alongside the burn, a Micro Hydro scheme is on view along with many different types of dry stone walls.

Other Details: Well stocked plant stall with a good variety of plants all home grown. WC available but, not suitable for disabled. There is a minimum of six visitors for the by arrangement openings.

Directions: Buses From Falkirk/Stirling to Cumbernauld then 147 to Kilsyth. 89 Glasgow to Kilsyth which has a stop at the bottom of Allanfauld Road a couple of minutes from the gardens. By train from Edinburgh/Glasgow/Stirling to Croy then take bus 147 to Kilsyth.

Disabled Access:
Partial

Opening Times:
Sunday
11 June 2:00pm - 5:00pm
Also by arrangement
1 April - 30 September
(minimum of 6 visitors)

Admission:
£6.50 includes entry to both gardens and homemade teas

Charities:
Strathcarron Hospice receives 40%, the net remaining to SG Beneficiaries

Colchicum at Aeolia

GLASGOW & DISTRICT

NEW PARTICKHILL GARDENS EAST
Glasgow G11 5AB
The Gardeners of Partickhill East T: 0141334 6277

52 Partickhill Road: this garden retains a beautiful herbaceous border. Of particular interest are the very old American Pillar roses, a double red lilac tree and *Campanula* 'Canterbury Bells' brought from Dundee in 1944. Roses and clematis adorn the front of the house. The garden is steeped in history having been with the same family since 1944.

9 Partickhill Court: across the lawn, framing a small pond, there are many shrubs and interesting specimen trees such as the Dawyck Beech, amelanchier, *Cornus contorversa* vareiagta, mulberry, crinodendron and *Eucryphia lucida*.

56 Partickhill Road: the principal garden is set to the rear of a Grade A listed villa built in 1841, lovingly restored by the current owners, retaining all the original features.The garden was designed and rebuilt in 2014, with three healthy trees being kept, a new vegetable garden set to the east of the plot and most of the previous rose bushes replanted surrounding the central lawn and pergola.

Other Details: Cream teas £3.00 at the local Bowling Club. Free maps at entrance.

Directions: From the M8 take junction 17 (A82) right at lights for Great Western Road, turn left onto Hyndland Road, right onto North Gardener Street and right onto Partickhill Road. Limited on street parking (free at time of publication).
Rail - To Hyndland Station (15 minute walk).
Bus - 44 & 15 to Cottiers, Hyndland Road (10 minute walk).

Disabled Access:
None

Opening Times:
Sunday 4 June
2:00pm - 5:00pm

Admission:
£5.00

Charities:
Homestart receives 20%, Adoption Scotland receives 20%, the net remaining to SG Beneficiaries

6 NEW PARTICKHILL GARDENS WEST

Glasgow G11 5AN
The Gardeners of Partickhill West

2 Banavie Road: a series of steps leads from a maritime themed patio area past a "hot" bed of red and orange plants, through a vegetable garden to a lawn and herbaceous border. The garden contains many fruit trees including step over apples, an old greengage and Victoria plum. The lawned front garden features many rhododendrons, azaleas, *Magnolia stellata* and a *Crinodendron hookerianum*.

69 Partickhill Road: this is a small Victorian urban garden, laid out in the 1860s. Its main feature is a terrace wall of that date. Unusually for this acid area it has been colonised by the lime loving Fairy Foxglove which loves the old lime mortar in the wall. The garden has significant steps.

64 Partickhill Road: the remains of Glasgow's out of town villas, some early town planning built round the West End's oldest house, believed to have been built in 1760. Some slopes and an attempt at rationalising the strange geometry results. Three versions of urban cottage gardens with not just the usual forsythia and rhododendrons. Mixed shrubberies with seasonal colour including livestock - or at least some half-way useful hens.

Other Details: Cream teas £3.00 at the local Bowling Club. Free maps at entrance.

Directions: From the M8 take junction 17 (A82) right at lights for Great Western Road, turn left onto Hyndland Road, right onto North Gardener Street and right onto Partickhill Road. Limited on street parking (free at time of publication).
Rail - To Hyndland Station (15 minute walk).
Bus - 44 & 15 to Cottiers, Hyndland Road (10 minute walk).

Disabled Access:
None

Opening Times:
Sunday 18 June
2:00pm - 5:00pm

Admission:
£5.00

Charities:
Scottish Refugee Council receives 20%, Marie Curie Scotland receives 20%, the net remaining to SG Beneficiaries

7 STRATHBUNGO GARDENS

March Street G41 2PX
The Gardeners of Strathbungo

An unexpected and interesting terrace cottage style garden in the city, showing what can be turned into a lovely colourful garden for all the occupants of the terrace to enjoy. Just across the road is the second garden, a verdant court garden taking full advantage of the limited light on offer. Streetscaping and inventive container planting are key features of these two distinct urban retreats.

Directions: From the south take the M74 to junction 1A Polmadie. Turn left onto Polmadie Road, then turn right at next traffic lights onto Calder Street. Proceed to Nithsdale Drive, then turn left into March Street, where ample parking can be found. From the M8, join the M74 and turn right into Polmadie Road at Junction 1A.

Disabled Access:
Partial

Opening Times:
Sunday 16 July
2:00pm - 5:00pm

Admission:
£5.00 including refreshments

Charities:
Association of Local Voluntary Organisations receives 20%, The Divine Innocence Trust receives 20%, the net remaining to SG Beneficiaries

ISLE OF ARRAN

Scotland's Gardens 2017 Guidebook is sponsored by **INVESTEC WEALTH & INVESTMENT**

District Organiser

Lavinia Gibbs	Dougarie, Isle of Arran KA27 8EB
	E: isle ofarran@scotlandsgardens.org

Treasurer

Lizzie Adam	Bayview, Pirnmill, Isle of Arran KA27 8HP

Gardens open on a specific date

Brodick Castle & Country Park, Brodick	Sunday 30 April	11:00am	- 4:00pm
Dougarie	Wednesday 5 July	2:00pm	- 5:00pm
Brodick Castle & Country Park, Brodick	Sunday 9 July	11:00am	- 4:00pm

Dougarie

Key to symbols

	New in 2017		Homemade teas		Accommodation
	Teas		Dogs on a lead allowed		Plant stall
	Cream teas		Wheelchair access		Scottish Snowdrop Festival

BRODICK CASTLE & COUNTRY PARK
Brodick, Isle of Arran KA27 8HY
The National Trust for Scotland T: 01770 302202
E: brodickcastle@nts.org.uk www.nts.org.uk

At any time of year the gardens are well worth a visit, especially in spring when the internationally acclaimed rhododendron collection bursts into full bloom. There are exotic plants and shrubs, a walled garden and a woodland garden to be enjoyed by garden enthusiasts, families and children. Venture out into the country park and discover wildflower meadows where Highland cows graze, woodland trails and tumbling waterfalls. There is something for everyone.

Other Details: National Plant Collection®: three rhododendron. Several Champion Trees. Dogs on leads welcome outside walled garden.
Tours with Head Gardener at 12noon and 2:00pm:
30 April - Focus on flowering rhododendrons.
9 July - Focus on summer colour and ongoing work in the garden.

Directions: Brodick two miles. Buses from Brodick Pier to Castle. Regular sailings from Ardrossan & Claonaig (Argyll). Info from Caledonian MacBrayne 01475 650100.

Disabled Access:
Partial

Opening Times:
Sunday 30 April
Sunday 9 July
11:00am - 4:00pm

Admission:
Normal NTS admission applies, donations welcomed for tours

Charities:
Donation to SG Beneficiaries

© NTS

DOUGARIE
KA27 8EB
Mr and Mrs S C Gibbs
E: office@dougarie.com

Most interesting terraced garden in castellated folly built in 1905 to celebrate the marriage of the 12th Duke of Hamilton's only child to the Duke of Montrose. Good selection of tender and rare shrubs and herbaceous border. Small woodland area with interesting trees including azara, abutilon, eucryphia, hoheria and nothofagus.

Other Details: Teas in 19th century boathouse. Plant stall.

Directions: Blackwaterfoot five miles. Regular ferry sailing from Ardrossan and Claonaig (Argyll). Info from Caledonian MacBrayne, Gourock 01475 650100.

Disabled Access:
None

Opening Times:
Wednesday 5 July
2:00pm - 5:00pm

Admission:
£3.50

Charities:
Pirnmill Village Association receives 40%, the net remaining to SG Beneficiaries

LANARKSHIRE

Scotland's Gardens 2017 Guidebook is sponsored by INVESTEC WEALTH & INVESTMENT

District Organisers

Nicky Eliott Lockhart   Stable House, Cleghorn Farm, Lanark ML11 7RW
Vanessa Rogers   1 Snowberry Field, Thankerton ML12 6RJ
                                     E: lanarkshire@scotlandsgardens.org

Area Organiser

Janis Sinclair   2 Meadowflatts Cottage, Meadowflatts Road,
                                     Thankerton ML12 6NF

Treasurer

Gordon Bell   9 Muirkirk Gardens, Strathaven ML10 6FS

Gardens open on a specific date

Cleghorn, Stable House, Cleghorn Farm	Sunday 5 March	2:00pm	- 4:00pm
The Quothquan Gardens, Biggar	Sunday 11 June	1:00pm	- 5:00pm
20 Smithycroft, Hamilton	Sunday 18 June	12:30pm	- 5:00pm
Dippoolbank Cottage, Carnwath	Sunday 25 June	2:00pm	- 6:00pm
Wellbutts, Elsrickle	Sunday 23 July	1:00pm	- 5:00pm
Dippoolbank Cottage, Carnwath	Sunday 30 July	2:00pm	- 6:00pm
The Walled Garden, Shieldhill	Sunday 6 August	2:00pm	- 5:00pm
Culter Allers, Culter Allers	Sunday 20 August	2:00pm	- 5:00pm

Gardens open by arrangement

Carmichael Mill, Hyndford Bridge	1 January - 31 December	01555 665880
St Patrick's House, Lanark	1 May - 30 June	01555 663800
The Scots Mining Company House, Leadhills	1 May - 30 September	01659 74235

Key to symbols

New in 2017		Homemade teas		Accommodation
Teas		Dogs on a lead allowed		Plant stall
Cream teas		Wheelchair access		Scottish Snowdrop Festival

GARDEN LOCATIONS IN LANARKSHIRE

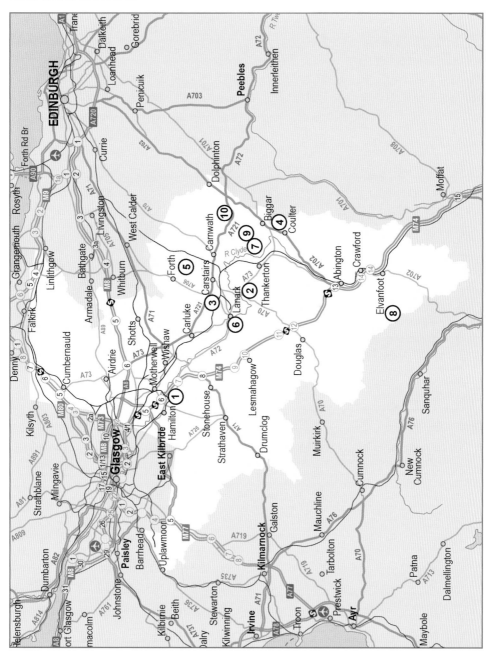

LANARKSHIRE

20 SMITHYCROFT
Hamilton ML3 7UL
Mr and Mrs R I Fionda
E: idafionda@hotmail.com

A plantswoman's award-winning garden which has developed into a mature oasis. Phormiums and clematis abound and there is a large range of unusual plants which only flourish in sheltered parts of Scotland.

Directions: Off the M74 at Junction 6. One mile on the A72. Garden is well signed.

Disabled Access:
Full

Opening Times:
Sunday 18 June
12:30pm - 5:00pm

Admission:
£4.00

Charities:
Mary's Meals receives 40%, the net remaining to SG Beneficiaries

CARMICHAEL MILL
Hyndford Bridge, Lanark ML11 8SJ
Chris, Ken and Gemma Fawell T: 01555 665880
E: ken.fawell@btinternet.com

Riverside gardens surrounding the only remaining workable water powered grain mill in Clydesdale. Diverse plant habitats from saturated to bone dry allow a vast range of trees and shrubs, both ornamental and fruit, with a vegetable garden. Herbaceous perennials, annuals and biennials with ornamental/wildlife pond complementing the landscape. Also, archaeological remains of medieval grain mills from circa 1200 and foundry, lint mill and threshing mill activity within the curtilage of the category B listed building.

Other Details: Admission includes entry to the mill which will be turning, river levels permitting.

Directions: Just off the A73 Lanark to Biggar road ½ mile east of the Hyndford Bridge.

Disabled Access:
Partial

Opening Times:
By arrangement on request

Admission:
£5.00, children over 12 £2.00

Charities:
Donation to SG Beneficiaries

CLEGHORN
Stable House, Cleghorn Farm, Lanark ML11 7RN
Mr and Mrs R Eliott Lockhart T: 01555 663792
E: eliottlockhart.nicky@gmail.com   www.cleghornestategardens.com

Eighteenth century garden which is gradually being renovated. Attractive walks through mature trees and shrubs. Recent replanting of a valley below a 12th century dam. Abundant snowdrops and visitors are welcome to return when the daffodils are in flower.

Directions: Cleghorn Farm is situated two miles north of Lanark on the A706.

Disabled Access:
Partial

Opening Times:
Sunday 5 March
2:00pm - 4:00pm
for the Snowdrop Festival

Admission:
By donation

Charities:
Marie Curie receives 40%, the net remaining to SG Beneficiaries

CULTER ALLERS
Culter Allers ML12 6PZ
The McCosh Family

The grounds of Culter Allers centre around its traditional one and a half acre walled garden, within which lies a productive vegetable and fruit garden with espalier fruit trees and berry bushes lining the walls. There are cut flower beds, an apple tree lined walk, a 'secret' herb garden, a wishing well and wide herbaceous borders revolving around an ornamental cherry and lawn. The policies of the house include winding woodland walks, fairy doors, a giant (small one) and an avenue of 125 year old lime trees leading to the village kirk.

Directions: In the village of Coulter, three miles south of Biggar on the A702.

Disabled Access:
Full

Opening Times:
Sunday 20 August
2:00pm - 5:00pm

Admission:
£4.00, accompanied children free

Charities:
Coulter Library Trust receives 40%, the net remaining to SG Beneficiaries

DIPPOOLBANK COTTAGE
Carnwath ML11 8LP
Mr Allan Brash

Artist's intriguing cottage garden. Vegetables are grown in small beds. There are herbs, fruit, flowers and a pond in woodland area with tree house and summer house. The fernery was completed in 2007. This is an organic garden which was mainly constructed with recycled materials.

Directions: Off B7016 between Forth and Carnwath near the village of Braehead on the Auchengray road. Approximately eight miles from Lanark. Well signposted.

Disabled Access:
None

Opening Times:
Sunday 25 June
Sunday 30 July
2:00pm - 6:00pm

Admission:
£4.00

Charities:
The Little Haven receives 40%, the net remaining to SG Beneficiaries

ST PATRICK'S HOUSE
Lanark ML11 9EG
Mr and Mrs Peter Sanders T: 01555 663800
E: peterjeansanders@gmail.com

A May or June visit to St Patrick's House garden will be rewarded with a stunning display of rhododendrons, azaleas, heathers and shrubs. Created over a fifty year period, the grounds of this five acre garden slope down to the River Clyde. Natural springs have been harnessed to create water features, a large contemporary pond with an arbour begs you to sit a while. Paths wend between beds of varied plantings and perennials, rockeries, woodland plants all add to the magic of this unexpected gem.

Other Details: Steep slopes in places, sturdy shoes recommended if wet.

Directions: A73 into Lanark, after Police Station turn right into Friar's Lane. At bottom of hill turn right onto St Patrick Road. Garden 0.25 mile on the left. A743 down Lanark High Street turn left onto Friar's Lane.

Disabled Access:
None

Opening Times:
By arrangement
1 May - 30 June

Admission:
£4.00

Charities:
Lanark Development Trust (Castlebank Regeneration Fund) receives 40%, the net remaining to SG Beneficiaries

NEW THE QUOTHQUAN GARDENS
Biggar ML12 6ND
The Gardeners of Quothquan Village

Lilyvale: Taking the twists and turns along the narrow paths of this intimate plantsman's gardens is rewarded with a large collection of unusual hardy perennials, alpines and mature shrubs. There is a woodland area with rhododendrons and azaleas, a fruit orchard and a vegetable garden to explore.

Curling Pond House: The garden is dominated by a large stream fed pond with its resident Moorhens. The banks are planted with colourful late spring flowers, Primula species abound. The garden features the former Shieldhill Castle curling rink, a pergola walk, specimen trees and shrubs and a sweeping perennial border.

Other Details: Children welcome. Dogs on a lead only allowed in Curling Pond field.

Directions: Quothquan is between A73 Lanark-Abington and the B7016 Carnwath-Biggar. The gardens are at opposite ends of the village but will be well signposted.

Disabled Access:
Partial

Opening Times:
Sunday 11 June
1:00pm - 5:00pm

Admission:
£4.00, accompanied children free

Charities:
Prostate Cancer UK receives 20%, Dumfriesshire and Cumbria Greyhound Rescue receives 20%, the net remaining to SG Beneficiaries

THE SCOTS MINING COMPANY HOUSE
Leadhills, Biggar ML12 6XS
Charlie and Greta Clark T: 01659 74235
E: clarkc@sky.com

The site is about 400 metres above sea level, which is high for a cultivated garden. The surrounding landscape is open moorland with sheep grazing. The garden is largely enclosed by dense planting, but the various walks allow views through the trees into the surrounding countryside. Historic Scotland in its register of "Gardens and designed landscapes" describes the garden as "An outstanding example of a virtually unaltered, small, 18th century garden layout connected with James Stirling, the developer of the profitable Leadhills mining enterprise, and possibly William Adam." Say goodbye to spring walking among what must be some of the last daffodils of the year.

Other Details: Homemade teas available by prior request.

Directions: On Main Street, Leadhills (B797) six miles from the M74 Junction 13 (Abington). Gate is in Station Road.

Disabled Access:
Partial

Opening Times:
By arrangement
1 May - 30 September

Admission:
£3.00

Charities:
Scots Mining Company Trust receives 40%, the net remaining to SG Beneficiaries

THE WALLED GARDEN, SHIELDHILL
Quothquan, Biggar ML12 6NA
Mr and Mrs Gordon T: 01899 221961

This 200 year old walled garden has been completely redesigned and planted in 2014/15. It has been designed as a contemporary take on a traditional walled garden and incorporates a modern rill, a lily tank, perennial borders, a sunken sitting area, raised beds for fruit and vegetable and a greenhouse leading to the original potting shed. The walled garden is surrounded by a mature woodland walk including a giant sequoia and a wildlife pond.

Directions: Turn off the B7016 between Biggar and Carnwath towards Quothquan. After about a mile, look for signs and turn right at the lodge.

Disabled Access:
Partial

Opening Times:
Sunday 6 August
2:00pm - 5:00pm

Admission:
£4.00

Charities:
Médecins Sans Frontières receives 40%, the net remaining to SG Beneficiaries

WELLBUTTS
Elsrickle, by Biggar ML12 6QZ
Mr and Mrs N Slater

At 960 feet the garden was started in 2000 from a two acre bare site around a renovated croft cottage. In an exposed and elevated position, the hedge and shrub planting gives some protection for the many new and now established varied herbaceous beds, whilst retaining the open views. There are two large natural ponds with ducks, a rill fed 'boggery', greenhouses, fish pond and covered areas for our fine collection of summer begonia baskets.

Other Details: Strawberry cream teas will be served in the garden using our collection of vintage china. No dogs please.

Directions: Parking on the main road (A721) then walk to the garden (approximately 200 yards). If available the adjacent field may be used to park, see signs.

Disabled Access:
None

Opening Times:
Sunday 23 July
1:00pm - 5:00pm

Admission:
£4.00

Charities:
Triple Negative Breast Cancer Research (Anne Konishi Memorial Fund) receives 40%, the net remaining to SG Beneficiaries

RENFREWSHIRE

Scotland's Gardens 2017 Guidebook is sponsored by **INVESTEC WEALTH & INVESTMENT**

District Organisers

Rosemary Leslie	High Mathernock Farm, Auchentiber Road, Kilmacolm PA13 4SP T: 01505 874032
Alexandra MacMillan	Langside Farm, Kilmacolm, Inverclyde PA13 4SA T: 01475 540423 E: renfrewshire@scotlandsgardens.org

Area Organisers

Helen Hunter	2 Bay Street, Fairlie, North Ayrshire KA29 0AL
Barbara McLean	49 Middlepenny Rd, Langbank, Inverclyde PA14 6XE

Treasurer

Jean Gillan	Bogriggs Cottage, Carlung, West Kilbride KA23 9PS

Gardens open on a specific date

Highwood, Kilmacolm	Sunday 14 May	2:00pm	- 5:00pm
Bridge of Weir Road Gardens, Kilmacolm	Sunday 21 May	2:00pm	- 5:00pm
Craig Hepburn Memorial Garden, Linwood	Sunday 11 June	2:00pm	- 5:00pm
Newmills Cottage, Nr Lochwinnoch/Newton of Belltrees	Sunday 25 June	2:00pm	- 5:00pm
Duchal, Kilmacolm	Saturday 15 July	2:00pm	- 5:00pm
St Vincents Hospice Garden, Howwood	Saturday 16 September	11:00am	- 3:00pm

Plant sales

Kilmacolm Plant Sale, Outside Kilmacolm Library	Saturday 22 April	10:00am	- 12:00pm
Kilmacolm Plant Sale, Outside Kilmacolm Library	Saturday 9 September	10:00am	- 12:00pm

Key to symbols

	New in 2017		Homemade teas		Accommodation
	Teas		Dogs on a lead allowed		Plant stall
	Cream teas		Wheelchair access		Scottish Snowdrop Festival

GARDEN LOCATIONS
IN RENFREWSHIRE

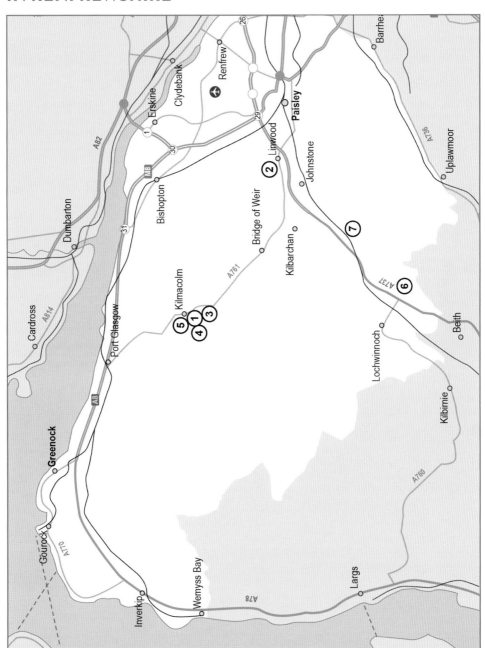

RENFREWSHIRE

1 **NEW BRIDGE OF WEIR ROAD GARDENS**
Kilmacolm PA13 4NN
Bridge of Weir Road Gardens

Beechwood: The garden was redesigned in 2004 to provide a sweeping lawn around the side of the house suitable for family use. The borders are well stocked and offer an interesting variety of shrubs and plants, including a eucalyptus tree.
Larchmont: Within the walled gardens are mature trees, rhododendrons and azaleas, wide lawns and herbaceous borders and a fine example of a late Victorian glasshouse
Shieldhall: For many years part of St Columba's School, returning to residential use in the 1990s. Since then the tarmac playground has been transformed into a well-stocked garden with mature shrubs and herbaceous plants, providing colour and interest throughout the year. The garden is on two levels with a meandering path leading you through both.

Directions: The gardens are within 50 yards of each other on the Bridge of Weir Road in the middle of Kilmacolm. Signage will be up on the day.

Disabled Access:
Partial

Opening Times:
Sunday 21 May
2:00pm - 5:00pm

Admission:
£4.00

Charities:
Ardgowan Hospice receives
40%, the net remaining to
SG Beneficiaries

---

2 **NEW CRAIG HEPBURN MEMORIAL GARDEN**
Stirling Drive, Linwood, Paisley PA3 3NB
Linwood High School
E: lesleyhinde@yahoo.com facebook.com/welovegardening14/

The Craig Hepburn Memorial Garden and Outdoor Learning Centre is located in Linwood High School. Our original garden with an outdoor classroom has been expanded to include community raised beds, an orchard, greenhouse, and presentation area. We work with all years in the school reconnecting them to the natural world whether it is through growing in our organic garden, encouraging biodiversity or learning about sustainability.

Directions: Exit M8 at St James Interchange and take A737. Take exit for Linwood onto A761, follow to Clippens Road and then Stirling Drive.

Disabled Access:
Partial

Opening Times:
Sunday 11 June
2:00pm - 5:00pm

Admission:
£3.50

Charities:
Accord Hospice receives
40%, the net remaining to
SG Beneficiaries

---

3 **DUCHAL**
Kilmacolm PA13 4RS
Lord Maclay

Eighteenth century walled garden particularly well planted and maintained, entered by footbridge over the Greenwater. Species trees, hollies, old fashioned roses, shrubs and herbaceous borders with fruit orchards and vegetable garden. Also in the garden are azaleas and a lily pond.

Directions: On the B788 one mile from Kilmacolm (this road links B786 Lochwinnoch Road and A761 Bridge of Weir Road). Greenock/Glasgow bus via Bridge of Weir. Knapps Loch stop is a ¼ mile from garden.

Disabled Access:
Partial

Opening Times:
Saturday 15 July
2:00pm - 5:00pm

Admission:
£5.00

Charities:
Ardgowan Hospice receives
40%, the net remaining to
SG Beneficiaries

HIGHWOOD
Kilmacolm PA13 4TA
Jill Morgan

Woodland walk around 50 acres of beautiful native bluebells in a delightful setting bordering the Green Water river with tumbling waterfalls. Stout waterproof footwear is essential as paths can be muddy. Dogs welcome on a lead. Fantastic opportunities for lovers of wild flowers and photography.

Other Details: Delicious home baked tea and plant sale. Fun duck race on the river for families at 3:30pm with rubber ducks available for purchase on the day.

Directions: Take B786 Lochwinnoch Road out of Kilmacolm and continue for approximately two miles then follow SG signs. From Lochwinnoch take B786 Kilmacolm road for approximately six miles, then follow SG signs.

Disabled Access:
Partial

Opening Times:
Sunday 14 May
2:00pm - 5:00pm
for Bluebells

Admission:
Donations welcome

Charities:
Orkidstudio receives 40%, the net remaining to SG Beneficiaries

KILMACOLM PLANT SALE
Outside Kilmacolm Library, Lochwinnoch Road, Kilmacolm PA13 4EL
Scotland's Gardens - Renfrewshire

Spring and end of season plant sales in the centre of Kilmacolm.

Directions: The plant sale will be held at the Cross outside the Library and Cargill Centre.

Disabled Access:
Full

Opening Times:
Plant sales
Saturday 22 April
Saturday 9 September
10:00am - 12:00pm

Admission:
Free, donations welcome

Charities:
Parklea "Branching Out" receives 40%, the net remaining to SG Beneficiaries

RENFREWSHIRE

6 **NEWMILLS COTTAGE**
Nr Lochwinnoch/Newton of Belltrees PA12 4JR
Patricia Allan

Surviving mill in a series of five built in 1864. Well established colourful garden on different levels sloping down to the burn. The garden is divided into different areas with pots and hanging baskets filling areas which cannot be planted. There is also a pond. Steps down the garden are steep but it can be accessed from a gate on the road if needed and can still be seen from the lower level. The garden has been extended since first opening in 2014 and Patricia has agreed to open once again despite the very wet opening in 2016!

Directions: Approach from Roadhead roundabout near Lochwinnoch (junction off A760/A737). Take turning by "Powerdoors" onto Auchengrange Hill. At T junction turn left onto Belltrees Road. Drive for 20 seconds then turn right. Single track road, garden on left after 1 mile.

Disabled Access:
Partial

Opening Times:
Sunday 25 June
2:00pm - 5:00pm

Admission:
£3.50, children under 16 free

Charities:
Kilbarchan Old Library receives 40%, the net remaining to SG Beneficiaries

7 NEW **ST VINCENT'S HOSPICE GARDEN**
Midton Road, Howwood PA9 1AF
St Vincent's Hospice Garden
E: katrina.vine@svh.co.uk

Created in 2015, this is a fully accessible garden which has been designed to be a tranquil and restful space. With a large wildlife pond and feature drystone walling, the garden has several seating areas - one known as "rest-a-while". There are different planting areas, including large herbaceous beds, raised sensory bed, memorial rose border underplanted with white heathers and a wildflower border with a pond teeming with frogs, newts and dragonflies.

Other Details: The Barn Tea Room will be open for teas, coffees, home baking and light refreshment with all proceeds going towards the running costs of the Hospice.

Directions: St Vincent's Hospice is signposted from the B787 between Johnstone and Howwood.

Disabled Access:
Full

Opening Times:
Saturday 16 September
11:00am - 3:00pm

Admission:
£3.00 and any additional donations welcome

Charities:
St Vincent's Hospice receives 40%, the net remaining to SG Beneficiaries

STIRLINGSHIRE

Scotland's Gardens 2017 Guidebook is sponsored by **INVESTEC WEALTH & INVESTMENT**

District Organiser

Mandy Readman	Hutchison Farm, Auchinlay Road, Dunblane FK15 9JS
	E: stirlingshire@scotlandsgardens.org

Area Organisers

Gillie Drapper	Kilewnan Cottage, Main Street, Fintry G63 0YH
Tracey Fisher	West Corner, The Cross, Kippen FK8 3DS
Maurie Jessett	The Walled Garden, Lanrick, Doune FK16 6HJ
Rosemary Leckie	Auchengarroch, 16 Chalton Road, Bridge of Allan FK9 4DX
Iain Morrison	Clifford House, Balkerach Street, Doune FK16 6DE
Fiona Wallace	Nether Spittalton, Coldoch, Blairdrummond FK9 4XD
Gillie Welstead	Ballingrew, Thornhill FK8 3QD
Clare Young	Merlo, Buchanan Castle Estate, Drymen G63 0HX

Treasurer

Rachel Nunn	9 Cauldhame Crescent, Cambusbarron FK7 9NH

Gardens open on a specific date

Kilbryde Castle, Dunblane	Sunday 26 February	1:30pm	-	4:30pm
Gargunnock House Garden, Gargunnock	Sunday 23 April	2:00pm	-	5:00pm
The Pass House, Kilmahog	Sunday 30 April	2:00pm	-	5:00pm
Milseybank, Bridge of Allan	Sunday 14 May	2:00pm	-	5:00pm
Dun Dubh, Aberfoyle	Sunday 21 May	2:00pm	-	5:00pm
Bridge of Allan Gardens, Bridge of Allan	Sunday 28 May	1:00pm	-	5:00pm
Shrubhill, Dunblane	Sunday 4 June	2:00pm	-	5:00pm
Thorntree, Arnprior	Sunday 25 June	2:00pm	-	5:00pm
The Mill House, Fintry	Saturday 10 June - Sunday 18 June (inclusive)	10:00am	-	5:00pm
Moon Cottage, Greenyards	Sunday 9 July	2:00pm	-	5:00pm
The Tors, Falkirk	Sunday 30 July	2:00pm	-	5:30pm
Little Carbeth, Killearn	Sunday 6 August	2:00pm	-	5:00pm
Kilbryde Castle, Dunblane	Sunday 17 September	2:00pm	-	5:00pm
Festive Floral Evening, Camphill Blair Drummond Trust	Thursday 23 November	7:00pm		

STIRLINGSHIRE

Gardens open regularly

Gargunnock House Garden, Gargunnock	5 February - 12 March (daily) & 13 March - 30 September (Mondays - Fridays)	11:00am - 3:30pm

Gardens open by arrangement

Arndean, by Dollar	15 May - 18 June	01259 743525
Duntreath Castle, Blanefield	1 February - 30 November	01360 770215
Gardener's Cottage Walled Garden, Killearn	1 May - 31 October	01360 551682
Kilbryde Castle, Dunblane	1 April - 30 September	01786 824897
Milseybank, Bridge of Allan	1 April - 31 May	01786 833866
Rowberrow, Dollar	1 February - 31 December	01259 742584
The Tors, Falkirk	1 May - 30 September	01324 620877
Thorntree, Arnprior	1 April - 15 October	01786 870710

Plant sales

Gargunnock House Garden Plant Sale, Gargunnock	Sunday 23 April	2:00pm - 5:00pm

Key to symbols

New in 2017	Homemade teas	Accommodation
Teas	Dogs on a lead allowed	Plant stall
Cream teas	Wheelchair access	Scottish Snowdrop Festival

GARDEN LOCATIONS IN STIRLINGSHIRE

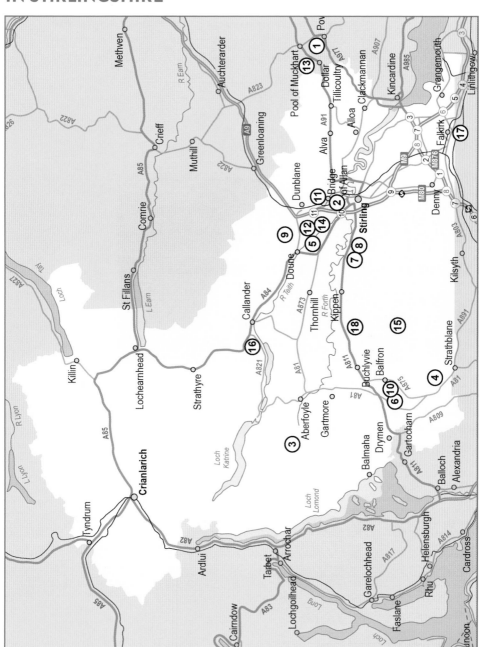

STIRLINGSHIRE

ARNDEAN
by Dollar FK14 7NH
Johnny and Katie Stewart T: 01259 743525
E: johnny@arndean.co.uk

This is a beautiful mature garden extending to 15 acres including the woodland walk. There is a formal herbaceous part, a small vegetable garden and orchard. In addition, there are flowering shrubs, abundant and striking rhododendrons and azaleas as well as many fine specimen trees. There is a tree house for children.

Other Details: Groups welcome.

Directions: Arndean is well sign posted off the A977.

Disabled Access:
Full

Opening Times:
By arrangement
15 May - 18 June

Admission:
£5.00, accompanied children free

Charities:
Marie Curie Cancer Care receives 40%, the net remaining to SG Beneficiaries

BRIDGE OF ALLAN GARDENS
Bridge of Allan FK9 4AT
The Bridge of Allan Gardeners
E: r.leckie44@btinternet.com

This year, there are five NEW gardens, as well as four who have opened in the past. Four are small gardens, same size of plot, but very different designs, all with varied planting. A new large garden has many species of rhododendrons, also an old Victorian well. Other larger gardens include a Victorian garden, with beautiful trees and shrubs, a vegetable garden and pond. A semi terraced garden divided into separate rooms with wild spaces, water features and sculptures. Finally, a Japanese inspired garden with a variety of acers, shrubs, specimen trees and vegetable garden.

Other Details: Tickets and maps available from all gardens. The addresses will be on the website nearer the time. Teas will be served in St Saviour's Church Hall, Keir Street from 1:30pm till 5:00pm.

Directions: Signposted from the village.

Disabled Access:
Partial

Opening Times:
Sunday 28 May
1:00pm - 5:00pm

Admission:
£5.00, accompanied children free

Charities:
St Saviour's Church receives 20%, Artlink Central receives 20%, the net remaining to SG Beneficiaries

DUN DUBH
Kinlochard Road, Aberfoyle FK8 3TJ
Callum Pirnie, Head Gardener T: 01877 382698
E: callumpirnie@gmail.com

A late Victorian garden of six acres undergoing restoration and development. It is set on a series of terraces and slopes which run down to the shores of Loch Ard with superb views west to Ben Lomond framed by stands of mature conifers. There is an enclosed, colour themed formal garden laid out on three terraces and a new Victorian style glasshouse overlooking a terraced kitchen and fruit garden. The formal paved terrace at the front of the house overlooks a newly developed rock garden and crag while the lower walk running from the boat house to the main lawn gives views across the Loch. A developing woodland garden leads on to a formal late summer herbaceous border and terraced heather garden. Featured on the *Beechgrove Garden* and *Scottish Field* in 2014.

Other Details: Car parking is limited to disabled badge holders and helpers, but there will be free transport to and from Aberfoyle car park throughout the afternoon. Parking on the road outside Dun Dubh is dangerous and prohibited. Guide Dogs only. **PLEASE NOTE:** It is the same day as the Stirling Marathon, please look out for diversions and heavy traffic in Stirling.

Directions: Follow the signs to the car park in the centre of Aberfoyle, look for the Garden Open signs. The minibus will leave from the bus stop beside the Tourist Office. Turn around time about 15 minutes.

Disabled Access:
Partial

Opening Times:
Sunday 21 May
2:00pm - 5:00pm

Admission:
£5.00, accompanied children free

Charities:
Help for Heroes receives 40%, the net remaining to SG Beneficiaries

DUNTREATH CASTLE
Blanefield G63 9AJ
Sir Archibald & Lady Edmonstone T: 01360 770215
E: juliet@edmonstone.com www.duntreathcastle.co.uk

Extensive gardens with mature and new plantings. Ornamental landscaped lake and bog garden. Sweeping lawns below formal fountain and rose parterre with herbaceous border leading up to an attractive waterfall garden with shrubs and spring plantings. Stunning display of snowdrops along the side of former drive. There is a woodland walk and a 15th century keep and chapel.

Other Details: Groups welcome.

Directions: A81 north of Glasgow between Blanefield and Killearn.

Disabled Access:
Full

Opening Times:
By arrangement
1 February - 30 November

Admission:
£4.00, accompanied children free

Charities:
All proceeds to
SG Beneficiaries

STIRLINGSHIRE

FESTIVE FLORAL EVENING
Camphill Blair Drummond Trust, Cuthil Brae, Stirling FK9 4UT
Blair Drummond Trust Ltd

By kind permission of Camphill Blair Drummond Trust, Stirlingshire District will be holding a festive floral evening in the drawing room of Blair Drummond House. A demonstration of Christmas floral decorations by Fiona Wallace of Bramble & Thyme and a selection of bespoke stalls selling something that "little bit different" i.e. books from local authors, handmade jewellery, paintings.

Other Details: Wine and Canapes will be served.
Tickets can be purchased from:
Mandy Readman E: mandy@tebhan.com T: 01786 821102
and Iain Morrison E: iainmorrison9@gmail.com T: 01786 841007

Directions: Six miles from the City of Stirling and three miles from the historic village of Doune. It will be signed from the A84 via Cuthil Brae.

Disabled Access:
Partial

Opening Times:
Thursday 23 November
7:00pm

Admission:
£20.00

Charities:
Camphill Blair Drummond
receives 40%, the net
remaining to SG Beneficiaries

GARDENER'S COTTAGE WALLED GARDEN
Ballochruin Road, Killearn, G63 9QB
Derek and Morna Knottenbelt T: 01360 551682
E: mornaknottenbelt@hotmail.com

The Walled Garden, acquired in 2013 by the present owners, has been planted with extensive herbaceous borders, box hedging, roses and many unusual plants. There is a White garden, an orchard, vegetable area, a long shrub border with primulas and gentians and alpine border with meconopsis. The Victorian Fernery, previously restored, has peach and pear trees, vegetables and a collection of salvias. There is a long season of interest with peonies, primulas and bulbs in spring to roses and herbaceous flowers in summer followed by substantial autumn flowers with rudbeckias, Michaelmas daisies and aconitums. Below the house a small area of mature conifers, rhododendrons and collection of ferns. There are fine views of the Campsie Hills and the garden is surrounded by mature conifers of the Designed Landscape of Carbeth.

Other Details: This garden won the Hidden Gardens of Killearn trophy in 2014 and 2015. Garden groups welcome.

Directions: From Stirling take the A811, turning to Balfron A875, through the village towards Killearn, over the bridge and take the next turning to the right signposted Balfron Station. The entrance to the drive is the second on the left. From Milngavie A81, drive through Killearn and after ½ mile take the next turning to the left signposted Balfron Station. Avoid Satnav.

Disabled Access:
Partial

Opening Times:
By arrangement
1 May - 31 October

Admission:
£5.00 includes garden tour
and tea/coffee and scones

Charities:
British Horse Society
Scotland receives 40%,
the net remaining to
SG Beneficiaries

GARGUNNOCK HOUSE GARDEN
Gargunnock FK8 3AZ
The Gargunnock Trustees T: 01786 860392
E: gargunnockgardens@btinternet.com

Large mature garden just five miles from Stirling, with Walled Garden, well established house garden, woodland walks with species and hybrid rhododendrons, massed plantings of azaleas and wonderful specimen trees. Snowdrops in February/March, over 40 varieties of daffodils in bloom in April and the glorious display of Azaleas and Rhododendrons in May. Later in the year it is a delight to see the late season colours from the many wonderful trees along the drive to the house in Autumn. The three acre Walled Garden is being fully restored with perennial borders, cut flower beds, kitchen garden with newly planted orchard. We have picnic benches and seating in the Walled Garden area. New arboretum of specialist trees was planted in spring 2016.

Other Details: Plant Stalls are in the Walled Garden. The garden will also be open on 23 April for details see entry for **Gargunnock House Garden Plant Sale.**

Directions: Five miles west of Stirling on A811, follow the Scotland's Gardens signs.

Disabled Access:
Full

Opening Times:
5 February - 12 March daily for the Snowdrop Festival & 13 Mar - 30 Sept Mons - Fris 11:00am - 3:30pm

Admission:
£4.00, accomp children free, cash in honesty box at car park

Charities:
Children's Hospice Assoc. and Gargunnock Community Trust both receive 20%, the net remaining to SG Beneficiaries

GARGUNNOCK HOUSE GARDEN PLANT SALE
Gargunnock FK8 3AZ
The Gargunnock Trustees T: 01786 860392
E: gargunnockgardens@btinternet.com

Major Plant Sale with a wonderful selection of azaleas, rhododendrons, many other shrubs, bulbs and herbaceous plants.

Garden will also be open, see entry for Gargunnock House Garden above.

Other Details: Homemade teas served in Gargunnock House.

Directions: Five miles west of Stirling on A811.

Disabled Access:
Full

Opening Times:
Plant sale Sunday 23 April 2:00pm - 5:00pm garden also open

Admission:
£5.00, accompanied children free

Charities:
Children's Hospice Association receives 20%, Gargunnock Community Centre receives 20%, the net remaining to SG Beneficiaries

KILBRYDE CASTLE
Dunblane FK15 9NF
Sir James and Lady Campbell T: 01786 824897
E: kilbryde1@aol.com www.kilbrydecastle.com

The Kilbryde Castle gardens cover some 12 acres and are situated above the Ardoch Burn and below the castle. The gardens are split into three parts: formal, woodland and wild. Natural planting (azaleas, rhododendrons, camellias and magnolias) is found in the woodland garden. There are glorious spring bulbs and autumn colour provided by clematis and acers. There will be some new plantings for additional late summer/autumn colour for 2017. Featured in *Scotland on Sunday* in September 2016.

Other Details: Cream teas on both 26 February and 17 September.

Directions: Three miles from Dunblane and Doune, off the A820 between Dunblane and Doune. On Scotland's Gardens' open days the garden is signposted from the A820.

Disabled Access:
Partial

Opening Times:
Sun 26 Feb 1:30pm - 4:30pm for the Snowdrop Festival Sun 17 Sep 2:00pm - 5:00pm Also by arrangement 1 April - 30 September

Admission:
Feb: £4.00 Sept: £5.00 accompanied children free

Charities:
Leighton Library receives 40%, the net remaining to SG Beneficiaries

STIRLINGSHIRE

10 NEW LITTLE CARBETH
Drumtian Road, Killearn G63 9QB
Ian and Agnes Bowie T: 01360 551595
E: little.carbeth@btinternet.com

A young garden with many interesting design features. Where there was once a field, sweeping lawns now fall down to a wildlife lochan with many varieties of primulas, unusual grasses and other water plants. There is also a wildflower meadow. A formal parterre by the house and many shrubs and specimen trees. A small but productive vegetable and herb garden and new orchard. There are lovely views all round the gardens.

Other Details: Parking will be signed a short distance from the house and teas will be in the garage area. There will also be a plant stall.

Directions: Turn down Drumtian Road in Killearn and Little Carbeth is about ½ mile on the left.

Disabled Access:
Full

Opening Times:
Sunday 6 August
2:00pm - 5:00pm

Admission:
£5.00, accompanied children free

Charities:
The Preshal Trust receives 40%, the net remaining to SG Beneficiaries

---

11 MILSEYBANK
Bridge of Allan FK9 4NB
Murray and Sheila Airth T: 01786 833866
E: smairth@hotmail.com

Wonderful and interesting sloping garden with outstanding views, terraced for ease of access. Woodland with bluebells, rhododendrons, magnolias and camellias, and many other unusual plants, including a big variety of meconopsis, and water features. This is a true plantsman's garden with several quiet corners to sit, admire and reflect. A garden to inspire you and give you ideas to take home.

Other Details: Teas at Lecropt Kirk Hall on 14 May only. Plant stall at Milseybank. Disabled parking only at the house, otherwise at the Kirk Hall or the Station car park.

Directions: Situated on A9, one mile from junction 11, M9 and ¼ mile from Bridge of Allan. Milseybank is at the top of the lane at Lecropt Nursery, 250 yards from Bridge of Allan train station.

Disabled Access:
Full

Opening Times:
Sunday 14 May
2:00pm - 5:00pm
Also by arrangement
1 April - 31 May

Admission:
£4.00, accompanied children free

Charities:
Strathcarron Hospice receives 40%, the net remaining to SG Beneficiaries

---

12 MOON COTTAGE
Greenyards, Dunblane FK15 9NX
Jeanie and David Ashton
E: macashton@btinternet.com

Moon Cottage has a fairly young garden. It has grown up over the past ten to fifteen years on the edge of farm land adjacent to a wood plantation. There are herbaceous beds, a wonderful variety of shrubs and trees, a vegetable patch, fruit trees and a pond. There is also a folly!

Other Details: The grass may be soft if it has been wet. Some paths are a bit rough.

Directions: One and a half miles on B824 from the Keir roundabout to Doune - at stone walled entrance to Greeenyards farm track on the right . (Do not go down to white cottages, Biggins, as per GPS. Take next track on right after half a mile). Coming from Doune take the B824 to Bridge of Allan the track entrance is on the left, about half mile past the David Stirling Memorial statue. Follow the yellow garden open signs.

Disabled Access:
Partial

Opening Times:
Sunday 9 July
2:00pm - 5:00pm

Admission:
£4.00, accompanied children free

Charities:
MND Scotland receives 40%, the net remaining to SG Beneficiaries

ROWBERROW
18 Castle Road, Dollar FK14 7BE
Bill and Rosemary Jarvis T: 01259 742584
E: rjarvis1000@hotmail.com

On the way up to Castle Campbell overlooking Dollar Glen, this colourful garden has several mixed shrub and herbaceous borders, a wildlife pond, two rockeries, alpine troughs, fruit and vegetable gardens, and a mini-orchard. The owner is a plantaholic and likes to collect unusual specimens. Rowberrow was featured on the *Beechgrove Garden* in 2011.

Directions: Pass along the burn side in Dollar, turn right at T junction, follow signs for Castle Campbell and Dollar Glen. Park at the bottom of Castle Road or in the Quarry car park just up from the house.

Disabled Access:
Partial

Opening Times:
By arrangement
1 February - 31 December

Admission:
£4.00, accompanied children free

Charities:
Hillfoot Harmony Barbershop Singers receives 40%, the net remaining to SG Beneficiaries

---

NEW SHRUBHILL
Dunblane, Perthshire FK15 9PA
Tiff and Michaela Wright
E: wrightrascals@btinternet.com

Two acres of mixed, informal planting of some unusual rhododendrons, azaleas, specimen trees and other shrubs. Beautiful all round views particularly over the Carse of Stirling and towards Ben Ledi and Ben Lomond. Herbaceous borders, meconopsis, late spring bulbs, water feature with a wide variety of primulas. Small walled garden predominantly for fruit and greenhouse with well established vine.

Other Details: Guide dogs only. Airbnb at the Bothy.

Directions: Two miles from Keir roundabout on the B824 on the left, just after the David Stirling Memorial, follow the signs and parking advice. One mile from A820 and on right.

Disabled Access:
Partial

Opening Times:
Sunday 4 June
2:00pm - 5:00pm

Admission:
£5.00, accompanied children free

Charities:
Crossroads Caring Scotland (West Stirling Branch) receives 40%, the net remaining to SG Beneficiaries

---

NEW THE MILL HOUSE
Kippen Road, Fintry, Stirlingshire G63 0YD
Mrs Katherine Cowtan T: 01360 860009
E: cowtan@weefoot.com

Delightful small country garden with interesting planting at the front of the house. Plants are chosen for their resistance to both deer and rabbits. Late spring bulbs, geraniums, poppies and other colourful herbaceous plants and shrubs.

Other Details: Opening during Forth Valley Art Beat (Open Studios) week, there will be an opportunity to see the artist's studio as well as the garden which provides a lot of inspiration. There may be other artists, country crafts and interesting activities on offer. Tea and coffee may be available depending on numbers.

Directions: Signed from the Kippen Road. Disabled parking only at the house, but there is parking at the Fintry Sports Club or on the road in the village nearby.

Disabled Access:
Partial

Opening Times:
Saturday 10 June - Sunday 18 June (inclusive)
10:00am - 5:00pm

Admission:
By donation

Charities:
All proceeds to
SG Beneficiaries

STIRLINGSHIRE

THE PASS HOUSE
Kilmahog, Callander FK17 8HD
Dr and Mrs D Carfrae

Well planted, medium-sized garden with steep banks down to a swift river. The garden paths are not steep. There are lovely displays of camellias, magnolias, rhododendrons, azaleas, alpines and shrubs. The Scotland's Gardens plaque awarded for 25 years of opening is on display.

Other Details: Tea/coffee and a biscuit for a donation if the weather is fine.

Directions: Two miles from Callander on the A84 to Lochearnhead.

Disabled Access:
None

Opening Times:
Sunday 30 April
2:00pm - 5:00pm

Admission:
£4.00, accompanied children free

Charities:
Crossroads Caring Scotland (West Stirling Branch) receives 40%, the net remaining to SG Beneficiaries

THE TORS
2 Slamannan Road, Falkirk FK1 5LG
Dr and Mrs D M Ramsay T: 01324 620877
E: dmramsay28@yahoo.co.uk   www.torsgarden.co.uk

An award winning Victorian garden of just over one acre with a secret woodland garden to the side and an orchard leading off to a wild area at the rear of the house. Many unusual maple trees, hydrangeas and rhododendrons are the main interest of this garden and two fine avenues of Chinese paperbark maples are especially noteworthy. Featured on the *Beechgrove Garden* for autumn colour in 2010, but the best time to see this garden is at the end of July or the beginning of August. *Scotland on Sunday* featured the house and garden in an article with many lovely photographs in 2015. We now have our own website with a link to our Facebook page.

Other Details: Enquiries and groups welcome. Large plant stall.

Directions: The B803 to the south of Falkirk leads to Glenbrae Road. Turn right at the traffic lights into Slamannan Road and The Tors is a Victorian building immediately on the left. The house is within 200 yards of Falkirk High Station.

Disabled Access:
Partial

Opening Times:
Sunday 30 July
2:00pm - 5:30pm
Also by arrangement
1 May - 30 September

Admission:
£4.00, accompanied children free

Charities:
Strathcarron Hospice receives 40%, the net remaining to SG Beneficiaries

THORNTREE
Arnprior FK8 3EY
Mark and Carol Seymour T: 01786 870710
E: info@thorntreebarn.co.uk   www.thorntreebarn.co.uk

The amazing views from Ben Lomond, to Ben Ledi and on to Stirling sold Thorntree to Carol and Mark 25 years ago. The garden evolved trying to keep a "cottage" feel. Carol sold old silver never used in years to build the dry stone wall. An apple arch was given to Mark to encourage him into the garden. The lawns are mown like a bowling green (or to a millimetre) by Mark. The courtyard includes flower beds. The saltire bed was designed in 2002 when Carol stopped growing dried flowers in a 20x20m square. The slightly sunken bed, all that they inherited on arrival, now holds Meconopsis. And so it evolves, Carol is now making a wooded area filled with primroses and Martagon lilies. Do come and see!

Other Details: Plants are for sale throughout the year. No dogs except guide dogs. On 25 June, there may be coffee/tea and a biscuit for a donation if the weather is fine.

Directions: A811. In Arnprior take Fintry Road, Thorntree is second on the right.

Disabled Access:
Full

Opening Times:
Sunday 25 June
2:00pm - 5:00pm
Also by arrangement
1 April - 15 October

Admission:
£4.00, accompanied children free

Charities:
Forth Driving Group RDA receives 40%, the net remaining to SG Beneficiaries

Each visit you make to one of our gardens in 2017 will raise money for our beneficiary charities:

In addition, funds will be distributed to a charity of the owner's choice.
For West Central Scotland, these include:

Accord Hospice

Adoption Scotland

Alzheimer Scotland

Appin Parish Church

Appin Village Hall

Ardgowan Hospice

Argyll Animal Aid

Artlink Central

Association of Local Voluntary
Organisations

British Horse Society Scotland

Camphill Blair Drummond

Children's Hospice Association
Scotland (CHAS)

Christchurch Episcopal Church,
Lochgilphead

Coulter Library Trust

Crossroads Caring Scotland
(West Stirling Branch)

Diabetes UK

Dumfriesshire and Cumbria
Greyhound Rescue

Erskine Hospital

Feedback Madagascar

Fenwick Church Hall
Development Fund

Forth Driving Group RDA

Friends of St Modan's

Gargunnock Community Centre

Gargunnock Community Trust

Help for Heroes

Hessilhead Wildlife Rescue Trust

Hillfoot Harmony
Barbershop Singers

Homestart

Hope Kitchen (Oban)

Horatio's Gardens

Kilbarchan Old Library

Lanark Development Trust
(Castlebank Regeneration Fund)

Leighton Library

Macmillan Cancer Support

Macmillan Nurses

Marie Curie

Mary's Meals

Médecins Sans Frontières

MS Therapy Centre (Oban)

Netherthird Community
Development Group

Orkidstudio

Perennial

Pirnmill Village Association

Plant Heritage

Prostate Cancer UK

Scots Mining Company Trust

Scottish Refugee Council

St Columba's Church

St Margaret's Parish Church, Dalry

St Saviour's Church

St Vincent's Hospice

Strathcarron Hospice

The Divine Innocence Trust

The Little Haven

The Red Cross, Dunoon Branch

The Scottish Dark Sky Observatory

Triple Negative Breast Cancer
Research (Anne Konishi
Memorial Fund)

University of Strathclyde
Ross Priory Gardens

SOUTH WEST SCOTLAND

Scotland's Gardens 2017 Guidebook is sponsored by **INVESTEC WEALTH & INVESTMENT**

DUMFRIESSHIRE

Scotland's Gardens 2017 Guidebook is sponsored by **INVESTEC WEALTH & INVESTMENT**

District Organiser

Sarah Landale	Dalswinton House, Dalswinton, Auldgirth DG2 0XZ E: dumfriesshire@scotlandsgardens.org

Area Organisers

Fiona Bell-Irving	Bankside, Kettleholm, Lockerbie DG11 1BY
Guy Galbraith	Stanemuir, Parkgate, Dumfries DG1 3NE
Liz Mitchell	Drumpark, Irongray, Dumfriesshire DG2 9TX

Treasurer

Harold Jack	The Clachan, Newtonairds DG2 0JL

Gardens open on a specific date

Craig, Langholm	Sunday 19 February	12:00pm	-	4:00pm
Barjarg Tower, Auldgirth	Thursday 23 February	10:00am	-	4:00pm
Barjarg Tower, Auldgirth	Friday 24 February	10:00am	-	4:00pm
Barjarg Tower, Auldgirth	Saturday 25 February	10:00am	-	4:00pm
Barjarg Tower, Auldgirth	Sunday 26 February	10:00am	-	4:00pm
Portrack, The Garden of Cosmic Speculation, Holywood	Sunday 30 April	11:00am	-	5:00pm
Drumpark, Irongray	Saturday 13 May	11:00am	-	5:00pm
Capenoch, Penpont, Thornhill	Sunday 14 May	2:00pm	-	5:00pm
The Crichton Rock Garden and Arboretum, Dumfries	Sunday 21 May	12:00pm	-	4:00pm
Dalswinton House, Dalswinton	Sunday 28 May	2:00pm	-	5:00pm
Dabton, Thornhill	Sunday 4 June	2:00pm	-	5:00pm
Holehouse, Thornhill	Sunday 4 June	12:00pm	-	3:00pm
Holehouse, Thornhill	Friday 9 June	3:00pm	-	6:00pm
Cowhill Tower, Holywood	Sunday 11 June	2:00pm	-	5:00pm
Westerhall, Langholm	Sunday 11 June	2:00pm	-	5:00pm
Dunesslin, Dunscore	Sunday 18 June	2:00pm	-	5:00pm
Glenae, Amisfield	Sunday 25 June	2:00pm	-	5:00pm
Dalgonar, Dunscore	Sunday 2 July	2:00pm	-	5:00pm
Whiteside, Dunscore	Saturday 15 July	11:00am	-	4:00pm
Whiteside, Dunscore	Sunday 16 July	11:00am	-	4:00pm
Newtonairds Lodge, Newtonairds	Sunday 30 July	2:00pm	-	5:00pm
Shawhead, Lochmaben	Sunday 13 August	1:00pm	-	5:00pm

DUMFRIESSHIRE

Gardens open by arrangement

Westwater Farm, Langholm	1 May - 30 September	01387 381004

Dalswinton House © Val Corbett

Key to symbols

New in 2017	Homemade teas		Accommodation		
 Teas	Dogs on a lead allowed		Plant stall		
Cream teas	Wheelchair access		Scottish Snowdrop Festival		

GARDEN LOCATIONS
DUMFRIESSHIRE

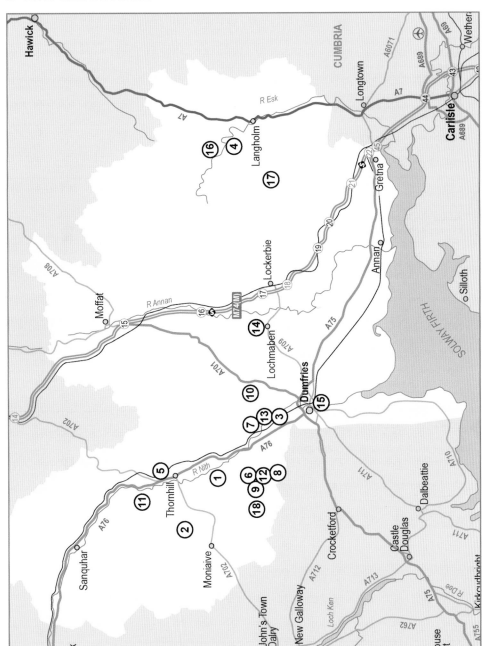

BARJARG TOWER
Auldgirth DG2 0TN
Mary and Archie Donaldson T: 01848 331545

Barjarg Tower lies on a gentle slope enjoying the lovely views of the surrounding Lowther hills. The original Tower House dates back to the late 16th century but has had various cleverly designed additions over the years. The gardens have undergone considerable development since they were last opened to the public, though the carpets of snowdrops in the surrounding woods remain a tribute to the care of earlier generations.

Other Details: Morning coffee and afternoon teas are available in Auldgirth and Penpont tearooms. Both are equidistant at some four miles from Barjarg. Wear Wellies or strong shoes for your visit.

Directions: Situated on the C125 half way between Auldgirth and Penpont. Driving from Auldgirth, the stone, arched entrance is on the left hand side with Barjarg engraved on sandstone.

Disabled Access:
Partial

Opening Times:
Thursday to Sunday
23 to 26 February
10:00am - 4:00pm
for the Snowdrop Festival

Admission:
There will be an honesty box for donations. As a guide a minimum of £3.00 per person

Charities:
Alzheimer's Research receives 40%, the net remaining to SG Beneficiaries

CAPENOCH
Penpont, Thornhill DG3 4TZ
Mr and Mrs Robert Gladstone
E: maggie.gladstone@gmail.com

There are rare trees throughout the grounds and the main garden is the remnant of that laid out in Victorian times. There is a pretty little raised knot garden called the Italian Garden and a lovely old Victorian conservatory. Parking is available at the house but you may prefer to park in Penpont Village and walk up the drive to Capenoch, as there are lovely bluebells and wild flowers in the oak woods on either side of the drive.

Other Details: There is a good variety of plants for sale in the old Walled Garden where Morag has the garden centre. This year homemade teas will be available in the conservatory.

Directions: Take the A702 west from Thornhill, drive through Penpont and the entrance to the house is at the lodge on the left hand side, just at the speed restriction sign.

Disabled Access:
Partial

Opening Times:
Sunday 14 May
2:00pm - 5:00pm

Admission:
£4.00, accompanied children free

Charities:
The Jo Walters Trust receives 40%, the net remaining to SG Beneficiaries

COWHILL TOWER
Holywood DG2 0RL
Mr and Mrs P Weatherall T: 01387 720304
E: cmw@cowhill.co.uk

This is an interesting walled garden. There are topiary animals, birds and figures and a beautiful woodland walk. Splendid views can be seen from the lawn right down the Nith Valley. There is also a variety of statues from the Far East.

Directions: Holywood one and a half miles off A76, five miles north of Dumfries.

Disabled Access:
Partial

Opening Times:
Sunday 11 June
2:00pm - 5:00pm

Admission:
£5.00, accompanied children free

Charities:
Maggie's Cancer Caring Centres receives 40%, the net remaining to SG Beneficiaries

CRAIG
Langholm DG13 0NZ
Mr and Mrs Neil Ewart T: 013873 70230
E: nmlewart@googlemail.com

Craig snowdrops have evolved over the last 30 or so years. Round the house and policies, a large variety have been planted with a varied flowering season stretching from the start of January until April and peaking mid-February. Large drifts of *Leucojum vernum* (Winter Snowflake) have started to naturalise here and along the riverbank a variety of snowdrops swept down by the river have naturalised in the adjacent woodland, known as the Snowdrop Walk.

Other Details: Each walk takes about twenty minutes. Wellies are essential. Wheelchair access down by the river is not possible but easier around the house. Teas will be available in the nearby Bentpath Village Hall from 2:00pm - 4:00pm.

Directions: Craig is three miles from Langholm on the B709 towards Eskdalemuir. The Village Hall is at Bentpath, one mile further towards Eskdalemuir.

Disabled Access:
Partial

Opening Times:
Sunday 19 February
12:00pm - 4:00pm
for the Snowdrop Festival

Admission:
£4.00, accompanied children free

Charities:
Kirkandrews Church receives 40%, the net remaining to SG Beneficiaries

DABTON
Thornhill DG3 5AR
The Duke and Duchess of Buccleuch T: 01848 330467
E: phunter@buccleuch.com

Nineteenth century house built of pink stone. Extensive walled garden. Ninety-five yards long herbaceous border, roses, island beds and shrubs, ponds with azaleas and primulas, woodland walk, vegetable garden and greenhouses.

Other Details: There will be a pipe band and country dance performances at intervals throughout the afternoon. Nearby Holehouse, only 15 minutes drive away is also open on 4 June 12 noon - 3:00pm.

Directions: Entrance off the A76 between Thornhill and Carronbridge.

Disabled Access:
Partial

Opening Times:
Sunday 4 June
2:00pm - 5:00pm

Admission:
£4.00, accompanied children free

Charities:
The Buccleuch and Queensberry Pipeband receives 20%, The Thornhill Scottish Country Dancers receives 20%, the net remaining to SG Beneficiaries

DALGONAR
Dunscore, Dumfries DG2 0SS
Judge and Mrs William Crawford T: 01387 820339
E: william@crawford.org

There are well-wooded policies with woodland paths and a traditional, very well maintained walled garden containing an unusual and beautiful sundial.

Directions: Half a mile north west of Dunscore, Dumfriesshire on the B729 road to Moniaive. Entrance through black gates on north side of the road.

Disabled Access:
Partial

Opening Times:
Sunday 2 July
2:00pm - 5:00pm

Admission:
£5.00, accompanied children free

Charities:
The Dunscore Gala receives 20%, Compassion in World Farming receives 20%, the net remaining to SG Beneficiaries

DUMFRIESSHIRE

7 DALSWINTON HOUSE
Dalswinton DG2 0XZ
Mr and Mrs Peter Landale T: 01387 740220

Late 18th century house sits on top of a hill surrounded by herbaceous beds and well established shrubs, including rhododendrons and azaleas overlooking the loch. Attractive walks through woods and around the loch. It was here that the first steamboat in Britain made its maiden voyage in 1788 and there is a life-size model beside the water to commemorate this. Over the past year, there has been much clearing and development work around the loch, which has opened up the views considerably.

Other Details: A new circular walk has recently been created through the woods at the back of the walled garden which leads to the village and round back to the main house. Wear Wellies.

Directions: Seven miles north of Dumfries off A76. Parking is available at the village hall.

Disabled Access:
Partial

Opening Times:
Sunday 28 May
2:00pm - 5:00pm

Admission:
£5.00, accompanied children free

Charities:
Kirkmahoe Parish Church receives 40%, the net remaining to SG Beneficiaries

8 DRUMPARK
Irongray DG2 9TX
Mr and Mrs Iain Mitchell T: 01387 820323
E: iain.liz.mitchell@googlemail.com

Well contoured woodland garden and extensive policies with mature azaleas, rhododendrons and rare shrubs among impressive specimen trees. Water garden with primulas and meconopsis. Victorian walled garden with fruit trees and garden produce. There is also a beautiful herbaceous border. All set in a natural bowl providing attractive vistas.

Other Details: The nearest place for teas and refreshments is either at the Auldgirth Tearoom or into Dumfries both equidistant at about five miles away.

Directions: From Dumfries by-pass, head north on A76 for ½ mile, turn left at the signpost to "Lochside Industrial Estates" and immediately right onto Irongray Road; continue for five miles; gates in sandstone wall on left (½ mile after Routin' Brig).

Disabled Access:
None

Opening Times:
Saturday 13 May
11:00am - 5:00pm

Admission:
£5.00, accompanied children free

Charities:
Loch Arthur Community (Camphill Trust) receives 40%, the net remaining to SG Beneficiaries

9 DUNESSLIN
Dunscore DG2 0UR
Iain and Zara Milligan
E: zaramilligan@gmail.com

Set in the hills with wonderful views, the principal garden consists of a series of connecting rooms filled with a great variety of herbaceous plants, beautifully designed and maintained. There is a substantial rock garden with alpines and unusual plants and a very pretty pond and a hill walk to view three cairns by Andy Goldsworthy.

Directions: From Dunscore, follow the road to Corsock. Approximately 1½ miles further on, turn right at the post box, still on the road to Corsock and at small crossroads ½ mile on, turn left.

Disabled Access:
Partial

Opening Times:
Sunday 18 June
2:00pm - 5:00pm

Admission:
£5.00, accompanied children free

Charities:
Alzheimer Scotland receives 40%, the net remaining to SG Beneficiaries

GLENAE

Amisfield DG1 3NZ
Mrs Victoria Morley T: 01387 710236
E: tottsmorley@btinternet.com

A beautiful, well-established, walled garden, well stocked with interesting plants, four small lawns surrounded by colourful herbaceous borders, a woodland garden and a restored Victorian glass-house.

Other Details: Refreshments will be available in some form!

Directions: 1½ miles north of Amisfield on A701. Turn left to Duncow and Auldgirth and 1 mile on right.

Disabled Access:
Partial

Opening Times:
Sunday 25 June
2:00pm - 5:00pm

Admission:
£4.00, accompanied children free

Charities:
Canine Concern Scotland Trust receives 40%, the net remaining to SG Beneficiaries

---

NEW HOLEHOUSE

Near Penpont, Thornhill DG3 4AP
Lord and Lady Norrie T: 01848 600303

A newly-established garden, beautifully and carefully landscaped and developed in, around, and through a farm steading over the past 12 years. Its secluded location high on a hillside offers some wonderful views. It is a garden of great variety including a labyrinth, pond, some lovely roses, shrubs and early trees and a working vegetable garden laid out beside the orchard. A great number of trees have been planted and these are really starting to take shape.

Other Details: Nearby Dabton, only 15 minutes drive away, is also open on 4 June, directions available. Teas at Dabton.

Directions: From Penpont Village crossroads, take Sanquhar Road, passing triangle on left after 2.1 miles. Carry on 1.2 miles and take next left in front of white farmhouse. Turn right at next T-Junction with three white cottages. Continue past farm on left. Holehouse is next on right.

Disabled Access:
Partial

Opening Times:
Sunday 4 June
12:00pm - 3:00pm
Friday 9 June
3:00pm - 6:00pm

Admission:
£5.00, accompanied children free

Charities:
All proceeds to
SG Beneficiaries

NEWTONAIRDS LODGE

Newtonairds DG2 0JL
Mr and Mrs J Coutts
www.newtonairds-hostasandgarden.co.uk

An interesting 1.2 acre plantsman's garden punctuated with topiary, trees and shrubs, surrounding a 19th century listed baronial lodge. The National Collection is integrated with a further 150 other hosta varieties on a natural terraced wooded bank.

Other Details: National Plant Collection®: *Hosta plantaginea* hybrids and cultivars. The plants, of which there is a great variety, are of exceptional quality and all grown and brought on in situ at Newtonairds Lodge.

Directions: From Dumfries take A76 north. At Holywood take B729 (Dunscore). After one mile turn left (Morrinton). After three miles red sandstone lodge is on right, behind black iron railings.

Disabled Access:
Partial

Opening Times:
Sunday 30 July
2:00pm - 5:00pm

Admission:
£4.50, accompanied children free

Charities:
Peter Pan Moat Brae Trust receives 40%, the net remaining to SG Beneficiaries

DUMFRIESSHIRE

13 PORTRACK, THE GARDEN OF COSMIC SPECULATION
Holywood DG2 0RW
Charles Jencks
www.charlesjencks.com

Forty major areas, gardens, bridges, landforms, sculptures, terraces, fences and architectural works. Covering thirty acres, the Garden of Cosmic Speculation uses nature to celebrate nature, both intellectually and through the senses, including the sense of humour. A water cascade of steps recounts the story of the universe; a terrace shows the distortion of space and time caused by a black hole; a "Quark Walk" takes the visitor on a journey to the smallest building blocks of matter and a series of landforms and lakes recall fractal geometry. Charles Jencks and his late wife, Maggie Keswick, conceived this unique garden in 1989 and it has been evolving ever since.

Other Details: Parking is in the fields adjacent to the gardens and will be clearly signed from the main A76. Please wear sensible footwear as it can get very muddy in the car park and gardens.
This garden opening is one of the most popular in the Scotland's Gardens calendar, so please bear with us during busy times. We would like to make sure that everyone is parked safely. Payment is at the gate once parked or by booking online in advance at - *http://portrack2017.eventbrite.co.uk*

Directions: Holywood 1½ miles off the A76, five miles north of Dumfries. Follow signs.

Disabled Access:
None

Opening Times:
Sunday 30 April
11:00am - 5:00pm

Admission:
£10.00, concessions £5.00, accompanied children free, cash payment only at the gate or full price tickets may be purchased in advance by booking online at *portrack2017.eventbrite.co.uk*

Charities:
Maggie's Cancer Caring Centres receives 40%, the net remaining to SG Beneficiaries

© Ming Thein 2015

© Ming Thein 2015

14 NEW **SHAWHEAD**
7 Vendace Drive, Lochmaben DG11 1QN
Mr and Mrs Ian Rankine T: 01387 811273
E: srankine298@btinternet.com

A young, four year old, garden situated on the edge of Lochmaben and with delightful views overlooking The Mill Loch. It has immaculately maintained and very many well furnished borders bursting with colour and a great variety of plants. There are well over 200 RHS Award of Garden Merit Cultivars and a collection of 150 *Phlox Paniculata* cultivars.

Other Details: The walk around Mill loch takes about 30-40 minutes from the house. Wear suitable walking shoes. For keen walkers, the nearby Castle Loch also has a lovely walk of about 3½ miles.

Directions: From Dumfries, turn left opposite The Crown Hotel, turn left at give way and then sharp left. From Lockerbie, take the right fork beside the Town Hall and after ½ mile, take left turn.

Disabled Access:
Partial

Opening Times:
Sunday 13 August
1:00pm - 5:00pm

Admission:
£7.00 includes homemade tea, accompanied children free

Charities:
Castle Loch, Lochmaben Community Trust receives 40%, the net remaining to SG Beneficiaries

---

15 **THE CRICHTON ROCK GARDEN AND ARBORETUM**
The Crichton University Campus, Bankend Road, Dumfries DG1 4ZL
The Crichton
E: elainecarruthers@easterbrookhall.co.uk

Over 100 acres of mature landscaped parkland in Dumfries makes up these famous grounds. The Rock Garden and Arboretum dating from the early 1900s house many unusual and striking plants. The extensive grounds offer enjoyable walking trails with stunning views of the surrounding countryside.

Other Details: Refreshments will be available in the Easterbrook Hall located at the centre of the Campus. A heritage walking route leaflet of the Crichton Estate will be available on arrival and will include directions of where to go.

Directions: Follow the B725 South out of Dumfries or, more easily, follow the signs for the hospital. Drive past the hospital on the right and continue on to the roundabout at the Easterbrook Hall Entrance.

Disabled Access:
Partial

Opening Times:
Sunday 21 May
12:00pm - 4:00pm

Admission:
£5.00, accompanied children free

Charities:
The Crichton Trust receives 40%, the net remaining to SG Beneficiaries

---

16 **WESTERHALL**
Bentpath, Langholm DG13 0NQ
Mrs Peter Buckley
E: mary.buckley@hotmail.co.uk

An extensive collection of azaleas, rhododendrons, rare shrubs and mature trees set in a landscape of follies, sculpture and stunning vistas. The redesigned walled garden contains a glasshouse with some exotic plants which have been collected from around the world.

Other Details: Selling plants this year are Allan Clark, a rhododendron specialist and award winner Helen Knowles from Tinnisburn Nursery.

Directions: From Langholm take the B709 towards Eskdalemuir. After approximately five miles in village of Bentpath, turn right by white house. Go down through the village, over a small/narrow bridge and turn right by the church. Carry on this road for approximately one mile. Parking at farm which will be signed.

Disabled Access:
Partial

Opening Times:
Sunday 11 June
2:00pm - 5:00pm

Admission:
£5.00, accompanied children free

Charities:
Westerkirk Parish Trust receives 40%, the net remaining to SG Beneficiaries

WESTWATER FARM
Langholm DG13 0LU
Mr and Mrs Charlie Clapperton T: 01387 381004
E: charlieclapperton@hotmail.com

In a wonderful, remote and romantic setting, the interesting walled garden adjacent to the house has both herbaceous plants and shrubs. There is also a woodland garden with a variety of bamboos and interesting trees. Dotted around the house and steadings are some fabulous pots .

Other Details: The beautifully restored steadings around the house, is home to some very special donkeys among other farm animals.

Directions: Thirteen miles from Lockerbie on the B7068 Lockerbie to Langholm road (five miles from Langholm). Entrance is signed Westwater on the left coming from Lockerbie. Keep to left fork for house.

Disabled Access:
Partial

Opening Times:
By arrangement
1 May - 30 September

Admission:
£3.00, accompanied children free

Charities:
All proceeds to
SG Beneficiaries

NEW WHITESIDE
Dunscore DG2 0UU
John and Hilary Craig T: 01387 820501
E: hjcraig19@gmail.com

The garden, which extends to several acres is 200m above sea level on a north facing slope with views across to Queensberry and the Lowther Hills. There are some mature trees around the house but the rest of the garden is relatively new, having been created from a bare hillside since 2000. There are shrubs, young trees, a rowan avenue, a walled vegetable garden, orchard and courtyard garden. Several burns run through the property and there is a pond and two duck enclosures.

Other Details: Tea, coffee and cake will be available in the courtyard. Wellies are advisable if it's wet. There may be a plant stall.

Directions: From Dunscore, take the Corsock road. Continue two miles on, turn right opposite the postbox. Continue on for 1¾ miles, over the humpback bridge and past the white farmhouse on the left. Whiteside is signed on the left.

Disabled Access:
None

Opening Times:
Saturday 15 July
Sunday 16 July
11:00am - 4:00pm

Admission:
£5.00, accompanied children free

Charities:
Dumfries Music Club receives 40%, the net remaining to SG Beneficiaries

KIRKCUDBRIGHTSHIRE

Scotland's Gardens 2017 Guidebook is sponsored by **INVESTEC WEALTH & INVESTMENT**

District Organiser

Julian and Theodora Stanning	Seabank, Merse Road, Rockcliffe DG5 4QH
	E: kirkcudbrightshire @scotlandsgardens.org

Area Organisers

Hedley Foster	Deer Pk, Fleet Forest, Gatehouse of Fleet DG7 2DN
Lesley Pepper	Anwoth Old Schoolhouse, Gatehouse of Fleet DG7 2EF
Sheila Pook,	11 Whitepark Drive, Castle Douglas DG7 1EQ
Vivien Scott	14 Castle Street, Kirkcudbright DG6 4JA
Audrey Slee	Holmview, New Galloway, Castle Douglas DG7 3RN
George Thomas	Savat, Meikle Richorn, Dalbeattie DG5 4QT

Treasurer

Duncan Lofts	Balcary Tower, Auchencairn, Castle Douglas DG7 1QZ

Gardens open on a specific date

Danevale Park, Crossmichael	Date to be advised	2:00pm	-	5:00pm
3 Millhall, Shore Road, Kirkcudbright	Sunday 16 April	2:00pm	-	5:00pm
Threave Garden, Castle Douglas	Sunday 7 May	11:00am	-	4:00pm
Barmagachan House, Borgue, Kirkcudbright	Sunday 21 May	2:00pm	-	5:00pm
Corsock House, Corsock, Castle Douglas	Sunday 28 May	2:00pm	-	5:00pm
Cally Gardens, Gatehouse of Fleet	Sunday 4 June	10:00am	-	5:30pm
Broughton House Garden, 12 High Street, Kirkcudbright	Thursday 8 June	6:00pm	-	9:00pm
Stockarton, Kirkcudbright	Sunday 11 June	2:00pm	-	5:00pm
Glenlivet with The Limes, Tongland Road, Kirkcudbright	Sunday 18 June	1:00pm	-	5:00pm
Seabank, The Merse, Rockcliffe	Sunday 25 June	2:00pm	-	5:00pm
Southwick House, Southwick	Sunday 2 July	2:00pm	-	5:00pm
Drumstinchall House with Drumstinchal Cottage, Dalbeattie	Sunday 9 July	2:00pm	-	5:00pm
Barmagachan House, Borgue	Sunday 16 July	2:00pm	-	5:00pm
Crofts, Kirkpatrick Durham	Sunday 23 July	2:00pm	-	5:00pm
Cally Gardens, Gatehouse of Fleet	Sunday 6 August	10:00am	-	5:30pm
Threave Garden, Castle Douglas	Sunday 6 August	6:00pm	-	10:00pm
3 Millhall, Shore Road, Kirkcudbright	Sunday 27 August	2:00pm	-	5:00pm

KIRKCUDBRIGHTSHIRE

Gardens open by arrangement

3 Millhall, Shore Road, Kirkcudbright	1 April - 30 September	shamash@freeuk.com
Anwoth Old Schoolhouse, Anwoth	15 February - 15 November	01557 814444
Brooklands, Crocketford	1 February - 1 October	01556 690685
Corsock House, Corsock	1 April - 30 June	01644 440250
Seabank, The Merse	1 June - 31 August	01556 630244
Stockarton, Kirkcudbright	1 April - 31 July	01557 330430
The Waterhouse Gardens at Stockarton, Kirkcudbright	1 May - 30 Septamber	01557 330430

Cally Gardens © Mary McIlvenna

Key to symbols

 New in 2017

 Teas

 Cream teas

 Homemade teas

 Dogs on a lead allowed

 Wheelchair access

 Accommodation

Plant stall

 Scottish Snowdrop Festival

GARDEN LOCATIONS
IN KIRKCUDBRIGHTSHIRE

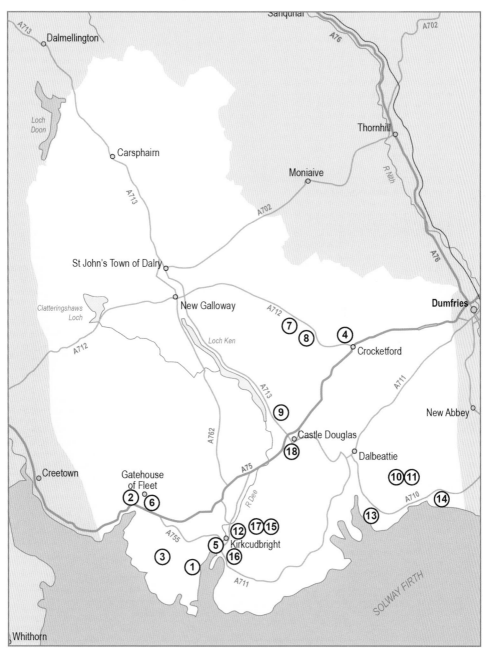

KIRKCUDBRIGHTSHIRE

1 3 MILLHALL
Shore Road, Kirkcudbright DG6 4TQ
Mr Alan Shamash
E: shamash@freeuk.com

Impressive five acre garden with a large collection of mature shrubs, including over 200 rhododendron species, many camellias, perennials, over 300 hydrangeas and many rare Southern Hemisphere plants. The garden is on a steep hillside running along the rocky shore of the Dee Estuary in Kirkcudbright Bay, close to the beach at the Dhoon and three miles from Kirkcudbright.

Directions: On the B727 between Kirkcudbright and Borgue on the west shore of the Dee Estuary. Parking at Dhoon beach public car park, about three miles south of Kirkcudbright. There is a five to ten minute walk to the house.

Disabled Access:
None

Opening Times:
Sundays 16 April & 27 August
2:00pm - 5:00pm
Also by arrangement
1 April - 30 September

Admission:
£4.00, accomp children free

Charities:
The Kirkcudbright Hospital League of Friends receives 20%, Alzheimer's Research UK receives 20%, the net remaining to SG Beneficiaries

---

2 ANWOTH OLD SCHOOLHOUSE
Anwoth, Gatehouse of Fleet DG7 2EF
Mr & Mrs Pepper T: 01557 814444
E: lesley.pepper@btinternet.com

Two acres of delightful cottage-style gardens behind the old schoolhouse and cottage in a picturesque setting opposite Anwoth old church (in ruins) and graveyard. Winding paths alongside a burn, informally planted with unusual woodland perennials and shrubs. Wildlife pond, fish pond, rock garden, wildflower area and viewpoint, vegetable garden.

Directions: Driving west on the A75, take the Anwoth turnoff about half a mile after Gatehouse of Fleet. Anwoth Church is about half a mile along the road and Anwoth Old Schoolhouse is a little further along, opposite Anwoth Old Church (in ruins).

Disabled Access:
None

Opening Times:
By arrangement
15 February - 15 November

Admission:
£3.00, accompanied children free

Charities:
Dogs for Good receives 40%, the net remaining to SG Beneficiaries

---

3 NEW BARMAGACHAN HOUSE
Borgue, Kirkcudbright DG6 4SW
Andy and Carolyn McNab T: 01557 870225

This new garden surrounds an 18th century house on a rocky knoll overlooking Wigtown Bay. It is profusely planted with a large variety of alpines, perennials and shrubs, including rhododendrons. Two themes are plants from SW China and Australasia e.g. meconoposis, Asian primulas, eucryphia, hebe. Many plants have been chosen for their wildlife value. The grounds also include an orchard, wall trained fruit, soft fruit area, potager and meadow. The woodland is rich in bird life. There is a 13th century motte.

Other Details: The plant stall features several species raised from seed by the owners.

Directions: From Borgue follow the coast (Carrick) road up hill past the church and down. Take the first and only right turn and follow the lane winding past farms for about ½ mile. Barmagachan House is on the left by a wood.

Disabled Access:
None

Opening Times:
Sunday 21 May
Sunday 16 July
2:00pm - 5:00pm

Admission:
£4.00, accompanied children free

Charities:
National Trust for Scotland (Threave Ospreys) receives 20%, Scottish Wildlife Trust receives 20%, the net remaining to SG Beneficiaries

BROOKLANDS

Crocketford DG2 8QH
Mr and Mrs Robert Herries T: Head Gardener John Geddes 01556 690685

Large old walled garden, richly planted with a wide variety of perennials, including many unusual species, soft fruit and vegetables. Mature woodland garden full of rhododendrons and carpeted with snowdrops in February and daffodils in spring.

Directions: Turn off the A712 Crocketford to New Galloway Road one mile outside Crocketford at the Gothic gatehouse (on the right travelling north).

Disabled Access:
Partial

Opening Times:
By arrangement
1 February - 1 October
including the Snowdrop
Festival (Groups only)

Admission:
£4.00, accompanied children free

Charities:
All proceeds to
SG Beneficiaries

BROUGHTON HOUSE GARDEN

12 High Street, Kirkcudbright DG6 4JX
The National Trust for Scotland T: 01557 330437 E: broughtonhouse@nts.org.uk
www.nts.org.uk/property/broughton-house-and-garden

Broughton House Garden is a fascinating townhouse garden that belonged to E A Hornel - artist, collector and one of the 'Glasgow boys'. Full of colour with mostly herbaceous plants, old apple trees, greenhouse with old pelargonium varieties and fruit and vegetable garden.

Other Details: Broughton House Garden at sunset. This event will offer visitors an evening of live music and refreshments (included in the entry price). It is an opportunity to meet the Head Gardener and see the garden in a different light!

Directions: Off A711/A755 on Kirkcudbright High Street. Stagecoach buses 500/X75 and 501 from Dumfries and Castle Douglas. By bike, NCN 7. Nearest train station Dumfries, then taxi/bus to Kirkcudbright.

Disabled Access:
Partial

Opening Times:
Thursday 8 June
6:00pm - 9:00pm

Admission:
£4.00 includes refreshments

Charities:
Donation to SG Beneficiaries

CALLY GARDENS

Gatehouse of Fleet DG7 2DJ
Mr Michael Wickenden T: 01557 815029
E: info@callygardens.co.uk   www.callygardens.co.uk

A specialist nursery in a densely planted 2.7 acre 18th century walled garden with old vinery and bothy, all surrounded by the Cally Oak Woods. Our collection of 3,500 varieties of plants can be seen and a selection will be available pot-grown. Excellent range of rare herbaceous perennials.

Other Details: The telephone at Cally Gardens provides a recorded message only.

Directions: From Dumfries take the Gatehouse turning off A75 and turn left through the Cally Palace Hotel gateway from where the gardens are well signposted.

Disabled Access:
Full

Opening Times:
Sunday 4 June
Sunday 6 August
10:00am - 5:30pm

Admission:
£3.50, accompanied children free

Charities:
ROKPA Tibetan Charity receives 40%, the net remaining to SG Beneficiaries

KIRKCUDBRIGHTSHIRE

CORSOCK HOUSE
Corsock, Castle Douglas DG7 3DJ
The Ingall Family T: 01644 440250

Corsock House Garden includes an amazing variety of types of designed landscape, from a strictly formal walled garden, through richly planted woodlands full of different vistas, artfully designed water features and surprises to manicured lawns showing off the Bryce baronial mansion. This is an Arcadian garden with pools and temples, described by Ken Cox as 'the most photogenic woodland garden in Scotland'.

Other Details: Larger guided tours are charged an additional £20.00 per tour.

Directions: Off A75 Dumfries fourteen miles, Castle Douglas ten miles, Corsock village ½ mile on A712.

Disabled Access:
Partial

Opening Times:
Sunday 28 May
2:00pm - 5:00pm
Also by arrangement
1 April - 30 June

Admission:
£5.00, accompanied children free

Charities:
Corsock and Kirkpatrick Durham Church receives 40%, the net remaining to SG Beneficiaries

---

CROFTS
Kirkpatrick Durham, Castle Douglas DG7 3HX
Mrs Andrew Dalton T: 01556 650235
E: jenniedalton@mac.com

Victorian country house garden with mature trees, a walled garden with fruit and vegetables and glasshouses, hydrangea garden and a pretty water garden. Delightful woodland walk, colourfully planted with bog plants, with stream running through.

Directions: A75 to Crocketford, then three miles on A712 to Corsock and New Galloway.

Disabled Access:
Partial

Opening Times:
Sunday 23 July
2:00pm - 5:00pm

Admission:
£4.00, accompanied children free

Charities:
Kirkpatrick Durham Church receives 40%, the net remaining to SG Beneficiaries

---

DANEVALE PARK
Crossmichael DG7 2LP
Mrs M R C Gillespie T: 01556 670223
E: danevale@tiscali.co.uk

First opening for snowdrops in 1951 these mature grounds have a wonderful display of snowdrops as well as aconites and many other wild flowers. Walks through the woods and alongside the River Dee, followed by an old fashioned afternoon tea, can make this a memorable day!

Other Details: In 2013 Mrs Gillespie was awarded The Diana Macnab Award for outstanding services to Scotland's Gardens.

Directions: On the A713 two miles north of Castle Douglas and one mile south of Crossmichael.

Disabled Access:
Partial

Opening Times:
Date for the snowdrop opening to be advised see SG website for details.
The garden will be open 2:00pm - 5:00pm

Admission:
£3.00

Charities:
Poppy Scotland receives 40%, the net remaining to SG Beneficiaries

NEW DRUMSTINCHALL COTTAGE WITH DRUMSTINCHALL HOUSE

Drumstinchall, Dalbeattie DG5 4PD
Ginny and Abel Quintanilla T: 01387 780571

A small informal quintessentially cottage style garden surrounded by farmland and hills, and with views to Criffel and Drumstinchall Loch. The main area has been reclaimed from agricultural land over the last seven years and continues to evolve, with the emphasis on growing a wide range of vegetables, herbs and fruit organically. Unusual varieties are combined with as many colourful wildlife friendly flowers as possible. There is a wildlife pond area and a few rescue chickens pottering about!

Other Details: An authentic Bolivian bread oven will be producing delicious treats to try and buy at Drumstinchall Cottage. Teas at Drumstinchall House.

Directions: From the A711 just east of Dalbeattie, take the B793 towards Southwick/Caulkerbush. After 4.2 miles take a right turn signposted Drumstinchall and follow this road for 0.8 miles to Drumstinchall House.

Disabled Access:
Partial

Opening Times:
Sunday 9 July
2:00pm - 5:00pm

Admission:
£5.00 includes entry to both gardens, accompanied children free

Charities:
Brooke | Action for Working Horses and Donkeys receives 40%, the net remaining to SG Beneficiaries

NEW DRUMSTINCHALL HOUSE WITH DRUMSTINCHALL COTTAGE

Drumstinchall, Dalbeattie DG5 4PD
Melanie and Mark Parry & Celia Hanbury T: 01387 780278
E: melanie@drumstinchall.co.uk

An extensive and established garden, surrounded by mature trees, with fine views to the sea two miles away. There are colourful herbaceous and mixed borders, and a rose garden in front of the house. A variety of paths wind their way through more borders, a rock garden, rhododendrons and azaleas, and past the ruin of the original house to a woodland walk around the edge of the garden. There is a vegetable garden, including a polytunnel and you can walk through the farmyard to the loch.

Directions: From the A711 just east of Dalbeattie, take the B793 towards Southwick/Caulkerbush. After 4.2 miles take a right turn signposted Drumstinchall and follow this road for 0.8 miles to Drumstinchall House.

Disabled Access:
Partial

Opening Times:
Sunday 9 July
2:00pm - 5:00pm

Admission:
£5.00 includes entry to both gardens (accompanied children free)

Charities:
Brooke | Action for Working Horses and Donkeys receives 40%, the net remaining to SG Beneficiaries

GLENLIVET WITH THE LIMES

Tongland Road, Kirkcudbright DG6 4UR
Alec and Doreen Blackadder T: 01557 332333
E: alec@alecblackadder.wanadoo.co.uk

This new town garden of half an acre on the edge of Kirkcudbright has been developed by the owners from scratch over the past nine years. It has a remarkably mature appearance already and is packed with colour and a huge variety of thriving plants, shrubs and trees, all carefully tended. There are two small ponds connected by a rill, with fountains at each end, herbaceous beds, gravel beds and a variety of statuary and garden structures. The garden is in a lovely position overlooking the River Dee.

Directions: Coming in to Kirkcudbright via the A711 and Tongland Bridge, on the outskirts of the town pass the Arden House hotel on the left. Glenlivet is about half a mile further on the right. It is exactly half a mile from the town centre crossroads on the Tongland Road. Parking is on the main road.

Disabled Access:
Partial

Opening Times:
Sunday 18 June
1:00pm - 5:00pm

Admission:
£5.00 includes entry to both gardens, accompanied children free

Charities:
Friends of Kirkcudbright Swimming Pool receives 40%, the net remaining to SG Beneficiaries

13 SEABANK
The Merse, Rockcliffe DG5 4QH
Julian and Theodora Stanning T: 01556 630244

The one and a half acre garden extend to the high water mark with fine views across the Urr Estuary, Rough Island and beyond. Mixed shrub and herbaceous borders surround the house and there is a new walled garden for fruit and vegetables. A plantswoman's garden with a range of interesting and unusual plants.

Directions: Park in the public car park at Rockcliffe. Walk down the road about fifty metres towards the sea and turn left along The Merse, a private road. Seabank is the sixth house on the left.

Disabled Access:
Partial

Opening Times:
Sunday 25 June
2:00pm - 5:00pm
Also by arrangement
1 June - 31 August

Admission:
£4.00, accompanied children free

Charities:
Marie Curie (DG5 Fundraising Group) receives 40%, the net remaining to SG Beneficiaries

14 SOUTHWICK HOUSE
Southwick DG2 8AH
Mr and Mrs R H L Thomas

The gardens at Southwick cover an extensive area displaying a wide range of plants set in a variety of garden styles, including an impressive selection of roses, hydrangeas and trees. The walled garden contains the large glasshouse in which fruit, vegetables and cut flowers are grown and is fronted by a scented rose bed. The potager is bounded by shrub and herbaceous borders, two of which have been completely redesigned for 2017. The hedged formal garden is centred by a lily pond and lawns surrounded by rose, hydrangea and herbaceous borders. Outwith the formal gardens the water garden features two connected ponds, one with an island reached by a Chinese style bridge. Trees, shrubs and lawns envelop the ponds and extend along the Southwick Burn across which a wildflower meadow has recently been established.

Directions: On the A710 near Caulkerbush. Dalbeattie seven miles, Dumfries seventeen miles.

Disabled Access:
Partial

Opening Times:
Sunday 2 July
2:00pm - 5:00pm

Admission:
£5.00

Charities:
Friends of Loch Arthur Community receives 40%, the net remaining to SG Beneficiaries

15 STOCKARTON
Kirkcudbright DG6 4XS
Lt. Col. and Mrs Richard Cliff T: 01557 330430

This charming garden was started in 1994. The aim has been to create small informal gardens around a Galloway farmhouse, leading down to a lochan, where there is a number of unusual small trees and shrubs. In 1996 a small arboretum of oak, including some very rare ones, was planted as a shelter belt.

Directions: On B727 Kirkcudbright to Gelston Road. Kirkcudbright three miles, Gelston 5 miles.

Disabled Access:
Partial

Opening Times:
Sunday 11 June
2:00pm - 5:00pm
Also by arrangement
1 April - 31 July

Admission:
£4.00, accompanied children free

Charities:
Friends of Loch Arthur Community receives 40%, the net remaining to SG Beneficiaries

THE LIMES WITH GLENLIVET
Kirkcudbright DG6 4XD
Mr and Mrs McHale

This one and a quarter acre plantsman's garden has a variety of different plant habitats: woodland, dry sunny gravel beds, rock garden, crevice garden and mixed perennial and shrub borders. There is also a large productive vegetable garden. The McHales like to grow most of their plants from seed obtained through various international seed exchanges. You can expect to see a large number of unusual and exciting plants. In June the meconopsis should be at their best.

Directions: In Kirkcudbright go straight along St Mary Street towards Dundrennan. The Limes is on the right, about ½ mile from the town centre crossroads, on the edge of the town i.e. ½ mile in the opposite direction from Glenlivet.

Disabled Access:
Partial

Opening Times:
Sunday 18 June
1:00pm - 5:00pm

Admission:
£5.00 includes entry to both gardens, accompanied children free

Charities:
Friends of Kirkcudbright Swimming Pool receives 40%, the net remaining to SG Beneficiaries

---

 THE WATERHOUSE GARDENS AT STOCKARTON
Kirkcudbright DG6 4XS
Martin Gould & Sharon O'Rourke T: 01557 331266
E: waterhousekbt@aol.com   www.waterhousekbt.co.uk

One acre of densely planted terraced cottage style gardens attached to a Galloway Cottage, three ponds surround the oak framed eco-polehouse. The Waterhouse is available to rent 52 weeks a year. Climbing roses, clematis and honeysuckles are a big feature as well as pond-side walk. Over 50 photos on our website, featured on BBC Scotland's *Beechgrove Garden* in 2007.

Directions: On B727 Kirkcudbright to Gelston Road - Dalbeattie Road. Kirkcudbright three miles, Castle Douglas seven miles.

Disabled Access:
None

Opening Times:
By arrangement
1 May - 30 September
Preferably Mondays or Fridays

Admission:
£3.00, accompanied children free

Charities:
Friends of Loch Arthur Community receives 40%, the net remaining to SG Beneficiaries

---

 THREAVE GARDEN
Castle Douglas DG7 1RX
The National Trust for Scotland T: 01556 502 575
E: rapolley@nts.org.uk   www.nts.org.uk/Property/Threave-Garden-and-Estate

Home of the Trust's School of Heritage Gardening. Spectacular daffodils in spring, colourful herbaceous borders in summer, striking autumn trees, interesting water features and a heather garden. There is also a working walled garden. For more information on the Scotland's Gardens event, please contact the property or visit *http://www.nts.org.uk/Events/*.

Other Details: Champion Trees: Acer platanoides 'Princeton Gold'. BBQ & Music in the Garden on 6 August. Cafe open daily. Plants and garden produce for sale. Self-catering accommodation available. Whilst dogs are welcome on the wider Threave estate, only assistance dogs are permitted in the garden.

Directions: Off A75, one mile west of Castle Douglas.

Disabled Access:
Full

Opening Times:
Sunday 7 May
10:00am - 5:00pm
Sunday 6 August
6:00pm - 10:00pm
for music & BBQ

Admission:
Normal NTS admission applies

Charities:
Donation to SG Beneficiaries

WIGTOWNSHIRE

Scotland's Gardens 2017 Guidebook is sponsored by **INVESTEC WEALTH & INVESTMENT**

District Organiser

Ann Watson	Doonholm, Cairnryan Road, Stranraer DG9 8AT
	E: wigtownshire@scotlandsgardens.org

Area Organisers

Eileen Davie	Whitehills House, Minnigaff, Newton Stewart DG8 6SL
Giles Davies	Elmlea Plants, Minnigaff, Newton Stewart DG8 6PX
Andrew Gladstone	Craichlaw, Kirkcowan, Newton Stewart DG8 0DQ
Shona Greenhorn	Burbainie, Westwood Avenue, Stranraer DG9 8BT
Janet Hannay	Cuddyfield, Carsluith DG8 7DS
Enid Innes	Crinan, Creetown, Newton Stewart DG8 7EP
Annmaree Mitchell	Cottage 2, Little Float, Sandhead DG9 9LD
Vicky Roberts	Logan House Gdns, Port Logan, by Stranraer DG9 9ND

Treasurer

George Fleming	Ardgour, Stoneykirk, Stranraer DG9 9DL

Gardens open on a specific date

Claymoddie Garden, Whithorn	Sunday 30 April	11:00am	-	5:00pm
Logan House Gardens, Port Logan	Sunday 14 May	1:00pm	-	4:30pm
Logan Botanic Garden, Port Logan	Sunday 21 May	10:00am	-	5:00pm
Balker Farmhouse, Stranraer	Sunday 28 May	2:00pm	-	5:00pm
Galloway House Gardens, Garlieston	Sunday 28 May	9:00am	-	5:00pm
Castle Kennedy and Gardens, Stranraer	Sunday 11 June	10:00am	-	5:00pm
Woodfall Gardens, Glasserton	Sunday 18 June	10:30am	-	4:30pm
Woodfall Gardens, Glasserton	Sunday 9 July	10:30am	-	4:30pm
Fernlea Garden with Lisieux Garden, Newton Stewart	Sunday 16 July	2:00pm	-	5:00pm
Ardwell House Gardens, Ardwell	Sunday 30 July	10:00am	-	5:00pm

Gardens open regularly

Ardwell House Gardens, Ardwell	1 April - 31 October	10:00am	-	5:00pm
Glenwhan Gardens, Dunragit	1 April - 31 October	10:00am	-	5:00pm

Gardens open by arrangement

Balker Farmhouse, Stranraer	1 May - 30 September	01776 702110
Craichlaw, Kirkcowan, Newton Stewart	On request	01671 830208

WIGTOWNSHIRE

Logan Botanic Garden

Key to symbols

 New in 2017

 Homemade teas

 Accommodation

 Teas

 Dogs on a lead allowed

 Plant stall

 Cream teas

 Wheelchair access

 Scottish Snowdrop Festival

GARDEN LOCATIONS
IN WIGTOWNSHIRE

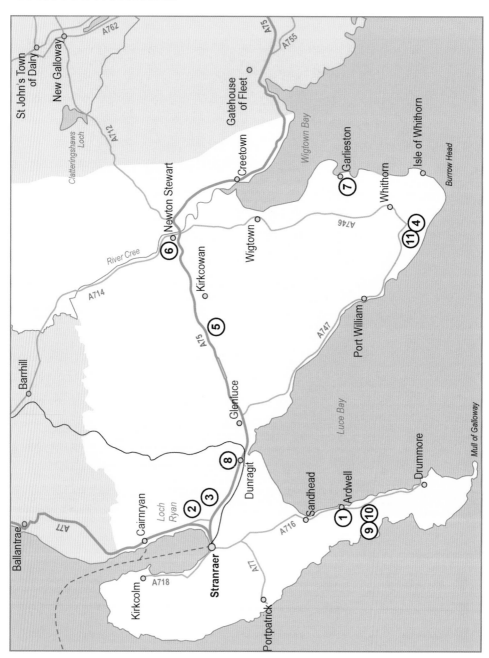

ARDWELL HOUSE GARDENS
Ardwell, Stranraer DG9 9LY
Mr and Mrs Christopher Brewis

Daffodils, spring flowers, rhododendrons, flowering shrubs, coloured foliage and rock plants. Moist garden at smaller pond and a 25-minute walk around larger pond with views over Luce Bay.

Other Details: Coach parties by arrangement.

Directions: A716 towards Mull of Galloway. Stranraer 10 miles.

Disabled Access:
None

Opening Times:
Sunday 30 July
1 April - 31 October
10:00am - 5:00pm

Admission:
£4.00, accomp. children free

Charities:
Ardwell Community Kirk receives 40% (for July opening), Maggie's receives 40% (for April -October openings), the net remaining to SG Beneficiaries

BALKER FARMHOUSE
Stranraer DG9 8RS
Davina, Countess of Stair T: 01776 702110

The house was restored and the garden, formerly a ploughed field, was started in 2003-4. It is now full of wonderful shrubs and plants for all seasons.

Other Details: There are gravel paths on the slope so it is not suitable for wheelchairs. There is a tearoom nearby at Castle Kennedy Gardens.

Directions: One and a half miles off A75, three miles from Stranraer - go through the farmyard to the blue gate.

Disabled Access:
None

Opening Times:
Sunday 28 May
2:00pm - 5:00pm
Also by arrangement
1 May - 30 September

Admission:
£4.00

Charities:
World Horse Welfare receives 20%, Canine Partners receives 20%, the net remaining to SG Beneficiaries

CASTLE KENNEDY AND GARDENS
Stranraer DG9 8SL
The Earl and Countess of Stair T: 01581 400225
www.castlekennedygardens.com

These famous 75 acres of landscaped gardens are located on an isthmus surrounded by two large natural lochs. At one end the ruined Castle Kennedy overlooks a beautiful herbaceous walled garden with Lochinch Castle at the other end. With over 300 years of planting there is an impressive collection of rare trees, rhododendrons, exotic shrubs and featuring many spectacular Champion Trees. The stunning snowdrop walks, daffodils, spring flowers, rhododendron and magnolia displays, and herbaceous borders make this a 'must visit' garden throughout the year.

Other Details: Champion Trees: 6 British, 11 Scottish, 25 for Dumfries and Galloway. Wildlife ranger events, Head Gardener guided walks, tree and family trails, bird hides, open air theatre, holiday cottages, charming tea room serving homemade teas and light lunches, plant centre and gift shop. Also open weekends Feb & Mar for the Snowdrop Festival and daily 1 Apr - 31 Oct, see website for further details.

Directions: A75 five miles E of Stranraer. Nearest train Stranraer. Local bus route.

Disabled Access:
Partial

Opening Times:
Sunday 11 June
10:00am - 5:00pm

Admission:
Adults £5.50, concessions £4.50, children £2.00, disabled free, families £12.00 (2 adults and 2 children) Special group discounts

Charities:
Homestart Wigtownshire receives 40%, the net remaining to SG Beneficiaries

CLAYMODDIE GARDEN
Whithorn, Newton Stewart DG8 8LX
Mrs Mary Nicholson T: 01988 500422
E: mary.claymoddie@aol.co.uk www.claymoddiegarden.com

This romantic five acre garden, designed and developed by the owner, an avid landscaper and plantsman, reflects half a century of dedicated work. It provides a range of timeless, intimate settings, both shady and sunny, for a vast range of plants from both hemispheres, all helped by the proximity of the Gulf Stream. Running through the lower part of the garden is the burn feeding a large pond which, along with the variety of plants and their backdrop of mature woodland, provides the perfect habitat for wildlife, in particular birds. There are changes in levels, but most of the garden is accessible to wheelchairs.

Other Details: Also open March to September, Friday-Sunday, 2:00pm-5:00pm or by appointment. There is normally no tearoom but Whithorn has several cafes.

Directions: From Whithorn: A746 south for 2 miles to Glasserton crossroads, then right onto the B7004. After 300 yards turn right up farm road signed *Claymoddie.*

Disabled Access:
Partial

Opening Times:
Sunday 30 April
11:00am - 5:00pm

Admission:
£5.00

Charities:
Whithorn Trust receives 40%, the net remaining to SG Beneficiaries

CRAICHLAW
Kirkcowan, Newton Stewart DG8 0DQ
Mr and Mrs A Gladstone T: 01671 830208
E: craichlaw@aol.com

Formal garden with herbaceous borders around the house. Set in extensive grounds with lawns, lochs and woodland. A path around the main loch leads to a water garden returning past a recently planted arboretum in the old walled garden. The best times to visit the garden are early February for snowdrops, May to mid-June for the water garden and rhododendrons and mid-June to August for herbaceous borders.

Other Details: Coach parties welcome.

Directions: Take the B733 for Kirkcowan off the A75 at the Halfway House eight miles west of Newton Stewart. Craichlaw House is the first turning on the right.

Disabled Access:
Partial

Opening Times:
By arrangement on request

Admission:
£4.00

Charities:
Donation to SG Beneficiaries

6 NEW FERNLEA GARDEN WITH LISIEUX GARDEN
Newton Stewart DG8 6LW
Mrs Jenny Gustafson and Mr & Mrs Ian Young

Fernlea Garden, Corvisel Road DG8 6LW:
A secluded town garden of a third of an acre. It was created ten years ago to complement a new house. There are many rare and unusual trees and shrubs. Two herbaceous borders, one with hot colours and the other pastels. A Chinese inspired corner, small pond, fruit trees including a Galloway pippin apple and soft fruit. There is a greenhouse with a productive grape vine from which wine is made. The upper part of the garden is hidden behind a tall beech hedge where there is a summer house.

Lisieux Garden, Gilmour Terrace DG8 6HR:
A small but colourful cottage style garden within an area bordered by high privet hedges and ancient rhododendrons. The bottom of the garden has several varieties of rowan and silver birch, and, most surprising, a 30 foot tall *Sequoia gigantea* (Redwood). The lawn is edged by deep borders with a wide range of shrubs, perennials, lilies and annuals such as sweet peas, misembryanthemums, cosmos, lavatera and sidalcea, etc. A small water feature and pond provides interest behind which a large collection of acers and conifers enjoy the dappled sunlight. We love our hostas, clematis, climbing roses and large HT rose bed.

Other Details: Teas and cakes served in the conservatory at Fernlea. Toilets available at Fernlea.

Directions: Turn right at the roundabout on the A75 if coming from Dumfries direction. Go left at the cattle market (opposite Crown Hotel), first through road on the right and Fernlea is the last house at far end on left.

Disabled Access:
Partial

Opening Times:
Sunday 16 July
2:00pm - 5:00pm

Admission:
£4.50, accompanied children free

Charities:
Host receives 20% and a charity to be advised will receive 20%, the net remaining to SG Beneficiaries

---

7 NEW GALLOWAY HOUSE GARDENS
Garlieston, Newton Stewart DG8 8HF
Galloway House Gardens Trust
www.gallowayhousegardens.co.uk

The garden is situated on the Solway Firth and benefits from the Gulf Stream. Visitors can wander through the arboretum on a network of hard and grass paths, which features handkerchief trees, soaring douglas firs, beeches, oaks, a particularly splendid horse chestnut, species rhododendrons and magnolias. Our walled garden, which is undergoing restoration, will be open on the day where refreshments will be served. Rigg Bay, which features an attractive sandy beach, adjoins the arboretum and our wilder woodland walk.

Other Details: The arboretum can be enjyed from a network of hard paths (no steps but some inclines).

Directions: South from Newton Stewart on the A714 and follow signs to Garlieston on B7004. At the first crossroads after passing the village sign go straight across on to the estate road then take the second right up to the pay and display car park.

Disabled Access:
Partial

Opening Times:
Sunday 28 May 9:00am - 5:00pm (gates close 8:00pm)

Admission:
Car parking £3.00, walled garden £2.50 per person (includes homemade refreshments), no additional charge for arboretum

Charities:
Galloway House Gardens receives 40%, the net remaining to SG Beneficiaries

GLENWHAN GARDENS
Dunragit, by Stranraer DG9 8PH
Mr and Mrs W Knott T: 07787 990702
www.glenwhangardens.co.uk

Described as one of the most beautiful gardens in Scotland, situated at 300 feet, overlooking Luce Bay and the Mull of Galloway, with clear views to the Isle of Man. Thirty-five years ago there was wild moorland, but with dedication and vision, you can now see glorious collections of plants from around the world. There is colour in all seasons and the winding paths, well placed seats, and varied sculptures, focusing around small lakes, add to the tranquil atmosphere. There is a 17 acre moorland wildflower walk, the chance to see red squirrels and a well marked Tree Trail.

Other Details: Thriving plant nursery and tearoom with delicious home produce. Parties catered for with notice. Disabled access available in most parts. Pond dipping and wildlife trails, moorland walks, easter egg hunt and children's quiz.

Directions: Seven miles east of Stranraer, one mile off A75 at Dunragit (follow brown VisitScotland signs).

Disabled Access:
Partial

Opening Times:
1 April - 31 October
10:00am - 5:00pm

Admission:
£5.00, season ticket £15.00, family ticket £12.00 (up to three children)

Charities:
Donation to SG Beneficiaries

LOGAN BOTANIC GARDEN
Port Logan, by Stranraer DG9 9ND
A Regional Garden of the Royal Botanic Garden Edinburgh T: 01776 860231
www.rbge.org.uk/logan

CELEBRATING 25 YEARS OF OPENING FOR CHARITY WITH SCOTLAND'S GARDENS!

At the south western tip of Scotland lies Logan which is unrivalled as the country's most exotic garden. With a mild climate washed by the Gulf Stream, a remarkable collection of bizarre and beautiful plants, especially from the southern hemisphere, flourish out of doors. Enjoy the colourful walled garden with its magnificent tree ferns, palms and borders along with the contrasting woodland garden with its unworldly gunnera bog. Visit the Logan Conservatory which houses a special collection of tender South African species.

Other Details: National Plant Collection®: Gunnera/Leptospermum/Griselinia. Champion Trees: Polylepis/Eucalyptus. Home baking, botanic shop, Discovery Centre, audio tours available and Logan Exhibition studio.

Directions: Ten miles south of Stranraer on A716 then 2½ miles from Ardwell.

Disabled Access:
Full

Opening Times:
Sunday 21 May
10:00am - 5:00pm

Admission:
£6.50, concessions £5.50, u16 free (includes donation to garden, for prices without donation check rbge.org.uk).

Charities:
RBGE receives 40%, the net remaining to SG Beneficiaries

LOGAN HOUSE GARDENS
Port Logan, by Stranraer DG9 9ND
Mr and Mrs Andrew Roberts

The Queen Anne house is surrounded by sweeping lawns and a truly spectacular woodland garden. Rare and exotic plants together with champion trees and fine species of rhododendrons provide an excellent habitat for an interesting variety of wildlife.

Other Details: Champion Trees: seven UK and eleven Scottish Champions.

Directions: On A716 thirteen miles south of Stranraer, 2½ miles from Ardwell village.

Disabled Access:
Partial

Opening Times:
Sunday 14 May
1:00pm - 4:30pm

Admission:
£4.00, children under 16 free

Charities:
Port Logan Hall receives 40%, the net remaining to SG Beneficiaries

WOODFALL GARDENS
Glasserton DG8 8LY
Ross and Liz Muir
E: woodfallgardens@btinternet.com   www.woodfall-gardens.co.uk

This lovely three acre 18th century triple walled garden has been thoughtfully restored to provide year round interest. Many mature trees and shrubs including some less common species; herbaceous borders and shrub roses surround the foundations of original greenhouses; grass borders; a parterre; extensive beds of fruit and vegetables; a herb garden; a small woodland walk. This unusual garden is well worth a visit.

Other Details: Teas on 18 June only. Woodfall is open all year by arrangement. Please contact us by email.

Directions: Two miles south-west of Whithorn at junction of A746 and A747 (directly behind Glasserton Church).

Disabled Access:
Partial

Opening Times:
Sunday 18 June
& Sunday 9 July
10:30am - 4:30pm

Admission:
£4.00, children free must be accomp. by responsible adult

Charities:
Glasserton Parish Church receives 20%, Macmillan Cancer Support receives 20%, the net remaining to SG Beneficiaries

Each visit you make to one of our gardens in 2017 will raise money for our beneficiary charities:

In addition, funds will be distributed to a charity of the owner's choice.
For South West Scotland, these include:

Alzheimer Scotland	Poppy Scotland
Alzheimer's Research	Port Logan Hall
Ardwell Community Kirk	RBGE
Brooke | Action for Working Horses and Donkeys	ROKPA Tibetan Charity
Canine Concern Scotland Trust	Scottish Wildlife Trust
Canine Partners	The Buccleuch and Queensberry Pipebank
Castle Loch, Lochmaben Community Trust	The Crichton Trust
Compassion in World Farming	The Dunscore Gala
Corsock and Kirkpatrick Durham Church	The Jo Walters Trust
Dogs for Good	The Kirkcudbright Hospital League of Friends
Dumfries Music Club	The Thornhill Scottish Country Dancers
Friends of Kirkcudbright Swimming Pool	Westerkirk Parish Trust
Friends of Loch Arthur Community	Whithorn Trust
Glasserton Parish Church	World Horse Welfare
Homestart Wigtownshire	
Kirkandrews Church	
Kirkmahoe Parish Church	
Kirkpatrick Durham Church	
Loch Arthur Community (Camphill Trust)	
Macmillan Cancer Support	
Maggie's Cancer Caring Centres	
Marie Curie (DG5 Fundraising Group)	
National Trust for Scotland (Threave Ospreys)	
Peter Pan Moat Brae Trust	

SOUTH EAST SCOTLAND

Scotland's Gardens 2017 Guidebook is sponsored by **INVESTEC WEALTH & INVESTMENT**

BERWICKSHIRE

Scotland's Gardens 2017 Guidebook is sponsored by **INVESTEC WEALTH & INVESTMENT**

District Organiser

Cilla Wills	Anton's Hill, Coldstream TD12 4JD
	E: berwickshire@scotlandsgardens.org

Treasurer

Freddy Wills	Anton's Hill, Coldstream TD12 4JD

Gardens open on a specific date

East Gordon Smiddy, Gordon	Sunday 25 June	11:00am	-	5:00pm
Lennel Bank, Coldstream	Sunday 2 July	10:30am	-	5:00pm
Netherbyres, Eyemouth	Sunday 16 July	2:00pm	-	5:00pm
Kames, Greenlaw	Sunday 23 July	2:00pm	-	5:00pm

Gardens open regularly

Bughtrig, Near Leitholm, Coldstream	1 June - 1 September	11:00am	-	5:00pm

Gardens open by arrangement

Lennel Bank, Coldstream	On request	01890 882297
Netherbyres, Eyemouth	1 May - 31 August	01890 750337

Key to symbols

	New in 2017		Homemade teas		Accommodation
	Teas		Dogs on a lead allowed		Plant stall
	Cream teas		Wheelchair access		Scottish Snowdrop Festival

GARDEN LOCATIONS IN BERWICKSHIRE

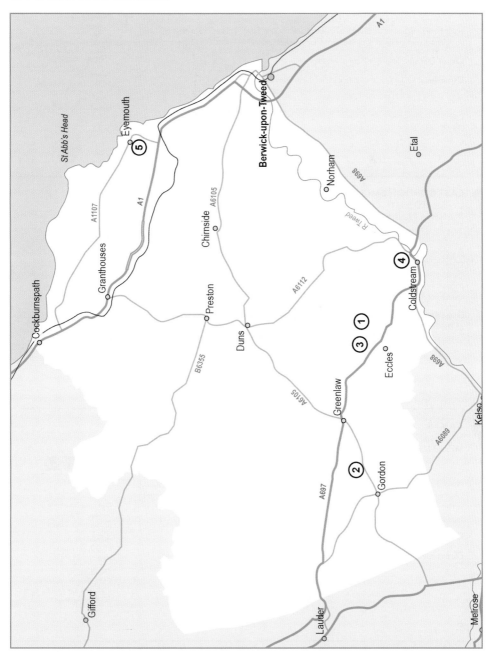

BERWICKSHIRE

 1 BUGHTRIG
Near Leitholm, Coldstream TD12 4JP
Mr and Mrs William Ramsay T: 01890 840777
E: ramsay@bughtrig.co.uk

A traditional hedged Scottish family garden with an interesting combination of sculpture, herbaceous plants, shrubs, annuals and fruit. It is surrounded by fine specimen trees which provide remarkable shelter.

Other Details: There will be plants for sale.

Directions: Quarter of a mile east of Leitholm on the B6461.

Disabled Access:
Partial

Opening Times:
1 June - 1 September
11:00am - 5:00pm

Admission:
£4.00, children £1.00

Charities:
Donation to SG Beneficiaries

---

 2 EAST GORDON SMIDDY
Gordon TD3 6JY
Martyn and Judith Welch

A garden newly created from farmland in 2008 with wonderful panoramic views towards the Cheviot Hills. Herbaceous borders, shrubbery, extensive vegetable garden and fruit trees. There is a pond, woodland and wildflower meadow. The whole garden is divided by mature hornbeam hedging, grass pathways and interesting corners to sit and contemplate.

Directions: On the A6105 between Gordon and Greenlaw at East Gordon. On top of the hill at the farm entrance.

Disabled Access:
Full

Opening Times:
Sunday 25 June
11:00am - 5:00pm

Admission:
£5.00, accompanied children free

Charities:
Sustrans receives 40%, the net remaining to SG Beneficiaries

---

 3 KAMES
Greenlaw TD11 3RD
Mr and Mrs D Jenkinson

An old and well established garden with shrubs and herbaceous plants, with a superb view of the Cheviot Hills. There is a very attractive large landscaped lake, together with a further pond, and a new woodland walk. The abandoned walled garden is currently six years into a restoration project and progressing well.

Other Details: Teas by the lake.

Directions: Take the A697 onto the B6461 signposted Leitholm to Kames.

Disabled Access:
Full

Opening Times:
Sunday 23 July
2:00pm - 5:00pm

Admission:
£5.00, accompanied children free

Charities:
CLIC Sargent receives 40%, the net remaining to SG Beneficiaries

LENNEL BANK
Coldstream TD12 4EX
Mrs Honor Brown T: 01890 882297

Lennel Bank is a terraced garden overlooking the River Tweed, consisting of wide borders packed with shrubs and perennial planting, some unusual. The water garden, built in 2008, is surrounded by a rockery and utilises the slope ending in a pond. There is a small kitchen garden with raised beds in unusual shapes. Different growing conditions throughout the garden from dry, wet, shady and sunny lend themselves to a variety of plants, which hopefully enhance interest in the garden.

Directions: On the A6112 Coldstream to Duns road, one mile from Coldstream.

Disabled Access:
None

Opening Times:
Sunday 2 July
10:30am - 5:00pm
Also by arrangement on request

Admission:
£5.00

Charities:
British Heart Foundation receives 40%, the net remaining to SG Beneficiaries

NETHERBYRES
Eyemouth TD14 5SE
Col S J Furness T: 01890 750337

A traditional Scottish walled garden, with a mixture of fruit, flowers and vegetables. It is thought to be the only elliptical walled garden in the world, dating from 1740. A pear tree planted at that time still survives, next to the largest rose in Berwickshire (R Kiftsgate).

Directions: Half a mile south of Eyemouth on the A1107 to Berwick.

Disabled Access:
Full

Opening Times:
Sunday 16 July
2:00pm - 5:00pm
Also by arrangement
1 May - 31 August

Admission:
£5.00, concessions £4.00, accompanied children free

Charities:
Gunsgreen House Trust receives 40%, the net remaining to SG Beneficiaries

EAST LOTHIAN

Scotland's Gardens 2017 Guidebook is sponsored by INVESTEC WEALTH & INVESTMENT

District Organiser

Frank Kirwan	Humbie Dean, Humbie, East Lothian EH36 5PW
	E: eastlothian@scotlandsgardens.org

Area Organisers

Bill Alder	Granary House, Kippielaw, Haddington EH41 4PY
Becca Duncan	St Michael's Lodge, Inveresk EH21 7UA
Mark Hedderwick	Gifford Bank, Gifford EH41 4JE
Beryl McNaughton	Macplants Berrybank Nursery, 5 Boggs Holdings, Pencaitland EH34 5BA
Ian Orr	6 Grannus Mews, Inveresk EH21 7TT
Julia Parker	Steading Cottage, Stevenson, Haddington EH41 4PU
Judy Riley	The Old Kitchen, Tyninghame House, Tyninghame EH42 1XW

Treasurer

Joan Johnson	The Round House, Woodbush, Dunbar EH42 1HB

Gardens open on a specific date

Shepherd House, Inveresk	Saturday 25 February	11:00am	4:00pm
Shepherd House, Inveresk	Sunday 26 February	11:00am	4:00pm
Winton House, Pencaitland	Sunday 9 April	12:00pm	4:30pm
Humbie Dean, Humbie	Wednesday 19 April	1:00pm	5:00pm
Humbie Dean, Humbie	Wednesday 3 May	1:00pm	5:00pm
Shepherd House, Inveresk	Saturday 6 May	11:00am	4:00pm
Shepherd House, Inveresk	Sunday 7 May	11:00am	4:00pm
Tyninghame House and The Walled Garden, Dunbar	Sunday 14 May	1:00pm	5:00pm
Humbie Dean, Humbie	Wednesday 17 May	1:00pm	5:00pm
Belhaven House with Belhaven Hill School, Dunbar	Sunday 28 May	2:00pm	5:00pm
Humbie Dean, Humbie	Wednesday 31 May	1:00pm	5:00pm
Broadwoodside, Gifford	Sunday 4 June	2:00pm	6:00pm
Humbie Dean, Humbie	Wednesday 14 June	1:00pm	5:00pm
Tyninghame House and The Walled Garden, Dunbar	Sunday 18 June	1:00pm	5:00pm
Humbie Dean, Humbie	Wednesday 21 June	1:00pm	5:00pm

EAST LOTHIAN

Longniddry Gardens, Longniddry	Sunday 25 June	1:00pm	- 5:00pm
East Lothian Garden Trail, East Lothian	Wednesday 28 June	1:00pm	- 6:00pm
East Lothian Garden Trail, East Lothian	Thursday 29 June	1:00pm	- 6:00pm
East Lothian Garden Trail, East Lothian	Friday 30 June	1:00pm	- 6:00pm
East Lothian Garden Trail, East Lothian	Saturday 1 July	1:00pm	- 6:00pm
East Lothian Garden Trail, East Lothian	Sunday 2 July	1:00pm	- 6:00pm
Humbie Dean, Humbie	Wednesday 5 July	1:00pm	- 5:00pm
Gullane Coastal Gardens, Gullane	Sunday 9 July	2:00pm	- 5:00pm
Humbie Dean, Humbie	Wednesday 19 July	1:00pm	- 5:00pm
Humbie Dean, Humbie	Wednesday 2 August	1:00pm	- 5:00pm

Gardens open regularly

East Lothian Garden Trail, East Lothian	28 June - 2 July	1:00pm	- 6:00pm
Shepherd House, Inveresk, Musselburgh	14 February - 9 March & 18 April - 13 July (Tue and Thu only)	2:00pm	- 4:00pm

Gardens open by arrangement

Stobshiel House , Humbie	1 March - 1 December	01875 833646

Key to symbols

 New in 2017

 Teas

 Cream teas

 Homemade teas

 Dogs on a lead allowed

 Wheelchair access

 Accommodation

 Plant stall

 Scottish Snowdrop Festival

GARDEN LOCATIONS
IN EAST LOTHIAN

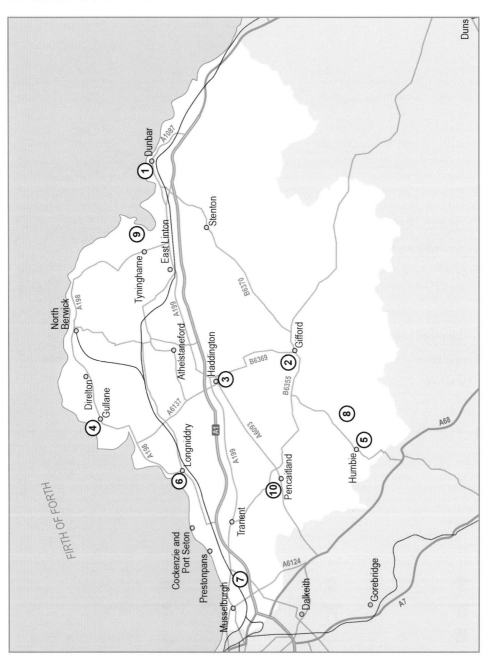

BELHAVEN HOUSE WITH BELHAVEN HILL SCHOOL
Belhaven Road, Dunbar EH42 1NN
Mr and Mrs Jon Bruneau and Mr Henry Knight

Belhaven House: has four acres of formal Georgian gardens, a walled vegetable and fruit garden, and a woodland with trees dating from the early 20th century. The garden has been associated with a succession of people interested in plants since the 19th century - being owned for a while by Sir George Taylor, a former director of Kew gardens. There are borders, garden terraces and troughs. Entry to the the garden is through the school playing field.

Belhaven Hill School: Originally called Winterfield House, the school has retained a formal garden accessed through an ornate gate and archway and laid to lawn with box-edged borders, some containing wild flowers. A gate from the playing field leads to the Belhaven House garden.

Other Details: Champion Trees: at Belhaven House - *Arbutus unedo, Davidia involucrata, Eucryphia nymansensis* and more.

Directions: Approaching Dunbar from the A1 on the A1087 Belhaven House is opposite Brewery Lane on the junction with Duke Street, the school entrance is a further 300 yards past a high stone wall.

Disabled Access:
Partial

Opening Times:
Sunday 28 May
2:00pm - 5:00pm

Admission:
£5.00, children under 12 free for admission to both gardens

Charities:
East Lothian Special Needs Play Schemes receives 40%, the net remaining to SG Beneficiaries

Belhaven Hill School

Belhaven House

BROADWOODSIDE
Gifford EH41 4JQ
Anna and Robert Dalrymple
www.broadwoodside.co.uk

The garden is planted in and around a farm steading saved from dereliction in 2000. While people often talk of starting a new garden with a blank canvas, Broadwoodside was more like painting by numbers - planting the garden has been like an exercise in 'colouring-in' with the layout determined by the footprint of existing buildings and the old walls surrounding them. But, unlike a picture in a frame, a garden is always a work in progress.

Directions: On the B6355 going out of Gifford towards Pencaitland, at the Golf Course junction.

Disabled Access:
Partial

Opening Times:
Sunday 4 June
2:00pm - 6:00pm

Admission:
£5.00, children free

Charities:
Leuchie House receives 40%, the net remaining to SG Beneficiaries

EAST LOTHIAN

3 NEW EAST LOTHIAN GARDEN TRAIL
East Lothian
The East Lothian Gardeners
E: ianandisabel@mac.com

Scotland's Gardens is proud to announce another East Lothian Garden trail after the first successful venture in 2014. This trail provides an opportunity to see twelve magnificent spacious gardens and well tended allotments in close proximity over a day or over multiple days.

Disabled Access:
Partial

Opening Times:
28 June - 2 July
1:00pm - 6:00pm

Admission:
Trail ticket £25.00, accompanied children under 16 free. £5.00 single garden entry.

Charities:
Trellis receives 20%, MND Scotland receives 20%, the net remaining to SG Beneficiaries

Blackdykes, North Berwick EH39 5PQ (Janey and Hew Dalrymple)
Bowerhouse, Dunbar EH42 1RE (Rebecca and Mark Tyndall)
Bowerhouse Walled Garden, Dunbar EH42 1RE (Moira and Ian Marrian)
Congalton House, North Berwick EH39 5JL (Clare and John Carson)
Fairnielaw House, Athelstaneford EH39 5BE (Alison and David Johnson)
Frostineb, Pathhead EH37 5TB (Henry and Caroline Gibson)
Garvald Grange, Garvald EH41 4LL (Caro and Hugo Straker)
Green House at Eskhill, Inveresk EH21 7TD (Lindsay and Robin Burley)
Musselburgh Allotments, Inveresk EH21 7TF (Secretary Alex Craigie)
Prestonhall Walled Garden, Pathhead EH37 5UG (Mrs Henry Callander)
Redcliff, Whittingehame, Haddington EH41 4QA (Joe and Jenny Harper)
The Hopes, Gifford EH41 4PL (Cressida and Robert Douglas Miller)

Other Details: Art and craft exhibition at Bowerhouse.

Admission: Season tickets for all twelve gardens over five days by advance purchase ticket are available from **http://www.scotlandsgardens.org/elgt2017** or by cheque, payable to Scotland's Gardens and accompanied by a stamped addressed envelope, to Ian Orr, 6 Grannus Mews, Inveresk EH21 7TT. E: ianandisabel@mac.com. £5.00 for last minute entry to a single garden on a single day. Please note: the gardens are open on all five days apart from The Hopes which will be open on 27 and 28 June and Musselburgh Allotments which will be open 1 and 2 July. See pages 36 - 37 for further details.

Directions: A map and full details of each garden are in the leaflet accompanying trail tickets.

Redcliff

Musselburgh Allotments

5 NEW **GULLANE COASTAL GARDENS**
Gullane EH31 2BH
The Gardeners of Gullane
E: jane.kirk13@btopenworld.com

A collection of beautiful and interesting gardens of various sizes and types (small to three acres) in Scotland's historic and pretty golfing village. Some overlook the majestic Firth of Forth or the golf courses and all are in walking distance of the village, with its 12th century church and its prize-winning beach. The gardens display a wide variety of herbaceous borders, roses and other shrubs and plants which enjoy Gullane's unique micro-climate.

Directions: Gullane is on the A198, five miles west of North Berwick.

Disabled Access:
Partial

Opening Times:
Sunday 9 July
2:00pm - 5:00pm

Admission:
£6.00, accompanied children free

Charities:
Leuchie House receives 40%, the net remaining to SG Beneficiaries

---

6 **HUMBIE DEAN**
Humbie EH36 5PW
Frank Kirwan T: 07768 996382
E: frank.kirwan@which.net www.humbiedean.com

A two acre ornamental and woodland garden at 600 feet which has been under renovation and major extension since 2008. The aim is to provide interest throughout a long season. A limited palette of plants with Hosta, primula, meconopsis and spring bulbs, herbaceous and shrubaceous planting, bluebell meadow mature and recent azalea and rhododendron planting. A short woodland walk has been created.

Other Details: Access-exit to the woodland walk is via multiple sets of steps.

Directions: Enter Humbie from the A68, pass the school and village hall on the left then immediately turn right into the lane. Take second left and Humbie Dean is on the left between two small bridges.

Disabled Access:
None

Opening Times:
Wednesday 19 April
Wednesday 3, 17 & 31 May
Wednesday 14 & 21 June
Wednesday 5 & 19 July
Wednesday 2 August
1:00pm - 5:00pm

Admission:
£5.00

Charities:
Mamie Martin fund receives 40%, the net remaining to SG Beneficiaries

EAST LOTHIAN

LONGNIDDRY GARDENS
EH32 0LF
The Gardeners of Longniddry

Longniddry is an attractive village with extensive green spaces and outstanding sea views. Our gardens, some large and some small, show a variety of trees, shrubs, herbaceous borders, summer bedding and overall garden designs. They are tended by enthusiastic gardeners some of whom are old hands and some recent converts to gardening, ensuring something for every visitor to enjoy.

Other Details: Tickets and maps will be available at three gardens at the main entrances to Longniddry. These gardens will be well signposted.

Directions: On the A198 from North Berwick (east) or Edinburgh (west). Access also from the B1348 (the coast road from Port Seton/Cockenzie) and the B1377 (from Drem).

Disabled Access:
Partial

Opening Times:
Sunday 25 June
1:00pm - 5:00pm

Admission:
£6.00, accompanied children free

Charities:
Leuchie House, North Berwick receives 20%, Teapot Trust receives 20%, the net remaining to SG Beneficiaries

---

SHEPHERD HOUSE
Inveresk, Musselburgh EH21 7TH
Sir Charles and Lady Fraser T: 0131 665 2570
E: annfraser@talktalk.net   www.shepherdhousegarden.co.uk

Shepherd House and its one acre garden form a walled triangle in the middle of the 18th century village of Inveresk. The main garden is to the rear of the house where the formality of the front garden is continued with a herb parterre and two symmetrical potagers. A formal rill runs the length of the garden, beneath a series of rose and clematis arches and connects the two ponds. There is a growing collection of specialist snowdrops which are mainly grown in beds and borders some of which will be displayed in our "Snowdrop Theatre". An addition to the garden in 2014 was a Shell House, designed by Lachlan Stewart. The garden has been featured in many magazines and in 2015 appeared on ITV in Alan Titchmarsh's *Britain's Best Back Gardens*. Charles and Ann have also published a book *Shepherd House Garden* which is for sale at Open Days, by application to Shepherd House or the website.

Other Details: Prints and cards by Ann Fraser will be on sale at weekend openings.

Directions: The garden is near Musselburgh. From the A1 take the A6094 exit signed Wallyford and Dalkeith and follow signs to Inveresk.

Disabled Access:
Partial

Opening Times:
Saturday 25 February
& Sunday 26 February
11:00am - 4:00pm
Also 14 February - 9 March
2:00pm - 4:00pm
for the Snowdrop Festival
Saturday 6 May
& Sunday 7 May
11:00am - 4:00pm
Also 18 April - 13 July
2:00pm - 4:00pm
(Tuesdays & Thursdays only)

Admission:
£5.00, accompanied children free

Charities:
Plant Life Scotland for Coronation Meadows receives 40%, the net remaining to SG Beneficiaries

STOBSHIEL HOUSE
Humbie EH36 5PD
Mr Maxwell and Lady Sarah Ward T: 01875 833646
E: stobshiel@gmail.com

A large garden to see for all seasons. Walled garden adjacent to the house, box-edged borders filled with bulbs, roses and lavender beds. There is also a rustic summerhouse, glasshouse, formal lily pond and castellated yew hedge. The shrubbery has rhododendrons, azaleas and bulbs. Growing in the water and woodland garden are meconopsis and primulas. Enjoy the beautiful woodland walks.

Directions: On the B6368 Haddington/Humbie road; sign to Stobshiel one mile.

Disabled Access:
None

Opening Times:
By arrangement
1 March - 1 December

Admission:
£5.00, children under 12 free

Charities:
Circle Scotland receives 40%, the net remaining to SG Beneficiaries

TYNINGHAME HOUSE AND THE WALLED GARDEN
Dunbar EH42 1XW
Tyninghame Gardens Ltd and Mrs C Gwyn

Splendid 17th century sandstone Scottish baronial house, remodelled in 1829 by William Burn. The gardens include herbaceous border, formal rose garden, Lady Haddington's Secret Garden with old fashioned roses and an extensive "wilderness" spring garden with rhododendrons, azaleas, flowering trees and bulbs. Grounds include a one mile beech avenue to the sea. The formal walled garden combines the lawn, sculpture and yew hedges, an "apple walk", extensive herbaceous planting including roses and peonies with an informal arboretum. The Romanesque ruin of St Baldred's Church commands views across the Tyne Estuary and Lammermuir Hills. Tyninghame has been awarded 'Outstanding' for every category in the *Inventory of Gardens and Designed Landscapes of Scotland.*

Other Details: Champion Trees: Two British and seven Scottish. Plant stall 14 May only.

Directions: Gates on the A198 at Tyninghame Village.

Disabled Access:
Full

Opening Times:
Sunday 14 May
Sunday 18 June
1:00pm - 5:00pm

Admission:
£5.00, accompanied children free

Charities:
RNLI Dunbar receives 40% (for the 14 May opening), Marie Curie receives 40% (for the 18 June opening), the net remaining to SG Beneficiaries

WINTON HOUSE
Pencaitland EH34 5AT
Sir Francis Ogilvy Winton Trust T: 01875 340222
www.wintonhouse.co.uk

The gardens continue to develop and improve. In addition to the natural areas around Sir David's Loch and the Dell, extensive mixed borders are taking shape for the terraces and walled garden. In spring a glorious covering of daffodils makes way for cherry and apple blossoms. Enjoy an informative tour of this historic house and walk off delicious lunches and home baking around the estate.

A visit to Winton House is a wonderful family day out. Their open day is essentially a family event with bouncy castle, archery, falconry displays, Luca's ice cream sold from a vintage Bentley, tours of the house, games on the lawn, treasure hunts, face painting etc.

Other Details: Home-baked teas and light lunches will be served at Café Winton.

Directions: Entrance off the B6355 Tranent/Pencaitland Road.

Disabled Access:
Full

Opening Times:
Sunday 9 April
12:00pm - 4:30pm

Admission:
£5.00
Guided House Tours £5.00/£3.00, children under 10 free

Charities:
Marie Curie receives 40%, the net remaining to SG Beneficiaries

EDINBURGH, MIDLOTHIAN & WEST LOTHIAN

Scotland's Gardens 2017 Guidebook is sponsored by **INVESTEC WEALTH & INVESTMENT**

District Organiser

Victoria Reid Thomas	Riccarton Mains Farmhouse, Currie EH14 4AR E: edinburgh@scotlandsgardens.org

Area Organisers

Nicky Lowe	2/17 Powderhall Rigg, Edinburgh EH7 4GA
Caroline Pearson	42 Pentland Avenue, Edinburgh EH13 0HY

Treasurer

Michael Pearson	42 Pentland Avenue, Edinburgh EH13 0HY

Gardens open on a specific date

41 Hermitage Gardens, Edinburgh	Saturday 22 April	2:00pm	- 5:00pm
41 Hermitage Gardens, Edinburgh	Saturday 6 May	2:00pm	- 5:00pm
Moray Place and Bank Gardens, Edinburgh	Sunday 7 May	2:00pm	- 5:00pm
Dr Neil's Garden, Duddingston Village	Saturday 13 May	2:00pm	- 5:00pm
Dr Neil's Garden, Duddingston Village	Sunday 14 May	2:00pm	- 5:00pm
101 Greenbank Crescent, Edinburgh	Sunday 21 May	2:00pm	- 5:00pm
Redcroft, Edinburgh	Sunday 21 May	2:00pm	- 5:00pm
Beech Lodge, Edinburgh	Saturday 27 May	2:00pm	- 5:00pm
Hunter's Tryst, Edinburgh	Sunday 28 May	2:00pm	- 5:00pm
Dean Gardens, Edinburgh	Sunday 4 June	2:00pm	- 4:00pm
The Glasshouses at the Royal Botanic Garden, Edinburgh	Sunday 11 June	10:00am	- 5:00pm
Colinton Gardens, Edinburgh	Sunday 2 July	2:00pm	- 5:00pm
Riccarton Mains Farmhouse, Currie	Sunday 9 July	2:00pm	- 5:00pm
45 Northfield Crescent, Bathgate	Saturday 29 July	2:00pm	- 5:00pm
9 Braid Farm Road, Edinburgh	Saturday 29 July	2:00pm	- 5:00pm
45 Northfield Crescent, Bathgate	Sunday 30 July	2:00pm	- 5:00pm
9 Braid Farm Road, Edinburgh	Sunday 30 July	2:00pm	- 5:00pm
39 Nantwich Drive, Edinburgh	Saturday 5 August	2:00pm	- 5:00pm
Craigentinny and Telferton Allotments, Edinburgh	Sunday 6 August	2:00pm	- 5:00pm

Gardens open regularly

Newliston, Kirkliston	3 May - 4 June (exc. Mon and Tues)	2:00pm	- 6:00pm

EDINBURGH, MIDLOTHIAN & WEST LOTHIAN

Gardens open by arrangement

101 Greenbank Crescent, Edinburgh	15 April - 31 August	0131 447 6492
Hunter's Tryst, Edinburgh	Daily	0131 477 2919
Newhall, Carlops	1 June - 31 August	01968 660206

9 Braid Farm Road

Key to symbols

 New in 2017

  Homemade teas

 Accommodation

 Teas

 Dogs on a lead allowed

 Plant stall

 Cream teas

 Wheelchair access

Scottish Snowdrop Festival

GARDEN LOCATIONS IN
EDINBURGH, MIDLOTHIAN & WEST LOTHIAN

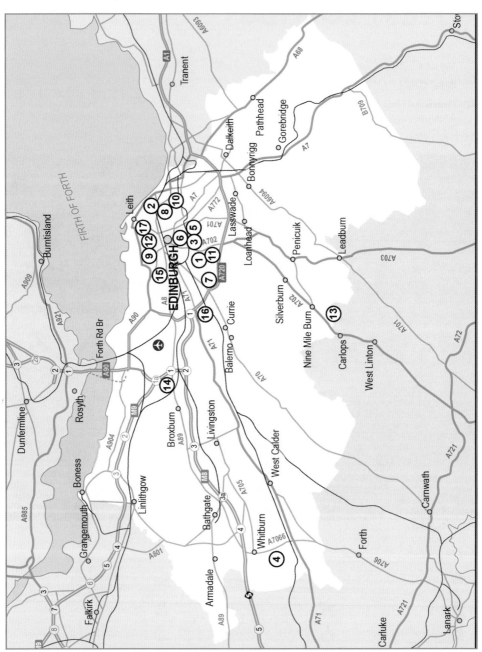

101 GREENBANK CRESCENT
Edinburgh EH10 5TA
Mr and Mrs Jerry and Christine Gregson T: 0131 447 6492
E: jerry_gregson@yahoo.co.uk

The front of the house is on a busy town bus route, but the back of the house is in the country, with views to the Pentland Hills and over the adjoining Braidburn Valley Park. The garden shows what can be done on a steeply sloped site, paths and steps join a variety of distinct areas and terraces, each with a different character. The aim is to have colour, contrast and interest all year round.

Other Details: This is a child friendly garden.

Directions: From Edinburgh centre, take the A702 through Morningside. Continue on and turn right at Greenbank Church to Greenbank Crescent. On the 5 and 16 bus routes, the stop is opposite Greenbank Row.

Disabled Access:
None

Opening Times:
Sunday 21 May
2:00pm - 5:00pm
Also by arrangement
15 April - 31 August

Admission:
£4.00, accompanied children free

Charities:
St Columba's Hospice receives 40%, the net remaining to SG Beneficiaries

---

NEW 39 NANTWICH DRIVE
Edinburgh EH7 6RA
Michael and Susan Burns

Large wildlife friendly garden, run on organic principles. Includes mini orchard, pond, mixed borders, greenhouse and secret garden. There are mini woodland walks and an allotment for vegetables a compost area, worm bin and rotary bin.

Other Details: Teas in the summer house at the pond.

Directions: No 19 bus to Craigentinny Road or no 26 bus to Kekewich Drive.

Disabled Access:
None

Opening Times:
Saturday 5 August
2:00pm - 5:00pm

Admission:
£4.00

Charities:
Garden Organic receives 40%, the net remaining to SG Beneficiaries

---

41 HERMITAGE GARDENS
Edinburgh EH10 6AZ
Dr and Mrs Tony Toft
E: toft41@hotmail.com

This relatively large city garden on the corner of Hermitage Gardens and Drive is at its best in spring with its rock garden, rhododendrons, camellias, acers, tulips and mature trees.

Other Details: Plant stall. Tea and cake £3.00. Parking is not restricted at weekends and there is disabled access from Hermitage Drive.

Directions: Buses 5,11,16,23.

Disabled Access:
Partial

Opening Times:
Saturday 22 April
& Saturday 6 May
2:00pm - 5:00pm

Admission:
£4.00

Charities:
Morningside Heritage Association receives 40%, the net remaining to SG Beneficiaries

45 NORTHFIELD CRESCENT
Longridge, Bathgate EH47 8AL
Mr Jamie Robertson T: 07885 701642
E: jamierobertson04@hotmail.co.uk

A delightful garden with a wide variety of shrubs, herbaceous, bedding and dozens of dahlia plants. Large pond with a small waterfall and a colourful decked area with an attractive selection of bedding plants. There is a vegetable patch with raised bed. A twelve foot by eight foot feature greenhouse showing award winning pot plants. The garden is the current holder of the Oatridge College award and has won several gold medals. The owner has won the *West Lothian Gardener of the Year* prize four times and is chairman of the Livingston and District Horticultural Society.

Directions:
From A71 - Turn right after Breith at traffic lights, go about a mile and turn right into the Crescent.
From Whitburn - Take A706 Longridge Road to Longridge and last left into the Crescent.

Disabled Access:
Partial

Opening Times:
Saturday 29 July
& Sunday 30 July
2:00pm - 5:00pm

Admission:
£3.00

Charities:
World Cancer Research receives 40%, the net remaining to SG Beneficiaries

---

9 BRAID FARM ROAD
Edinburgh EH10 6LG
Mr and Mrs R Paul T: 0131 447 3482
E: raymondpaul@btinternet.com

A fabulous medium sized town garden of different styles. Cottage garden with pond. Mediterranean courtyard and colourful decked area with water feature and exotic plants. Mosaics and unusual features throughout.

Directions: Near Braid Hills Hotel, on the 11 and 15 bus routes.

Disabled Access:
Partial

Opening Times:
Saturday 29 July
& Sunday 30 July
2:00pm - 5:00pm

Admission:
£5.00, accompanied children free

Charities:
Prostate Cancer receives 40%, the net remaining to SG Beneficiaries

---

BEECH LODGE
10 Church Hill, Edinburgh EH10 4BQ
Dr Anthony Ayles

Approximately one acre garden concealed inside a high wall in Church Hill Edinburgh. The garden contains a large lawn, white box garden, and large pond with bridge. There is also a doocot and beehives.

Directions: Turn east at the T-junction off Morningside Road, initially along Church Hill Place which becomes Church Hill. It is two thirds of the way down on the right behind a high Beech hedge.

Disabled Access:
Full

Opening Times:
Saturday 27 May
2:00pm - 5:00pm

Admission:
£4.00

Charities:
Marie Curie receives 20%, PF counselling receives 20%, the net remaining to SG Beneficiaries

7 **NEW COLINTON GARDENS**
Edinburgh EH13 0HY
David and Lindsay Maclure, Michael and Caroline Pearson, David and Margaret Robinson

Three Colinton gardens on the north side of the village, two of which surround early cottage-style houses by Sir Robert Lorimer. They are mature gardens with interest and colour in all seasons. There are herbaceous borders, rockeries, ponds and water features. Plants to be seen, hopefully if the weather is kind, will include *Meconopsis napaulensis, Carpentaria californica, Cornus kousa,* Oriental poppies, crinodendron, marsh orchids, anenomes, salvias and a large specimen of blue abutilon. As a backdrop, a wonderful vista of the Pentland Hills.

The gardens are located at:
21 Pentland Avenue EH13 0HY
42 Pentland Avenue EH13 0HY and
16 Gillespie Road EH13 0LL

Other Details: Homemade teas will be served at 21 Pentland Avenue and there will be a Plant Stall at 42 Pentland Avenue.

Directions: Access to all the gardens may be made from Pentland Avenue which leads off Gillespie Road which runs from Colinton village to the Lanark Road crossroads.

Disabled Access:
Partial

Opening Times:
Sunday 2 July
2:00pm - 5:00pm

Admission:
£5.00, accompanied children free

Charities:
Guide Dogs for the Blind receives 20%, Mercy Ships UK receives 20%, the net remaining to SG Beneficiaries

---

8 **CRAIGENTINNY AND TELFERTON ALLOTMENTS**
Telferton Road, off Portobello Road, Edinburgh EH7 6XG
The Gardeners of Craigentinny and Telferton
www.craigentinnytelferton.btck.co.uk

Established in 1923, this independent allotment site is a tranquil and charming space. Hidden away in a built up area, the local community benefit from growing their own vegetables and fruit. Come and enjoy tea, homebaking and chat with our friendly plot holders.

Other Details: Various workshops will be organised for the day.

Directions: Park on Telferton Road. Lothian Regional Transport buses 15, 26, 45.

Disabled Access:
Partial

Opening Times:
Sunday 6 August
2:00pm - 5:00pm

Admission:
£3.00, accompanied children free

Charities:
The Craigentinny Telferton Allotments receives 40%, the net remaining to SG Beneficiaries

DEAN GARDENS
Edinburgh EH4 1QE
Dean Gardens Management Committee
www.deangardens.org

Nine acres of semi-woodland garden with spring bulbs on the steep banks of the Water of Leith in central Edinburgh. Founded in the 1860s by local residents, the Dean Gardens contains part of the great structure of the Dean Bridge, a Thomas Telford masterpiece of 1835. Lawns, paths, trees, and shrubs with lovely views to the weir in the Dean Village and to the St Bernard's Well. There is also a children's play area.

Other Details: There will be live music along with teas and cakes

Directions: Entrance at Ann Street or Eton Terrace.

Disabled Access:
Partial

Opening Times:
Sunday 4 June
2:00pm - 4:00pm

Admission:
£3.00, accompanied children free

Charities:
All proceeds to
SG Beneficiaries

DR NEIL'S GARDEN
Duddingston Village EH15 3PX
Dr Neil's Garden Trust
E: info@drneilsgarden.co.uk www.drneilsgarden.co.uk

Wonderful secluded, landscaped garden on the lower slopes of Arthur's Seat including conifers, heathers, alpines, physic garden, herbaceous borders and ponds. Also Thompson's Tower with the Museum of Curling and beautiful views across Duddingston Loch.

Directions: Kirk car park on Duddingston Road West and then follow signposts through the Manse Garden.

Disabled Access:
Partial

Opening Times:
Saturday 13 May
& Sunday 14 May
2:00pm - 5:00pm

Admission:
£3.00

Charities:
Dr Neil's Garden Trust receives 40%, the net remaining to SG Beneficiaries

---

HUNTER'S TRYST
95 Oxgangs Road, Edinburgh EH10 7BA
Jean Knox T: 0131 477 2919
E: jean.knox@blueyonder.co.uk

Well stocked and beautifully designed mature, medium-sized town garden comprising herbaceous/shrub beds, lawn, vegetables and fruit, water feature, seating areas and trees. This is a garden that has been transformed from a wilderness thirty years ago and continues to evolve. This hidden treasure of a garden was featured on *The Beechgrove Garden* in June 2015 and on *The Instant Gardener* in June 2016.

Directions: From Fairmilehead crossroads head down Oxgangs Road to Hunter's Tryst roundabout, last house on the left. Take buses 4, 5, 18 or 27. The bus stop is at Hunter's Tryst and the garden is opposite.

Disabled Access:
None

Opening Times:
Sunday 28 May
2:00pm - 5:00pm
By arrangement on request

Admission:
£4.00

Charities:
Lothian Cat Rescue receives 40%, the net remaining to SG Beneficiaries

MORAY PLACE AND BANK GARDENS
Edinburgh EH3 6BX
The Residents of Moray Place and Bank Gardens

Moray Place: Private garden of three and a half acres in Georgian New Town. Shrubs, trees and beds offering atmosphere of tranquillity in the city centre.

Bank Gardens: Nearly six acres of secluded wild gardens with lawns, trees and shrubs with banks of bulbs down to the Water of Leith. Stunning vistas across Firth of Forth.

Other Details: Disabled access Moray Place only.

Directions: Moray Place - enter by north gate in Moray Place.
Bank Gardens - enter by the gate at top of Doune Terrace.

Disabled Access:
Partial

Opening Times:
Sunday 7 May
2:00pm - 5:00pm

Admission:
£4.00

Charities:
The Euan Macdonald
Centre for Motor Neurone
Disease Research receives
40%, the net remaining to
SG Beneficiaries

NEWHALL
Carlops EH26 9LY
John and Tricia Kennedy T: 01968 660206
E: tricia.kennedy@newhalls.co.uk

Traditional 18th century walled garden with huge herbaceous border, shrubberies, fruit and vegetables. Stunning glen running along the North Esk river in the process of restoration (stout shoes recommended). Large pond with evolving planting. Young arboretum and collection of *Rosa pimpinellifolia*. As seen in *Scottish Field, Gardens Monthly* and *Scotland on Sunday*.

Other Details: Coffee/tea and homebaking by arrangement. Light lunches for groups available by prior arrangement.

Directions: On the A702 Edinburgh/Biggar, half mile after Ninemileburn and a mile before Carlops. Follow signs.

Disabled Access:
Partial

Opening Times:
By arrangement
1 June - 31 August

Admission:
£5.00

Charities:
All proceeds to
SG Beneficiaries

NEWLISTON
Kirkliston EH29 9EB
Mr and Mrs R C Maclachlan T: 0131 333 3231
E: mac@newliston.fsnet.co.uk

Eighteenth century designed landscape with good rhododendrons and azaleas. The house, designed by Robert Adam, is also open.

Directions: Nine miles west of Edinburgh city centre, four miles south of the Forth Road Bridge, off the B800 between Newbridge and Kirkliston.

Disabled Access:
Partial

Opening Times:
3 May - 4 June
2:00pm - 6:00pm
(exc. Mon and Tues)

Admission:
£4.00

Charities:
Children's Hospice
Association receives 40%,
the net remaining to
SG Beneficiaries

15 REDCROFT
23 Murrayfield Road, Edinburgh EH12 6EP
James and Anna Buxton T: 0131 337 1747
E: annabuxtonb@aol.com

A walled garden surrounding an Arts and Crafts villa which provides an unexpected haven off a busy road. Planted and maintained with shape and texture in mind. Acid soil and relative shelter allow a wide range of plants to be grown. In May there should be a fine display of colour from rhododendrons and other flowering shrubs, trees in flower and plenty of tulips and other bulbs, both in the beds and in pots.

Other Details: Our chosen charity is Canine Partners Scotland which provides specially trained dogs to help wheelchair users.

Directions: Murrayfield Road runs north from Corstorphine Road to Ravelston Dykes. There is easy parking available which is free. Buses 26, 31 and 38; get off at Murrayfield Stadium.

Disabled Access:
Full

Opening Times:
Sunday 21 May
2:00pm - 5:00pm

Admission:
£4.00

Charities:
Canine Partners in Scotland receives 40%, the net remaining to SG Beneficiaries

---

16 NEW RICCARTON MAINS FARMHOUSE
Currie EH14 4AR
Mr and Mrs Michael Reid Thomas
E: ricmains@gmail.com

A large garden divided into sections and constructed from scratch over the last 40 years by the present owners. Terraces, herbaceous, roses, woodland and vegetables.

Directions: A71 from Edinburgh; follow directions for Heriot Watt University and the entrance to the garden is on the east side of the roundabout.
Bus - LRT nos 45, 25 or 34.

Disabled Access:
Partial

Opening Times:
Sunday 9 July
2:00pm - 5:00pm

Admission:
£5.00

Charities:
Oxfam receives 40%, the net remaining to SG Beneficiaries

---

17 THE GLASSHOUSES AT THE ROYAL BOTANIC GARDEN EDINBURGH
20A Inverleith Row, Edinburgh EH3 5LR
Royal Botanic Garden Edinburgh T: 0131 248 2909
www.rbge.org.uk

The Glasshouses with 10 climatic zones are a delight all year round. The Orchids and Cycads House brings together primitive cycads which dominated the land flora some 65 million years ago, and a diverse range of orchids, the most sophisticated plants in the world. In summer, giant water lilies, *Victoria amazonica*, are the star attraction in the Tropical Aquatic House. Plants with vibrant flowers and fascinating foliage thrive in the Rainforest Riches House and the complex ecosystems of life in the world's deserts are explored in the Arid Lands House. A large collection of gingers, (Zingiberaceae), one of the largest collections of vireya rhododendrons in the world and a case housing carnivorous plants are among other attractions.

Other Details: Includes donation to garden, prices without donation see website.

Directions: Off the A902. Lothian Buses 8, 23 and 27 stop close to East Gate entrance on Inverleith Row. The Majestic Tour Bus stops at Arboretum Place.

Disabled Access:
Full

Opening Times:
for the Glasshouses
Sunday 11 June
10:00am - 5:00pm

Admission:
£5.50, concessions £4.50,
(to glasshouses)
children under 16 free

Charities:
Donation to SG Beneficiaries

ETTRICK & LAUDERDALE

Scotland's Gardens 2017 Guidebook is sponsored by **INVESTEC WEALTH & INVESTMENT**

District Organiser

To be advised	E: ettrick@scotlandsgardens.org

Area Organisers

Jenny Litherland	Laidlawstiel House, Clovenfords, Galashiels TD1 1TJ
Camilla Warre	Peace Cottage, Synton Parkhead, Ashkirk TD7 4PB

Treasurer

Diana Muir	Torquhan House, Stow TD1 2RX

Gardens open on a specific date

Bemersyde, Melrose	Sunday 23 April	2:00pm	- 5:00pm
Laidlawstiel House, Clovenfords	Wednesday 24 May	1:00pm	- 5:00pm
Laidlawstiel House, Clovenfords	Wednesday 14 June	1:00pm	- 5:00pm
Lowood House , Melrose	Sunday 2 July	2:00pm	- 6:00pm
Harmonyand Priorwood Gardens, Melrose	Saturday 29 July	10:00am	- 5:00pm
Harmony and Priorwood Gardens, Melrose	Sunday 30 July	1:00pm	- 5:00pm

Key to symbols

 New in 2017

 Teas

 Homemade teas

 Dogs on a lead allowed

 Wheelchair access

 Accommodation

 Plant stall

 Scottish Snowdrop Festival

Cream teas

GARDEN LOCATIONS IN ETTRICK & LAUDERDALE

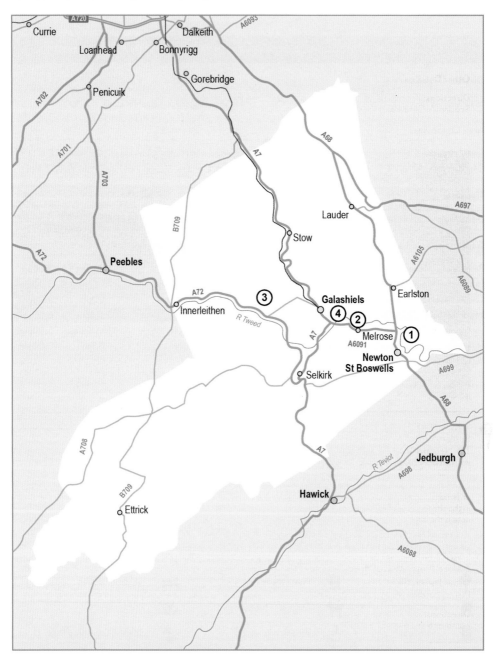

BEMERSYDE
Melrose TD6 9DP
The Earl Haig

Disabled Access:
Partial

CELEBRATING 75 YEARS OF OPENING FOR CHARITY WITH SCOTLAND'S GARDENS!

Sixteenth century peel tower reconstructed in the seventeenth century with added mansion house. Glorious show of daffodils around the house. Woodland garden and walks along the River Tweed - good footwear required.

Other Details: Discover the 800 year old Covin tree.

Directions: From A68 follow signs to Scott's View and then follow the yellow Scotland's Gardens signs to Bemersyde.

Opening Times:
Sunday 23 April
2:00pm - 5:00pm

Admission:
£4.00, accompanied children free

Charities:
PoppyScotland receives 40%, the net remaining to SG Beneficiaries

HARMONY AND PRIORWOOD GARDEN
St Mary's Road, Melrose TD6 9LJ
The National Trust for Scotland T: 01896 822493
www.nts.org.uk/property/priorwood-gardens-and-dried-flower-shop/

Disabled Access:
Full

Harmony Garden: The walled garden extends to approximately 1.5 hectares (3 acres) of ornamental and vegetable garden ground as well as working glasshouses. The gardens are in the shadow of Melrose Abbey and enjoy fine views of the Eildon Hills. Of particular note is the large mature herbaceous border along the eastern wall and the tennis lawn.

Priorwood Gardens: Extending to 0.8 hectares (2 acres), Priorwood was the first garden in Scotland devoted entirely to the cultivation of flowers for drying and preservaton. There is a heritage orchard containing over 90 apple varieties, including the local 'White Melrose' thought to date to before 1600. Gardener conducted tours.

Other Details: Produce from the vegetable garden sold at Harmony Garden. Plants, cuttings and dried flower arrangemnents can be purchased at Priorwood.

Directions: Off A6091, in Melrose, opposite the Abbey. First bus (X72) from Edinburgh and Peebles.

Opening Times:
Saturday 29 July
Sunday 30 July
1:00pm - 5:00pm

Admission:
Free, donations for open day welcome.

Charities:
Donation to SG Beneficiaries

ETTRICK & LAUDERDALE

LAIDLAWSTIEL HOUSE
Clovenfords, Galashiels TD1 1TJ
Mr and Mrs P Litherland

Walled garden containing herbaceous border, fruit, and vegetables in raised beds. There are colourful rhododendrons and azaleas as well as splendid views down to the River Tweed.

Other Details: Self-service teas/coffees.

Directions: A72 between Clovenfords and Walkerburn, turn up the hill signposted for Thornielee. The house is on the right at the top of the hill.

Disabled Access:
None

Opening Times:
Wednesday 24 May &
Wednesday 14 June
1:00pm - 5:00pm

Admission:
£4.00, children free

Charities:
CLIC Sargent receives
40%, the net remaining to
SG Beneficiaries

LOWOOD HOUSE
Melrose TD6 9BJ
Mr and Mrs Alexander Hamilton

Entry beside Lowood Bridge, past a tiny lodge then a half mile drive through a small wood and park. Lowood House sits on the south bank of the Tweed and has been added to over the years in a somewhat haphazard fashion. South of the house is a large garden with some nice shrubs, trees and a lot of roses, including climbing and rambling roses. Features are a sunken garden, woodland walk, a walk through the park by the lochan, a river walk, a secret garden and a walled garden mainly used as a kitchen garden.

Directions: Entrance from the B6374 at the south end of the single lane Lowood Bridge leading from Melrose to Gattonside.

Disabled Access:
Full

Opening Times:
Sunday 2 July
2:00pm - 6:00pm

Admission:
£4.00, accompanied children
free

Charities:
MND Scotland receives
40%, the net remaining to
SG Beneficiaries

PEEBLESSHIRE

Scotland's Gardens 2017 Guidebook is sponsored by **INVESTEC WEALTH & INVESTMENT**

District Organiser

Rose Parrott	An Sparr, Medwyn Road, West Linton EH46 7HA
	E: peeblesshire@scotlandsgardens.org

Area Organisers

John Bracken	Gowan Lea, Croft Road, West Linton EH46 7DZ
Graham Buchanan-Dunlop	The Potting Shed, Broughton Pl, Broughton ML12 6HJ
Rosalind Hume	Llolans, Broughton ML12 6HJ
Lesley McDavid	Braedon, Medwyn Road, West Linton EH46 7HA

Treasurer

John Bracken	Gowan Lea, Croft Road, West Linton EH46 7DZ

Gardens open on a specific date

Kailzie Gardens, Peebles	Sunday 26 February	Dawn	-	Dusk
Glen House, Innerleithen	Sunday 28 May	11:00am	-	4:00pm
Stobo Japanese Water Garden, Stobo	Wednesday 31 May	3:00pm	-	7:30pm
Stobo Japanese Water Garden, Stobo	Thursday 1 June	3:00pm	-	7:30pm
8 Halmyre Mains, West Linton	Sunday 4 June	10:00am	-	12:00pm
West Linton Village Gardens, West Linton	Sunday 16 July	2:00pm	-	5:00pm
Peebles Gardens, Peebles	Sunday 6 August	2:00pm	-	5:00pm
Glen House, Innerleithen	Sunday 24 September	11:00am	-	4:00pm
Dawyck Botanic Garden, Stobo	Sunday 8 October	10:00am	-	5:00pm

PEEBLESSHIRE

Gardens open regularly

Portmore, Eddleston	5 July - 30 Aug (Weds only)	1:00pm - 5:00pm
The Potting Shed, Broughton	14 June - 19 July (Weds only)	11:00am - 5:00pm

Gardens open by arrangement

Portmore, Eddleston	1 June - 31 August	07825 294388

Plant sales

8 Halmyre Mains, West Linton	Sunday 4 June	10:00am - 12:00pm

West Linton, The Cottage

Key to symbols

New in 2017	Homemade teas	Accommodation
Teas	Dogs on a lead allowed	Plant stall
Cream teas	Wheelchair access	Scottish Snowdrop Festival

GARDEN LOCATIONS IN PEEBLESSHIRE

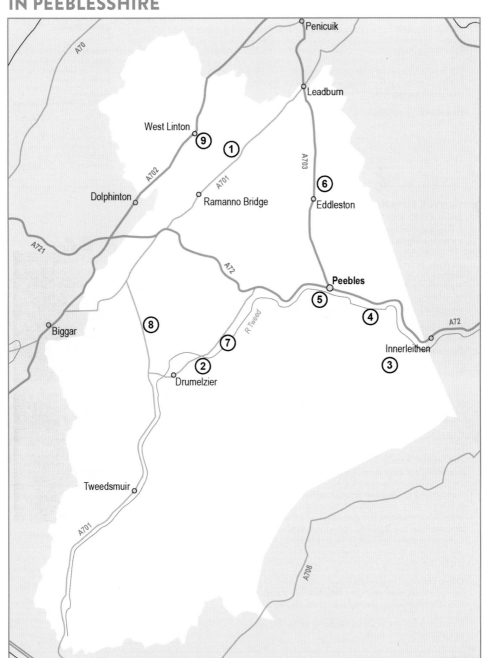

PEEBLESSHIRE

1 8 HALMYRE MAINS
West Linton EH46 7BX
Joyce Andrews and Mike Madden T: 07774 609 547
E: agentromanno@gmail.com

We have decided to carry out a much needed overhaul of many of the beds in the garden and therefore we will not have a main summer opening in 2017 whilst these beds re-establish.

We shall still have our popular spring plant sale on the 4 June with a large selection of plants, mostly grown here, and you are very welcome to have a look around at the changes in the garden.

Directions: Five miles South of Leadburn Junction on the A701 (Moffat).

Disabled Access:
Full

Opening Times:
Plant sale Sunday 4 June
10:00am - 12:00pm
garden also open.

Admission:
£2.00, accompanied children
free

Charities:
Lamancha & District
Community Association
receives 40%, the net
remaining to SG Beneficiaries

---

2 DAWYCK BOTANIC GARDEN
Stobo EH45 9JU
A Regional Garden of the Royal Botanic Garden Edinburgh T: 01721 760 254
www.rbge.org.uk/dawyck

Stunning collection of rare trees and shrubs. With over 300 years of tree planting, Dawyck is a world-famous arboretum with mature specimens of Chinese conifers, Japanese maples, Brewer's spruce, the unique Dawyck beech and Sequoiadendrons from North America which are over 45 metres tall. Bold herbaceous plantings run along the burn. Range of trails and walks. Fabulous autumn colours.

Other Details: National Plant Collection®: Larix and Tsuga. Open for the Snowdrop Festival 1st February - 13 March. A range of trails and walks are on offer. Visit the new hydro-electric scheme at the Scrape Burn. Lunches and teas using local produce are available in the cafe overlooking scenic woodland. Open February to November, see website for details.

Directions: Eight miles southwest of Peebles on B712.

Disabled Access:
Partial

Opening Times:
Sunday 8 October
10:00am - 5:00pm

Admission:
£6.50, concessions £5.50,
children u16 free (includes
donation, for prices without
donation check rbge.org.uk).

Charities:
Donation to SG Beneficiaries

---

3 GLEN HOUSE
Glen Estate, Innerleithen EH44 6PX
The Tennant Family T: 01896 830210
E: info@glenhouse.com www.glenhouse.com

Surrounding the outstanding Scots Baronial mansion designed by David Bryce in the mid-19th century, Glen House gardens are laid out on a series of shallow terraces overhanging the glen itself, which offers one of the loveliest 'designed landscapes' in the Borders. The garden expands from the formal courtyard through a yew colonnade, and contains a fine range of trees, long herbaceous border and pool garden with pergola, all arranged within the curve of slopes sheltering the house.

Other Details: The gardens range over a series of terraces and therefore gives very limited access to wheelchair users. Visitors are welcome to bring a picnic and enjoy the delightful views. Refreshments will also be available.

Directions: Follow B709 out of Innerleithen for approx. 2½ miles. Turn right at signpost for Glen Estate.

Disabled Access:
Partial

Opening Times:
Sunday 28 May
& Sunday 24 September
11:00am - 4:00pm

Admission:
£5.00, accompanied children
free

Charities:
The Conservation Foundation
receives 40%, the net
remaining to SG Beneficiaries

KAILZIE GARDENS
Peebles EH45 9HT
Lady Buchan-Hepburn T: 01721 720007
E: angela.buchanhepburn@btinternet.com www.kailziegardens.com

CELEBRATING 50 YEARS OF OPENING FOR CHARITY WITH SCOTLAND'S GARDENS!

Semi-formal walled garden with shrubs and herbaceous borders, rose garden and excellent display of plants in large Victorian greenhouses. Woodland and burnside walks among spring bulbs, snowdrops, bluebells, rhododendrons and azaleas. The garden is set among fine old trees including a larch planted in 1725. Osprey watch with live CCTV recordings of Ospreys nesting in the recently extended nature centre. Kailzie has been featured on *Landward* and the *Beechgrove Garden*.

Other Details: Champion Trees: Larch planted 1725. Wild garden and woodland walks open throughout the year, including for the Snowdrop Festival 30 January - 13 March. The walled garden opens 6 March - 30 October. Children's play area. Garden Cafe open daily during the summer months. Prices vary: see website.

Directions: Two and a half miles east of Peebles on B7062.

Disabled Access:
Partial

Opening Times:
Sunday 26 February
Dawn - Dusk for the
Snowdrop Festival

Admission:
£3.50, under 5s free

Charities:
Erskine Hospital receives
40%, the net remaining to
SG Beneficiaries

NEW PEEBLES GARDENS
Peebles EH45 9DX
Peebles Gardens T: 07813700786
E: cloudberryflowers@gmail.com www.facebook.com/cloudberryflowers

A group of four gardens will be opening for the first time in the beautiful borders town of Peebles. The gardens are all different, varying in their size and the varieties of plants grown. You will find well established herbaceous borders, mature shrubs, roses, areas for moisture loving plants, soft fruit and vegetable beds, a cutting garden full of annual flowers, water features, a Scottish border and displays of container grown plants. The gardeners are all enthusiastic amateurs who are passionate about their gardens and would love to share them with you.

Other Details: Parking is difficult at all of the gardens. A bus will run between the gardens and public car parks (toilet facilities available). Please check website for further details nearer the time.

Directions: From Peebles yellow signs direct you to the gardens at Frankscroft, south of the river, Innerleithen Road, near Peebles Hydro, and Connor Ridge.

Disabled Access:
Partial

Opening Times:
Sunday 6 August
2:00pm - 5:00pm

Admission:
£5.00

Charities:
Sandpiper Trust receives 20%,
MIND receives 20%, the net
remaining to SG Beneficiaries

PORTMORE
Eddleston EH45 8QU
Mr and Mrs David Reid T: 07825 294388
www.portmoregardens.co.uk

Lovingly created by current owners over the past 20 years the gardens surrounding the David Bryce mansion house contain mature trees and offer fine views of the surrounding countryside. Large walled garden with box-edged herbaceous borders planted in stunning colour harmonies, potager, rose garden, pleached lime walk and ornamental fruit cages. The Victorian glasshouses contain fruit trees, roses, geraniums, pelargoniums and a wide variety of tender plants. Italianate grotto. Water garden with shrubs and meconopsis and woodland walks lined with rhododendrons, azaleas and shrub roses. Starred in *Good Gardens Guide* and featured in Kenneth Cox's book *Scotland for Gardeners* and *Beechgrove Garden*.

Other Details: Self service refreshments on Wednesday openings. Homemade cream teas for groups over 15 people by prior arrangement.

Directions: Off A703 one mile north of Eddleston. Bus 62.

Disabled Access:
Partial

Opening Times:
5 July - 30 August
1:00pm - 5:00pm
(Wednesdays only)
Also by arrangement
1 June - 31 August

Admission:
£6.00

Charities:
Soldiers Off The Street
receives 40%, the net
remaining to SG Beneficiaries

PEEBLESSHIRE

7 STOBO JAPANESE WATER GARDEN
Home Farm, Stobo EH45 8NX
Hugh and Georgina Seymour T: 01721 760245
E: hugh.seymour@btinternet.com

Secluded woodland garden. While water is probably the main feature of the garden now, the layout echoes facets of a more conventional Japanese garden - stepping stones, humpback bridges, the 40 feet waterfall, azaleas and rhododendrons, acers and other specialist trees and shrubs, many of far eastern origins. Several Japanese lanterns and a tea house still remain from when the garden was created in the early years of the last century. Recently featured in the October issue of *The English Garden Magazine.*

Other Details: Self service tea/coffee available. Guided tours available for groups of 12 or more - also lunches /tea/coffee. B&B at Home Farm House. Some areas may be slippery or rough under foot so please wear appropriate footwear (and use alternative paths). There is ongoing work on trees and shrubs.

Directions: Off B712. Follow signs for Stobo Castle then yellow signs on the drive.

Disabled Access:
Partial

Opening Times:
Wednesday 31 May
& Thursday 1 June
3:00pm - 7:30pm

Admission:
£5.00, accompanied children free

Charities:
Marie Curie receives 40% (May opening), Lynn & Manor Kirk receives 40%, (June opening) the net remaining to SG Beneficiaries

---

8 THE POTTING SHED
Broughton Place, Broughton, Biggar ML12 6HJ
Jane and Graham Buchanan-Dunlop T: 01899 830574
E: buchanandunlop@btinternet.com

A one acre garden, begun from scratch in 2008, on an exposed hillside at 900 feet. It contains herbaceous plants, climbers, shrubs and trees, all selected for wind resistance and ability to cope with the poor, stony soil. There are (usually) fine views to the Southern Uplands.

A selection of plants propagated from those in the garden will be for sale.

Other Details: Lunch and tea available at Laurel Bank in Broughton Village. T: 01899 830462.

Directions: Signposted from the main A701 Edinburgh - Moffat Road, immediately north of Broughton Village.

Disabled Access:
Partial

Opening Times:
14 June - 19 July
11:00am - 5:00pm
(Wednesdays only)

Admission:
£4.00, accompanied children free

Charities:
Macmillan Centre at Borders General Hospital receives 40%, the net remaining to SG Beneficiaries

---

9 WEST LINTON VILLAGE GARDENS
West Linton EH46 7EL
West Linton Village Gardeners T: 01968 660328
E: parrott@btinternet.com

Once again a selection of gardens in the village will be opening. The gardens all vary in their size, design, planting styles and individual features with wide herbaceous borders, specimen trees, greenhouses full of pelargoniums and show begonias, an impressive hosta collection and an organic vegetable and fruit garden with a 'no dig' policy. Like most gardeners they are more than happy to talk about their gardens and offer advice come rain or shine.

Other Details: This year there will be a 'Garden and Historical Trail'. The village is a conservation area and has many points of interest which will be high lighted as you walk to the gardens. We hope you will enjoy this little extra.

Directions: Take the A701 or A702 and follow road signs to West Linton. The hall where we take the admission fee, teas and plant sale is in the centre of the village and will be signposted.

Disabled Access:
Partial

Opening Times:
Sunday 16 July
2:00pm - 5:00pm

Admission:
£5.00

Charities:
The Ben Walton Trust receives 20%, Margaret Kerr Unit Borders General Hospital receives 20%, the net remaining to SG Beneficiaries

ROXBURGHSHIRE

Scotland's Gardens 2017 Guidebook is sponsored by **INVESTEC WEALTH & INVESTMENT**

District Organiser

Sally Yonge	Newtonlees House, Kelso TD5 7SZ
	E: roxburghshire@scotlandsgardens.org

Area Organiser

Marion Livingston	Bewlie House, Lilliesleaf, Melrose TD6 9ER

Treasurer

Peter Jeary	Kalemouth House, Eckford, Kelso TD5 8LE

Gardens open on a specific date

West Leas, Bonchester Bridge	Sunday 4 June	2:00pm	- 6:00pm
Westerhouses, Bonchester Bridge	Sunday 25 June	1:00pm	- 5:00pm
Easter Weens, Bonchester Bridge	Sunday 2 July	2:00pm	- 5:30pm
Pirnie House, Fairnington	Saturday 8 July	2:00pm	- 5:00pm
Yetholm Village Gardens, Town Yetholm	Sunday 9 July	1:00pm	- 5:30pm
West Leas, Bonchester Bridge	Sunday 30 July	2:00pm	- 6:00pm

Gardens open regularly

Floors Castle, Kelso	10 January - 23 December	10:30am	- 4:00pm
Monteviot, Jedburgh	1 April - 31 October	12:00pm	- 5:00pm

Gardens open by arrangement

West Leas, Bonchester Bridge	On request	01450 860711

Key to symbols

	New in 2017		Homemade teas		Accommodation
	Teas		Dogs on a lead allowed		Plant stall
	Cream teas		Wheelchair access		Scottish Snowdrop Festival

GARDEN LOCATIONS
IN ROXBURGHSHIRE

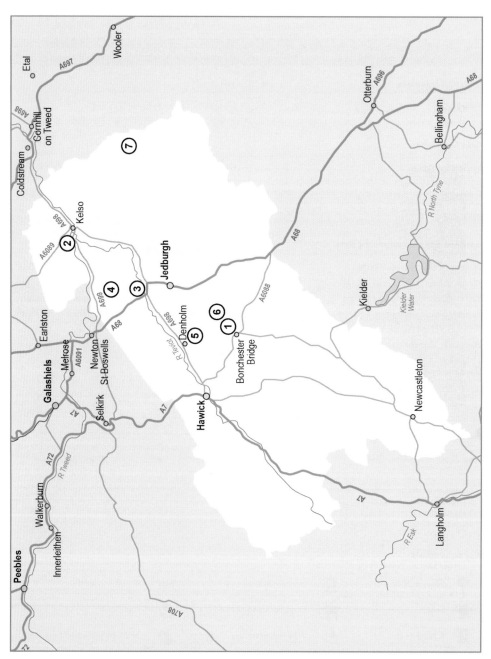

EASTER WEENS
Bonchester Bridge, Hawick TD9 8JQ
Roger and Alison Curtis

Formal garden set within former stable courtyard and informal grounds surrounding, designed by Percy Cane in 1958. Terraced rhododendron bank, vegetable gardens and woodland walks. Terraced parterre planted in 2005. Recently acquired revolving summer house with adjacent developing borders. There is a pear-shaped walled garden approximately a half mile to the south, accessed through grazed parkland.

Other Details: Tea and homemade cakes. Vintage lawnmowers.

Directions: The property is on the B6357 on the Jedburgh side of Bonchester Bridge, just north of Bonchester Care Home. Parking is available in the farm yard.

Disabled Access:
Partial

Opening Times:
Sunday 2 July
2:00pm - 5:30pm

Admission:
£5.00, children £1.00

Charities:
Maggie's Cancer Caring Centres, Edinburgh receives 20%, Hobkirk Church receives 20%, the net remaining to SG Beneficiaries

FLOORS CASTLE
Kelso TD5 7SF
The Duke of Roxburghe T: 01573 223333
www.floorscastle.com

The Gardens are situated within the grounds of Floors Castle. Meander through to the formal Millennium Parterre and soak up the spectacular visions of colour, texture and the most delicious scents around the four herbaceous borders in one of the finest Victorian kitchen gardens in Scotland. New perennial gardens, fruit cage and glasshouse access. Terrace Cafe, Castle Kitchen deli shop and play area. Explore the Grounds which offer woodland and riverside walks from Easter to October.

Other Details: Walled and Millennium Garden open daily all year. Terrace Cafe open daily all year and free to access. Please check our website for possible closures.

Directions: Floors Castle can be reached by following the A6089 from Edinburgh; the B6397 from Earlston or the A698 from Coldstream. Go through Kelso, up Roxburgh Street to the Golden Gates.

Disabled Access:
Partial

Opening Times:
10 January - 23 December
10:30am - 4:00pm

Admission:
Castle, Gardens & Grounds:
£12.50
Garden tickets available

Charities:
Donation to SG Beneficiaries

ROXBURGHSHIRE

3 MONTEVIOT

Jedburgh TD8 6UQ
Marquis & Marchioness of Lothian T: 01835 830380
www.monteviot.com

A series of differing gardens including a herb garden, rose garden, water garden linked by bridges, and river garden with herbaceous shrub borders of foliage plants. The Garden of Persistent Imagination has been recently created and planted with rose and clematis avenues leading to a Moonstone Gate.

Other Details: House open 1 - 29 July 1:00pm - 5:00pm

Directions: Turn off A68, three miles north of Jedburgh on to B6400. After one mile turn right

Disabled Access:
Partial

Opening Times:
1 April - 31 October
12:00pm - 5:00pm

Admission:
£5.00, children under 16 free. RHS members free with membership card

Charities:
Donation to SG Beneficiaries

4 NEW PIRNIE HOUSE

Fairnington, Kelso TD5 8NS
Christopher and Lorna Blunt

An informal country garden with well planted mixed borders, some unusual plants and specimen trees, a woodland border and a walled fruit and vegetable garden; stunning views to the Cheviot hills.

Directions: Access from A68 north of Ancrum, turn right signed Fairnington. Or from Maxton follow signs to Fairnington. Or from Kelso take the A699 and turn off towards Fairnington. Roads will be signed.

Disabled Access:
Full

Opening Times:
Saturday 8 July
2:00pm - 5:00pm

Admission:
£5.00

Charities:
Cancer Research UK receives 40% (Funds to ovarian cancer research), the net remaining to SG Beneficiaries

5 WEST LEAS

Bonchester Bridge TD9 8TD
Mr and Mrs Robert Laidlaw T: 01450 860711
E: ann.laidlaw@west-leas.co.uk

The visitor to West Leas can share in the exciting and dramatic project on a grand scale still in the making. At its core is a passion for plants allied to a love and understanding of the land in which they are set. Collections of perennials and shrubs, many in temporary holding quarters, lighten up the landscape to magical effect. New dams and water features and woodland planting ongoing for 2017.

Other Details: Opening on 4 June for early summer colour and 30 July for high summer colour.

Directions: Signposted off the Jedburgh/Bonchester Bridge Road.

Disabled Access:
Partial

Opening Times:
Sunday 4 June
Sunday 30 July
2:00pm - 6:00pm
Also by arrangement on request

Admission:
£4.00

Charities:
Macmillan Cancer Support, Borders Appeal receives 40%, the net remaining to SG Beneficiaries

⑥ NEW WESTERHOUSES
Bonchester Bridge, Hawick TD9 8TG
Mr and Mrs Philip Kerr

Wonderful garden developed over the last ten years, surrounding an old Borders farmhouse and steading, set within the "Teviot Valley Special Landscape Area". Challenging conditions at 750 ft high on heavy, wet clay. From rough grassland to hornbeam hedges and borders full of shrubs, perennials, alpines and a few plantaholic's gems, plus new woodland area. Fabulous views towards Bonchester Hill, Ruberslaw and, on clear days, the Moffat Hills.

Directions: Six miles south of Jedburgh, three miles east of Bonchester Bridge, one mile north of Chesters. From Jedburgh head south on A68, turn right onto B6357, signposted Bonchester Bridge, after three miles take Chesters turn-off and Westerhouses is 1.5 miles down this road on the left.

Disabled Access:
Partial

Opening Times:
Sunday 25 June
1:00pm - 5:00pm

Admission:
£4.00, accompanied children free

Charities:
Southdean Hall (SC044518) receives 40%, the net remaining to SG Beneficiaries

⑦ YETHOLM VILLAGE GARDENS
Town Yetholm TD5 8RL
The Gardeners of Yetholm Village

The villages of Town and Kirk Yetholm are situated at the north end of the Pennine Way and lie close to the Bowmont Water in the dramatic setting of the foothills of the Cheviots. A variety of gardens with their own unique features and reflecting distinctive horticultural interests will be open. The Yew Tree Allotments running along the High Street will open again, providing an ever popular feature with their unique water collection and distribution system. The short walking distance between the majority of the gardens provides magnificent views of the surrounding landscape to include Staerough and The Curr which straddle both the Bowmont and Halterburn Valleys where evidence of ancient settlements remains.

Other Details: Champion Trees: The Old Yew Tree in Yew Tree Lane. Attractions include the ever popular music, local wood-turning products at Almond Cottage, home baking and produce stall. An excellent plant stall supported by Woodside Walled Garden Centre is also planned for the afternoon. Tickets are available in the local village hall. Dogs on leads allowed. Cream teas £2.00.

Directions: Equidistant between Edinburgh and Newcastle. South of Kelso in the Scottish Borders take the B6352 to Yetholm Village. Ample parking is available along the High Street.

Disabled Access:
Partial

Opening Times:
Sunday 9 July
1:00pm - 5:30pm

Admission:
£4.00, children under 10 free

Charities:
Riding for the Disabled Association - Borders Group receives 40%, the net remaining to SG Beneficiaries

CHARITIES SUPPORTED

Each visit you make to one of our gardens in 2017 will raise money for our beneficiary charities:

Helping Horticulturists In Need Since 1839

**In addition, funds will be distributed to a charity of the owner's choice.
For South East Scotland, these include:**

Borders and Kirkton Manor
& Lyne Churches

British Heart Foundation

Cancer Research UK

Canine Partners in Scotland

Children's Hospice Association
Scotland (CHAS)

Circle Scotland

CLIC Sargent

Dr Neil's Garden Trust

East Lothian Special Needs
Play Schemes

Erskine Hospital

Garden Organic

Guide Dogs For the Blind

Gunsgreen House Trust

Hobkirk Church

Lamancha & District Community
Association

Leuchie House

Lothian Cat Rescue

Macmillan Cancer Support,
Borders Appeal

Macmillan Centre at Borders
General Hospital

Maggie's Cancer Caring Centres

Mamie Martin Fund

Margaret Kerr Unit Borders
General Hospital

Marie Curie

Mercy Ships UK

MIND

Morningside Heritage Association

Oxfam

PF Counselling Service

Plant Life Scotland for
Coronation Meadows

Prostate Cancer UK

RBLS (Borders Area)

Riding for the Disabled Association -
Borders Group

RNLI (Dunbar)

Sandpiper Trust

Scottish Motor Neurone

Soldiers Off The Street

Southdean Hall

St Columba's Hospice

Sustrans

Teapot Trust

The Ben Walton Trust

The Conservation Foundation

The Craigentinny Telferton
Allotments

The Euan Macdonald Centre for
Motor Neurone Disease Research

World Cancer Research

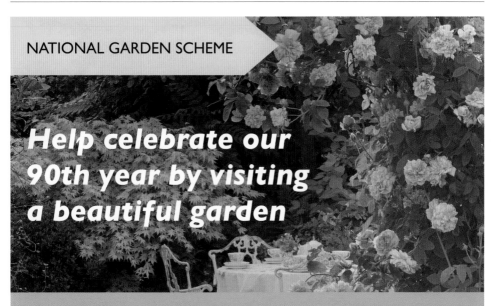

NATIONAL GARDEN SCHEME

Help celebrate our 90th year by visiting a beautiful garden

For more information on our 3,800 gardens open for charity in England and Wales, visit our website **www.ngs.org.uk** or telephone **01483 211535**

The National Gardens Scheme. Registered charity number 1112664

Plant Sales

Your opportunity to purchase from an enviable collection of plants at truly wonderful prices

All proceeds help support the work of the Royal Botanic Garden Edinburgh

Edinburgh – **Sunday 14th May from 2pm-4pm**
Benmore – **Sunday 28th May from 12-4pm**
Dawyck – **Sunday 28th May from 10am-3pm**
and Sunday 8th October from 10am-12noon

www.rbge.org.uk
The Royal Botanic Garden Edinburgh is a charity registered in Scotland (number SC007983)

www.rchs.co.uk

Join Scotland's National Horticultural and Gardening Society today and support the future of horticulture and gardening in Scotland.

Annual Spring Show, Prestigious Horticultural Awards, Talks, Trips, Garden Advice, Gardening for Children, Organic Allotment, Social Events and so much more.....

Scottish Charity Number SC 006522

The Caley
Royal Caledonian Horticultural Society

Meet Connor. At the age of 10 he became the man of the house.

Connor's dad died of a stroke at age 42.

He was the picture of health.

It was the last thing anyone expected.

Make the end a new beginning.

A gift in your Will can mean life to those suffering from chest, heart and stroke illness in Scotland.

The funding that gifts in Wills provide is crucial to our work.

We are Scotland's Health Charity

Research • Advice • Support • Action

Chest Heart & Stroke Scotland

FundRaising
Standards Board

0300 1212 555 | gifts@chss.org.uk | www.chss.org.uk

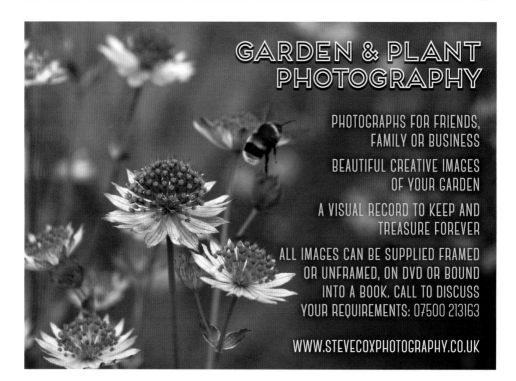

Supporting gardening in the heart of communities

Royal
Horticultural
Society

Sharing the best in Gardening

RHS in Scotland
Community Outreach Team
scotland@rhs.org.uk
rhs.org.uk /communities

Registered Charity No: 222879/SCO38262

Every one of our retirement homes comes with a 40 acre garden. And a team of gardeners.

Remember Flower Power? It's alive and well in the gardens at Inchmarlo.

You can enjoy the handiwork of our green-fingered workers everywhere (they do the spadework so you don't have to).

Then, slightly off the well-manicured path, our woods are home for red squirrels, deer and all kinds of birds.

And while woodland and gardens surround the village, the whole estate is surrounded by the regal grandeur of Royal Deeside.

Homes at Inchmarlo range from one-bedroom apartments to four-bedroom houses, all well proportioned and all carefully designed for retirement living.

An added comfort is Inchmarlo House. This magnificent Georgian mansion is now a Care Home, so as your needs change help and support is right on your doorstep.

Here too is a private lounge for homeowners' events and a bar/restaurant serving dishes inspired by Michelin starred chefs.

Call +44 (0) 1330 826242 or email dawn.ronaldson@inchmarlo-retirement.co.uk to find out more.

Then come and see why Inchmarlo is the ideal spot to put down some roots.

PINECREST

New 2 bedroom Homes for Sale.

INCHMARLO
RETIREMENT VILLAGE

Where Gracious Living Comes naturally

GET INVOLVED WITH SCOTLAND'S GARDENS

OPEN YOUR GARDEN

Opening your garden is a fun and rewarding experience, as one of our openers put it, "Well worth all the hard work for such a fantastic day." Many gardens open year after year; some for more than 80 years! Try it - you might just get hooked too.

BUY OUR GUIDEBOOK

This lists all the garden openings, trails and events for the year.

HELP WITH THE OPEN DAYS

- Welcome visitors at the gate
- Bake some delicious homebaking to sell
- Serve the teas and sell plants
- Find out how people heard about us
- Grow plants to sell on the day
- Take photos

HELP TO PROMOTE SCOTLAND'S GARDENS

- Would you write an article for a newspaper?
- Could you help by tweeting?
- Are you a dedicated Facebook follower?
- Would you like to write a blog for us?

VISIT A GARDEN

A lovely way to see other people's gardens; get design ideas, enjoy the home baking, discover new ways to deal with slimey slugs and also raise money for charity.

COME TO AN EVENT

Take part in one of our workshops, enjoy the Snowdrop Festival, come to a plant sale, or explore a garden trail.

Or, just let all your friends and family know about Scotland's Gardens and encourage them to visit us at **WWW.SCOTLANDSGARDENS.ORG**

GARDENS OPEN ON A SPECIFIC DATE

January

Date to be Advised
Kirkcudbrightshire   Danevale Park, Crossmichael

February

Sunday 19 February
Ayrshire   Blair House, Dalry
Dumfriesshire   Craig, Langholm
Perth & Kinross   Kilgraston School, Bridge of Earn

Thursday 23 February
Dumfriesshire   Barjarg Tower, Auldgirth

Friday 24 February
Dumfriesshire   Barjarg Tower, Auldgirth

Saturday 25 February
Dumfriesshire   Barjarg Tower, Auldgirth
East Lothian   Shepherd House, Inveresk

Sunday 26 February
Dumfriesshire   Barjarg Tower, Auldgirth
East Lothian   Shepherd House, Inveresk
Peeblesshire   Kailzie Gardens, Peebles
Stirlingshire   Kilbryde Castle, Dunblane

March

Sunday 5 March
Fife   Lindores House, By Newburgh
Kincardine & Deeside   Ecclesgreig Castle, St Cyrus
Lanarkshire   Cleghorn, Stable House, Lanark

Saturday 11 March
Angus & Dundee   Langley Park Gardens, Montrose

Sunday 12 March
Angus & Dundee   Lawton House, Inverkeilor

April

Sunday 9 April
East Lothian   Winton House, Pencaitland

Thursday 13 April

Ross, Cromarty, Skye & Inverness — Dundonnell House, Little Loch Broom

Saturday 15 April

Fife — Backhouse at Rossie Estate, By Collessie

Sunday 16 April

Aberdeenshire — Auchmacoy, Ellon

Fife — Cambo Gardens Spring Plant Sale, Kingsbarns

Kirkcudbrightshire — 3 Millhall, Shore Road, Kirkcudbright

Perth & Kinross — Megginch Castle, Errol

Wednesday 19 April

Argyll — Crarae Garden, Inveraray

East Lothian — Humbie Dean, Humbie

Saturday 22 April

Edinburgh, Midlothian and West Lothian — 41 Hermitage Gardens, Edinburgh

Moray & Nairn — Brodie Castle, Brodie

Renfrewshire — Kilmacolm Plant Sale, Kilmacolm

Sunday 23 April

Argyll — Benmore Botanic Garden, Benmore

Argyll — Crarae Garden, Inveraray

Dunbartonshire — Kilarden, Rosneath

Ettrick & Lauderdale — Bemersyde, Melrose

Moray & Nairn — Brodie Castle, Brodie, Forres

Stirlingshire — Gargunnock House Garden, Gargunnock

Stirlingshire — Gargunnock House Garden Plant Sale, Gargunnock

Saturday 29 April

Fife — The Tower, 1 Northview Terrace, Wormit

Sunday 30 April

Aberdeenshire — Westhall Castle, Oyne, Inverurie

Argyll — Arduaine Garden, Oban

Dumfriesshire — Portrack, The Garden of Cosmic Speculation, Holywood

Isle of Arran — Brodick Castle & Country Park, Brodick

Stirlingshire — The Pass House, Kilmahog, Callander

Wigtownshire — Claymoddie Garden, Whithorn

May

Monday 1 May

Ayrshire — Culzean, Maybole

Wednesday 3 May

East Lothian — Humbie Dean, Humbie

Thursday 4 May

Angus & Dundee — Inchmill Cottage, Glenprosen, nr Kirriemuir

Saturday 6 May

Aberdeenshire	Castle Fraser Garden, Sauchen
Argyll	Kames Bay, Kilmelford
East Lothian	Shepherd House, Inveresk
Edinburgh, Midlothian and West Lothian	41 Hermitage Gardens, Edinburgh
Lochaber	Canna House Walled Garden, Isle of Canna

Sunday 7 May

Aberdeenshire	Castle Fraser Garden, Sauchen
Angus & Dundee	Brechin Castle, Brechin
Argyll	Kames Bay, Kilmelford
Ayrshire	Craigengillan Estate and Scottish Dark Sky Observatory,
East Lothian	Shepherd House, Inveresk, Musselburgh
Edinburgh, Midlothian and West Lothian	Moray Place and Bank Gardens, Edinburgh
Fife	Kellie Castle Spring Plant Sale, Pittenweem
Kirkcudbrightshire	Threave Garden, Castle Douglas
Perth & Kinross	Fingask Castle, Rait

Friday 12 May

Angus & Dundee	Angus Plant Sale, Logie

Saturday 13 May

Argyll	Dalnashean, Port Appin
Argyll	Knock Cottage, Lochgair
Dumfriesshire	Drumpark, Irongray
Edinburgh, Midlothian and West Lothian	Dr Neil's Garden, Duddingston Village

Sunday 14 May

Angus & Dundee	Dalfruin, Kirriemuir
Argyll	Dalnashean, Port Appin
Argyll	Knock Cottage, Lochgair
Dumfriesshire	Capenoch, Penpont, Thornhill
East Lothian	Tyninghame House and The Walled Garden, Dunbar
Edinburgh, Midlothian and West Lothian	Dr Neil's Garden, Duddingston Village
Fife	St Fort Woodland Garden with Tayfield and Willowhill, Newport-on-Tay
Perth & Kinross	Branklyn Garden, Perth
Renfrewshire	Highwood, Kilmacolm
Stirlingshire	Milseybank, Bridge of Allan
Wigtownshire	Logan House Gardens, Port Logan

Wednesday 17 May

East Lothian	Humbie Dean, Humbie
Kincardine & Deeside	Crathes Castle Garden, Banchory
Ross, Cromarty, Skye & Inverness	Inverewe Garden and Estate, Poolewe

Thursday 18 May

Angus & Dundee	Inchmill Cottage, Glenprosen

Friday 19 May

Perth & Kinross	Rossie House, Forgandenny

Saturday 20 May

Argyll	Braevallich Farm, by Dalmally
Argyll	Strachur House Flower & Woodland Gardens, Strachur

Sunday 21 May

Angus & Dundee	Dundee & Angus College Gardens, Dundee
Angus & Dundee	Dunninald Castle, Montrose
Argyll	Braevallich Farm, by Dalmally
Argyll	Strachur House Flower & Woodland Gardens, Strachur
Dumfriesshire	The Crichton Rock Garden and Arboretum, Dumfries
Dunbartonshire	Ross Priory, Gartocharn
Edinburgh, Midlothian and West Lothian	101 Greenbank Crescent, Edinburgh
Edinburgh, Midlothian and West Lothian	Redcroft, Edinburgh
Fife	Earlshall Castle, Leuchars
Fife	Kirklands, Saline
Kincardine & Deeside	Inchmarlo House Garden, Inchmarlo
Kirkcudbrightshire	Barmagachan House, Borgue
Renfrewshire	Bridge of Weir Road Gardens, Kilmacolm
Ross, Cromarty, Skye & Inverness	Aultgowrie Mill, Aultgowrie
Ross, Cromarty, Skye & Inverness	Skye Forest Gardens, Rhuba Phoil,
Stirlingshire	Dun Dubh, Kinlochard Road, Aberfoyle
Wigtownshire	Logan Botanic Garden, Port Logan

Wednesday 24 May

Ettrick & Lauderdale	Laidlawstiel House, Clovenfords
Ross, Cromarty, Skye & Inverness	House of Gruinard, Laide

Thursday 25 May

Aberdeenshire	Leith Hall Garden, Huntly

Friday 26 May

Angus & Dundee	The Shrubbery, Dundee
Perth & Kinross	Rossie House, Forgandenny

Saturday 27 May

Angus & Dundee	Gallery, Montrose
Angus & Dundee	The Shrubbery, Dundee
Argyll	Maolachy's Garden, Lochavich
Edinburgh, Midlothian and West Lothian	Beech Lodge, Edinburgh
Kincardine & Deeside	Drum Castle Garden, Drumoak
Ross, Cromarty, Skye & Inverness	Oldtown of Leys Garden, Inverness

Sunday 28 May

Angus & Dundee	The Shrubbery, Dundee
Argyll	Maolachy's Garden, Lochavich

Dumfriesshire	Dalswinton House, Dalswinton
East Lothian	Belhaven House with Belhaven Hill School, Dunbar
Edinburgh, Midlothian and West Lothian	Hunter's Tryst, Edinburgh
Fife	46 South Street, St Andrews
Glasgow & District	44 Gordon Road, Netherlee
Kincardine & Deeside	Drum Castle Garden, Drumoak
Kirkcudbrightshire	Corsock House, Corsock
Lochaber	Ardverikie with Aberarder, Kinlochlaggan
Moray & Nairn	Balnabual Cottage, Dalcross
Peeblesshire	Glen House, Innerleithen
Ross, Cromarty, Skye & Inverness	Hugh Miller's Birthplace Cottage & Museum, Cromarty
Stirlingshire	Bridge of Allan Gardens, Bridge of Allan
Wigtownshire	Balker Farmhouse, Stranraer
Wigtownshire	Galloway House Gardens, Garlieston

Wednesday 31 May

East Lothian	Humbie Dean, Humbie
Peeblesshire	Stobo Japanese Water Garden, Stobo

June

Thursday 1 June

Angus & Dundee	Inchmill Cottage, Glenprosen
Peeblesshire	Stobo Japanese Water Garden, Stobo
Perth & Kinross	Bradystone House, Murthly
Ross, Cromarty, Skye & Inverness	Dundonnell House, Little Loch Broom
Ross, Cromarty, Skye & Inverness	Gorthleck, Stratherrick
Ross, Cromarty, Skye & Inverness	Inverewe Garden and Estate, Poolewe

Saturday 3 June

Angus & Dundee	Arbroath Collection of Gardens, Arbroath
Argyll	Knock Cottage, Lochgair

Sunday 4 June

Aberdeenshire	Kildrummy Castle Gardens, Alford
Aberdeenshire	Tillypronie, Tarland
Argyll	Fasnacloich, Appin
Argyll	Knock Cottage, Lochgair
Dumfriesshire	Dabton, Thornhill
Dumfriesshire	Holehouse, Near Penpont
East Lothian	Broadwoodside, Gifford
Edinburgh, Midlothian and West Lothian	Dean Gardens, Edinburgh
Fife	Lindores House, By Newburgh
Fife	Three Gardens in Blebo Craigs, Blebo Craigs
Glasgow & District	Partickhill Gardens East, Glasgow
Kirkcudbrightshire	Cally Gardens, Gatehouse of Fleet
Peeblesshire	8 Halmyre Mains, West Linton
Perth & Kinross	Explorers Garden, Pitlochry

Ross, Cromarty, Skye & Inverness	Field House, Belladrum, Beauly
Roxburghshire	West Leas, Bonchester Bridge
Stirlingshire	Shrubhill, Dunblane, Perthshire

Wednesday 7 June

Aberdeenshire	Cruickshank Botanic Gardens, Aberdeen

Thursday 8 June

Kirkcudbrightshire	Broughton House Garden, Kirkcudbright
Perth & Kinross	Bradystone House, Murthly

Friday 9 June

Dumfriesshire	Holehouse, Near Penpont

Saturday 10 June

Angus & Dundee	Forfar Open Garden, Forfar
Ayrshire	Holmes Farm, Drybridge
Caithness, Sutherland, Orkney & Shetland	Amat, Ardgay
Glasgow & District	Greenbank Garden, Clarkston
Ross, Cromarty, Skye & Inverness	Malin, Glenaldie
Stirlingshire	The Mill House, Fintry

Sunday 11 June

Aberdeenshire	Birken Cottage, Burnhervie
Ayrshire	Holmes Farm, Drybridge
Caithness, Sutherland, Orkney & Shetland	Amat, Ardgay
Caithness, Sutherland, Orkney & Shetland	Duncan Street Gardens, Thurso
Dumfriesshire	Cowhill Tower, Holywood
Dumfriesshire	Westerhall, Bentpath
Dunbartonshire	Geilston Garden, Cardross
Edinburgh, Midlothian and West Lothian	The Glasshouses at the Royal Botanic Garden Edinburgh
Fife	Craigrothie Village Gardens,
Glasgow & District	Greenbank Garden, Clarkston
Glasgow & District	Kilsyth Gardens, Kilsyth
Kincardine & Deeside	Kincardine, Kincardine O'Neil
Kirkcudbrightshire	Stockarton, Kirkcudbright
Lanarkshire	The Quothquan Gardens, Biggar
Perth & Kinross	Bonhard House, Perth
Perth & Kinross	Mill of Forneth, Forneth
Renfrewshire	Craig Hepburn Memorial Garden, Linwood
Ross, Cromarty, Skye & Inverness	Malin, Glenaldie
Stirlingshire	The Mill House, Fintry
Wigtownshire	Castle Kennedy and Gardens, Stranraer

Monday 12 June

Stirlingshire	The Mill House, Fintry

Tuesday 13 June

Stirlingshire	The Mill House, Fintry

Wednesday 14 June

East Lothian	Humbie Dean, Humbie
Ettrick & Lauderdale	Laidlawstiel House, Clovenfords
Stirlingshire	The Mill House, Fintry

Thursday 15 June

Angus & Dundee	Inchmill Cottage, Glenprosen
Perth & Kinross	Bradystone House, Murthly
Stirlingshire	The Mill House, Fintry

Friday 16 June

Stirlingshire	The Mill House, Fintry

Saturday 17 June

Angus & Dundee	Kilry Village Gardens, Kilry
Caithness, Sutherland, Orkney & Shetland	Orkney Garden Festival: Secret Gardens of Kirkwall
Perth & Kinross	The Bield at Blackruthven, Tibbermore
Stirlingshire	The Mill House, Fintry

Sunday 18 June

Angus & Dundee	Kilry Village Gardens, Kilry
Caithness, Sutherland, Orkney & Shetland	Orkney Garden Festival: Trail One
Dumfriesshire	Dunesslin, Dunscore
East Lothian	Tyninghame House and The Walled Garden, Dunbar
Fife	Culross Palace Garden, Culross
Fife	Greenhead Farmhouse, Greenhead of Arnot
Fife	Kinghorn Village Gardens
Glasgow & District	Partickhill Gardens West, Glasgow
Kincardine & Deeside	Ecclesgreig Castle, St Cyrus
Kincardine & Deeside	Finzean House, Finzean
Kirkcudbrightshire	Glenlivet with The Limes, Kirkcudbright
Lanarkshire	20 Smithycroft, Hamilton
Stirlingshire	The Mill House, Fintry
Wigtownshire	Woodfall Gardens, Glasserton

Tuesday 20 June

Caithness, Sutherland, Orkney & Shetland	The Quoy of Houton, Orphir
Fife	The Fife Garden Trail

Wednesday 21 June

East Lothian	Humbie Dean, Humbie
Fife	The Fife Garden Trail

Thursday 22 June

Fife	The Fife Garden Trail
Perth & Kinross	Bradystone House, Murthly
Ross, Cromarty, Skye & Inverness	Brackla Wood, Culbokie

Saturday 24 June

Argyll	Dal an Eas, Kilmore
Ayrshire	Netherthird Community Garden, Netherthird
Caithness, Sutherland, Orkney & Shetland	Orkney Garden Festival: Hoy Garden Trail, Hoy
Fife	The Tower, Wormit
Moray & Nairn	Haugh Garden, College of Roseisle
Perth & Kinross	Abernethy Open Gardens, Abernethy
Perth & Kinross	Blair Castle Gardens, Blair Atholl
Perth & Kinross	Wester House of Ross, Comrie

Sunday 25 June

Angus & Dundee	Newtonmill House, by Brechin
Argyll	Dal an Eas, Kilmore, Oban
Ayrshire	Barnweil Garden, Craigie
Berwickshire	East Gordon Smiddy, Gordon
Caithness, Sutherland, Orkney & Shetland	Orkney Garden Festival: Trail Two, Orkney
Dumfriesshire	Glenae, Amisfield
East Lothian	Longniddry Gardens
Fife	Backhouse at Rossie Estate, By Collessie
Fife	Pittenweem: Gardens in the Burgh
Kincardine & Deeside	Clayfolds, Bridge of Muchalls, Stonehaven
Kirkcudbrightshire	Seabank, Rockcliffe
Lanarkshire	Dippoolbank Cottage, Carnwath
Perth & Kinross	Kincarrathie House, Perth
Perth & Kinross	Wester House of Ross, Comrie
Renfrewshire	Newmills Cottage, Nr Lochwinnoch/Newton of Belltrees
Ross, Cromarty, Skye & Inverness	House of Aigas and Field Centre, By Beauly
Roxburghshire	Westerhouses, Bonchester Bridge
Stirlingshire	Thorntree, Arnprior

Tuesday 27 June

Fife	The Fife Garden Trail

Wednesday 28 June

Aberdeenshire	Haddo House, Methlick, Ellon
East Lothian	East Lothian Garden Trail
Fife	The Fife Garden Trail

Thursday 29 June

Aberdeenshire	Leith Hall Garden, Huntly
East Lothian	East Lothian Garden Trail
Fife	The Fife Garden Trail
Perth & Kinross	Bradystone House, Murthly

Friday 30 June

East Lothian	East Lothian Garden Trail

July

Saturday 1 July

Ayrshire	The Gardens of Fenwick, Fenwick
East Lothian	East Lothian Garden Trail

Sunday 2 July

Berwickshire	Lennel Bank, Coldstream
Caithness, Sutherland, Orkney & Shetland	Bighouse Lodge, by Melvich
Dumfriesshire	Dalgonar, Dunscore
Edinburgh, Midlothian and West Lothian	Colinton Gardens, Edinburgh
East Lothian	East Lothian Garden Trail
Ettrick & Lauderdale	Lowood House , Melrose
Fife	Earlshall Castle, Leuchars
Fife	Wormistoune House, Crail
Kirkcudbrightshire	Southwick House, Southwick
Moray & Nairn	10 Pilmuir Road West , Forres
Roxburghshire	Easter Weens, Bonchester Bridge

Tuesday 4 July

Fife	The Fife Garden Trail

Wednesday 5 July

Caithness, Sutherland, Orkney & Shetland	The Castle & Gardens of Mey, Mey
East Lothian	Humbie Dean, Humbie
Fife	The Fife Garden Trail
Isle of Arran	Dougarie
Kincardine & Deeside	Drum Castle Garden, Drumoak

Thursday 6 July

Fife	The Fife Garden Trail
Perth & Kinross	Bradystone House, Murthly

Saturday 8 July

Angus & Dundee	Hospitalfield Gardens, Westway
Fife	Crail: Small Gardens in the Burgh
Roxburghshire	Pirnie, Fairnington

Sunday 9 July

Aberdeenshire	Bruckhills Croft, Rothienorman
Ayrshire	Golf Course Road Gardens, Girvan
East Lothian	Gullane Coastal Gardens, Gullane
Edinburgh, Midlothian and West Lothian	Riccarton Mains Farmhouse, Currie
Fife	Crail: Small Gardens in the Burgh
Isle of Arran	Brodick Castle & Country Park, Brodick
Kirkcudbrightshire	Drumstinchall Cottage, Drumstinchall
Roxburghshire	Yetholm Village Gardens, Town Yetholm
Stirlingshire	Moon Cottage, Greenyards
Wigtownshire	Woodfall Gardens, Glasserton

Tuesday 11 July

Fife	The Fife Garden Trail

Wednesday 12 July

Caithness, Sutherland, Orkney & Shetland	The Castle & Gardens of Mey, Mey
Fife	The Fife Garden Trail
Kincardine & Deeside	Drum Castle Garden, Drumoak

Thursday 13 July

Fife	The Fife Garden Trail
Perth & Kinross	Bradystone House, Murthly

Saturday 15 July

Angus & Dundee	Gallery, Montrose
Argyll	Caol Ruadh, Colintraive
Dumfriesshire	Whiteside, Dunscore
Moray & Nairn	Knock House, Rafford
Renfrewshire	Duchal, Kilmacolm

Sunday 16 July

Argyll	Caol Ruadh, Colintraive
Ayrshire	Carnell, By Hurlford
Berwickshire	Netherbyres, Eyemouth
Dumfriesshire	Whiteside, Dunscore
Fife	Balcarres, Colinsburgh
Glasgow & District	Strathbungo Gardens
Kincardine & Deeside	Douneside House, Tarland
Kirkcudbrightshire	Barmagachan House, Borgue
Moray & Nairn	Knock House, Rafford
Peeblesshire	West Linton Village Gardens, West Linton
Ross, Cromarty, Skye & Inverness	Aultgowrie Mill, Aultgowrie
Wigtownshire	Fernlea Garden with Lisieux Garden, Newton Stewart

Wednesday 19 July

East Lothian	Humbie Dean, Humbie
Kincardine & Deeside	Drum Castle Garden, Drumoak

Thursday 20 July

Perth & Kinross	Bradystone House, Murthly
Ross, Cromarty, Skye & Inverness	Dundonnell House, Little Loch Broom

Saturday 22 July

Aberdeenshire	Middle Cairncake, Cuminestown
Moray & Nairn	Haugh Garden, College of Roseisle
Ross, Cromarty, Skye & Inverness	2 Durnamuck, Little Loch Broom

Sunday 23 July

Aberdeenshire	Drumrossie Mansion House, Insch
Aberdeenshire	Middle Cairncake, Cuminestown

Berwickshire	Kames, Greenlaw
Fife	Balcaskie with Kellie Castle, Pittenweem
Fife	Boarhills Village Gardens, St Andrews
Fife	Falkland Palace and Garden, Falkland
Fife	Kellie Castle with Balcaskie, Pittenweem
Kirkcudbrightshire	Crofts, Kirkpatrick Durham
Lanarkshire	Wellbutts, Elsrickle
Ross, Cromarty, Skye & Inverness	House of Aigas and Field Centre, By Beauly

Wednesday 26 July

Kincardine & Deeside	Drum Castle Garden, Drumoak

Thursday 27 July

Aberdeenshire	Leith Hall Garden, Huntly
Perth & Kinross	Bradystone House, Murthly

Saturday 29 July

Angus & Dundee	The Herbalist's Garden at Logie, Logie House, Kirriemuir
Argyll	2 Broadcroft Lane, Rothesay
Caithness, Sutherland, Orkney & Shetland	House of Tongue, Tongue
Edinburgh, Midlothian and West Lothian	45 Northfield Crescent, Longridge
Edinburgh, Midlothian and West Lothian	9 Braid Farm Road, Edinburgh
Ettrick & Lauderdale	Harmony Garden with Priorwood Garden, Melrose
Fife	The Tower, Wormit

Sunday 30 July

Aberdeenshire	Alford Village Gardens, Alford
Angus & Dundee	The Herbalist's Garden at Logie, Kirriemuir
Argyll	2 Broadcroft Lane, Rothesay
Dumfriesshire	Newtonairds Lodge, Newtonairds
Edinburgh, Midlothian and West Lothian	45 Northfield Crescent, Longridge
Edinburgh, Midlothian and West Lothian	9 Braid Farm Road, Edinburgh
Ettrick & Lauderdale	Harmony Garden with Priorwood Garden, Melrose
Glasgow & District	Horatio's Gardens, Queen Elizabeth Hospital
Lanarkshire	Dippoolbank Cottage, Carnwath
Roxburghshire	West Leas, Bonchester Bridge
Stirlingshire	The Tors, Falkirk
Wigtownshire	Ardwell House Gardens, Ardwell

August

Wednesday 2 August

East Lothian	Humbie Dean, Humbie

Thursday 3 August

Angus & Dundee	Inchmill Cottage, Glenprosen

Saturday 5 August

Edinburgh, Midlothian and West Lothian	39 Nantwich Drive, Edinburgh

Sunday 6 August

Caithness, Sutherland, Orkney & Shetland	Langwell, Berriedale
Edinburgh, Midlothian and West Lothian	Craigentinny and Telferton Allotments, Edinburgh
Kincardine & Deeside	Glenbervie House, Drumlithie
Kirkcudbrightshire	Cally Gardens, Gatehouse of Fleet
Kirkcudbrightshire	Threave Garden, Castle Douglas
Lanarkshire	The Walled Garden, Shieldhill
Peeblesshire	Peebles Gardens, Peebles
Perth & Kinross	Drummond Castle Gardens, Crieff
Stirlingshire	Little Carbeth, Killearn

Wednesday 9 August

Aberdeenshire	Haddo House, Methlick

Saturday 12 August

Caithness, Sutherland, Orkney & Shetland	Springpark House, Thurso
Lochaber	Canna House Walled Garden, Isle of Canna

Sunday 13 August

Aberdeenshire	Pitmedden Garden, Ellon
Caithness, Sutherland, Orkney & Shetland	Springpark House, Thurso
Dumfriesshire	Shawhead, Lochmaben
Kincardine & Deeside	Fasque House, Laurencekirk

Thursday 17 August

Angus & Dundee	Inchmill Cottage, nr Kirriemuir
Ross, Cromarty, Skye & Inverness	Dundonnell House, Little Loch Broom

Saturday 19 August

Angus & Dundee	12 Glamis Drive, Dundee
Caithness, Sutherland, Orkney & Shetland	The Castle & Gardens of Mey, Mey
Moray & Nairn	Haugh Garden, College of Roseisle

Sunday 20 August

Angus & Dundee	12 Glamis Drive, Dundee
Dunbartonshire	Dean Cottage with Ortona, Helensburgh
Lanarkshire	Culter Allers, Culter Allers
Ross, Cromarty, Skye & Inverness	2 Durnamuck, Little Loch Broom

Thursday 24 August

Aberdeenshire	Leith Hall Garden, Huntly

Sunday 27 August

Caithness, Sutherland, Orkney & Shetland	The Garden at the Auld Post Office B&B, Spittal-by-Mybster
Kirkcudbrightshire	3 Millhall, Shore Road, Kirkcudbright
Ross, Cromarty, Skye & Inverness	Highland Liliums, Kiltarlity

September

Saturday 2 September
Ross, Cromarty, Skye & Inverness   Old Allangrange, Munlochy

Sunday 3 September
Dunbartonshire   Hill House Plant Sale, Helensburgh

Thursday 7 September
Angus & Dundee   Inchmill Cottage, Glenprosen

Saturday 9 September
Renfrewshire   Kilmacolm Plant Sale, Kilmacolm
Ross, Cromarty, Skye & Inverness   2 Durnamuck, Little Loch Broom

Sunday 10 September
Moray & Nairn   Gordonstoun, Duffus

Saturday 16 September
Renfrewshire   St Vincents Hospice Garden, Howwood

Sunday 17 September
Stirlingshire   Kilbryde Castle, Dunblane

Thursday 21 September
Angus & Dundee   Inchmill Cottage, Glenprosen
Ross, Cromarty, Skye & Inverness   Dundonnell House, Little Loch Broom

Saturday 23 September
Aberdeenshire   Tarland Community Garden, Aboyne

Sunday 24 September
Peeblesshire   Glen House, Innerleithen

Saturday 30 September
Kincardine & Deeside   Crathes Castle Garden, Banchory

October

Sunday 1 October
Aberdeenshire   Kildrummy Castle Gardens, Alford
Fife   Hill of Tarvit Plant Sale and Autumn Fair, Cupar

Sunday 8 October
Peeblesshire   Dawyck Botanic Garden, Stobo

November

Thursday 23 November
Stirlingshire   Festive Floral Evening, Camphill Blair Drummond Trust

GARDENS OPEN BY ARRANGEMENT

Aberdeenshire

Airdlin Croft, Ythanbank, Ellon	21 May - 31 July
An Teallach, Largue, Huntly	1 June - 31 August
Birken Cottage, Burnhervie	1 May - 31 July
Blairwood House, Blairs	18 June - 27 August
Bruckhills Croft, Rothienorman	18 February - 19 March and 1 July - 31 July
Grandhome, Danestone	1 April - 31 October
Hatton Castle, Turriff	On request
Laundry Cottage, Culdrain	On request
Middle Cairncake, Cuminestown	1 June - 10 September

Angus & Dundee

3 Balfour Cottages, Menmuir	3 May - 17 May
Gallery, Montrose	1 June - 31 August
Kirkton House, Kirkton of Craig	1 May - 30 September

Argyll

Barochreal, Kilninver, Oban	1 May - 30 September
Dal an Eas, Kilmore, Oban	15 April - 10 September
Eas Mhor, Cnoc-a-Challtuinn, Clachan Seil	1 May - 30 September
Kinlochlaich Gardens, Appin	16 October - 2 March
Knock Cottage, Lochgair	15 April - 15 June
Maolachy's Garden, Lochavich	28 January - 12 March
Seafield, Hunter's Quay	1 June - 31 August

Ayrshire

Burnside, Drongan	1 April - 31 August
Glenapp Castle, Ballantrae	17 March - 22 December
High Fulwood, Stewarton	1 May - 31 August

Berwickshire

Lennel Bank, Coldstream	On request
Netherbyres, Eyemouth	1 May - 31 August

Caithness, Sutherland, Orkney & Shetland

Cruisdale, Sandness	On request
Keldaberg, Cunningsburgh	1 June - 31 October
Lindaal, Tingwall	1 June - 30 September

Nonavaar, Levenwick	14 April - 3 September

Dumfriesshire

Westwater Farm, Langholm	1 May - 30 September

East Lothian

Stobshiel House , Humbie	1 March - 1 December

Edinburgh, Midlothian & West Lothian

101 Greenbank Crescent, Edinburgh	15 April - 31 August
Hunter's Tryst, 95 Oxgangs Road, Edinburgh	1 January - 31 December

Fife

Helensbank, Kincardine	1 June - 31 July
Kirklands, Saline	1 April - 30 September
Logie House, Crossford, Dunfermline	1 April - 31 October
Rosewells, Pitscottie	1 April - 30 September
St Fort Woodland Garden, St Fort Farm, Newport-on-Tay	1 May - 30 November
Teasses Gardens, near Ceres	1 April - 30 September
The Tower, 1 Northview Terrace, Wormit	1 April - 30 September
Willowhill, Forgan, Newport-on-Tay	1 April - 31 August
Wormistoune House, Crail	1 April - 30 September

Glasgow & District

Kilsyth Gardens, Allanfauld Road, Kilsyth	1 April - 30 September

Kirkcudbrightshire

3 Millhall, Shore Road, Kirkcudbright	1 April - 30 September
Anwoth Old Schoolhouse, Anwoth, Gatehouse of Fleet	15 February - 15 November
Brooklands, Crocketford	1 February - 1 October
Corsock House, Corsock, Castle Douglas	1 April - 30 June
Seabank, The Merse, Rockcliffe	1 June - 31 August
Stockarton, Kirkcudbright	1 April - 31 July

Lanarkshire

Carmichael Mill, Hyndford Bridge, Lanark	1 January - 31 December
St Patrick's House, Lanark	1 May - 30 June
The Scots Mining Company House, Leadhills, Biggar	1 May - 30 September

Moray & Nairn

10 Pilmuir Road West , Forres	28 January - 12 March
Haugh Garden, College of Roseisle	1 May - 31 August

Peeblesshire

Portmore, Eddleston	1 June - 31 August

Perth & Kinross

Carig Dhubh, Bonskeid	1 May - 30 September
Glenlyon House, Fortingall	On request
Hollytree Lodge, Muckhart	1 April - 31 October
Kirkton Craig, Abernyte	15 May - 31 August
Latch House, Abernyte	1 May - 31 August
Mill of Forneth, Forneth	1 May - 30 September
Pitcurran House, Abernethy	1 April - 30 September
The Garden at Craigowan, Ballinluig	15 April - 30 June
The Steading at Clunie, Newmill of Kinloch	29 April - 7 May and 14 June - 28 June

Ross, Cromarty, Skye & Inverness

Dundonnell House, Little Loch Broom	3 April - 31 October
Glenkyllachy Lodge, Tomatin	1 May - 30 October
House of Aigas and Field Centre, By Beauly	1 April - 28 October
Leathad Ard, Upper Carloway, Isle of Lewis	1 April - 30 September
The Lookout, Kilmuir, North Kessock	1 May - 31 August

Roxburghshire

West Leas, Bonchester Bridge	On request

Stirlingshire

Arndean, by Dollar	15 May - 18 June
Duntreath Castle, Blanefield	1 February - 30 November
Gardener's Cottage Walled Garden, Killearn,	1 May - 31 October
Kilbryde Castle, Dunblane	1 April - 30 September
Milseybank, Bridge of Allan	1 April - 31 May
Rowberrow, Dollar	1 February - 31 December
The Mill House, Fintry	10 June - 18 June
The Tors, Falkirk	1 May - 30 September
Thorntree, Arnprior	1 April - 15 October

Wigtownshire

Balker Farmhouse, Stranraer	1 May - 30 September
Craichlaw, Kirkcowan	On request

GARDENS OPEN ON A REGULAR BASIS

Aberdeenshire

Fyvie Castle, Fyvie	5 January - 22 December

Angus & Dundee

Gallery, Montrose	1 June - 31 August (Tuesdays only)
Pitmuies Gardens, Guthrie	1 April - 30 October

Argyll

Achnacloich, Connel	1 April - 31 October (Saturdays only)
Ardchattan Priory, North Connel	1 April - 31 October
Ardkinglas Woodland Garden, Cairndow	Daily
Ardmaddy Castle, by Oban	Daily
Ascog Hall, Ascog	1 April - 30 September
Barguillean's "Angus Garden", Taynuilt	Daily
Crinan Hotel Garden, Crinan	1 May - 31 August
Druimneil House, Port Appin	1 April - 31 October
Inveraray Castle Gardens, Inveraray	1 April - 31 October
Kinlochlaich Gardens, Appin	3 March - 15 October
Oakbank, Ardrishaig	1 May - 31 August

Berwickshire

Bughtrig, Near Leitholm	1 June - 1 September

Caithness, Sutherland, Orkney & Shetland

Highlands, East Voe	1 May - 30 September
Lea Gardens, Tresta	1 March - 31 October (exc. Thursdays)
Nonavaar, Levenwick	14 April - 3 September (Fri and Sun only)
Norby, Burnside	Daily

Dunbartonshire

Glenarn, Rhu	21 March - 21 September

East Lothian

Shepherd House, Inveresk, Musselburgh	14 February - 9 March and 18 April - 13 July (Tue and Thu only)

Edinburgh, Midlothian & West Lothian

Newliston, Kirkliston	3 May - 4 June (exc. Mon and Tues)

Fife

Glassmount House, By Kirkcaldy	1 May - 30 September (Mon - Sat only)
Willowhill, Forgan	5 August - 26 August (Saturdays only)

Lochaber

Ardtornish, By Lochaline	Daily

Moray & Nairn

Burgie, Between Forres and Elgin	1 April - 31 October

Peeblesshire

Portmore, Eddleston	5 July - 30 August (Wednesdays only)
The Potting Shed, Broughton	14 June - 19 July (Wednesdays only)

Perth & Kinross

Ardvorlich, Lochearnhead	1 May - 1 June
Bolfracks, Aberfeldy	1 April - 31 October
Braco Castle, Braco	28 January - 31 October
Glendoick, by Perth	1 April - 31 May
Glenericht House Arboretum	Daily
Fingask Castle	30 January - 9 March (Mondays - Thursdays only)

Ross, Cromarty, Skye & Inverness

Abriachan Garden Nursery, Loch Ness Side	1 February - 30 November
Attadale, Strathcarron	1 April - 28 October (exc. Sundays)
Balmeanach House, Balmeanach	2 May - 6 October (Tue and Fri only)
Bhlaraidh House, Glenmoriston	13 April - 30 September (Thur - Sun only)
Dunvegan Castle and Gardens	1 April - 15 October
Highland Liliums	Daily
Leathad Ard, Upper Carloway	15 May - 2 September (exc. Sundays)
Oldtown of Leys Garden, Inverness	Daily
The Lookout, Kilmuir	1 May - 31 August (Sundays only)

Roxburghshire

Floors Castle, Kelso	10 January - 23 December
Monteviot, Jedburgh	1 April - 31 October

Stirlingshire

Gargunnock House Garden, Gargunnock	5 February - 12 March (Daily) and 13 March - 30 September (Mon - Fri only)

Wigtownshire

Ardwell House Gardens, Ardwell	1 April - 31 October
Glenwhan Gardens, Dunragit	1 April - 31 October

INDEX OF GARDENS

W

Y

INDEX OF ADVERTISERS

OUR GUIDEBOOK FOR 2018

ORDER NOW
and your copy will be posted to you on publication.

Send order to:

Scotland's Gardens, 23 Castle Street, Edinburgh EH2 3DN

Please send me ____ copy / copies of our **Guidebook for 2018**, price £5.00 plus £2.00 UK p&p, as soon as it is available.

I enclose a cheque / postal order made payable to Scotland's Gardens.

Name _____

Address _____

_____

Postcode _____

Copies of our Guidebook for 2018 may also be purchased on our website:
www.scotlandsgardens.org